INDIAN DEMOCRACY'S PARADOXES

"DOES THE HUMAN BEING REASON? NO; HE THINKS, MUSES, REFLECTS, BUT DOES NOT REASON...THAT IS, IN THE TWO THINGS WHICH ARE THE PECULIAR DOMAIN OF THE HEART, NOT THE MIND, POLITICS AND RELIGION. HE DOESN'T WANT TO KNOW THE OTHER SIDE. HE WANTS ARGUMENTS AND STATISTICS FOR HIS OWN SIDE, AND NOTHING MORE." – MARK TWAIN

PRAHALAD RAO

BLUEROSE PUBLISHERS
India | U.K.

Copyright © Prahalad Rao 2024

All rights reserved by author. No part of this publication may be reproduced, stored in a retrieval system or transmitted in any form or by any means, electronic, mechanical, photocopying, recording or otherwise, without the prior permission of the author. Although every precaution has been taken to verify the accuracy of the information contained herein, the publisher assume no responsibility for any errors or omissions. No liability is assumed for damages that may result from the use of information contained within.

BlueRose Publishers takes no responsibility for any damages, losses, or liabilities that may arise from the use or misuse of the information, products, or services provided in this publication.

For permissions requests or inquiries regarding this publication, please contact:

BLUEROSE PUBLISHERS
www.BlueRoseONE.com
info@bluerosepublishers.com
+91 8882 898 898
+4407342408967

ISBN: 978-93-5989-404-1

Cover design: Tahira
Typesetting: Tanya Raj Upadhyay

First Edition: March 2024

DEDICATION

This book is dedicated to those humans who believe in reasoning that resides in their conscience. To those politicians and religious leaders who denounce ill-will and dedicate to wellbeing of the people. Both these qualities produce the best leaders and the citizens, the shining symbol of democracy.

DISCLAIMER

Views expressed by the author in this book are based on his personal understanding of the past and perception of the present. This book neither intends nor suggests any attribution of whatsoever nature to anyone or to any policy or program or system existing or envisaged nor this book intends or suggests to hurt sentiments of any person or state or political bodies or religious bodies or political or religious leaders or body of any other nature or defame any of them whatsoever and any construction of the writings in this book otherwise is sole to the person so construing. The author or the publisher will not be liable for any civil or criminal proceedings under the laws of the country.

GRATITUDES

My gratitude to Dr. Sharda, K.Ananth Raman, Royal Hotel, Hyderabad, V.Laxma Reddy, T.S.Murthy, A.R.Venkataraman, P.P.S.Puri, A.S.Dhupia, R.B. Mathur and Lalit Chand, whose guidance, benevolence and humanism in my initial years of service will shine in my heart for ever, C.V.Nair, D. Sankaraguruswamy, Dr. Uddesh Kohli, B.M. Pant, M. Prasad, T.N. Thakur, A.A. Khan, Dr. K. K. Govil and Raji Phillips who gave confidence and lent support to me during my most testing time of life.

My gratitude to senior Indian Administrative Officers (IAS) who headed the organizations, account and audit service officers, eminent engineers, eminent finance & legal experts with whom I had the opportunity to work in one or the other capacity during my thirty years of service in Public Financial Institutions. Gratitudes to A.K.Sah and Shahzad Bahadur for giving me opportunity to develop my career as a consultant post retirement. My gratitude and special thanks to Dr.J.T.Verghese who offered me chance for continuity of my consultancy job with continued guidance and advice.

My association with all of them helped imbibe in me their direction, dedication to the cause of economic development, virtues, values, compassion and affection that became bedrock of my life.

My gratitude to Scholars, Journalists, Thinkers, Philosophers, Historians, Bankers, Economists, Professionals, Socialists and Environmentalists within and outside the country whose writings on Google website helped me to understand the width and depth of subjects selected for this book. I have disclosed the sources of valuable writings relied upon under "References". No copyright infringement is intended. Author reiterates his grateful thanks to all of them.

My special thanks to Google for providing inspiration with invaluable sources of information that helped me in completing this book.

In particular, my gratitude to Arun Kumar Sarna who gave me strong standing support during my association with him in service in multi-national consultancy Services Company as well as throughout thereafter.

My gratitude to K. G. Dewan, Sadiq Shafiq and Boben Anto whose ever helping hand remained a sustainable strength to me.

Grateful thanks to M/s BLUE ROSE PUBLISHESERS PRIVATE LIMITED, the Publishers without whose cooperation, guidance and advice, this book wouldn't have reached the readers.

Thanks to my friends, relatives and my family members for their continued encouragement. Their suggestions and support were a great strength for me in completing this book.

13TH JUNE, 2023   Prahalad Rao

TABLE OF CONTENTS

DEDICATION iii

DISCLAIMER iv

GRATITUDES v

THE DEMOCRACY PARADOX - WHAT GREAT WRITERS SAID 1

PART 01 PARADOXES - A REFLECTION 11

PART 02 DIVERSITY & DIVISION PARADOX 66

PART 03 FUNDAMENTAL DUTIES PARADOX 115

PART 04 GOVERNANCE AND CITIZENS' MORAL VALUES PARADOX 152

PART 05 HUMAN DEVELOPMENT PARADOX 179

REFERENCES 246

ABOUT THE AUTHOR 257

LIST OF BOOKS PUBLISHED BY PRAHALAD RAO 263

THE DEMOCRACY PARADOX - WHAT GREAT WRITERS SAID

Wikipedia states:

"The Democratic Paradox is a collection of essays by the Belgian political theorist Chantal Mouffe, published in 2000 by Verso Books. The essays offer further discussion of the concept of radical democracy that Mouffe explored in Hegemony and Socialist Strategy, co-Ied by Ernesto Laclau. In this collection, Mouffe deals with the specific conflicts between the post-Marxist democratic theory that she and Laclau theorized in Hegemony and Socialist Strategy and the competing democratic theories proposed by Jürgen Habermas and John Rawls. Verso's UK blog characterizes The Democratic Paradox as Mouffe's most accessible review of her perspectives on radical democracy.[1]

Synopsis: The eponymous paradox of democracy that this collection of essays deals with is the internal conflict within modern liberal democracy that is created by the union of two separate strands of political thought: the tradition of classical liberalism and the tradition of democratic theory, forming the institution of liberal democracy.

We are dealing with a new political form of society whose specificity comes from the articulation between two different traditions. On one side we have the liberal tradition constituted by the rule of law, the defence of human rights and the respect of individual liberty; on the other the democratic tradition whose main ideas are those of equa identity between governing and governed and popular sovereignty. There is no necessary relation between those two distinct traditions but only a contingent historical articulation....Let's not forget that, while we tend today to take the link between liberalism and democracy for granted, their union, far from being a smooth process, was the result of bitter struggles. — *Mouffe, The Democratic Paradox, pp. 2-3*[2]

Mouffe sees Radical Democracy as a means for continuing to sustain the balance between the values of liberalism and democracy. This balance is accomplished through the agonistic practice of valuing and sustaining dissent in the democratic process as a more important goal than consensus. This point is where Radical Democratic theory diverges from both Habermas and Rawls, as it contradicts Habermas's quest for rational consensus and Rawls's project for political liberalism. Mouffe describes the importance of the radical democratic alternative in a 2009 interview, saying that "The aim of a pluralist democracy is to provide the institutions that will allow them to take an agonistic form, in which opponents will treat each other not as enemies to be destroyed, but as adversaries who will fight for the victory of their position while recognising the right of their opponents to fight for theirs. An agonistic democracy requires the availability of a choice between real alternatives."[3]"

Reasoning?

In Hinduism:

'The category of reason is used in Hindu spiritual and philosophy in different senses. One can discern two broad usages: one, as a faculty of the mind that is, as an instrument of philosophical reflection and, two, as logic, that is, an instrument of argumentation. There is no exact Sanskrit synonym for the word "reason." The term buddhi is often used to denote reason as a faculty of the mind, and words like manana and vicāra are used to denote the act of reflection or contemplation. Anumāna is inference; it is one of the six pramāṇas or valid means of knowledge and is accepted by all the six schools of Hindu philosophy (darśana). The word Nyāya, after which is named one of the six schools of Hindu philosophy, means logic. Tarka and yukti are also words used to denote logic. These different words are used to denote different dimensions of reason.

In Islam

Verily, in the creation of the heavens and earth, and the alternation of the night and the day, and the ships which sail through the sea with benefits for people, and what Allah has sent down from the heavens of rain, giving life thereby to the earth after its lifelessness and dispersing therein every creature, and in His directing of the winds and the clouds controlled between the heaven and the earth are signs for a people who use reason. Surat al-Baqarah 2:164

In Christianity

Paul commands us to think about what he says. Use your mind. Engage your reasoning powers when you hear the word of God. Jesus warned what happens if we don't and what blessing may come if we do. In the parable of the soils, he said concerning the seed sown on the path: "When anyone hears the word of the kingdom and *does not understand it*, the evil one comes and snatches away what has been sown in his heart." Understanding with the mind is not optional. Our lives hang on it. And concerning the seed sown on good soil, he says, "This is the one who hears the *word and understands it*. He indeed bears fruit and yields, in one case a hundredfold, in another sixty, and in another thirty" (Matthew 13:23).

Democratic Reason

Individual decision making can often be wrong due to misinformation, impulses, or biases. Collective decision making, on the other hand, can be surprisingly accurate. In Democratic Reason, Hélène Landemore demonstrates that the very factors behind the superiority of collective decision making add up to a strong case for democracy. She shows that the processes and procedures of democratic decision making form a cognitive system that ensures that decisions taken by the many are more likely to be right than decisions taken by the few. Democracy as a form of government is therefore valuable not only because it is legitimate and just, but also because it is smart.

Landemore considers how the argument plays out with respect to two main mechanisms of democratic politics: inclusive deliberation and majority rule. In deliberative settings, the truth-tracking properties of deliberation are enhanced more by inclusiveness than by individual competence. Landemore explores this idea in the contexts of representative democracy and the selection of representatives. She also discusses several models for the "wisdom of crowds" channelled by majority rule, examining the trade-offs between inclusiveness and individual competence in voting. When inclusive deliberation and majority rule are combined, they beat less inclusive methods, in which one person or a small group decide. Democratic Reason thus establishes the superiority of democracy as a way of making decisions for the common good. - Hélène Landemore.

Inclusion is a central tenet in deliberative democratic theory and an important indicator of the quality of a deliberative mini-public (DMP). Empirical measures of deliberation assess the quality of a deliberative exchange according to criteria drawn from deliberative theory; the discourse quality index is one well-known example. Despite the importance of inclusion in deliberative theory, existing measures do not account for this aspect of deliberative quality. This paper introduces and uses a measure for assessing the inclusiveness of deliberation called "deliberative uptake". This paper describes the new measure and applies it to the case of Ireland's Convention on the Constitution, a forum in which both citizens and politicians were included as members. The results suggest that politician members were more likely to receive deliberative uptake for their ideas than their citizen counterparts. In addition, women and men received similar levels of deliberative uptake throughout the Convention.

In India, this theory was well understood and practised within the Parliament and outside during the period 1950-1975. It was blacked out during 1975-77 and deliberative dictator theory was found more convenient by the party in power during that period. Fortunately, the theory was recaptured and re-established by the people of the country throwing out the deliberative dictator theory. That was the golden day in the Indian Democracy providing full breathing capacity to the citizens. The Panchayat Raj which became integral part of the Constitution of the country rejuvenated the continuance of the deliberative democratic theory.

This is flourishing at the villages, talukas and districts levels but gradually sinking in the Parliamentary body, metros and cities. The reason could be attributed to misunderstanding and misuse of the word 'inclusiveness' occurring in the theory. This has been gaining its strength since recent past leading a paradoxical theory. The extent of damage it has inflicted on the decency and dignity of the Parliamentary body is enormous. The paradoxical theory has hit hard both the ruling party and the parties in opposition inventing a new kind of instrument or process to disregard and disrespect the deliberative democratic theory due to, a large extent, exclusion of the inclusiveness.

The political system in the Parliament is working poles apart missing the cohesiveness and common sense. Inclusiveness in the deliberative democratic theory is the golden basis and fundamental to the democratic functioning. Time now that the both the ruling parties [coalition] and the parties in the opposition come together in auguring more inclusiveness in the theory failing which the pillars of the democracy may start shaking up. Because, the non-inclusiveness that is what generally being expressed is not because of that reason but because of reorienting the theory of confrontation in deliberative democratic process that has seeped down among the parties' members and the citizens in general. The hallucinating signal has started showing up. In medical terms, according to Online Dictionary, hallucination means – 'A sense perception in the absence of an external cause. Hallucinations may involve sights (visual hallucinations), sounds (auditory), smells (olfactory), tastes (gustatory) and touch (tactile) or size (dimensional). Hallucinations should be distinguished from delusions-which are mistaken ideas.

Wikipedia states – 'Confrontation is an element of conflict wherein parties confront one another, directly engaging one another in the course of a dispute between them. A confrontation can be at any scale, between any number of people, between entire nations or cultures, or between living things other than humans. Metaphorically, a clash of forces of nature, or between one person and his own causes of internal turmoil, might be described as a confrontation.

It has been noted that the term confrontation has "a negative image, largely because people tend to confront others not about pleasant things but about painful, unpleasant things" and that it also "suffers from the stigma of being overly aggressive in both nature and intent".[1] An examination of a hypothetical confrontation is the basis of confrontation analysis (also known as dilemma analysis), an operational analysis technique used to structure, understand and think through multi-party interactions such as negotiations. It is the underpinning mathematical basis of drama theory.[2]'

Confrontation happens among other living beings due to rage and provocation but among the human beings, it is happening consciously creating a state of confusion in the orderly conduct of the democratic functioning system. In fact, it should have been in reverse order, in that, the humans having a higher level of Consciousness should have more cooperated with the sense of inclusiveness that has capacity to minimize the confrontational attitude but as we have been witnessing the confrontation is being given greater consideration at the Parliamentary level, religious level, societal level and citizens level. It is said that the water runs downwards and not upwards; that is what could be considered when the confrontation at higher platforms flows down below at various levels stated before. So, one confrontation multiplies several confrontations which are its basic character. It is not that we cannot coalesce but we don't have time to think towards that possibility, the reason being the confrontation prevails in a highly charged atmosphere in the country as it is happening at the upper levels.

Such precept does not occupy the minds of the learned people such as the persons holding high positions in the governance system or the learned Members of the Parliamentary body or the teaching and lecturing professional. It is so because we think that the learning is different from personal behaviour, teaching and lecturing. This is the hard rock that prevents the passage of the learning process down below people. In life, there is a great gap between the ideal and the practical; between precept and practice. It is not always easy for anyone except for great souls like Gandhiji—to practice what they preach. For example, a father may tell his son that he should rise early and set about his daily duties. But he may not set an example himself and he may get up late. Seeing this, his son is not likely to follow any advice is always easy to offer advice, but difficult to follow such advice. Hence, if one wants to improve others one must set an example. A good man may be illiterate. But he can guide and be a model to even educated people by showing how he got the quality of Goodness. He does not talk about such quality but acts well and thus induces others to follow his example. Thus it is better to act well and show the way rather than talk well and be stagnant.

Such situations promote more confrontation than using the standard of knowledge one possesses for exemplification to others that bring a sense of awareness of difference between the confrontation and cooperation or inclusiveness. Let us not blame the common people for what they do or talk about for; they are doing and talking about what they have been able to comprehend from the visual acts of the learned people reflected through the electronic or presented in a printed form. They find from what they have seen or read about the public figures and politician does not match with what they find such people in real life, especially, talking is common while walking on the talk is rare. Such practice gets imbibed among the people who believe talking is better than acting. The core understanding that God has gifted to humans is more misused than using it for the benefit of the people to follow what others talked out and have actually been practising. Once this ignites in the human mind, the behavioural pattern from the top to bottom undergo sea change intended for increasing the strength of the democratic system of functioning. This is the first lesson for obviating the theory of confrontation. Act good Zone, talk good oneself and set a life of practice by oneself that is how one can change the hearts of the millions.

A carriage system works on two or multi wheels but not on one wheel; so the deliberative democratic theory cannot work on one wheel but on multi wheels and, if one wheel is to be invented for the carriage, it is bound to fall flat on the ground. This creates paradoxical conditions highly harmful for the functioning of the democracy, the functionality of democracy being art of balancing as against unbalancing. In life, there is a great gap between the ideal and the practical; between precept and practice.

Diversity, equity, and inclusion are three closely linked values held by many organizations that are working to be supportive of different groups of individuals, including people of different races, ethnicities, religions, abilities, genders, and sexual orientations. The same definition should have an automatic extension in all the spheres of life of the people in democratic functioning. However, in general, inclusive means to include or encompass all individuals or groups, while exclusive means to exclude or restrict access to certain individuals or groups. Understanding the difference between these two words is crucial in creating a welcoming and accepting environment.

Conversely, majoritarianism is a political philosophy or ideology with the agenda asserting that a majority based on a religion, language, social class, or other category of the population, is entitled to a certain degree of primacy in society, and has the right to make decisions that affect the society. This traditional view has come under growing criticism and liberal democracies have increasingly included constraints on what the parliamentary majority can do, in order to protect citizens' fundamental rights. A parliament that gives law-making power to any group that holds a majority of seats may be called a majoritarian parliament. Such is the case in the Parliament of the United Kingdom and the Parliament of India) and many other chambers of power.

Under a democratic majoritarian political structure, the majority would not exclude any minority from future participation in the democratic process. Majoritarianism is sometimes pejoratively referred to by its opponents as "ochlocracy" or "tyranny of the majority". Majoritarianism is often referred to as majority rule, which may refer to a majority class ruling over a minority class, while not referring to the decision process called majority rule. Majority rule is a belief that the majority community should be able to rule a country in whichever way it wants. However, due to active disempowerment of the minority or minorities, in many cases what is claimed as the majority with the right to rule is only a minority of the voters.

"MAN IS A HOSTAGE TO THE CAGE OF CULTURAL PROGRAMMING AND THE MASS HALLUCINATION OF THE PROPAGANDIST'S NARRATIVE ILLUSION." — JAMES SCOTT, SENIOR FELLOW, THE CENTER FOR CYBER INFLUENCE OPERATIONS STUDIES

The Unity in Diversity is also based on multi wheel and not on one wheel carriage system; the multi wheel system is stronger than one wheel system carriage, more so when it encompasses the inclusiveness with liberty to discharge the role as majoritarian and minority with the latter playing as an opponent which means the opposition has to work in the legislature and outside the legislature. In the legislature, the opposition party is mainly controlling the goals of the government through parliamentary devices, forcing the government to achieve the proper direction and to think the people's questions in a priority manner. Also important is that the majority has to accord due place and respect to the minority in the parliament proceedings that facilitates bridging the fine gap that otherwise exists between the majority and the minority.

THIS IS THE ULTIMATE JOY OF INDIA'S UNITY IN DIVERSITY

Chandrayaan-3 mission: United in joy... a nation cheers its touchdown on surface of Moon [TNN / Updated: Aug 24, 2023, 06:33 IST]

Nation is celebrating its monumental achievement of Chandrayaan-3 landing on Moon. Pained to note that some political parties are making mockery of it saying the present government has taken credit for what was done by their predecessors. ISRO was established on August 15, 1969. It was established by Vikram Sarabhai. ISRO succeeded its predecessor organisation named Indian National Committee for Space Research (INCOSPAR), which was established in 1962.

A house is built brick by brick. So was also about ISRO. ISRO is the transformation of the past into the present form. ISRO is now a huge family of great Scientists, Scholars and Astronauts of multi-religions and multi-languages. ISRO is an organization and not a political body.

How can we divide the achievements of ISRO as belonging to one political set up at the initial stage, another political set up as it marched ahead and yet another political set up as it entered futuristic India and made a monumental achievement? Doing that is undermining one's own wisdom. **"Knowing yourself is the beginning of all wisdom." — Aristotle**

R. K. Laxman, a great Cartoonist is no more. He used to make cartoons of the political leaders and events of the day through the 'Common Man' in the left corner of the front page of Times of India. He would have made a fitting Cartoon on the petty statements of the politicians when the country has made a monumental achievement, if he were to be alive today. His Common Man is the one shown below and one can see him on Google Website in various forms of political zigzagging during days the Cartoonist was alive.

."BUT LIKE INFECTION IS THE PETTY THOUGHT: IT CREEPS AND HIDES, AND WANTS TO BE NOWHERE--UNTIL THE WHOLE BODY IS DECAYED AND WITHERED BY THE PETTY INFECTION... THUS SPOKE ZARATHUSTRA." — FRIEDRICH NIETZSCHE.

Truth has one face while the untruth has many faces. Truth does not seek for any excuse while the untruth always searches for an excuse. Truth cannot be divided; it is the same for one and all. To believe what is told by one is false by the other, then the essence of truth stands washed out. When the other considers a false as a truth, one who told the truth has to distrust the other. Both know democracy works on trust. What Pakistan admitted recently about Pulawama bared what the other said about against his own country and about soldiers killed? At least, common sense given by God in everyone would have been applied by the other what is truth and what is false in matters like National Security and National Interest; not doing so is like sending a bouquet to the hostile country. There is no strong opposition political party or parties possessed with political consensus rather they are acting like strong opponents that makes wide difference in understanding what is known as political wisdom............

Freedom of Speech is like breathing for the body; choking it or misapplication of it makes the body to lose the Life for ever. Misapplication or abuse of freedom can also be attributed to a severe virus that entrenches the body of the Constitution like the one that happens to humans. We have reached seventy three years of our country becoming Republic. A child when it is admitted in nursery class ascends to higher classes according to enlargement of its knowledge and reaches a respectable level of education for the good of itself and the country in which it is born. This simple thinking has not understood by the political parties. A leader's maturity needs to be much larger than a child's maturity. The wisdom, political maturity and meaningful interaction, should be the hallmark of the parliamentary system in democracy.

The statement a politician or a political party makes must be based on the facts and not fictions. When I am driving a car, I see another car coming opposite to me but if I say opposite car is coming in wrong lane, I must know myself before saying so whether I am driving in right lane. Whether I was driving the car in the right lane or whether the opposite car was driving in the wrong lane will be known when both cross the other if such crossing results in an accident when it is the law that alone decides who was driving in the right or wrong lane but if farsightedness would been applied by one or the other, the crossing would not have resulted in any accident. This state of farsighted mind or maturity is missing among the politicians and political parties in our country that drives them to the corner of confrontation when the corner of reconciliation adjacent there to is available for alternative solution.

<u>"To find fault is easy; to do better may be difficult." This insightful quote by Plutarch encapsulates the human tendency to criticize and complain effortlessly, while actually taking action to improve or surpass the existing standards requires considerable effort and determination. At its core, this quote emphasizes the importance of not only identifying flaws and deficiencies but also striving to enhance them, thus highlighting the significance of active participation and personal responsibility.</u> In our society, it is all too common to witness people readily pointing out flaws and inadequacies without contributing any meaningful solutions or constructive ideas. It is a convenient stance to adopt – to loudly voice grievances and find fault with whatever does not meet our expectations or standards. However, while identifying problems can serve as a catalyst for change, it alone does not resolve anything. Merely criticizing without striving to do better perpetuates a cycle of dissatisfaction and stagnation. To truly make a difference, one must embrace the challenging journey of striving for improvement. This requires more than just a desire for change; it necessitates commitment and the willingness to put in the hard work required to surpass or rectify what is seen as inadequate. Taking the initiative to go beyond finding faults and instead focusing on creating solutions and improvements can be demanding, but the rewards are immeasurable. Interestingly, this quote by Plutarch also brings to light a philosophical concept known as the "perfectibility of man" – the belief that humans have innate qualities that enable them to continuously strive for improvement. This concept emphasizes the transformative power of individuals and their ability to transcend existing limitations. It challenges the notion that finding fault is the end goal, instead arguing that seeking improvement is an inherent human trait that sets us apart from other species. By comparing and contrasting the act of finding fault with the pursuit of doing better, we realize that finding fault tends to be reactionary and passive, while striving for improvement demands active involvement and personal growth. It is far easier to criticize shortcomings from a distance than it is to roll up our sleeves and actively contribute towards a solution. Yet, as Plutarch suggests the easy road of fault-finding leads to complacency and perpetuates the very flaws we seek to correct. Ultimately, this quote serves as a reminder that our true potential lies not in our ability to find fault in others or the

world around us, but in our capacity to translate those criticisms into tangible actions that drive progress. It is through the dedication and perseverance to do better that we can effect positive change in both our own lives and society as a whole. In conclusion, Plutarch's quote is a powerful reflection on human behavior and societal norms. It highlights the ease of finding fault and the difficulty of actively doing better. By introducing the philosophical concept of the perfectibility of man, we delve deeper into the significance of striving for improvement. It is a call to action, reminding us that in order to make a meaningful impact, we must transcend the realm of criticism and actively contribute to the betterment of ourselves and our surroundings. Let us embrace the challenge and embark on the journey of doing better." [Emphasis added]

> Anas reported: The Messenger of Allah, peace and blessings be upon him, said, "Blessed is he who is occupied with his own Faults over the Faults of people."
>
> (Source: Musnad al-Bazzār 6237)

The common sense of understanding each other is gifted by God to human and, even, to other livings on Mother Earth. This is so because the Other Living Beings also fight fiercely each other but have also ability to come to mutual understanding which is governed by the natural Doctrine of Reconciliation. Let us use it for further betterment and not for detriment. Betterment flows like clean water while detriment tries to block the flowing water in a river. Misunderstanding multiplies the misreading in minds in human that has the capacity to create blockage in the human body like the detriment creates blocking the flowing water. The human has both the options but important of them is that one should not structure the misunderstanding inasmuch as unstructured misunderstanding keeps the door of the human heart open that has capacity to restore the understanding among human as it existed originally. Human ego undermines the reconciliation effort. Ego should consult the Conscience adjacent to the Soul that counsels using ego in reconciliation generates negativity while not using it generates positivity – the affinity - the Hope of Life to Live.

PART 01
PARADOXES - A REFLECTION

"If you do not take an interest in the affairs of your government, then you are doomed to live under the rule of fools." - Plato

"Religion is regarded by the common people as true, by the wise as false and by rulers as useful." – Seneca

India is moving towards becoming an intelligent and industrious nation in the world but unmoving in its communal conflagration. Religious right is crossing the Constitutional limit. Religion is for me and my family within my home and place of my worship, ignorance of which is blinding us to know how to distinguish between religion and human. Every citizen's welfare is the only way to make the nation great. The ultimate truth of development of a country is the upbringing of the downtrodden to a level of respect and wellbeing of its people and security of the country. A democratic nation is built not by one Faith but by all the Faiths living therein together as an integral part of the nation.

Seventy five years after Independence and seventy three years after becoming Republic, as an octogenarian, I am forced to question myself whether we fought for the Independence and Republican democracy to test our inter-relationship fighting capacity or to endow the citizens with those golden principles pronounced in the Preamble of our Constitution? Former is showing a demonic face while the latter is depressing and disgruntling in the storm evolving and spreading every morning; the democratic dust. This dust is becoming so thick that we are almost blinded to understand the very meaning of life through the democratic process we have chosen for; we have been accumulating the dust as against democratic way of life. For this, everyone is blameworthy because everyone is more eager to be part of the dust than democratic evolution. The dust used in the sense of democratic functioning is increasing aggressive tones of caste, creed, religion, selfishness, corruption, black money, drug addiction, upmanship, self-contradictions and trafficking, infighting for expanding the space for liquor sale {an anti-thesis of Father of Nation} in the society, none of them is conducive and capable to provide self-sustenance, self-evolving, self-dignity and minimum means of livelihood to the neediest citizens through speedier economic development of the country.

Why is it so? Because we have chosen a wrong path in the democratic race in place of the path decorated with jewels enunciated in the Preamble. The opposition political parties think it is their birth right to criticise anything and everything integral to democracy while the ruling political party thinks what all it is doing is for the betterment of the citizens of the country. Both are true in their own understanding because there is no democratic testing code to measure whether what was done or is being done is for the citizen's welfare and in their best interests. That crops up contradictions in the style of functioning of the democracy. Futuristic democracy in India otherwise would remain just in words. **"The future depends on what you do today." -** — Mahatma Gandhi

How should we describe of what has been happening since recent past in our country? Politics acts as an invisible instigator for reasons of mutual party or personal mistrust, the object of which is to enjoy the lit fire with pretending expressions. Politics is omnipresent, more so, in miscreation in society. Search for an opportunity for doing that is the essence of the breathing of politics, that is what the politicians think today. Saying that 'Be silent and Do silently is only the wishful thinking. Silence is the strength seems to be a foregone saying which now seems to be substituted by 'Be violent. Be violating. Violence is the strength.' Silence soothes while violence simmers the Conscience. We boast we are educated, highly educated, engaged in educating illiterate, in innovations and inventions for the betterment of our country. We seem to have forgotten what is education or higher education or innovation or invention?

Education helps citizens to meet basic job qualifications and makes them more likely to secure better jobs'. What is Education For? Relevant here to reproduce excerpts from an Article "What is Education for? By Sir Ken Robinson, Kate Robinson - March 2, 2022 posted on the Website: "edutopia":

"………So, what does it mean to be educated now? Well, I believe that education should expand our consciousness, capabilities, sensitivities, and cultural understanding. It should enlarge our worldview. As we all live in two worlds—the world within you that exists only because you do, and the world around you—the core purpose of education is to enable students to understand both worlds. In today's climate, there is also a new and urgent challenge: to provide forms of education that engage young people with the global-economic issues of environmental well-being…….."

This we have forgotten altogether and have considered education as the matter of policy of the party in power. Absence of this foundational meaning and essence of education after the country became Republic led to evolving educational policy according to whims and fancies of the politicians at relevant times according to their political ideologies that caused immense injury to the basic concept of education and has fractured into pieces which is promoting and encouraging unseemly acts both by the politicians and the religious leaders. In every civilization and centuries, there were educated and uneducated communities. Yet, their foundational understanding of togetherness to survive each other was uppermost in their minds. That way, each community realized the truth of life. Our educated ancestors enlightened the communities they lived with while today we are though boast highly educated, we are uneducated, the simple reason being we are indifferent to each other which generates a more unhealthy society. The distance about the education that ought to have been maintained from political ideology or religion has been blurred, if not, erased whereby free for all voices started echoing in the country. Today, even issues that ought to have remained within the realm of religious practices are spilling over in the public domain. The schools, the children and the parents are the victims of the changing philosophy and ideologies of education whereby we seem to have lost meaning of inherited integrated knowledgeable education. The political parties that assume power accord first priority on changing the existing policy in schools and colleges. What education policy was there in the morning was not there by the evening. That is the state of affairs.

The ancestral knowledge and wisdom that stood the test even during seven hundred years that country was ruled by the invaders forming a strong foundation of integrated education was considered not worthwhile to continue. So, what we built over the years after becoming democracy is now standing without any foundation that is being reshuffled by the political party assuming the power rather than keeping updated the historical events and facts retaining the foundation as it stood prior thereto. This is downgradation of our own self-respect that is spurting indiscipline, disorder, and violence, revengeful attitudes among the youngsters that erupts ultimately in the society and among the Faiths. It is wrong to say our youngsters are misguided by someone or the other within and from outside our country because that is happening due to our sinking foundation of education, the strongest of which were to be protected, including conduct, character, courage, confidence, conviction, discipline, mutual understanding and orderliness. Education inculcated euphoria that turned most of us into negativity without understanding the basic meaning of that word. Online Free Dictionary defines 'euphoria', among others, as 'an exaggerated state of happiness, with no foundation in truth or reality.'

Let us understand and appreciate: is it expected of an educated person to remain unconscious or conscienceless when he or she or they venture upon ugliest acts, an insult to the education, learning and earning and, above all, being educated, an insult to self. These essences are burnt within when one or many want to flare up a social or religious or cultural issues in the given circumstances or situation. Mutual love and appreciation is the live wire of life.

Time now that we the citizens of the country belonging to different Faiths and lived together for centuries must give message to the politicians and the religious leaders that their affinity to each other in seizing a chance or opportunity to create social and religious tensions must stop. Also that, we the citizens of the country should increase their affinity towards respecting each other and each other's' Faiths. Any injury to a Faith, psychological or physical inflicted by any citizen of another Faith, must be taken immediate cognizance by the law enforcement authorities and prosecution process must be initiated without waiting for any signal from somewhere or the other.

The greatest weakness of our democracy lies here. One who is assigned with a duty to obey the rule of law ignoring any red signal from anywhere? That is duty and rest is disobedience of rule of law whether it is governance, administration and enforcing mechanism; law does not suggest looking at the green or red signal. Addition to their various privileges and powers, the politicians have acquired the art of signalling, red or green {Yellow color is used to 'wait' until appearance of red or green} which they click for the law enforcing authorities and for their opportunistic times. This is known as mockery of duty in democracy. They click the signal to wait till the flaring up the tension. Tension and clashes would have crossed the limits of their control. It is like not using kerosene to lit up the lamp in the night and using it when sun rises in the sky.

The complexities of Faiths are not created by God but by humans through the ages that necessitated in the given time(s). One is faithful to his or her Faith when one embraces God through one's perception and path of prayer as per one's own Faith. As believed in all the Faiths, Creator is ONE. The difference is different incarnations of the Creator according to the needs of the time(s). Those who berate one Faith over the other are ignorant of the genesis of the Faith deserving condemnation. So say our ancestral Holy Scriptures and Saints. Also, according to them, God is happy when contentious issues are mutually settled that gives a heavenly feeling and unhappy when such issues are made quarrelsome that gives a hell like feeling. This is ascertainable by anyone from one's own Conscience within wherein resides the righteousness bestowed by God upon humans.

Should we say we have not undergone any change at all from the practices our ancestors followed for centuries in the past? That has not happened in any belief or faith because the entire Earth environmental operation has been undergoing change from time immemorial. We have changed and continue to change that is the call of the hour we are living. The day we understand we are one among our different Faiths, one among our different cultures, one among our different languages, one among our different political and religiosity, we can say we understood what is 'oneness' which generates highest order of strength psychologically and physically to make us stand together to secure our own better living conditions as well as the interests of our country until our last drop of blood. That is what I believe, every citizen wants to be which we could realize through our own conscience that leads us to a happiest moment of life for everyone regardless of the bickering by the political and religious leaders which works like breathing for their body, the latter is loaded with selfishness for power and money while the former unites us to protect each other's interests in every aspect of our and our nation's growth and welfare.

The religious leaders will change, the political parties will change and the people will change that is part of the democratic life but such change should be one that originates not in individualized but collective form or individuals' integrated voice culminating into a national voice, whether there is threat to the security of our nation or there is a peacetime. That way, we would be able to build strength to stand up to the challenges whether internal or external, thus hold our head high within the country and the world. This message should be made clear within and outside by the citizens of the country in words, actions and deeds. That is reverberation of oneness of the country.

Faiths and politics are part and parcel of economic development, welfare and security of everyone in the country. Democracy has only one meaning – Be good to all and do well to all, the foundation of prosperity of one and everyone. Enlightening everyone in every Faith through religious teachings and guidance, education, culture and economic welfare both by the religion and the state is the sacred and sole object and duty of democracy. All efforts otherwise would become futile, fruitless, frustrating, fighting each other; an invitation to the frightening futuristic democracy. This onus lies on every generation which is none but in our lineage that would reap what we sow today.

In writing this book, I am not guided by the statistical development of India which is changing and open to distortions by the political parties in power to best suit their taste.. We also found the ruling political parties, late seventies onwards, befooling the people presenting the progress said to have been made to ameliorate the poverty and misery of the people of the country through this or that measure, scheme. This became a routine recital whenever we found change in the ruling political party. The governing system presents its achievement and print and electronic media at the pains of the public money. Who believes it if the reality speaks in different language. It so continues, how long not known for; even now, we continue to talk about them and introduce newer kinds of welfare schemes to better their living conditions. What does it mean? It means more musical noise than the sound; rhetoric rather than realistic.

I have not made any specific study but seen in the reports and news items that we had not been sincere in our efforts so far to build a self-sustaining nation to make its citizens self-confident to self-create, self-advance in life with self-dignity, the only one that is the decider of real economic and security strength. There is an impression that all the political parties that ruled the country all these years found more gracious to place self-interests before the interests of the nation and the people and such self-interest also included misutilization of the public funds for promotion of the interests of the political parties and the politicians. This, if continued, would have catastrophic effect for the Future India.

There seems some uneasiness growing within the calmness of the sentiments of the people of our country like dust trying to swarm vastness of the Earth. Its origin is known to none because what we see on the surface are its tiny particles. This is what appeared to me while reading daily newspapers that are reporting about religious and castes conflicts in the society on one or the other account, such as, irresponsible and nonsensical speeches, propagation of conversions, showing ferocity in interfaith relationships including interfaith marriages, the cruelty of rapes including killing the victim, targeting to tarnish the images of someone or the other baiting them to one or other evil designed acts, roaring debates upon them on the free for all the TV channels, the street corner talks by a group of people of all faiths, all playing the part of flying balloons in the air in different colors attracting those watching them from earth which way the balloons will be moving about.

These are, according to me, the offshoots working behind the politico-religious individualized or combined hard pushers yearning to see eagerly the actions and reactions among the political leaders, religious leaders, learned and scholars, youths and the common people. They have words in their pocket to defend their utterance not known to the common man. This is becoming perfunctory acknowledged unmindfully as happenings with sounds of warnings one could hear from here and there that strict action would be taken. When something of this kind happens once, should stop at once, once the warning is honoured and action is taken. That does not happen because it has acquired the character of habituation and routineness.

About the avoidable controversies we are used to create to keep our names shining in the media which, in essence, is like beating the drum without sound, substance and sensibility in the era in which we are living which calls for only One Voice, that is, betterment of the living conditions of the people irrespective of the Faiths they belong, through speediest education and economic development. This essential breathing for the survival of the human body is being pushed to secondary status just to divert the needs of the people keeping one or the other controversy floating in the air.

Quietness enhances the dignity of the person and the religion he or she belongs while Quarrelsomeness shows inborn hatredness of the person making such utterances. Above all, such utterances, in my view, are formulated in the mind of the person uttering when he or she is idling the time that is equal to a devil's workshop. Such sayings present to the people a most awkward and uglier thinking mindset of the person{s} that should shame self for; the people in the country know what is what and who is who. The meaning of DOCTRINE is a principle or position or the body of principles in a branch of knowledge or system of belief: dogma that remains more preserved among the citizens.

There is a saying "Before you condemn someone else for a wrongful act, check your behaviour and see if you too, have committed an act similar or even worse than the act that person has done. Then you won't be in a position to judge." – Ellen J. Barrier.

It is high time both print and electronic media to highlight the needs for essence of survival of the people of the country than highlighting such ill-conceived utterances that has no solution in hand to solve the peoples' problems. Media also needs to appreciate highlighting such speeches works like pouring oil in the fire with emerging emotional reactions. Media itself is integral part {Fourth Pillar} of the Democracy enriched with vast knowledge built up over seventy five years deals such matter with valuable suggestions to soften the heating up situation. Also, in my personal view, the Media is one forum that has the responsibility and the right to correct the wrong statements being made by the politicians that injures the sentiments of the majority of the people. It is Media that can remind the politicians the limits of their talking in the public gatherings relating to whatever matter and suggestively insulting the other political party (ies) for self-importance and self-advocated popularity. The political parties need to be subjected to close scrutiny to stop them to search for escapism. It needs to needle the person to prove the context and basis for such utterances that shows the velocity and velour of the media so that the people come to know the truth, whether it is biased, malicious or in reality. This would help dispel once and for all times the recurring recriminations in the society for which the people of the country would be grateful to media..

Hon'ble Supreme Court of India has recognized that the traditional words or usages have the force of law. More so, the constitution of the country does not confer any right expressly or impliedly to use the words and terms which are intertwined with religious relationships, as one likes for reason of their sensitivity and inherently prohibits making such statements. They seem to avoid understanding the Soul and Spirit of the Constitution and judicial interpretations by the highest Court of Law of the country rather more eager to turn its pages to find more misunderstandings, if any, which they could use as stick at every given opportunity.

"A flower does not think of competing with the flower next to it. It just blossoms." Zen Shin.

There is no Holy Scripture in any Faith that denies freedom, liberty to live, follow religious commands according to human decency and dignity envisaged therein and to love all and be loved by all. This is the beginning and end of the message to humans of every Faith so long the human is ordained to live on Mother Earth. Human wants to cross the limits laid down by God or Holy Scriptures that are outside the limits of humanity, an act against the very Nature. The rest of it is ignorance. The ignorance cannot be removed by chanting and reciting but by understanding the love filled and spirited strength contained in such chanting and recital – the foundation of humanity.

If the taste of a food item is sweet by its very nature, better to eat it as sweet and not to interpret as bitter, that bitterness lies on tongue of the person eating the sweet but not in sweet he or she is eating. This is necessary to understand the difference between the sweetness and the bitterness that is possible only when such person consults a dietician or doctor to confirm it; otherwise his or her tongue will only have the taste of bitterness throughout life.

Good words and deeds remain behind us when we depart from Mother Earth, accumulate them as many as one can while on Mother Earth for; they are the ornaments we will be wearing while leaving Mother Earth and the people for whom we said good words and done good deeds remember us forever, their wishes are conveyed to "ALMIGHTY". This should be the Lifecycle of everyone, so I wish.

Swami Chinmayananda used to explain: there is one electricity running through all the various equipments the light bulb, the fan, the refrigerator, the elevator, the TV, the microphone etc. There is one gold running through the gold ornaments, the bangle, the earring, the necklace, the anklet, etc. The one saptak of seven svara, and endlessly evolving ragas with countless compositions. How many expressions can there be of that one-ness? Innumerable. The expression is limited only by human imagination! The Indian culture dazzles, fascinates, and invites one to a journey of exploration. The one ānanda pursued in all of its diversity.

Let us first understand what is paradox? Britannica states '**paradox**, apparently self-contradictory statement, the underlying meaning of which is revealed only by careful scrutiny. The purpose of a paradox is to arrest attention and provoke fresh thought. The statement "Less is more" is an example. Francis Bacon's saying, "The most corrected copies are commonly the least correct," is an earlier literary example. In George Orwell's anti-utopian satire *Animal Farm* (1945), the first commandment of the animals' commune is revised into a witty paradox: "All animals are equal, but some animals are more equal than others." Paradox has a function in poetry, however, that goes beyond mere wit or attention-getting. Modern critics view it as a device, integral to poetic language, encompassing the tensions of error and truth simultaneously, not necessarily by startling juxtapositions but by subtle and continuous qualifications of the ordinary meaning of words'….

Wikipedia states 'A **paradox** is a logically self-contradictory statement or a statement that runs contrary to one's expectation.[1][2] It is a statement that, despite apparently valid reasoning from true premises, leads to a seemingly self-contradictory or a logically unacceptable conclusion.[3][4] A paradox usually involves contradictory-yet-interrelated elements that exist simultaneously and persist over time.[5][6][7] They result in "persistent contradiction between interdependent elements" leading to a lasting "unity of opposites".[8]

In logic, many paradoxes exist that are known to be invalid arguments, yet are nevertheless valuable in promoting critical thinking,[9] while other paradoxes have revealed errors in definitions that were assumed to be rigorous, and have caused axioms of mathematics and logic to be re-examined. One example is Russell's paradox, which questions whether a "list of all lists that do not contain themselves" would include itself, and showed that attempts to found set theory on the identification of sets with properties or predicates were flawed.[10][11] Others, such as Curry's paradox, cannot be easily resolved by making foundational changes in a logical system.[12]

Examples outside logic include the ship of Theseus from philosophy, a paradox that questions whether a ship repaired over time by replacing each and all of its wooden parts, one at a time, would remain the same ship.[13] Paradoxes can also take the form of images or other media. For example, M.C. Escher featured perspective-based paradoxes in many of his drawings, with walls that are regarded as floors from other points of view, and staircases that appear to climb endlessly.[14]

In common usage, the word "paradox" often refers to statements that are ironic or unexpected, such as "the paradox that standing is more tiring than walking".[15]

Let us then know what reflection is? Taylor & Francis Online defines reflection 'Reflection is widely endorsed by professional bodies and practitioners are required to document professional learning to evidence standards of professionalism. Due to the lack of a consensual definition for reflection, there is confusion regarding 'what reflection is'. Prior to the development of an empirical evidence base that explores reflection, it is important to develop a consensually agreed concept and definition to guide experimental research. The aim of this systematic review is to understand the concept of reflection by performing a synthesis of existing conceptually oriented qualitative studies. Fourteen sources were included in a thematic synthesis that resulted in the construction of four analytical themes: cognitive, integrative, iterative and active. These themes were explored in relation to existing research and a novel definition of reflection was proposed. It is hoped that this review will encourage further enquiry into the concept and process of reflection.

Paradox reflection births perplexity. The perplexity is a confused state of mind. According to Charles Loring Brace [(June 19, 1826 – August 11, 1890) was an American philanthropist who contributed to the field of social reform. He is considered a father of the modern foster care.] – 'When a child of the streets stands before you in rags, with a tear-stained face, you cannot easily forget him. And yet, you are perplexed what to do. The human soul is difficult to interfere with. You hesitate how far you should go.'

What is said before about the perplexity is to be seen from psychological but not physiological angle [*Physiological* relates to the physical and chemical processes of the body, and may be used to describe physical diseases or disorders. *Psychological* relates to the processes of the mind, and may be used to describe mental illnesses]. Can we stretch this analogy to what we are going through in the paradox among the political parties and religious bodies? Example of the child quoted before is the real in cities and metros but not in the towns and rural areas. It is so on account of denial of opportunies to live with minimum food and shelter in metros while in rural areas such scenes are out of sight – they live their life within what they earn but never beg. Begging is a professional function organized by the gangs in cities.

The governments say they are providing both the facilities to the deprived children in the cities and metros which are more of political show than a sustainable solution. This comes only through education and creating earning capacity to such children. The politicians are more interested in digging the holes for diverting the resources meant for welfare and freebies. Would they help or hamper the progression of the democracy in future according to prevailing ground realities? Are we preparing such opportunities also for passing them over to the coming generations? That would be day the democracy would be doomed. This is not the concern either of the politicians or the religious bodies as they seem to think. This is where we are stuck up because of our apathy and anguish that has engulfed us in our social life and national outlook.

What Quote has to do with reflection of perplexity? The Quote incorporates the child as the focal point. Who is a child? A human of a particular age. Who is the focal point in a democratic country, like ours? Citizen or citizens of different religions, age groups and of different social levels like richest, rich, middle class, poor and poorest. Both the political and religious bodies are well aware of these people but reflect perplexity towards them how to make them equal in their social standing, the crux of the democracy born from the synthesized words embedded in our Constitution. Both also know this. The heading of this Part 'Paradox Reflection' is intended to express how both the bodies reflex the perplexity in the context of our country for; either or both of them have not been able to understand the meaning of reflection enlightened in the Quote stated before even after our country becoming republic seventy three years ago. The reflection of the poor or poorest child is staring today at both of them; yet both are driving paradoxly believing words uttered by them are weightier than what brings out in reality of the larger part of our people; for the emptiness looks like beads of words while reality reflects the bare thread.

They don't accept this but keep insisting what they said is true and what others think about them is untrue. This stance continues and changes once in five years when citizens are counted with highest value on the eve of every state or national elections. Both do remember them at this hour lest they may lose the fight that comes once in five years, an opportunity to capture power and make self-prosperity. They shower all they have in their words, pocket and hands on the people who feel proud of the democracy that has conferred them such a high status without knowing at what lowest level they are still living in society although the contesting candidates know the truth. Any paradox thinking by the political bodies, the candidates and the religious bodies is considered excusable due to silence of the concerned that is independent in words but dependent in deeds. This was how our election system progressed for over seventy years of republic leaving least doubt that it would continue for years to come.

The Election Commission of India [ECI} is an independent body constitutionally which is a fact and not a fiction but the appointment of its Chief and Members being vested in the Executive, it always stands overshadowed. It is also a constitutional body but without constitutional bones that have strength to withstand the outside pressures. This strength lost its weight by reason of one Article in the Part dealing with the Election Commission that has made the ECI a boneless constitutional body. Being a constitutional body, it has yet been made to look at the ray passing through the governing system.

Time we delete this provision and accord ECI its due constitutional base so as to make it to stand on its own leg. This is so because the source of election financing originates only from the provision that is contained in the Representation of Peoples' Act, 1951 whereas the governing system believes there is no need to look at that provision and announces the sources for election funding as best suited to the governing system, not even having any prior consultation with ECI whereas the ECI is required to make prior consultations with the government on certain matters specified in the Act. Another interesting part is that powers to make rules under the RPA, 1951 solely vest in the government whereas the Laws {Acts} enacted for various purposes empower the bodies named therein to make rules for administration of the Law or the Act concerned. ECI is thus to act only through its Codes and Official Instructions in the administration of the RPA, 1951. Why such discrimination or paradox has been made to exist cannot be answered by a common man.

The Supreme Court of India has provided express authority for the ECI's approach to interpreting and augmenting India's electoral law. In the case of Mohinder Singh Gill & Anr. v. The Chief Election Commissioner, the Court commented, "the framers of the Constitution took care to leaving scope for exercise of residuary power by the Commission, in its own right, as a creature of the Constitution, in the infinite variety of situations that may emerge from time to time in such a large democracy as ours." And, further, "Once the appointment is made by

the President, the Election Commission remains insulated from extraneous influences, and that cannot be achieved unless it has an amplitude of powers in the conduct of elections – of course in accordance with the existing laws. But where these are absent, and yet a situation has to be tackled, the Chief Election Commissioner has not to fold his hands and pray to God for divine inspiration to enable him to exercise his functions and to perform his duties or to look to any external authority for the grant of powers to deal with the situation.(Mohinder Singh Gill & Anr. v. The Chief Election Commissioner, December 2, 1977.).

Unacknowledged excuse is money needed for election financing. Our forefathers who drafted the Constitution gave a direct message that the elections are not of individual citizens or of the capitalists but of the State and, if we ask the capitalists, they would think of earning twice the amount they contributed through quid pro quo deals, so also, is the case of politicians who are keen to exploit a given situation for the sake of self and for the political party one belongs. This process builds up competition among the political parties, the capitalist and the ministerial community using the civil servants as the best made conduit, the civil servants also having a pie in the amass and servility to their ministers. When the country was under rein of foreigners, the civil servants were patriotic as natives but now the natives having secured Independence and having made the country a Republic, believed more beneficial being close to the person holding the power. If mother poisons the child, who else is there to protect the child. The citizens of the country are the children of Mother Land whose welfare rests with the governing system and those associated with governance. Such sentimentality resides in those who have regard, respect and duty towards the citizens of the country that resides in the Conscience of human adjacent to the Soul, God.

The only answer to brighten the future of the country is to find an alternative mode for election financing doing away financing through quid pro quo deals which makes everyone corrupt including the entire governing system even though we may say with comfort that the laws of the country permit such method of contributions such as by companies and trusts etc. Are the laws unchangeable or we wanted to change the laws more for the benefit of the political parties and not for the piousness of the process of the democratic system?

I am eighty seven years old at the time of writing this book and have seen in my life how the elections financing revolves. For this reason, I have made my humble submissions in my book 'Freebies and Welfare Schemes A Fiscal Disaster & Suggested Framework for Electing Financing' [ISBN: 978-93-5704-9702] published in February, 2023. I also submitted the Suggested Framework including the governing rules to the Chief Election Commissioner of India with request to float a Consultative Paper for public opinion and contribution. The practice followed in our country is that the government invites suggestions from the citizens, the citizens take pains to make suggestions but the government remains silent placing the suggestions in a properly made file. Citizens are wiser than the governance, the judicial and administration functioning in the country and have enriched knowledge compared to those in those positions for; the positions they hold are for specific period whereas the citizens' experience is based on the changing situations and their knowledge gained through experiences life make them practical in place of preaching.

These paradoxes are inflicting avoidable injuries in the body of the democracy. If a picture of a cat is placed before me and asked whether it is cat or not, I should say it is cat and cannot say it is cat but not the one I assumed to be the cat without disclosing my assumptions. If I am standing in the middle of flooded river and the people are watching me from the two sides of the river banks and, if one bank side people want to swim to save me, I should not say I want the people standing on the other side of the bank of the river to save me. Time is most critical that leaves hardly any choice to anyone. So, one should not stand in the middle of the democratic structure that is one's lack of commitment to the cause of the democracy.

"Whatever you can do or dream you can do, begin it. Boldness has genius, power, and magic in it. Begin it now." — Johann Wolfgang von Goethe.

The Constitution is one for all the citizens of the country. The parliament and the judiciary are continuing to amplify the expression and spirit of the constitution in terms of laws and rulings. The political parties and the religious bodies seem to want such laws and rulings to be best suited and more favourable to their thoughts which are paradoxes within themselves. Can we discern homogeneity which is the antonym of paradox the way we are conducting ourselves in political and religious fields? Differences are as important in a democracy as are common or mutual. The right of reconciliation of difference exists in democratic system but not in autocratic and dictatorship systems, both having no space for consideration to 'difference [s]' let alone reconciliation. Even in democracy, differences beyond the limit of reconciliation compel breaking up of the understandings, relationship and mutuality.

The atmosphere of democracy in the country is worrisome due to increasing pollution of the political and religious noise, acts and deeds. Lack of respect to the rule of law and obligation to discharge the Fundamental Duties are also responsible for the birth of the negative effects in the atmosphere. There is also distinction in their application, one overlooks what is being done by the VVIPs and VIPs while the other captures what is done by the very ordinary persons [VOPs]. This has become a thumb rule that is creating a burning sensation in the society in general. First upholds and the second attacks any breach of the rule of law and duties. Let us take it a democracy paradox because answer lies outside the thinking of the ordinary person. Law enforcing authority thinks as the sole judge in such situations.

Party Systems in India: Patterns, Trends and Reforms

*

Mahendra Prasad Singh

**

Krishna Murari

Party Systems in India: Patterns, Trends and Reforms

Mahendra Prasad Singh[*]

Krishna Murari[**]

Lack of explicit constitutional compulsions has given a long rope to the politicians and the people of the country. Founders of the constitution thought that the democracy would mature over the time; the political system and the people would be capable of laying sound democratic foundation. That did happen during the first two decades of the country becoming republic. Signs of ruptures started showing up thereafter and headed towards unhealthy and amoral practices late seventies onwards unstoppable shaking the foundation throwing up dangers to the democratic structure of the country. Here is how?

Making up the Constitutional Gaps/Abeyances	
Constitutional Gaps/Abeyances	Submissions made by me in my book 'India's Futuristic Democracy – Threats of Constitutional Gap & Digital Era' – December, 2022 [Represent the Sum of the Gap/Abeyance. To understand the Sum, the logic and reasoning contained in the said book may be read together.]
A. Empowering Election Commission of India {ECI} for deregistration of the political parties	Election Commission registers the political party fulfilling the prescribed criteria. Once registered, the party takes for granted that the role of the Election Commission is over and the party is free to conduct its internal affairs and system as it likes. It should not be so. The object of registration of the political party under a particular law or rules is to regulate the functioning of the political party according to its internal regulations as it happens in the case of the companies registered under the Companies Act or the societies registered under the Societies Registration Act 1860. This part of enforcement does not exist today and I have not come across where the Election Commission debarred or disqualified the politically party on the grounds of its failure to function according to its internal rules forming part of the registration with the Election Commission whereas the companies or the firms registered under the Companies Act or the societies stated before are bound to follow literally the internal rules governing them, failing which the Iity which registered the parties pursues such failures, prosecute and punish the defaulters that includes both fine and imprisonment under the Companies Act as well as the Societies Registration Act. Why not so in the case of the political parties?
B. Limiting the number of political parties on identical political ideology basis but not based on religion, castes, creed and	The submission made before for enacting law on the Political Parties should include provisions for limiting the number of political parties considered expedient for the sake of transparency, prevention of corrupt practices in the elections and for easing the present burden placed upon

Making up the Constitutional Gaps/Abeyances	
Constitutional Gaps/Abeyances	Submissions made by me in my book 'India's Futuristic Democracy – Threats of Constitutional Gap & Digital Era' – December, 2022 [Represent the Sum of the Gap/Abeyance. To understand the Sum, the logic and reasoning contained in the said book may be read together.]
classes that act in opposite direction in the democratic structure.	the ECI including heavily increasing statutory and administrative expenditure from the public funds. It is submitted that at the national level, there could be only the political parties recognized in the order of their placement in the records of ECI at national level parties. The remaining national political parties not recognized on ECI records must merge with national recognized parties based on their inter-se closeness and fairness of their ideologies that eliminates the process of fractioning of the political parties, thus being followed.
C. Election Financing by the State – A crucial consideration for upholding the values and virtues of elections but none seems to be interested in them, the absence of which will drive the fate our democracy to a great uncertainty and may jeopardize the democracy itself.	Appendix to this book is a suggestive self-contained framework based on the views I could find from the articles on the website and according to my own understanding. The essence is not to suggest I have done something to solve the problem of election financing but to bring home to all the stakeholders that the present method{s} practised for election financing are illogical viewed from any angle, the same being of concealing nature open for enormous misuse in the process of elections as if the funds used by the parties and the candidates though are said to be according to permitted laws and rules, in rea they are not to so for two reasons; one that there is no mechanism to assess the funds applied or used for elections are within the total funds available at the disposal of the parties according to the their declarations and second that thereby the political parties and the candidates have their own inbuilt channels invisible to anyone to route the illegally held funds in the election process, an open field for both the political parties and their candidates.
D. Term of office of the Prime Minister needs to be defined which is presently remain open with no regard or limitation on the period of office.	To bring vibrancy in the government, it is considered desirable for the majority political party or in coalition to elect its Leader for appointment as Prime Minister for a period of not more than five years. It will be further desirable if young blood is injected after every five years that is bound to bring new blood culture that is incumbent for establishing good governance for the benefit of the people as well as to ensure the security of the nation. Those who ruled the country for a long period of ten or more than that period perforce established their own blood culture which may be good for an individual but not for the citizens, the society and the nation for, its limitations are made to be hidden opening scope for explosion. Electing any member of a majority political party or in coalition beyond five years not only would have greater stress and strain upon the incumbent, depending upon the age of such member, also limits to see the new horizon for furthering the interests of the people and the country whereas the younger blood would drive and encourage new energy and enthusiasm normally found among the newly elected

Making up the Constitutional Gaps/Abeyances	
Constitutional Gaps/Abeyances	**Submissions made by me in my book 'India's Futuristic Democracy – Threats of Constitutional Gap & Digital Era' – December, 2022 [Represent the Sum of the Gap/Abeyance. To understand the Sum, the logic and reasoning contained in the said book may be read together.]**
	member compared to the existing one whom the party may like to continue for the next five years and so on. Also a question is how the political party graduates and prepares its young blood to assume higher level of responsibilities within the party and the national as well? This is not being cultivated in our country.
E. Updating or Revision of existing Rules of Business of Parliament	Review of the Parliament Business Rules should include introduction of restrictions on boycotting, walkouts, usage of language, damage to property of the Parliament, Introducing, besides orientation course, roles and responsibilities of the parliamentarians; Organizing Annual Outing Meets for parliamentarians for not more than three days; Creation of a separate Parliamentary Security Academy under the Iity of the Presiding Officers for orientating parliament working system, security management and enforcement, training in changing technologies in their application for management and enforcement of security, Organizing Annual Conference of Secretary General level officers of Parliament and State Assemblies. Upgradation of existing Bureau of Parliament Studies and Training to the level of an Institute known as "Indian Parliament Studies, Research and Training Institute" {IPSRTI} with the same existing objects or additional objects as considered necessary as existing in other countries such as EU countries and UK.
F. ECI recommendations for Reforms in Election Laws pending with the Central government	All this I am submitting to draw the kind attention of the governance and the parliament that greater urgency needs to be accorded in such matters in the best interests of conducting fair and transparent elections and, with that understanding, it is imperative that there should be a prescribed time limit for the governance to consider the recommendations made by the Commission. Even after five years of submission of the recommendations, if the same are still sleeping in the cup boards of the concerned Iity, it amounts to a prejudicial act and the parliament and the commission need to be informed of the status for the pendency for such a long time. Whether or not what is in the interest or disinterest of the political parties arising from the recommendations stands subordinate to the implementation of the recommendations as cleared by the government seen in the context of much higher consideration of the interest involved in conduct of the elections and interests of the country but not the other way which seems to be the main cause for prolonged withholding of the clearance /approval. This pattern needs to change making suitable provision in the relevant law prescribing the time limit within which the government needs to accord its clearance or response to the recommendations and, if that is not

Making up the Constitutional Gaps/Abeyances	
Constitutional Gaps/Abeyances	**Submissions made by me in my book 'India's Futuristic Democracy – Threats of Constitutional Gap & Digital Era' – December, 2022 [Represent the Sum of the Gap/Abeyance. To understand the Sum, the logic and reasoning contained in the said book may be read together.]**
	ensured, it should be deemed that the government has no objection to the recommendations, on the expiry of the prescribed time limit to be prescribed as submitted above.
G. Independent Law for the political parties	For convenience, I humbly urge all the stakeholders to have a glance at the document titled: "Strasbourg, 14 December 2020 Study No. 881/2017 CDL-AD(2020)032 Or. Engl. EUROPEAN COMMISSION FOR DEMOCRACY THROUGH LAW (VENICE COMMISSION) OSCE OFFICE FOR DEMOCRATIC INSTITUTIONS AND HUMAN RIGHTS (OSCE/ODIHR) GUIDELINES ON POLITICAL PARTY REGULATION 2ND EDITION Approved by the Council of Democratic Elections at its 69th online meeting (7 October 2020) and Adopted by the Venice Commission at its 125th online Plenary Session (11-12 December 2020) on the basis of comments by OSCE/ODIHR Core Group of Experts on Political Parties Mr Josep Maria CASTELLA ANDREU (Member, Spain) Mr Pieter van DIJK (Expert, Former Member, the Netherlands) Mr Nicolae ESANU (Substitute Member, Republic of Moldova) Mr Ben VERMEULEN (Member, the Netherlands) posted on the Website which may be of help in systematizing and synthesising our existing law, rules and regulations in that respect. Amount of efforts that would have gone into in formulating these Guidelines for the benefit and safeguarding the democratic credentials are worthy of acknowledgement and high appreciation by the democratic countries including our own country. It is worth emulating in India to the extent considered as relevant in the context of the Indian democracy. On 1 January 2020, the population of the European Union (EU) with 27 Member States was estimated at 447.7 million. The system of government in states in India closely resembles that of the Union. There are 28 states and 8 Union territories in the country.
H. Defection of elected member(s) from one political party to another political – Amendment of Oath of Office in place of making laws on Defections which encourage defections rather than demolishing them.	Seen from what has been happening in defections among the political parties, the unpleasant situations that confront the Presiding Officers as well as approaching the Hon'ble High Court or the Hon'ble Supreme Court by the aggrieved member at the national or state level, it appears the extant law on defections is not serving its intent and purpose envisaged therein abusing or misusing the provisions of law based more on the interpretations than the substance of the law. The process the political parties have been adopting to hide and control its members from possible defections has reached a stage which amounts insulting the democracy and the people of the country when such members of the party are abruptly shifted and placed in palatial hotels and resorts to

Making up the Constitutional Gaps/Abeyances	
Constitutional Gaps/Abeyances	**Submissions made by me in my book 'India's Futuristic Democracy – Threats of Constitutional Gap & Digital Era' – December, 2022 [Represent the Sum of the Gap/Abeyance. To understand the Sum, the logic and reasoning contained in the said book may be read together.]**
	keep them away from the political party engaged in inducement of the members. The system invites hundreds of crores of the rupees for inducement either arranged from out of the black money or by involving the big corporates. The symptoms of defection has assumed the symptoms of a serious disease in the political system making the whole system as jocular openly and unashamedly with electronic media playing as a spring board for publicity and the viewer's thinking what kind of democracy we are running round the country shocking those who voted for members awaiting for defection. It also seems such opportunities are availed by the intended defectors to earn huge unearned money overnight.
	Modifications to the Form of Oath or Affirmation specified in Third Schedule have been made in past by the parliament. There are no restrictions in the constitution that specifies the said Form for various dignitaries for amendment of the Form of Oath or Affirmation specified in Third Schedule. Modifications to the Form of Oath or Affirmation specified in Third Schedule have been made in past by the parliament. If the Legislature and Executive continue to overlook the immediate need for the amendment of the Constitution that the Defector or Defectors duly elected from one Political Party to another Political Party during his or her or their tenure as Member of the Parliament or State Legislature, such member {s} should take the Oath of Affirmation as modified and specified below subject to the same being passed by the parliament as in the past {Modifications suggested are underlines}:
	Form of oath or affirmation to be made by a member of Parliament:—
	"I, A.B., having been elected (or nominated) a member of the Council of States (or the House of the People) do swear in the name of God/solemnly affirm that I will bear true Faith and allegiance to the Constitution of India as by law established, that I will uphold the sovereignty and integrity of India and that I will Faithfully discharge the duty upon which I am about to enter."].
	<u>I further do swear in the name of God/solemnly affirm that I, during my tenure as member of the Parliament as such, will not defect from the political party on whose credentials I have been elected by the people of India to be member of parliament , as such, to any other political party whose credentials I have not attested or subscribed to as a member as such and, I further swear that if I contravened this swearing I have taken as aforesaid that will be deemed my defecting from the political party to which I belonged to another political to which I did not belong at the</u>

Making up the Constitutional Gaps/Abeyances	
Constitutional Gaps/Abeyances	**Submissions made by me in my book 'India's Futuristic Democracy – Threats of Constitutional Gap & Digital Era' – December, 2022 [Represent the Sum of the Gap/Abeyance. To understand the Sum, the logic and reasoning contained in the said book may be read together.]**
	<u>time I filed my nomination papers. I shall be further deemed to have resigned forthwith from the date of such defection and cease to be member so elected as such.</u> Form of oath or affirmation to be made by a member of Parliament:— "I, A.B., having been elected (or nominated) a member of the Legislative Assembly (or Legislative Council), do swear in the name of God that I will bear true Faith and allegiance to the Constitution of India as by law established, that I will uphold the sovereignty and integrity of India and that I will Faithfully discharge the duty upon which I am about to enter."] <u>I further do swear in the name of God/solemnly affirm that I, during my tenure as member of the Legislative Assembly (or Legislative Council) as such, will not defect from the political party on whose credentials I have been elected by the people of India to be member of Legislative Assembly (or Legislative Council), as such, to any other political party whose credentials I have not attested or subscribed to as a member as such and, I further swear that if I contravened this swearing I have taken as aforesaid that will be deemed my defecting from the political party to which I belonged to another political to which I did not belong at the time I filed my nomination papers, I shall be further deemed to have resigned forthwith from the date of such defection and cease to be member so elected as such.</u> Article 13(4) of the constitution specifies that nothing in this article shall apply to any amendment of this Constitution made under article 368. Article 368 (3) specifies nothing in article 13 shall apply to any amendment made under this article. Right to Freedom is part of the Fundamental Rights. But this right will have no effect with respect to amendments to the constitution made under Article 368, as submitted above. Therefore, the modification to the existing Form of Oath or Affirmation specified in Third Schedule will not violate the Right to Freedom contemplated under Part III – Fundamental Rights of the elected member covered under the Form of Oath or Affirmation specified in the said Schedule. This is an alternative mode for precluding the defections by incorporating self-made statement by a member in the relevant Form of Oath or Affirmation as aforesaid. The modification suggested to the existing Oath of Affirmation is to make it voluntary for the defecting member(s) to resign to be a member as such according to Oath he has taken. This does not involve legislative or legal implications or wrangles

Making up the Constitutional Gaps/Abeyances		
Constitutional Gaps/Abeyances	**Submissions made by me in my book 'India's Futuristic Democracy – Threats of Constitutional Gap & Digital Era' – December, 2022 [Represent the Sum of the Gap/Abeyance. To understand the Sum, the logic and reasoning contained in the said book may be read together.]**
	that is happening today because the members themselves are reluctant to further amend the relevant Article/Schedule of the Constitution which suggests they feel highly comfortable with the existing law with freedom to earn unearned money under the disguise of defection in lakhs and crores overnight amassed by the political party inducing him or her or them for defections with full protection by shifting such member or members to resorts to make them feel as homely as the situation demanded. Amendment to the existing Form of Oath or Affirmation as submitted above can be made in ordinary course as an amendment to the Constitution under Article 368 as done in several cases in the past.
I. Qualification Requirements for electing as a Member of Parliament or the Legislative Assembly/Council	With this background, it is submitted that:-
a. Minimum Qualification Requirement should be Tenth Class passed both for Parliament and the Legislative Assembly. In addition:
i. That in the case of Member of Parliament, such member would have served as a Member of Legislative Assembly for a period of not less than three years.
i. That in the case of Member of Legislative Assembly such member would have served as the Member of Panchayati Samiti for not less than three years.
b. Upper Age limit in the case of Member of Parliament should be 65 {Sixty Five} years; based on his or her date of birth incorporated in the Tenth or equivalent class Board Examination Certificate issued by competent Board.
c. Accordingly, on the date of filing of the nomination papers and its acceptance by the ECI, the candidate's age should be not more than 60{Sixty} years.
d. Upper Age limit in the case of Member of Legislative Assembly should be not more than 60 {Sixty} years based on his or her date of birth incorporated in the Tenth or equivalent class Board Examination Certificate issued by competent Board.
e. Accordingly, on the date of filing of the nomination papers and its acceptance by the ECI, the candidate's age should be not more than 55 {Fifty Five} years.
The Qualification and upper Age limit suggested above, if considered in order, or such other period (s) as considered appropriate, may be prescribed by law pursuant to Article 84 (c) of the constitution. It is also

Making up the Constitutional Gaps/Abeyances	
Constitutional Gaps/Abeyances	**Submissions made by me in my book 'India's Futuristic Democracy – Threats of Constitutional Gap & Digital Era' – December, 2022 [Represent the Sum of the Gap/Abeyance. To understand the Sum, the logic and reasoning contained in the said book may be read together.]**
	submitted that the suggestions made above have twin objects; firstly that the Qualification Requirement is not guided or based on higher educational qualification, if any or background and secondly, the upper age limit would automatically widen the scope for accommodating or absorbing the upcoming young people or politicians. This is also the basic feature of the Constitution that cannot be ignored, the reasons being that the democracy starts aging itself that weaken basic strength of the country in political maturity, economic development, national interest and the security interests of the country if the prevalent practice with unlimited freedom and privilege about the age limit and qualification requirements, constitutionally required to be prescribed but delayed and continue to be delayed for reasons of selfishness that about which we talk too much when it comes to the fact that the interests of the country and democracy should be before self-interest. There are no two definitions or meanings of self-interest; what applies in the latter case also equally apply in the former case.
J. Election Manifestos of the political parties – Boundary Limits	This provided the following points on the same:- 1. The election manifestos cannot be considered as a corrupt practice according to the Section 123 of The Representation of People's Act, 1951; and distributing freebies interrupts the process of a fair election. 2. The election commission must issue the model code of conduct as follows to en- sure free and fair election as it has done in the past; 3. If the election manifesto is made before the election dates are announced then the ECI has no authority to regulate, however, an exception can be made in exceptional cases. 4. The meetings with the political parties were conducted to maintain a balance between the rights of the political parties to announce their manifestos and maintain a level field for fair elections. 5. ECI made guidelines to political parties to ensure the spirit and directive principles of state policy are abided by for declaring welfare policies without exaggerated promises which prima facie seems objectionable. 6. Whether single-phase or multiphase election manifestos must not be released during the probationary period as per Section 126 of the Representation of People's Act, 1951. In sub-sector Para 4 of para I general conduct- The current model code of conduct at the time the above was ordered by the Supreme Court has good provisions such as "All parties and

Making up the Constitutional Gaps/Abeyances	
Constitutional Gaps/Abeyances	**Submissions made by me in my book 'India's Futuristic Democracy – Threats of Constitutional Gap & Digital Era' – December, 2022 [Represent the Sum of the Gap/Abeyance. To understand the Sum, the logic and reasoning contained in the said book may be read together.]**
	candidates must not indulge in corrupt activities, bribing, intimidation, impersonation of voters, canvass- sing within 100 meters of the polling station during the last 48 hours after the date fixed for the closure of the poll is announced, transportation or conveyance of voters." In Para VII Party in Power The party at center or state shall not misuse official power to sanction funds/grants, lay any foundation stone, make the promise of infrastructure development projects, and make any specific appointments in the government after election dates are announced to influence the voter.
	Addition to the above, I wish to add that Freebies included in the Manifestos are denied under the Constitution other than free legal aid. The constitutional provisions and N.K.Singh Committee Report are dealt in great detail in the book ''Freebies and Welfare Schemes A Fiscal Disaster & Suggested Framework for Election Financing' [February, 2023]. Except free legal aid, all kinds of Freebies including providing of utilities services freely are outside the constitutional ambit. Hence, in my personal view, freebies other than the one stated before are not permissible under the constitution and relevant governing laws as to free utilities services. The matter is subjudice before the Hon'ble Supreme Court. Other than what I have submitted in the above book, I refrain from any further comments on the subject matter.
K. Enforcement of Fundamental Duties	In the ultimate analysis, when in the Indian Constitution there is a separate part which deals with fundamental duties, then there must be some effective mechanism for their proper implementation so that the ultimate objectives can be achieved for which purpose it was inserted in the Constitution by an amendment. It might be urged that there are no specific legislative entries corresponding to these fundamental duties. Although Article 248 along with Entry 97 of the Union List of the Constitution of India being a residuary entry, everything relating to fundamental duties can be brought under it. Generally, we, the people are much more aware about our rights not our duties. So, if some stringent piece of legislation is there along with punishment then we can only be duty-bound otherwise not. The National Commission to Review the Working of the Constitution has also recommended some steps relating to fundamental duties.........................
L. Performance of Judiciary and the urgency for Reforms	1. I have the following points that I am submitting for kind consideration of the authorities and the readers in this regard:

	Making up the Constitutional Gaps/Abeyances	
	Constitutional Gaps/Abeyances	**Submissions made by me in my book 'India's Futuristic Democracy – Threats of Constitutional Gap & Digital Era' – December, 2022 [Represent the Sum of the Gap/Abeyance. To understand the Sum, the logic and reasoning contained in the said book may be read together.]**
		2. The ground for the long pendency of the criminal cases relied upon by the judiciary is stated to be lack of equivalent infrastructure and manpower including presiding judicial officers. This tussle has now acquired commona between the judiciary and government, each finding most convenient to seek an excuse and blame each other. It is not appreciated in such circumstances what kind of wrong an accused person in the criminal case has committed in addition to those as have been alleged in the Charge Sheet, the burden of bearing the effects of the ongoing tussle aforesaid?
		3. Both the government and the judiciary seem to consider that the accused person deemed to be part of such tussle and should bear with the circumstances including the long period of pendency while the accused thinks how he could be so when the matter is between the government and judiciary which fact is ignored. Should it not evoke humanistic consideration?
		4. In exchange of words orally and in writing or through observations on the given occasions such as seminars, conferences, inaugurations by the high government officials and judiciary regarding the reasons for long pendency of criminal cases, the single factor that escapes their kind attention - where does the accused stand in such situations and what could have been his financial, physical and mental condition having been forced upon to learn to travel with longer or if necessary longest period to wait for the justice, not knowing when judgment is passed after lapse of long time, whether or not criminality existed in the allegations made by the prosecuting agencies and to face conviction if criminality is proved or stand discharged if the criminal is not proved?
		5. Let us think of the consequences in both the conditions. If the accused person is convicted and sentenced to imprisonment or fine or both on the basis of the proof of his or her criminality or if the accused is discharged due to lack of proof of criminality, the former needs to undergo imprisonment for the period specified in the Order of the Hon'ble Court over and above the sufferance he or she had undergone for twenty five years, end of which the Order is pronounced whereas if he or she were to be faced with the same sentence or fine or both within a period of maximum five years, which should be the norm according to natural justice, he or she could have completed the period of the imprisonment long before the date on which the Order was pronounced on completion of the trial end of twenty five years. In the latter case i.e. where the accused is discharged for want of proof at the end of the

Making up the Constitutional Gaps/Abeyances	
Constitutional Gaps/Abeyances	**Submissions made by me in my book 'India's Futuristic Democracy – Threats of Constitutional Gap & Digital Era' – December, 2022** [Represent the Sum of the Gap/Abeyance. To understand the Sum, the logic and reasoning contained in the said book may be read together.]
	period of twenty five years, he would have not only become old aged, also would have lost all his physical, financial and mental strength having travelled for so long time through the judicial system and would have been left with bones visible to anyone having lost the flesh in the body for the aforesaid reasons. The famous proverbs say **"Justice Delayed is Justice Denied"**, all that remains now for the sake of quoting. This is the fact of life of the criminal accused persons that continues to persist. There is no door to knock at; so remain in the room with blinded eyes whether or not criminality exists and wait for the time till the judicial system takes its own time. 6. Looking at the zonal map of India, one can find that India is divided into six zones namely North Zone, South Zone, East Zone, West Zone, Central Zone and North East Zone. All these zones include 28 states and 8 union territories. Each zone is comprised of certain number of states and union territories. North Zone: Himachal Pradesh, Punjab, Uttarakhand , Uttar Pradesh and Haryana. East Zone: Bihar, Orissa, Jharkhand, and West Bengal. West Zone: Rajasthan , Gujarat, Goa and Maharashtra. Goa. South Zone: Andhra Pradesh, Karnataka, Kerala and Tamil Nadu. Central Zone: Madhya Pradesh and Chhattisgarh North East Zone – Assam, Sikkim, Nagaland, Meghalaya, Manipur, Mizoram, Tripura and Arunachal Pradesh {Source: Maps of India.com – Zonal Maps} PILs presently are filed in the Hon'ble High Courts and/or Hon'ble Supreme Court. There is need to establish independent PIL Special Courts {PILSCs} (status of High Court) in each Zone to deal with Public Interest Litigations (PILs) that are taking considerable time and efforts of the Hon'ble High Courts and the Hon'ble Supreme Court. The appeals in all such cases will lie with the Hon'ble Supreme Court. It is my submission that if such an arrangement is made, the need for the Hon'ble High Courts (Existing) and the Hon'ble Supreme Court to entertain PIL cases direct would not be necessary and appeals, if any, against the orders passed by the PILSCs proposed for being set up could be considered by the Hon'ble Supreme Court. This would reduce the case load, the time and efforts on the PIL cases both at the existing Hon'ble High Courts and the Hon'ble Supreme Court. PILs have

Making up the Constitutional Gaps/Abeyances	
Constitutional Gaps/Abeyances	**Submissions made by me in my book 'India's Futuristic Democracy – Threats of Constitutional Gap & Digital Era' – December, 2022 [Represent the Sum of the Gap/Abeyance. To understand the Sum, the logic and reasoning contained in the said book may be read together.]**
	become as a matter of routine cases in the country and hence need for urgent consideration of proposed courts in each Zone. Also to be appreciated is that PILs add to the burden already building up with the entry of new cases every day among the Hon'ble High Courts and Hon'ble Supreme Court. It is believed High Court level PIL courts would strengthen the democratic system with the timely intervention of such courts, as also generate greater confidence among the people of the country from the points of view expeditious disposal and timely relief to the people. Within each Zone, PILSCs may be set up at the following places that take into consideration easy accessibility and avoidance of considerable inconvenience to the people in the existing system: North Zone: NCT of Delhi East Zone: Kolkata West Zone: Mumbai South Zone: Chennai Central Zone: Bhopal North-East Zone: Guwahati Above Zones include the UT within each Zone. Modality: a. Hon'ble Supreme Court will have jurisdiction over all the PILSCs. b. Appeals from PILSCs lie with the Hon'ble Supreme Court. c. Existing High Courts will not entertain any PIL from the date of operationalization of the PILSC in the respective Zones. d. PILSCs will be set up by the Central Government based on Standard and Uniform Norms as may be laid down. e. PILSC will be headed by a Single Judge of Hon'ble High Court status similar to the Special Court at Mumbai for disposal of cases arising under the securities scam in 1992 under a Special Act. f. PILSCs being at par with Hon'ble High Courts, the Pay, Allowances, and Perks etc. of Hon'ble Judge of PILSCs will be at par with those of the Hon'ble High Courts. g. Once the PILSCs are set up by the Central Government including the entire expenditure according to the Standard and Uniform Norms, the Annual Capital and Maintenance Expenditure of these Courts will be met by the State from the revenue earned by PILSCs with additional funding, if necessary, in whose jurisdiction the PILSCs are set up and

Making up the Constitutional Gaps/Abeyances	
Constitutional Gaps/Abeyances	**Submissions made by me in my book 'India's Futuristic Democracy – Threats of Constitutional Gap & Digital Era' – December, 2022 [Represent the Sum of the Gap/Abeyance. To understand the Sum, the logic and reasoning contained in the said book may be read together.]**
	will be included in its Annual Budget, fifty {50} percent of which will be shared by the central government and paid to the State concerned as grant. h. This will ensure even spread of PILSCs based on Zones and will provide new employment opportunities and various other avenues for creating earning capacity to the local people. i. In case of conflicts of judgements on a subject matter of PILs, the Hon'ble Supreme Court could deal all such cases en bloc as is presently being done. j. It is anticipated that with the setting up of PILSCs, the pendency in the existing Hon'ble High Courts as also the Hon'ble Supreme Court will be reduced substantially, say in the rage of 20-25 percent and in due course of time such reduction in pendency may go up to 30-35 percent, once PILSCs are fully operationalized. k. Expenditure in setting up the PILSCs will almost be equivalent to the saving of expenditure in the existing Hon'ble High Courts and Hon'ble Supreme Court which would effectively offset the proposed expenditure for setting up the PILSCs in each Zone. PLSCs will also be generating revenue for the State. l. This will also increase the professional Advocates in the places where PILSCs are established who would be having their own their own Junior Advocates and Office Assistants that would add to the employment opportunities mentioned {h} above.

The founding fathers made the Constitution according the circumstances then existed with as much farsightedness as they could think of. The constitution is an ever moving document with capacity to absorb the changing situations taking place in the country. The Articles therein provide the best insights for the generations to come with positivity in their thoughts, acts and deeds. A mistake or omission is part the English Dictionary; however, what is more important is to search for their right meaning so that the human understanding is guided with such understanding. Nobody likes being criticized. But how you handle it makes all the difference. If you lock up and become defensive, you're likely to waste a lot of time feeling bad--and repeating the same behavior that was a problem to begin with. But if you can learn to take it in stride, with some genuine reflection on how you can use it as a basis for improvement, you can come to realize that criticism can actually be a gift.

"The final proof of greatness lies in being able to endure criticism without resentment." --*Elbert Hubbard*

Criticism is to be welcomed for self-improvement and self-correction. The gaps or abeyances I have referred to before are genuine mistakes or omissions because they were awaiting judicial testimony and wisdom of their application in the routine life of democracy. We cannot call democratic process under a given Constitution as static which will be like standing on the roof and wanting to see only dark clouds hovering. Online Free Dictionary defines hovering as 'to remain floating, suspended, or fluttering in the air: gulls hovering over the waves. 2. To remain or linger in or near a place: hovering around the speaker's podium. 3. To remain in an uncertain state; waver: hovered between anger and remorse.

This was the case when we failed to identify and recognize the gaps or abeyance embedded in the Article of the Constitution believing that the structure of democracy stood erected; forgetting at the same time that the standing of the structure is the sole consideration for functioning of the democracy. The structure is alterable[The structure is alterable [within the ambit of the Doctrine of Basic Features or Structure pronounced by the Hon'ble Supreme Court] according to the changing times.] according to the changing times. We utterly failed to understand how the structure could stand without substructures. The substructure here is considered to be the gaps or abeyances whereby we became more concerned with the structure but not the substructures that hold the structure together. The messiness and disorderliness that is prevailing today in the country, more so, in the Parliament and the Rule of Law. A human thinks he is not bound by anything around that is where the drowsiness started developing in our country. Online Dictionary defines 'drowsiness' as 'Feeling abnormally sleepy or tired during the day is commonly known as drowsiness. Drowsiness may lead to additional symptoms, such as forgetfulness or falling asleep at inappropriate times. What are the causes of drowsiness? A variety of things may cause drowsiness. This was the kind of an attitude that we developed within us discarding the need for governing substructures for the smoothened working of the democracy. If someone tells a child you start learning English from alphabet 'Z' but the child says I cannot reach alphabet 'Z' unless I pass through the alphabets from the beginning. This is what we thought about the democracy.

The judicial process peeps into the gaps or abeyances but put them to test or evolutionize bridgeable gaps or abeyances once something is challenged by a citizen seeking for its clarity and maintainability. The gaps or abeyances I have been able to identify listed before are the concretization of the blanks that should afford to be filled through laws or amendment of the extant laws which function lies within jurisdiction of the Legislature or the Rulings of the highest Court of Law.

As a humble citizen of the country, I wish to submit that the gaps or abeyance in the Constitution are to be given greatest urgency and made up earliest the possible. Their absence so far has been giving birth to utter indiscipline and ugliest posture of the functioning of the Parliament due to which the lower rung of the governance and rule of law is dangerously threatened in the country. The country looks as if playground for the politicians, religious leaders and citizens, the games they started playing has been injurious and hurting the very sustenance of the democracy. The ruling parties should be concerned with what best could be done for safeguarding the democracy and should not accord undeserving attention especially where the games are of provocative and non-playable nature. Good criticisms should be embraced and taken to heart to correct what is lacking for the better future. Good criticisms are like raining in the drought affected field. These produce purposeful and positive actions for further improvement. It is ignorance to consider all the criticisms are bad or intolerable. Such formation in one's mind creates counter criticism that encourages more misunderstanding than understanding. The negative criticism is harmful when it is made under the stress of prejudicial thoughts. If one considers good criticism as bad one, he needs to think to shed antagonism. Failures to make up the gaps or abeyance may cause fractures in the democratic system which are already showing signs of their presence in the governing system and the political parties in the opposition.

It is pertinent here to refer to one of the most important recommendations Dr. C. Kashyap [a former Secretary-General of 7th Lok Sabha, 8th Lok Sabha and 9th Lok Sabha and Lok Sabha Secretariat (Lower House of Parliament of India) from 1984 to 1990 had made in his Paper "WORKING OF PARLIAMENT AND NEED FOR REFORMS – 2000" which is dealt in more details in Part 02 of this book:

"While executive power of the Union is co-extensive with its legislative power, the constituent power under the Constitution belongs exclusively to Parliament. The responsibility of Parliament, therefore, becomes much greater in the case of Constitution (Amendment) Bills. As such, instead of the Constitution Amendments being presented to Parliament like ordinary pieces of legislation in the form of Bills for introduction sometimes at very short notice, it would be desirable if Parliament is associated right from the initial stages of formulation of proposals for constitutional reform, i.e., the actual drafting of a Constitution Amendment Bill may be taken up only after the principles involved have been thrashed out in a parliamentary forum and subjected to appropriate a prior scrutiny by the constituent power. The proposed involvement of Parliament and a prior scrutiny can be achieved through the device of a Constitution Committee of Parliament which may be constituted by resolution or otherwise as a standing joint Committee of the two Houses. The members of the Committee may be elected by the respective Houses. Rather than delay, this might expedite the process of constitutional reforms besides bestowing greater ability, legitimacy and wider acceptability to the reform proposals. As an alternative, after a Constitution Amendment Bill has been formulated but before it has been introduced, it may be subjected to a prior scrutiny of the „Constitution Committee". If this is done, even the Government would be saved many an embarrassment."

Seventy three years have elapsed since the country became republic but no thought has ever been considered on the need or otherwise of an independent Committee of Parliament on amendment of the Constitution recommended by Dr. C. Kashyap. This has resulted in two serious problems.

One, introduction of a constitutional amendment bill direct by the Executive in the parliament has suffered most worst embarrassing situations where the learned Members found inadequacy of time for scrutiny of such Bills due to pushing the Bill abruptly or in haste. This might have served the immediacy of the ruling party to table the Bill but it failed to understand an important parliamentary ethical consideration that the Bill had to be passed through the process envisaged under the Conduct of Rules of the parliament which insists for the according sufficient time for the members to subject the Bill to strict scrutiny both from the point of view of personal views as well as the party's views.

This procedure was meticulously followed during the twenty five years of the constitution becoming in force. The later periods saw rushing of the Bills without affording requisite time to the members and passing the Bills on majority rule. This cut the root of the democratic spirit where a systematic and sound debate and deliberations are fundamental in the matter of the amendment of the constitution have been ignored for self-interests. This situation continued to worsen in later years thereby inviting the genuine reservations of the members, especially those sitting in the Opposition. This started turning into a quarrelsome House whereby the differences and chaotic conditions took precedence over the very purpose of the sailing through the Bills. Due to this, many times, such Bills were referred to Select Committee inordinately delaying the subject matter in hand which could have been well achieved had the due process of Conduct Rules was followed. Establishment of a Constitution Committee stated before would have minimized the need for referring the Bill to the Select Committee. The present confrontations between the ruling party and the opposition parties were the birth of such attitudes on the part of the ruling party. Another avenue that was well established to brief the opposition political parties on agenda of the parliament, more so, the constitution amendments, on the eve of the session of the parliament has been put aside.

Second, Dr. Kashyap had anticipated such developments to come in course of the time which was the reason for his recommendation for having an independent Constitution Amendment Committee to review and study the gaps or abeyances found in the constitution which the political parties which ruled the country since seventy three years took best advantage of such gaps or abeyances to avoid most needed reforms in the constitutional workingbrought out before.

It has been like running a horse without any break resulting in the collapse of horse to reach the point of place. That is what has been happening in the case of our constitution which has been made to run and run thoughtlessly without any specialist or expert inputs for maintaining it hale and healthy. This purpose will be well served if the parliament accords due consideration to the recommendation made by Dr. C. Kashyap. Such Committee may also be empowered to review the abeyance or gaps found in the constitution based on the detailed study how the ruling parties exploited them to their advantage rather than the foremost interests of the nation.

Indian democracy is a system of alternatives—of alternative parties, alternative policies, principles, approaches and alternative leaders. In this system, today's Opposition party could be tomorrow's ruling party and vice-versa. A vigilant and functioning Opposition, therefore, has a positive and constructive role to play in the parliamentary system. The existence and effectiveness of the Opposition, in fact, accords greater legitimacy and strength to the Government. The Opposition provides constructive criticism of the policies and programmes of the Government and also keeps an unremitting vigil on the ruling party by highlighting any of its acts of commission or omission. The success of democracy thus depends not only on how the Government performs but also on how responsive the Opposition is. Both the Government and the Opposition are aware that their presence rests on electoral support; thus, while criticizing the governmental policies, the Opposition pursues a supportive approach and extends its constructive cooperation in carrying out those policies, which are dictated by national interests and particularly those which involve the principle of continuity of policies. This has not been happening because the political parties came into power of late have not appreciated the sanctity of the Parliament and the purity of the debates, the exquisite character of the parliamentary proceedings rather they are getting more concerned to safeguard the political party or parties in coalition which predominating its mind than the need for sustenance of the aforesaid character and qualities which alone has the capacity to provide continued strength and stability to the democratic functioning.

Every Member of Parliament, before taking his/her seat in the House, is required to make the prescribed oath or affirmation as laid down in the Constitution. As an elected representative of the people, a Member of Parliament is entrusted with onerous responsibilities. He is the representative and the leader of the people at one and the same time. As a representative, he reflects the hopes and aspirations of the people in the House and also conveys the message of the Government to the people. As a leader, it is his bounden duty to make the voice of the people heard, their expectations fulfilled, grievances redressed, and urges understood by the Government. He is the vital link between the Government and the society. A Member of Parliament therefore fulfils a wide variety of roles and performs several functions, both inside and outside the House. Within the House, of course, he performs the classical roles ascribed to him by virtue of his elected position. In the constituency role, he functions as a safety valve, allowing citizens to express themselves in a way that might not otherwise be possible. He is an information provider to those who approach him seeking advice or information. A member is also a prominent local/regional dignitary. He functions as an active advocate too for local and provincial causes. In a different role, a member is a benefactor serving as the provider of some benefits or other to the needy. He is at once a powerful and influential friend to his constituents. Over and above all those, he is the promoter of constituency interests. How successful a parliamentarian is, depends ultimately on how well he is able to categorize priorities and then discharge the functions to the satisfaction of all concerned.

Role of Members of Parliament

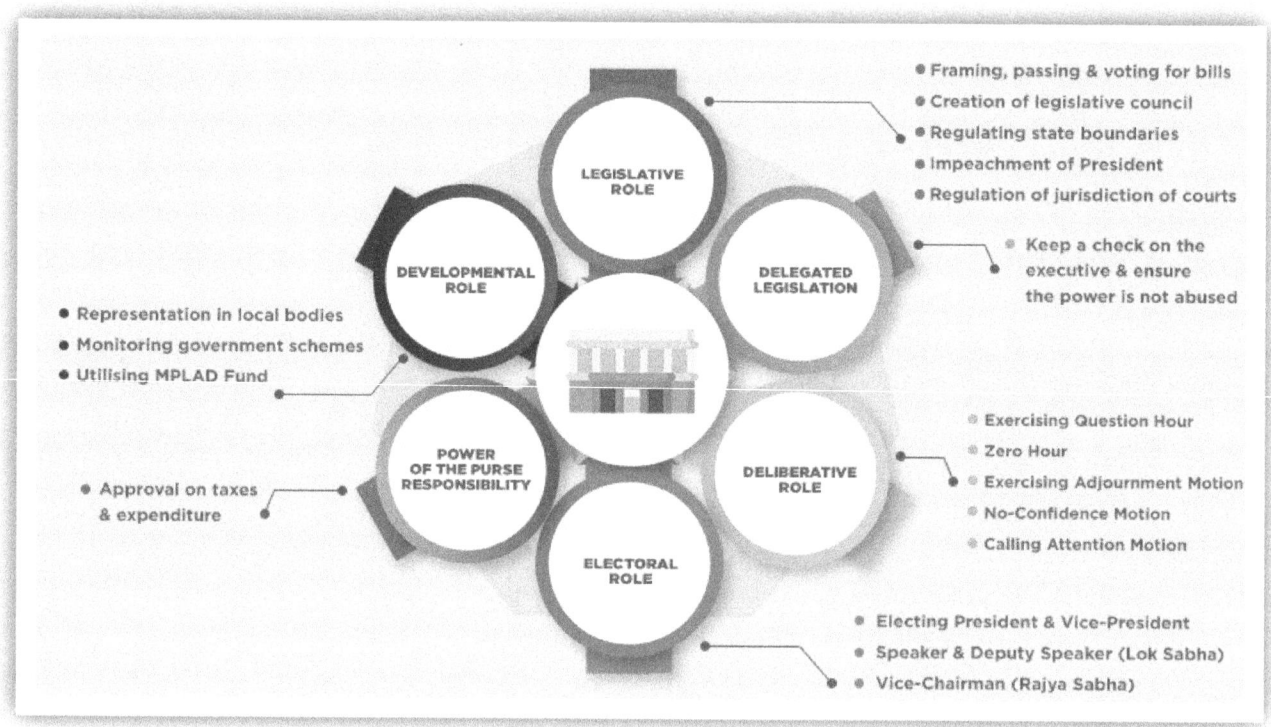

Ruling party is a governing party in a democratic system of government. A party becomes ruling party only when it attains majority in elections.

An Opposition Party refers to a position in the Indian parliament (both Lok Sabha and Rajya Sabha). The political party that secures the second largest number of seats in the general elections in the upper or lower houses will be designated as the opposition party.

Political parties are an inseparable part of modern democracy, and the conduct of elections is largely dependent on their behaviour. Although a large number of candidates contesting the elections are independent, political parties offer candidates organizational support and a broader election campaign to help the voters make choices. In India, political pluralism prevails and is all pervasive in the Government as well as the Opposition. Over the years, the party system in the country has undergone an evolution from the one-party dominance of the 1950s and early 1960s to plural and the coalition politics of the present. The prevalence of a multi-party system, including small and regional parties, enables a large number of political entities to participate in the elections to the Lok Sabha and the State Legislative Assemblies. Parties that wish to contest local, State or national elections are required to be registered by the Election Commission.

Dissecting the Evasiveness of Inner Party Democracy - Vivek Mishra, Ambar Ghosh - Liberal Studies, Vol. 4, Issue 1, January–June 2019 –Posted on the Google Website] – [Excerpts]:

"The Imperative

It must be stated right at the onset why inner-party democracy is critical for the survival and consolidation of democracy in India. It is a no-brainer to understand that the political parties are the most prominent drivers of the political discourse in a multiparty democracy. It is the parties, which provide political leadership, mobilize the electorate during the elections and perform crucial functions like agenda-setting and political propagation based on a wide range of issues impinging on the aforementioned factors. Moreover, the political parties are the organizationally coherent, functional units that compete for capturing state power and hold the levers of power and resources, once they manage to win the popular mandate. Hence, the question that naturally arises is whether the institution, which works as a lynchpin for the democratic order to thrive, is itself truly democratic in its working internally or not. The need for an innerparty democracy that is strictly followed has been reiterated by a plethora of notable political leaders in India. ………………………..

Absence of a Credible Regulatory Framework:

It is curious to observe that despite the enormous role that the political parties play in the democratic discourse in India, constitutional and legal regulations to monitor the functioning of these parties is conspicuously limited and in some instances, non-existent.27 The Section 29 A of the Representation of the People Act 1951 merely mandates the registration of political parties. Hence, the Election Commission of India (ECI) is rendered powerless in ensuring that the political parties conduct fair and regular internal elections for choosing its office bearers.28 In the landmark Indian National Congress versus Institute of Social Welfare Case, the Supreme Court judgment has reiterated that the ECI cannot take punitive action against the registered parties for violating the principle of inner party democracy.29 [Emphasis added]

The political inaction, notwithstanding, there is a slew of recommendations on electoral reforms given by several government constituted committees like Dinesh Goswami Committee, Tarkunde Committee and Indrajit Gupta Committee which strongly argued for more transparent working of the political parties in India.30 The 1999 Law Commission Report strongly recommended the introduction of a regulatory framework for governing the internal structures and inner party democracy of the political parties.31 Even, a draft; Political Parties (Registration and Regulation of Affairs) Act, 2011 was submitted to the Law Ministry which envisaged the creation of an Executive Committee for every political party whose members would be elected by the members of the local committees of the state units of the party, who themselves would elect the office bearers of the party from amongst themselves, without accepting any nomination.32 But, any significant development in making it legally binding for the parties to strictly observe internal democracy in its functioning has not been initiated by any political party or ruling coalition in power so far.

Democratising the Drivers of Democracy

In order to ensure an effective legal regime to guarantee genuine adherence to the principle of inner party democracy in India, the two fundamental factors – institutional as well as functional, which impede the consolidation of democratic culture in the parties, needs to be adequately addressed. One needs to be mindful of the fact that the menace of centralization of power that has a corrosive influence on the internal democracy of the parties, cannot be done away with, by only ensuring free and fair organizational elections in the parties. Such efforts should be complemented by other commensurate measures in order to ensure that the cascading impact of money and muscle power and rampant defections and crossovers can be effectively mitigated. But, it is highly improbable that the incumbent political leadership of parties in India, who are the biggest beneficiaries of such shortcomings in the electoral system, would genuinely initiate any meaningful step for ushering in robust electoral reforms.

Therefore, any momentous landmark legislation in advancing the goal of equal opportunity for political participation in India seems difficult to perceive in the near future. Rather, it is the non-elected apex judicial body, the Supreme Court, which has till now issued a number of advisory recommendations in the path of such electoral reforms.33 <u>It is for the interest of advancing the substantive objectives of Indian democracy that the Supreme Court must step up its jurisdiction in order to make a leeway for initiating structural reforms in the functioning of the party as well as in the conduct of the election campaign under the efficient watch of another non-elected body, the ECI.</u> [Emphasis added]

However, it is of pivotal importance to take cognizance of the fact that mere legal regulatory framework would never be a sufficient condition to bring about a seismic transformation in the working of the political parties in India. As the electorate remains the fulcrum of political vicissitudes in a democracy, a change in the psyche and the views of the people worldwide would be the biggest facilitator of any such reform. If the electoral salience for such reforms increases amongst the people, the parties would gradually but definitely feel pressurized to mend their ways. The element of sycophancy for "branded" candidates, easy lure for short-term political patronage and lack of information regarding the background and credibility of the candidates among the electorates, have deepened the pathologies in the functioning of the electoral democracy in India. Only when the electorate will be conscious enough to understand that democracy is much more than just passively voting in elections at periodic intervals, a holistic democratization of the political landscape in general and functioning of the political parties in particular would be possible."

The issues highlighted in the Article stated before, I believe, would stand resolved as much as possible if the constitutional Gaps/Abeyances stated before are made up earliest. Failure to do so is likely to cause irreparable injuries to our democracy. Articles and books will continue to be written and published on the serious shortcomings in the parliamentary system of democracy as found and listed before as well as may be found hereafter. Efforts will go futile if the

Parliament/Government/Higher Courts of Law continue to overlook the urgency to address those Gaps/Abeyances that would revitalize our democracy in its every sense compared to autocratic/dynastic democracy being ascribed by some of the countries on our democracy.

We claim we are the largest democracy in the world. Unless we are constitutionally strong, our other strengths though worthy of high praise, are as weak as our democracy is today. What is constitutionally strong? Making its spirit to work in real that gives us confidence and conviction. Every Article in the Constitution has a spirit of purpose to be achieved. True, its interpretation and ruling comes within the judicial wisdom of review. The gaps or abeyances noticeable become subject to judicial review on a petition made by a citizen. The parties that ruled our country during the last over seventy three years of republic continued to take a stance of there being no provision that enables it to act upon important concerns. Example, the provision relating to Elections. The Constitution makers empowered the parliament to make laws on every aspect of elections. When it came to most pressing problems faced on elections, such as enactment of law for the political parties or financing the elections, the governments of the day argued the lack of provisions in the constitution. This is known as selfishness and recklessness.

The correct understanding of the constitutional provisions gets blinded when the legislature and judicial review become unable to decipher the pricking gap or abeyance that we consider as preventing achieving our intentions. The entire outlook on such matters revolves on the stature and standing of the political parties, more so, the ruling political parties. If something starts pricking me in the body, I go to a doctor and seek his diagnosis and treatment. If I were to neglect that pricking in my body, I am permitting the pricking to grow further causing a more serious injurious harmful condition in my body. That is where we are standing today in our democratic working system. This sought for diagnosis as and when there were outward and inward pricking in the democratic body. We overlooked them wantonly believing that treatment of such pricking may block rule of escapism from performing important constitutional obligations we should have discharged rather than disregarded them. I have given the examples of such pricking as considered to be coming within the meaning of constitutional gaps and abeyances. Today, we are standing midst of not one but many such pricking in the constitutional body.

What is the pricking that is creating more problems than solutions in our democratic functioning? Why we disregarded fulfilling the obligations knowing the fact that they have been causing considerable pricking in our constitutional working system? Why we didn't fulfil the following constitutional obligations:

➢ Empowering Election Commission of India {ECI} for deregistration of the political parties; Limiting the number of political parties on identical political ideology basis but not based on religion, castes, creed and classes that act in opposite direction in the democratic structure?

- Election Financing by the State – A crucial consideration for upholding the values and virtues of elections but none seems to be interested in them, the absence of which will drive the fate our democracy to a great uncertainty and may jeopardize the democracy itself?
- Term of office of the Prime Minister needs to be defined which is presently remain open with no regard or limitation on the period of office?
- Updating or Revision of existing Rules of Business of Parliament?
- ECI recommendations for Reforms in Election Laws pending with the Central government?
- Independent Law for the political parties including Internal Regulation?;
- Defection of elected member(s) from one political party to another political – Amendment of Oath of Office in place of making laws on Defections which encourage defections rather than demolishing them?
- Qualification Requirements for electing as a Member of Parliament or the Legislative Assembly/Council?
- Election Manifestos of the political parties – Boundary Limits?
- Enforcement of Fundamental Duties; and
- Performance of Judiciary and the urgency for Reforms?

Above is the sum of the constitutional abeyances and gaps that beg for instant action stated individually before.

These very governments sought making laws and rules as most suited to their interests and convenient in the governance including the political parties. The Act [s] was made by the Parliament on the elections including the mode of registration of political parties, means and methods of financial resources to be raised by the political parties for election expenses. The Representation of Peoples Act, 1951 is the only Act that contains provisions in this regard. But the governments of the day made it a practice to empower the political parties to mobilize resources for their expenses for elections through various ways; most of them were done as part of the Finance Bill without any corresponding amendment to the RPA, 1951and were independently published in the Gazette of India. The RPA 1951specifies the power in the matter and doing something outside it amounts to overriding the provisions of that Act that renders the liberalization granted to the political parties for financing elections questionable rather inconsistent there having been no amendments to the said Act.

In [2014] 3 S.C.R. 1 2 COMMERCIAL TAX OFFICER, RAJASTHAN v. M/S BINANI CEMENT LTD. & ANR. (Civil Appeal No. 336 of 2003) FEBRUARY 19, 2014 [H.L. DATTU AND S.A. BOBDE, JJ.], the Hon'ble Supreme Court ruled as follows on Interpretation Statues:

"………..Interpretation of Statues:

General entry over specific - Held: Where a Statute contains both a general provision as well as specific provision, the latter must prevail - In other words, where a general statute and a specific statute relating to the same subject matter cannot be reconciled, the special or specific statute ordinarily will control - The principle finds its origins in the latin maxim of generalia specialibus non derogant, i.e., general law yields to special law should they operate in the same field on same subject. Rule of Harmonious Construction - Conflict between independent provisions of law - Held: When there is an apparent conflict between two independent provisions of law, the special provision must prevail - This rule has application in construction of taxing statutes along with the proposition that the provisions must be given the most beneficial interpretation - While determining the question whether a statute is a general or a special one, focus must be on the principal subject-matter coupled with a particular perspective with reference to the intendment of the Act - With this basic principle in mind, the provisions must be examined to find out whether it is possible to construe harmoniously the two provisions - Once it is held that intention of the legislation is to exclude the general provision then the rule "general provision should yield to special provision" is squarely attracted - The rule of statutory construction that the specific governs the general is not an absolute rule but is merely a strong indication of statutory meaning that can be overcome by textual indications that point in the other direction. …………….."

One hand, the political parties that ruled our country for the past seventy three years, find one or the other excuse to make up the vacuum in the political parties working system including election financing, on the other hand, the ECI whom the Hon'ble Supreme Court considered having all the powers on earth in the matters of elections, disciplining of political parties, election financing and so on. The ruling parties avoided their best to hold on to any regulation on the working of political parties, more so, election financing while the Hon'ble Supreme Court though showered the powers vested in the ECI under the constitution are all embracive, the Hon'ble Court reiterated that the ECI cannot take punitive action against the registered parties for violating the principle of inner party democracy.

Let us consider a company registered under the Companies Act in force at the relevant time with the Registrar of Companies [ROC}, the prerequisites for which are the Memorandum of Association [MOA] that contains Main, Ancillary and Other Objects and the Articles of Association [AOA] that contains the internal regulations of the company. The said Act makes provisions for initiating strict action including punitive action for not adhering to the internal regulations by a company including interventions by the Ministry of Corporate Affairs where it found some kind of mismanagement by the company. So also is the case with the societies registered under the Societies Registration Act, 1860 where under the Act empowers the Registrar of Societies [ROS] to take punitive actions against the Executive Committee for non-adherence to approved regulations. Then, why it cannot be so in the case of political parties registered under the Representation of Peoples Act, 1951. It is the humble submission of the author to the Hon'ble Supreme Court to review its decision stated before and empower the ECI to initiate action including cancellation of registration of the party concerned and punitive action as may be laid down where the political party is not adhering to its internal regulations registered with the ECI. This will go a long way in disciplining the working of the political parties which have, otherwise, consider themselves as kingdoms unassailable by any one. The RPA 1951, as in the case of the Acts stated before, also include the punitive powers for failure on the part of the political parties to perform their functions according to their Internal Rules registered with ECI as per the requirement of the applicable law.

The above submissions need to be appreciated by the Hon'ble Supreme Court taking into consideration that there is no other law that permits ECI to deregister or to initiate punitive actions. This has, as submitted before, already caused irreparable damage to the democracy which solely works on the basis of the disciplined political parties but, in the absence any powers to ECI, the tendency of indiscipline is growing among the political parties. My submission, in this context is, whether there is any other law that empowers ECI to deregister/derecognize the political parties that are working in contravention of their own internal regulations. That has made ECI armless to act upon in such situations since both the empowerments, namely, deregistration and initiating punitive actions are denied to ECI under the rulings of the Hon'ble Supreme Court. Both these powers are very vital powers for the ECI to enforce discipline among the political parties, the absence of which is promoting more indiscipline among them. Is it not salutary in the working of the democracy? If not, it implies that the political parties can do deleterious acts as they wish. ECI would be a mere onlooker due to lack of above powers under any other law or judicial ruling.

The cruces of the democracy are self-discipline, self-regulation, decency, dignity, mutual respect etc. If these ethical mandates are not contained in the governing Acts, Rules and Byelaws of the governance of the political parties, the democracy will start working haywire. This is precisely the present status of our democracy for the reasons submitted before which are supposed to act as teeth of the democracy. Mere decoration of a home with luxurious items and articles without its foundation and outside walls being strong is like holding the gold piece in hand not knowing when it would fall to the ground. That is how the democratic framework functions; its ignorance not only makes the democracy ignoble, also throws out wide playground for the political parties, the citizens and including the governance system. We are right now standing in such playground where the rules of the games are thrown out and individualized dictates assume the status of rules of the games.

As an ordinary citizen of the country, I feel sometimes standing in a simmering condition when I find our democratic framework continues shaking even after the country became republic seventy three years back. The obvious reason for this, in my personal view, is we jumped into the river without thinking first how to return to the bank that has the strength to prevent floods; so in our anxious moment of democracy and freedom, we forgot to establish a strong bank along the river of democracy started overflowing the bank for want of the basic controlling points over the political and religious bodies, the politicians and the people, the impact of which is so high today that we are struggling to know, let alone do, how and why it is so happening. Unless we first make up the constitutional gaps or abeyances which ought to have been in place well at the commencement of the Constitution, we will continue to not only struggle, also sometimes think whether our democratic framework would be safe for the future generation. There is no supporting effort to show that the governments that ruled the country so far have ever gone into the aspects of the constitutional gaps or abeyances allowing them to widen further and further. How the highly learned and scholarly communities felt not inclined to point out such gaps and abeyances outright on the face of the government and in both Houses of Parliament?

"TO ME, ONE OF THE PROOFS THAT THERE IS MORAL GOVERNANCE IN THE UNIVERSE IS THE FACT THAT WHEN PEOPLE AND GOVERNMENTS WORK INTELLIGENTLY AND FAR-SIGHTEDLY FOR THE GOOD OF OTHERS, THEY ACHIEVE THEIR OWN PROSPERITY, TOO." - BARBARA WARD, BARONESS JACKSON OF LODSWORTH

Every human wants to keep his or her mental and physical body hale and healthy that gives him or her strength to survive and to achieve his or her ambitions in life. The Constitution of our country also needs to be accorded same level of understanding. Humans are indifferent in themselves but the constitution is made up not by one but by hundreds of genius humans that made it to stand steady so far common to all the citizens. It is illogical to expect our forefathers to have covered every aspect of the constitutionalisation. Constitutionalisation involves the attempt to subject all governmental action within a designated field to the structures, processes, principles, and values of a 'constitution'. Constitutionalisation is the term used for the attempt to subject the exercise of all types of public power, whatever the medium of its exercise, to the discipline of constitutional procedures and norms. Last seventy three years of republic prove that we had been concerned only with the body of the Constitution but not its structures, processes, principles, and values. That forced us in more misunderstanding of its spirit rather than its soul. The political leaders including those who occupied as ruling party sought to split the essence of the constitutional values insisting their own understanding to prevail, the unanimity on constitutional values continue to miss that has been encouraging constitutional squabbling until the judicial review sets the line straight.

Let us take the examples of secularism and conversion. The term "Secular" means being "separate" from religion, or having no religious basis. A secular person is one who does not owe his moral values to any religion. His values are the product of his rational and scientific thinking. Secularism means separation of religion from political, economic, social and cultural aspects of life, religion being treated as a purely personal matter. It emphasized dissociation of the state from religion and full freedom to all religions and tolerance of all religions. It also stands for equal opportunities for followers of all religions, and no discrimination and partiality on grounds of religion. The definition of religion is a controversial and complicated subject in religious studies with scholars failing to agree on any one definition. Oxford Dictionary defines religion as the belief in and worship of a superhuman controlling power, especially a personal God or Gods.

Whereas, over a period of time, the word "Secular" sought to be expanded by the political and religious communities to cover the religion, caste and creeds for equal or same treatment to one and all that gave birth to contesting contentions weighing that word from any and every angle whenever the state initiated certain policies and practices for the betterment of the society, the different religions, castes and creeds having construed them as a bane rather than a boon for them. This concept further dragged into the political games the political parties and the politicians started playing in the local, state and national level election process according to the sounds of the music best suited to embrace and enchant the people through the relationship of religion, caste and creeds. Thus, we have been able to carry forward the concept of "Secular" to this extent and, it is not known, to what extent it would be carried further in future. Undisguised understanding of that word accords its true meaning, none is interested to understand so and continue to place his or her socialized title interests first corrupting the transparency of the process of elections, the basic feature of the constitution for safeguarding and protection of democracy.

Now about the conversion. No Holy Scripture of any religion in India permit conversion from one religion to another. This is expressly prohibited therein. Then what prompted us to talk about the conversion. "When the Constituent Assembly [CAD] discussed the religious freedom clause once more in December 1948, the use of the word 'propagate' generated more discontent and confusion; hence, several members moved amendments to remove the term or revise the clause. However, rather than being a debate about the disagreements and the proposed amendments, the meeting took the form of a seemingly random sequence of statements of opinion by Assembly members, who neglected to respond to each other and eventually did not even defend their own objections to the clause.

The history of every Nation also loudly speaks of the forceful conversions of their subjects by the Rulers of the day into their own religion with ulterior motives. This practice did not stop there but continues today, to prevent which, some of the states have enacted laws. The type of conversions that occurred in the recent past was forceful conversions consequent on the invasion of the country by the Kingdoms of different religions. This cannot be taken as attesting conversion as a precedent or a right.

Tajamul Hussain, a Muslim representative in CAD, suggested replacing the words "practise and propagate religion" by "practise religion privately." "Why should you interfere with my religion," he asked, "and why should I interfere with your religion?" Supposing I honestly believe that I will attain salvation according to my way of thinking, and according to my religion, and you Sir, honestly believe that you will attain salvation according to your way, then why should I ask you to attain salvation according to my way, or why should you ask me to attain salvation according to your way?

(CAD, 3 December 1948). If we accept this proposition, he asked, then "why propagate religion?" "Do not demonstrate it for the sake of propagating," he continued: "Do not show to the people that this is your religion for the sake of showing." Hussain's conclusion was clear: "If you start propagating religion in this country, you will become a nuisance to others. So far it has become a nuisance" (CAD, 3 December 1948). Clearly, this Indian Muslim shared the objections against granting a constitutional right to propagate religion and found interfering with the religions of others objectionable.

Rev Stanislaus vs Madhya Pradesh, 1977 SCR (2) 611 is a matter where the Hon'ble Supreme Court of India considered the issue whether the fundamental right to practise and propagate religion includes the right to convert, held that the right to propagate does not include the right to convert and therefore upheld the constitutional validity of the laws enacted by Madhya Pradesh and Odisha legislatures prohibiting conversion by force, fraud or allurement.

Our entire traditions and practices in life, as we say, are based upon the Holy Scripts of our religion[s]. As submitted before, no Holy Script of any religion in India permits conversion from one religion to another. This gains further strength from what was debated upon in the CAD that strongly opposed the conversion. <u>The message Tajamul Hussain, a Muslim representative in CAD, has given on replacing the words "practise and propagate religion" by "practise religion privately" stated before</u> is an eye-opener to us that stands shining and valid for ever. Let us adopt the message as part of our life for the betterment of the present and future generations, if necessary by amending the Constitution. Doing contrary exhibits pettiness on the part of the religions concerned and such religions not only are self-shaming, also disrespecting their own Holy Scriptures.[Emphasis added].

The Hon'ble Supreme Court ruled that in making its decision that persons above the age of 18 in India are free to choose the religion of their choice. The Hon'ble Court also ruled that the Centre and states to take stringent action against forced religious conversion carried out through intimidation or by luring people using gifts and monetary benefits. This is because Conscience, unlike religious belief which lays down established practices to be recognized, can never have a set standard which may be attributed to a class of citizen. Humans' Conscience is bound to yield different approaches to moral, ethical, legal and political issues. A child is born with Conscience and belongs to a religion to which its parents belong. The child's Conscience will thus be dictated by the religious, moral and ethical practices followed by its parents. Choice is free will whereas Conscience is "Deep within his Conscience man discovers a law which he has not laid upon himself but which he must obey. Its voice, ever calling him to love and to do what is good and to avoid evil, sounds in his heart at the right moment . . . . For, man has in his heart a law inscribed by God.. . His Conscience is man's most secret core and his sanctuary. There he is alone with God whose voice echoes in his depths." Conscience, then, is the judgment of reason whereby the human person, guided by God's grace, recognizes the moral qua of a concrete act. In all we say and do, we are obliged to follow faithfully what we know to be just and right.

To believe that one can convert from his or her religion to another religion according to one 'Conscience' suffers in its essence because Conscience stands above the religion, yet to plead that one can convert according to one's Conscience does not stand to reason for; the Conscience is not confined only to the religion but covers many other matters that one comes across in his or her life. In all these cases, one is guided in his or her act or thoughts whether one is 'right' or wrong'. That is the leading light of the Conscience that may relate to one's any personal matter. Let us not confuse co-relating Conscience and religion conversion. Conversion is ordinarily bound by one's choice or free will that also needs to have the consent of the Conscience which has the power to overrule the free will, the latter is legalistic concept while the former is the dictate of God made law. The Conscience by itself negates the conversion concept. All the conversions are made either under the rulers of the day in the past or by luring helpless human offering so called gifts, promises etc. in the present. Sad part is that the religious leaders and politicians involve in conversions for their selfish motives predominated with demographic calculations which itself is against Conscience of the religion. Let us live as we are born without tampering each other's birth on Mother Earth – that is the call of the Nature.

I have touched so much about conversion because it has assumed a state of paradox on account of the political and religious greed that is disturbing the normal human environment that maintains the peace and tranquil among the humans in the democratic set up. The human, to whatever religion he or she belongs wants peace of mind and tranquil to progress and prosper in life.

Article 18 of the universal declaration of HR {Human Rights} declares the freedom of religion in the following terms:

"Everyone has the right to freedom of thought, Conscience and religion; this right includes freedom to change his religion or belief, and freedom, either alone or in community with others and in public or private, to manifest his religion or belief in teaching, practicing, worship and observance."

The freedom to change religion is expressly recognized by this Article. Seven states abstained from voting; and Saudi Arabia was one amongst them. The objection raised by Saudi Arabia was that Article 18 incorporating the freedom to change religion is against the tenets of Islam………………………………….

In Stainislaus Rev. v. State of M.P, Supreme Court held that the right to propagate one's religion means the right to communicate a person's beliefs to another person or to expose the tenets of that faith, but would not include the right to 'convert' another person to the former's faith because the latter person is "equally entitled to freedom of Conscience" which words precede the word 'propagate'.

Article 25 of the Indian Constitution guarantees freedom of religion to all citizens. The right to religion does not include the right to convert other people to a particular religion, especially through fraud, deception, coercion, allurement and other means, the Home Ministry told the Hon'ble

Supreme Court on Monday [November 29, 2022]. The Ministry said the word 'propagate' in Article 25 (right to freedom of religion) does not include the right to convert.

This constitutional obligation has to be respected by all the religions and citizens covered by the religions besides the State. The freedom of religion guaranteed under Article 25 of the Constitution has to be construed as one in which the citizen was born on and from the date of proclamation of the Constitution of India and, accordingly, such freedom is specific to the religion to which the citizen belonged to on and from the said date. The Conscience mentioned in the said Article stood annexed to the citizen as on the date of the Constitution or born thereafter in that religion. Here, the ruling given by the Hon'ble Supreme Court is to be understood, according to me, as in relation to one religion and other religion or among the religions of the citizens of the country and not merely that it applies only to the State. If it is to apply only to the State, as is being talked about today, then the State is supposed to intervene through appropriate course provided in the constitution if there is abuse of one religion against another religion or among group of religions. What is happening in our country has been that there are open criticisms among the religions that acts against the very basic fibre of 'equal treatment to every religion' thereby the ruling also ipso facto applies to all the religions and the citizens belonging to those religions in the country. The Conscience is not a commodity that can be exchanged from one hand to another hand or from one person to another person. It is static as created by God and remains incorporated in the citizen's religion to which the citizen belongs.

&

. A wrong is done when the original standing was tampered that cannot be taken to mean that if such wrong if taken up for correction is tampering of history. The correction done in such cases also stands as part of the history for future generations. One need to understand that the wrong done in the past is also an integral part of history when the citizens of given time would understand that the correction done is in order inasmuch as the history was also twisted when the originality was brutalized, the restoring of the originality in such cases does not amount to hurting the sentiments of any particular religion. That is how corrections of historical wrongs need to be considered as valid and acceptable to one and all.

Other Living Beings on Mother Earth in whom also God resides and which also have Consciousness and Conscience as ascertainable from the behavioural pattern live according to natural law which, according to the practice these beings follow, do not allow them to cross their original birth into the birth of any other Living Being while living on Mother Earth. For humans also, Live and Let Live according to one's own birth and Faith is the lone call of Mother Earth.

Democracy without education is like capturing wild creatures in a jungle. It is pertinent to reproduce below an Article 'Democracy has limited relevance without education: SC judge' published in The Times of India – Mangalore – TNN 24 April, 2022: [Excerpts]

Justice S Abdul Nazeer, judge, Supreme Court of India said, "Democracy has always found education as its greatest support and constant company. Without education, democracy has limited relevance and effectiveness, and without democracy, education loses its meaning."

He was addressing the 40th annual convocation of Mangalore University, here on Saturday. Governor and chancellor of the university, Thawar Chand Gehlot, presided over the event. Speaking on the subject 'Correlation between education and democracy', Justice Nazeer said that democracy and education share a reciprocal relation, and one cannot thrive without another.

Democracy also believes in giving freedom to the people, but if they are not educated, then their freedom may lead to anarchy and indiscipline, he said. He pointed out how education also plays a crucial role in the electorate. "Democracy can function well, only when the people are educated and conscious of their rights and duties. Education helps people to judge right and wrong, and what is just and unjust. Otherwise, a small group will assume control over the government of the state, and begin to exploit the masses," he said. He further said that education believes in giving freedom to the people. In a democratic country, people elect their representatives to work for a quality life, and to ensure inclusive growth opportunities for them. "The quality of public representatives, in turn, depends on the quality of the people who vote for them. So the root cause of problems as well as solutions lies with the voters. They must be properly educated to choose their leaders," he said. [Emphasis added]

One can listen to defending and justifying arguments of the political parties as to what was wrong with them the way they have been conducting today but none of them seem to have thought their arguments are like bare body which is not conducive to continue with inviting the jocularity by the people of the country and the other countries as well. Is jocularity in the ear of the listener? Jocularity seems to be in the ear of the listener, and what the 18th century found ludicrous was no laughing matter at the end of the 19th. One can be jocular about things but when alarm is caused the jocularity has to stop and seriousness must take over. [Online Dictionary]

The reason for the present state of political atmosphere in the country preoccupied more by political and policy differences between ruling parties and the opposition political parties. The differences are driven more towards increasing criticism, accusations turning into, as it seems, inimical relationship, the outcome of which is highly disturbing seen through the mirror of good democratic functioning. The lost opportunities that opened up both for the ruling and opposition to engage in a deliberation based on constructive approach in both the Houses of Parliament in the past are marking a different direction. Both the sides have reached a stage of refusal to reconcile with visible adamant attitude that is adversely affecting the normal business process in both the Houses, the functional costs of which are enormous and are met from the public expenditure. At this time, it looks the political parties are assuming such public expenditure also as 'freebies' with which they are used to in the election campaigns. Time also to strictly enforce at the Conduct of Business Rules of both the Houses and the written Directions of the Presiding Officers.

"THE PRINCIPLE OF NO WORK NO PAY"

August 2, 2019inbatvUncategorized

The division bench of the Supreme Court comprising of Justice Ashok Bhushan and Navin Sinha on July 13, 2019 in a matter titled 'Chief Regional Manager, United India Insurance Company Limited v. Siraj Uddin Khan'[1] has observed that the principle of 'No Work No Pay' can be applied even when the employee was not kept away from the work by any order of the employer. Hon'ble SC reiterated that under the settled principle, the one who remained absent without leave or any justification cannot be directed to claim wages for that particular period.

Dies non or Dies non juridicum is a generally accepted Latin phrase/maxim for the principle of No work No Pay [2]. The principle of 'No Work No Pay' is an implied condition of the contract of employment. The said principle is the basic dictum of industrial relations. In simpler words it means, a person is generally employed to get the assigned work performed, and in a situation where the employee fails to perform the said work, s/he is not entitled to any payment or remuneration. Generally, the absence of workers from the workplace is also covered under this principle. However, it is pertinent to note that such failure in the performance of work should not happen at the instance of any circumstance/failure on the part of the employer.[Emphasis added]

The principle of 'No Work No Pay' finds its root in the Indian Constitution and is a logical corollary as well as the extension of the principle of 'Equal Pay For Equal Work' as enshrined in Art. 39 of the Constitution of India. It aims to establish social justice in action. Though this principle is not laid down in any labor or service laws expressly but a result of judicial creativity, it has assumed great industrial importance to maintain cordial and harmonious relations between the employer(s) and employee(s).[Emphasis added]

Online Dictionary states 'The word 'election' simply refers to the act of choosing someone for an official job, in a formal and organised manner, mostly done by way of voting. But in any society having a popular Government, the word is typically comprehended in its political sense of electing a representative in a modern representative Democracy'. Who is a Member of Parliament? Those elected or nominated (by the President) to either house of Parliament are referred to as members of Parliament (MPs).

The Roles & Responsibilities of MPs:

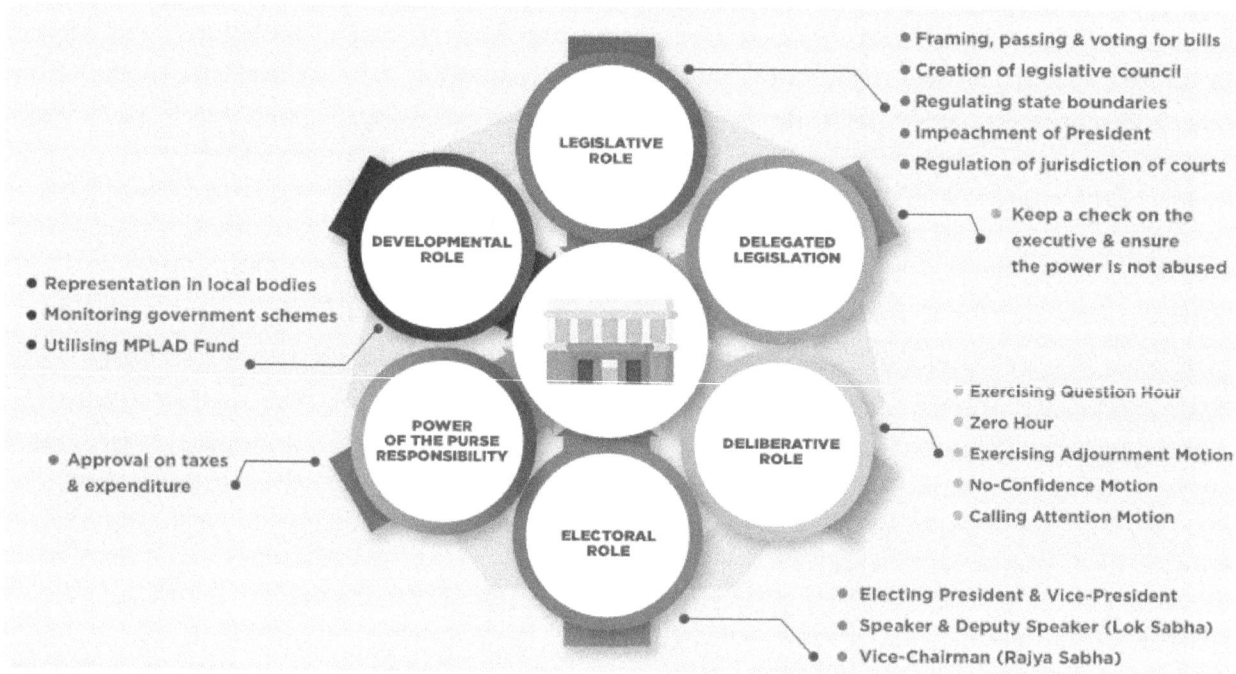

My research from the available information on the Google Website shows that the relationship between the voters and their elected representatives is neither contractual nor legal but a democratic contract. Democratic means 'We must accept the results of a democratic election (=an election in which all people can vote). The social contract and economic contract are part of the democratic contract. So also is the political contract. These contracts need not be in writing between the governments and the people but the very fact that the government promises several kinds of social and economic programmes that create an implied binding force between the governments and the people although not enforceable in law by virtue of being covered under the Directive Principles of the State Policy. Nevertheless, the democratic contract engages the elected representatives to fulfil the promises in the ruling party Manifesto. In a democratic set up, the roles and responsibilities may not amount to having any legal force but they are integral part of the moral and democratic obligation to be fulfilled by the elected representatives. These functions are, therefore, to be inferred as democratic contract between the elected representatives and the voters who are not limited to those elected the representatives but all the voters who participated and voted in the elections.

One may ask is it practicable?

Third Schedule of the Constitution of India specifies the Oath to be taken by a Member of Parliament as follows:

Form of oath or affirmation to be made by a Member of Parliament:—

"I, A.B., having been elected (or nominated) a member of the Council of States (or the House of the People) do swear in the name of God that I will bear true faith and allegiance to the Constitution of India as by law established, that I will uphold the sovereignty and integrity of India and that I will faithfully discharge the duty upon which I am about to enter."] [Emphasis added]

So also is the case of Members of Legislative Assembly for whom the Form of Oath to be made is as specified in the Third Schedule. This form of Oath also includes 'duty upon which I am about to enter'.

The Manifesto of the political parties, however, stands on a different footing and whether or not it has a legalistic character is yet to be established.

However, the Roles and Responsibilities of MPs shown above do place a responsibility to perform the roles and, for doing that, the MPs are paid pay, allowances and perks from the Consolidated Fund which implies that if the MPs lack in performance of the their roles may also, if not directly, indirectly attract the principle of 'No work No Pay' elucidated before which is although relatable to the employer and the employees in terms of the contract existed but does not bring the non-performance of the roles by the MPs or failure of a responsibility within its ambit. Fact, however, remains that their roles and responsibilities have direct relationship towards fulfillment of the voters' interests of various nature shown above for which they are paid representatives from the said Fund which indirectly suggests foregoing of their salaries, allowances and fees to which they are entitled to for the day or for a specific period during which they did not perform their roles. This is a democratic legislative but not a legal obligation. The principle of 'No Work No Pay' has to be construed as applicable in such cases also subject, however, to the approval of the Presiding Officers and its incorporating as a provision in the Rules of Conduct of Business of both the Houses. The roles and responsibilities of the MPs also need to be measured according to the said principle. Their failure to perform the constitutionally assigned roles cannot justify their entitlement to the pay and allowances for the period they failed to fulfil. This is my personal view based on the reasoning submitted.

The 'duty' consists of Roles and Responsibilities of the Member of the Parliament/Member of the Legislative Assembly stated before. Thus, the Oath establishes a constitutional commitment on the part of the Member of Parliament/Legislative Assembly. Article 106 of the Constitution of India provides that the members of either House of Parliament shall be entitled to receive salaries and allowances as may from time to time be determined by Parliament. The Salary, Allowances and Pension of Members of Parliament Act, 1954, enacted in pursuance to the constitutional provision, governs the salaries and allowances of the members. The oath is either a declaration of fact or a promise with wording associated to something considered sacred as a sign of truth. The Oath of Office includes an affirmation to discharge one's duties faithfully and never show favouritism

It is submitted that it is practicable considering the above provisions of the Constitution and on the basis of the ruling of the Hon'ble Supreme Court that 'The principle of 'No Work No Pay' finds its root in the Indian Constitution and is a logical corollary as well as the extension of the principle of 'Equal Pay For Equal Work' as enshrined in Art. 39 of the Constitution of India. The rights of the MPs are those contained in the Rules of Conduct of Business but do not include those specifically stated in the Speaker's Directions of 1970 [namely, In order to keep the area and passages within the Parliament House Estate free and open for members of Parliament without any obstruction or hindrance, the following activities are prohibited within the area of the Parliament House Estate— (i) holding of any public meeting; (ii) assembly of five or more persons; (iii) carrying of fire-arms, banners, placards, lathies, spears, swords, sticks, brick-bats; (iv) shouting of slogans; (v) making of speeches, etc. (vi) processions or demonstrations; (vii) picketing or dharna; and (viii) any other activity or conduct which may cause or tend to cause any obstruction or hindrance to members of Parliament.] The non-compliance of the above directions (iv), (v), (vi) and (vii) are non-permissible activities on the part of MPs that amount to absence from the duty liable to the application of the principle 'No Work No Pay' [Emphasis added]

"The Importance of Oaths
Oaths play a vital role in maintaining trust, integrity, and accountability within legal and professional contexts. By taking an oath, individuals publicly declare their commitment to honesty and fulfilling their obligations. This not only instills confidence in others but also serves as a deterrent against dishonesty and unethical behavior.

From a business owner's perspective, oaths can be particularly significant. When employees, partners, or contractors take an oath, they are more likely to act in the best interest of the company and its stakeholders. Oaths create a sense of responsibility and encourage individuals to uphold ethical standards, maintain confidentiality, and fulfil their contractual obligations.

Furthermore, oaths can have legal implications. If someone breaks an oath, they may face legal consequences, such as perjury charges or breach of contract claims. This provides a legal recourse for parties who have been harmed by the dishonesty or failure to fulfil obligations of others.

In summary, an oath is a solemn pledge to tell the truth or perform a duty, often accompanied by a calling upon a higher power to witness the statement. Oaths are commonly used in legal, professional, and business settings to ensure honesty, integrity, and accountability. As a business owner, understanding the legal definition and importance of oaths can help you foster a culture of trust and ethical behavior within your organization. By encouraging employees and partners to take oaths when necessary, you can promote a sense of responsibility and ensure that everyone is committed to upholding their obligations." [Source: Fitter Law » Insight » Legal Dictionary » The Legal Definition of Oath: Importance, Examples, and Legal Consequences]

The crucial considerations both with respect to the Members of Parliament/Legislative Assembly, the government employees and the public sector and private sector employees are 'duty to be performed' and 'remuneration to be paid/received'. There is no provision under any law or in the Rules of Conduct of Business of both the Houses that the principle of 'No Work No Pay' does not apply to the Members of Parliament/Legislative Assembly. The application of the said principle stands on parity in both the cases. Then, could we say that the principle applies to others stated before but not to the Members of Parliament/Legislative Assembly and, if so, whether or not it amounts to discrimination, the same having been rooted under the constitution according to the ruling of the Hon'ble Supreme Court also stated before. Whether or not this practice is presently in vogue is not ascertainable from the Google Website. I accordingly presume that the practice not in vogue.

There are sufficient grounds based what have been submitted before to extend the principle 'NWNP' to the Members of Parliament/Legislative Assembly. There is, therefore, an urgent need on the part of the Presiding Officers of both the Houses to give due attention and consideration on this issue, if the practice is not in vogue. The Members of Parliament/Legislative Assembly are the elected representatives of the people of the country who are expected to set an example by them rather than by compulsion. Their roles and responsibilities are within the ambit of the Constitution of India, so also is the case of the employees who are working in government sector, public sector and private sector. There being no law or any provision in the Rules of Conduct of Business of both the Houses that excludes the said Principle, the application of the Principles assumes greater importance and urgency. This is not to be construed as any kind of intent to denigrate the status of the MPs/MLAs rather it begs for bringing a level of parity between them and the employees to whom the Principle is made to apply automatically. It will, otherwise, will remain dormant in the application of the provisions of the constitution.

Today, the proceedings in both the Houses of Parliament are televised and observed by all ages of people including adults and children. Examples we set in the Houses are the moral and binding examples. The conduct and behavioural pattern of the Hon'ble Members of Parliament/Assembly have a direct reflection in the eyes of the viewers. If these are good, the children and adults, the future generation, will pursue them as an example to the people of their times.

"If you set a poor example for your children, you'll teach them to be just like you." — Frank Sonnenberg, the Path to a Meaningful Life.

The constitutional spirit and the judicial system should guide for settlement of irreconcilable issues through proper process as it is happening today in many matters among citizens, institutions, organizations, states and centre. Likewise, this path is open to the political parties to put forth their points of views but the political parties, as noted before, being functioning in a way as small kingdoms, shy to recourse to such approach or consider themselves above the rule of law. The differences pervade in every aspect of life of human being or juristic person [juristic person. a body recognized by the law as being entitled to rights and duties in the same way as a natural or human person, the common example being a company]. A journey of a thousand miles begins with a single step.

"Peace cannot exist without justice, justice cannot exist without fairness, fairness cannot exist without development, development cannot exist without democracy, and democracy cannot exist without respect for the identity and worth of cultures and peoples." Rigoberta Menchú Tum.

'Opposition unity' is the latest jargon in the lexicon of political scientists and commentators. The putative argument is that a single joint opposition candidate against the ruling alliance represents the best shot at victory in the upcoming national election. In other words, it posits that India's political diversity must be reshaped and reoriented to a two-Alliance democracy in each state. The clamour for this fuzzy notion of 'Opposition unity' is unsound in practice and in theory……

Let me also touch here the distinction, if any, in the freedom of speech as between the Members of Parliament and the ordinary citizens.

The Indian constitution grants varied fundamental freedoms to the citizens of India. Right to freedom of speech and expression is one of the fundamental freedoms protected under article 19(1) (a) of the Indian constitution and many international treaties to which India is a party. Article 19(1)(a) guarantees the citizens of India freedom of speech and expression. This can be in the form of written texts, word of mouth or any other form of communication. The mode can be anything from the following- oral/ written/ electronic/ broadcasting/ press or others. Besides, in the case of Maneka Gandhi v. Union of India, it was also confirmed by the Hon'ble Supreme Court that freedom of speech and expression was not limited by geographical limitations or boundaries and claimed that Article 19(1)(a) encompasses both the right to speak and the freedom to express in India as well as abroad. Freedom of expression is also inclusive of Freedom of Press. Although it is nowhere expressly mentioned in the Constitution. However, it is implicitly present as a right under the meaning of freedom of speech and expression Freedom of the press is essential to freedom of expression, which forms the backbone of political freedom and genuine functioning of democracy. In the case of Romesh Thappar v. State of Madras, the court affirmed that the enforcement of pre-censorship on a journal constituted an infringement on the freedom of the press, which is an essential part of Article 19(1)(a). The judgment also added that free political dialogue is necessary if a democratic government is to work properly. "When it comes to democracy, liberty of thought and expression is a cardinal value that is of paramount significance under our constitutional scheme. -- Supreme Court of India, Shreya Singhal v. Union of India, March 24, 2015.

"In parliamentary language the term privilege applies to certain rights and immunities enjoyed by each House of Parliament and Committees of each House collectively and by members of each House individually. The object of parliamentary privileges is to safeguard the freedom, the nobility and the dignity of Parliament. Privileges are necessary for the proper exercise of the functions entrusted to Parliament by the Constitution. They are enjoyed by individual members, because the House cannot perform its functions without unimpeded use of the services of its members; and by each House collectively for the protection of its members and the vindication of its own Iity and dignity.

In modern times, parliamentary privilege has to be viewed from a different angle than in the earlier days of the struggle of Parliament against the executive authority. Privilege at that time was regarded as a protection of the members of Parliament against an executive authority not responsible to Parliament. The entire background in which privileges of Parliament are now viewed has changed because the Executive is now responsible to Parliament. The foundation upon which they rest is the maintenance of the dignity and independence of the House and of its members.

In interpreting these privileges, therefore, regard must be had to the general principle that the privileges of Parliament are granted to members in order that "they may be able to perform their duties in Parliament without let or hindrance". They apply to individual members "only insofar as they are necessary in order that the House may freely perform its functions. They do not discharge the member from the obligations to society which apply to him as much and perhaps more closely in that capacity, as they apply to other subjects". Privileges of Parliament do not place a Member of Parliament on a footing different from that of an ordinary citizen in the matter of the application of laws unless there are good and sufficient reasons in the interest of Parliament itself to do so.

The fundamental principle is that all citizens, including members of Parliament, have to be treated equally in the eye of the law. Unless so specified in the Constitution or in any law, a Member of Parliament cannot claim any privileges higher than those enjoyed by any ordinary citizen in the matter of the application of law ………..''[Source: CHAPTER XI Powers, Privileges and Immunities of Houses, their Committees and Members]. It will thus be seen that the distinction is made between the Members of Parliament and the ordinary citizens under the Privileges based on Rules of Procedure and precedents. But for that, as noted before, the footing between the two is one and the same. That is, the MPs enjoy the immunities and privileges guaranteed in the Constitution and the Rules of Procedures of both the Houses of Parliament; to that extent the distinction exists between the MPs and the ordinary citizens.

"IF YOU LOVE FREEDOM, THEN YOU ARE GOING TO HAVE TO PAY FOR IT. NOT ONLY BY PAYING TAXES BUT BY MAKING THE COMMITMENT TO LIVE BY THE PRINCIPLES THAT ARE ESSENTIAL FOR FREEDOM TO SURVIVE. THAT INCLUDES RESPECTING THE RULE OF LAW AND IF YOU HAVE SET THAT ASIDE FOR POLITICAL REASONS, THEN YOU ARE A THREAT TO OUR DEMOCRACY AND OUR FREEDOMS." — RJ INTINDOLA – (GANDOLFO) – 2018

Let us remember unless we make best efforts to join the fractured political parties into a unifying form, soonest the possible, democracy would continue to remain in a state of uncertainty with increasing fragmentations prevailing over the political common sense - the political paradox. Seventy three years of our Republic have shown more inclination in fragmentation than unity. Those times were different and, if we continue them as precedents, self-elimination is not far from truth. The underlying principal cause for the divisioning is not differences in ideologies of the parties which concept stand negated when coalitions started emerging but it is the deep rooted selfishness that is undermining the unity among the political parties, particularly, the dynastic political parties. Dynastic parties are playing different kinds of games to repossess the power to which they are addicted and feel like fish out of water without that. They are resorting to playing any kind of political or social disturbing games to uphold themselves as the worthy system of democracy with the main object of tarnishing the image of ruling party.

Paradoxes in Indian democracy also exist in the matter of gender equality, almost in every walk of life including the political participation. The women in metros, cities, districts and talukas towns are gradually rising to their duties and obligations in the democracy but that is not identifiably evolving in the rural areas that represent major component of the country mainly due to educational disabilities and dominance of the male community as a matter of traditional compulsions. Doing away existence of such compulsion has been hard job, the same having psychologically rooted. The new generation in the rural areas is showing signs of upward movement in their social life which is being reciprocated by the male generation with the change of guard in the families. This needs to be given a push up opening up more opportunities in the rural areas for women participation, the education being given the highest priority. Hope is the belief things will work, especially when it seems otherwise. It helps us stay calm and peaceful when something less than desirable emerges. Hope believes we will get through it. Hope remembers the times we made it through. Hope teams with faith and believes in the impossible. Let us hope it happens to women in rural areas.

I am raising an important issue at this stage. If we are saying we are democratic country, we are saying so based on the symptoms and not the systems of democracy. The principles and systems to smoothen the democracy are yet to be evolved and defined in terms of law. None wants to swim in Muddy River yet we want to swim in that river whereby we are unable to differentiate the muddy river and the normal river mainly because of irresistible desire to be in power or nearer to the power – a paradox unexplainable. So, our democracy at best could be considered as a paradoxical and not a normal or principled democracy. Until the elected representatives realize that they are there to serve the people selflessly, they represent true democrats while those who place selfish motives before the serving the people are untrue and anti-democrats. Our elected representatives have given so far prominence to the latter than the former. This happened because the wealth they make through selfish motives to contest and win the elections are devoid of decency and dignity of life and, if this continues, the values and virtues of the democracy would further decline and downgrade. A democratic nation stands on the strong footing of the values and virtues of democracy as the standing stone for futuristic democracy; not a sand stone. When we think of our own future, we should think first about the future of democracy and nation. Without fulfilment of the latter, the former cannot be fulfilled rather it would turn into a desert. This can be ensured through the State funding the elections failing which the stream of illegal money will widen coupled with the freebies culture that is likely to endanger the fiscal strength of the nation.

A nation should think of concretising the course of democracy which is not happening because we believe present democracy is valid for me as long as I am alive; let future generations take care of it themselves that is none of my concern. Ancestors protected the civilizations through practising values, virtues and culture for the benefit of the future generations, so also was the wish of our forefathers who made the constitution not confined to the present but more importantly for the future generations. This simple message has not entered into our thoughts which are the reasons for our searching the surface rather than depth of the democracy. Seventy three years of our republic was a long period to have understood basic credentials of democracy stated before [as constitutional abeyances or gaps which continue to remain in the deep bore wells] to act as the cradle for our futuristic democratic journey.

NDTV Website posted an Article: "Is It Necessary?" PM Requests Couples To Not Hold Weddings Abroad- In his Mann Ki Baat radio broadcast, PM Modi said while shopping for weddings, people should give importance to products made in India only – News India Updated: November 26, 2023:

"Prime Minister Narendra Modi on Sunday said he is troubled by the trend of some "big families" conducting weddings abroad, and urged people to hold such celebrations on Indian soil so that the country's money does not leave its shores. In his Mann Ki Baat radio broadcast, PM Modi said while shopping for weddings, people should give importance to products made in India only.

"The wedding season as well has commenced now. Some trade organisations estimate that there could be a business of around ₹ 5 lakh crore during this wedding season. While shopping for weddings, all of you should give importance to products made in India only," he said.

And yes, since the topic of marriage has come up, one thing has been troubling me off and on for a long time... and if I don't open up my heart's pain to my family members, who else do I do it with? Just ponder... these days a new milieu is being created by some families to go abroad and conduct weddings. Is this at all necessary?" PM Modi said.

He stressed that if people celebrate the festivities of marriages on Indian soil, amid the people of the country, the country's money will remain in the country.

The people of the country will get an opportunity to render some service or the other at such weddings, he pointed out.

Even poor people will tell their children about your wedding. Can you expand this mission of 'Vocal for Local'? Why don't we hold such wedding ceremonies in our own country?" Modi said. "It is possible that the kind of system you want may not be there today, but if we organise such events, systems will also develop. This is a topic related to very big families. I hope this pain of mine will definitely reach those big families," the prime minister said.

In his remarks, PM Modi also asserted that when the people at large take charge of nation-building, no power in the world can stop that country from moving forward. Today, it is clearly visible in India that many transformations are being led by the 140 crore people of the country, he said.

"We have seen a direct example of this during this festive season. Last month in 'Mann Ki Baat' I had laid emphasis on 'Vocal for Local' i.e. buying local products. Within the last few days, business worth more than ₹ 4 lakh crore has been done in the country on Diwali, Bhaiya Dooj and Chhath," he said.

And during this period, tremendous enthusiasm was seen among the people in buying products Made in India, PM Modi said.

"Now even our children, while buying something at the shop, have started checking whether Made in India is mentioned on them or not. Not only that, nowadays, people do not forget to check the country of origin while purchasing goods online," he said.

PM Modi said that just as the very success of 'Swachh Bharat Abhiyan' is becoming its inspiration, the success of 'Vocal for Local' is opening the doors to a 'developed India - prosperous India'.

"This campaign of 'Vocal for Local' strengthens the economy of the entire country. The Vocal for Local campaign is a guarantee of employment. This is a guarantee of development; this is the guarantee of balanced development of the country," he said.

This provides equal opportunities to both urban and rural people, he added. "This also paves the way for value addition in local products, and if ever, there are ups and downs in the global economy, the mantra of Vocal for Local also protects our economy," PM Modi asserted.

It is the second consecutive year when the trend of buying some goods through cash payments on the occasion of Deepawali is gradually on the decline, he said.

"That means, people are making more and more digital payments now. This is also very encouraging. You can do one more thing. Decide for yourself that for one month you will make payments only through UPI or any digital medium and not through cash," he said.

The success of the digital revolution in India has made this absolutely possible. And when one month is over, please share your experiences and your photos with me. I wish you all the best in advance from now itself," PM Modi said.

Post a comment (Except for the headline, this story has not been edited by NDTV staff and is published from a syndicated feed.)"

"……In a country like India, marriage is regarded as a one-time event in life by the people which is usually sanctified and glorified with much social approval. As we all know that marriage is considered as a heavenly alliance between the two individuals, therefore, in this bond, two human beings enter into the world of emotional, physical, mental and spiritual union through the marriage vows. Marriage is again taken as a social necessity and marrying children is the primary responsibility of parents in India. It is believed that sons should be married as soon as they start earning whereas daughters should be married as soon they become young in early twenties. Marriage is not only an important social institution but the stepping stone to build the family unit and is the most significant legal contract of each society. However, in this contemporary society, even the meaning of marriage has changed thereby making it more complex and a different affair for the entire human race. Factors like urbanization, new legislative measures and influence of the western societies are flipping the minds of the Indian people towards love marriages, livein -relationships and break-up in relationship thereby affecting the entire society………….

Each form of marriage was exclusive in ancient times. Matrimonial laws were preserved and followed without any disagreement. Though contemporary Hindu marriage has its own issues that challenge the long-standing methods but still marriage as an institution has stayed alive in the face of societal turmoil. It is of no doubt that our Indian society is passing through a cultural clash between Indian and western ethos in modern times. In this scenario, attempts have been continuously made by the families, laws and other agencies to provide freedom to personal liberty and to exercise the right to live an independent life whereby people can choose their spouse and other priorities in life. To conclude, time has changed along with the forms of marriage. But marriage is still considered as a sacred bond in present society. This knotting process of two individuals not only involves the couple only but the two families of the bride and the bridegroom as well. Be it arrange marriage or love marriage, marriage is just an institution to fulfil some responsibilities towards each other, towards one's family and society at large. Therefore, love marriage vs. arranged marriage is just a question that prevails in the mind of people now and then who are either not satisfied with a relationship or are scared to live with an unknown partner for the rest of their life." [Source: www.ijcrt.org © 2022 IJCRT | Volume 10, Issue 2 February 2022 | ISSN: 2320-2882]

"There are few things Indians love as much as weddings. While dictionaries may define weddings simply as "marriage ceremonies", in India, they represent much more. Indian weddings are extravagant celebrations that go beyond the conventional understanding of marriage ceremonies. In fact, a modest wedding is considered an oxymoron in the Indian context.

Spread across about three weeks, between late November and mid-December, close to four million weddings are expected to be held in India. Collectively, these weddings are projected to bring in a staggering $51 billion. This thriving industry sees Indians spending over $7 billion on jewellery, booking hotel rooms worth $600 million and purchasing apparels worth over a billion dollars each year.

Destination weddings: The epitome of grandeur

While weddings in India are known for their opulence, the most extravagant among them are the big, fat destination weddings. India, with over 7,90,000 high-net-worth individuals, including 161 billionaires, has become a land of the rich and famous. The flourishing economy and celebrity endorsements have further amplified aspirations.

High-profile Indian families have taken destination weddings to a global level. Chartering flights, renting gondolas in Venice, hiring Michelin-starred chefs in Rome and even shutting down famous casinos in Monte Carlo are not uncommon for these elite celebrations. In 2022, popular destinations included Paris in France, Istanbul in Turkey, Tuscany and the Amalfi Coast in Italy. This year's itinerary features Rome and Lake Como in Italy, Cancun in Mexico and Budapest in Hungary.

Challenges for the Indian wedding business

Despite the glamour associated with international destination weddings, it poses a challenge for the Indian wedding business. While the average wedding can cost anywhere from $3,000 to $1, 20,000, extravagant destination weddings can range from one to five million dollars. With over 600 thousand dollars spent on a two-day hotel booking for guests, the trend threatens the domestic wedding industry.

Government initiatives

Recognising the impact of destination weddings on the domestic economy, India's Ministry of Tourism has launched a campaign to promote weddings within the country. Prime Minister Narendra Modi has also voiced concerns about the trend, questioning the necessity of going abroad for weddings.

For many Indians, destination weddings may not be necessary, considering the diverse and picturesque locations within the country. States like Rajasthan, Goa, Uttarakhand and Tamil Nadu offer beautiful landscapes and historical palaces, making India an ideal choice for destination weddings. As the debate continues, the grandeur and economics of Indian weddings remain a fascinating aspect of the country's cultural and economic landscape." [Source: Vantage | 'Why foreign weddings are not good news for India' - The Vantage Take November 28, 2023] - [Views expressed in the above piece are personal and solely that of the author. They do not necessarily reflect First post's views.]

I sought the help of Google to ascertain how many marriages of people of foreign countries have taken place in India; I found no information available which means none. This does not involve NRIs but two Indian citizens going to a country for solemnizing the marriage as a matter of high dignity or prestige they are holding in society in India. There is no instance I could find whether similar foreign citizens coming to India for solemnizing the marriage. Does it suggest that rich people holding high dignified and prestigious status are only in India? It cannot be so which means the Indian rich and prestigious community considers it a status symbol and wants to show something not ordinarily done by the people in general nor any foreign citizen seems to believe in such status.

Contrast the above two Articles to contest whether it is desirable going to a foreign country for the marriage of sons and daughters of rich families in India, about which the PM spoke. PM's understanding becomes more understandable if one have a relook at the second Article stated before for; it brings out the truth as to its impact on the Indian Wedding Industry, hence to the economy which may be negligible, yet contributable to the economy.

Also to be considered about what PM spoke in his Man Ki Baat that it brought home the message in clear terms from the point of pride and dignity being an Indian and signifying that pride and dignity as Indian as such when he referred to vocal for local. PM's talk needs to be taken in a larger context of saving precious foreign exchange for speedier economic development of the country. Such events being happening in India randomly, imposition of conditions thereon does not seem to be advisable since the government itself has already issued an advisory.

Nevertheless, it underpins the role of black money holding by the Indians in various forms which includes banks in the foreign countries for which there is a separate law to deal with. With due respects to such citizens of India who are going abroad for solemnizing the marriage of their son or daughter, it would be more appropriate from Indianness and high morality point of view that the difference between overall expenditure incurred abroad for such purpose and the overall expenditure which would have been incurred for the same purpose if the marriages were to be done within the country [as computed in the second Article noted before] would have been sufficient enough to perform the mass marriages of the socially poorest of the poor people in the country that enhances the dignity, prestige and honour of such people to a much higher level. Issue involved is much larger, that is, self-affection one attaches to being Indian and the self-pride that one cultivates as an Indian. This should be the personal privilege and pride for every Indian compared to the status of dignity and prestige that should always be subordinate to the former.

PART 02
DIVERSITY & DIVISION PARADOX

"Unity, not uniformity, must be our aim. We attain unity only through variety. Differences must be integrated, not annihilated, not absorbed." – Mary Parker Follett (1868-1933) – American social worker, management consultant, and philosopher.

By now we are able to understand about the diversity. Within it, there lies another word known as 'division'. It is bit confusing to understand what is diversity and division when we subject to a comparison. I believe, there is hardly any scope for us to be divisive on diversity for; diversity is ingrained in us since eleventh century or so onwards when the foreigners started invading our country by the Kings from Greek, Persian countries, Mughals and English. This period stretched over 700-800 years domination by these kings, one after another. It was so because we were more divided within with hundreds of kingdoms within the country, each fighting against the other.

A story goes as under:

One day two cats stole a piece of bread from the kitchen of a house. But there arose a problem of dividing their share. Both of them agreed to take an equal share of the bread. They tried to divide the bread into two equal parts but failed. None of them agreed to take a small part of the bread. Indeed they couldn't come to a result rather they began to quarrel and changed a lot of words. At last finding no acceptable way the two cats decided to go to a monkey who was popular as the wisest animal in the forest. The two cats went to the monkey and requested him to divide the bread into two equal parts. The monkey was veritably clever. He understood their problem. He assured the two cats to do the same.

The monkey brought a pair of scales and cut the bread in such a way that it wasn't ever equal. As a result, he had to cut a bit of the bigger part of the bread and ate the excess also, he scaled again. This time the lower piece was proved bigger than another piece. He cut the bigger piece again to make the two equal and ate the additional. In this way, the monkey continued his eating and the two pieces of bread got lower and lower and finally, the monkey eats all the bread. The cats lost their bread for their foolishness, due to fighting with each other and believing in some third one.

Parts of India have been subject to Muslim rule from the period of Muhammad ibn Qasim till the fall of the Mughal Empire. While there is a tendency to view the Muslim conquests and Muslim empires as a prolonged period of violence against Hindu culture, in between the periods of wars and conquests, there were harmonious Hindu-Muslim relations in most Indian communities, and the Indian population grew during the medieval Muslim times. No populations were expelled based on their religion by either the Muslim or Hindu kings, nor were attempts made to annihilate a specific religion.

According to Romila Thapar, with the onset of Muslim rule all Indians, higher and lower caste were lumped together in the category of "Hindus". While higher-caste Indians regarded lower castes to be impure, they were now regarded as belonging to a similar category, which partly explains the belief among many higher caste Indians "Hinduism in the last one thousand years has been through the most severe persecution that any religion in the world has ever undergone." ....

Romila Thapar states that the belief in a severe persecution in the last millennium brushes away the "various expressions of religious persecution in India prior to the coming of the Muslims and particularly between the Śaiva and the Buddhist and Jaina sects". She questions what persecution means, and if it means religious conversions, she doubts that conversions can be interpreted as forms of persecution. It is quite correct to mention that Muslim iconoclasts destroyed temples and the broke images of Hindus, states Thapar, it should also be mentioned that Muslim rulers made donations to Hindu sects during their rule.[200]

During the Islamic rule period, states David Lorenzen, there was state-sponsored persecution against Hindus, yet it was sporadic and directed mostly at Hindu religious monuments.[202] According to Deepa Ollapally, the Mughal emperor Aurangzeb was clearly discriminatory towards Hindu and all other non-Muslims, displaying an "unprecedented level of religious bigotry", but perhaps this was a consequence of the opposition he faced from a number of his family members[203]. During the medieval span, she states, "episodes of direct religious persecution of Hindus were rare", as were communal riots between Hindus and Muslims.[204]

By any measure, 700-800 years occupation of our country by the foreign invaders was a long period that implies the invasions were succeeded, wealth was looted but those belonging to them who were left behind found themselves in a state of fixation that lead to their permanent settlement in our country. The social, political, cultural, and religious movements that arose in various parts of India during the medieval period attempted to bind the people together in a harmonious cord. The religious movement of Medieval India had a huge impact on the country's literature and language. Rulers such as Akbar were heavily influenced by Bhakti and Sufi Philosophers, leading him to take a secular stance on religion.

It is truly amazing what can be accomplished when individuals with different talents and experiences come together to enrich workplaces, neighbourhoods, political parties, churches, and so on. There is a richness that is evident when group members respect the differences that exist and work fervently to use those dissimilarities for a common good; each person committed to doing the best that they can as they seek to guarantee outstanding overall performance. There is beauty in diversity.

There seems to be a natural/normal tendency for us as humans to look at each other with "jaundiced eyes"; focused on identifying and magnifying differences in a negative and counter-productive way.

This seems to be especially so as nations prepare for general elections. Politicians tend to highlight differences between themselves and their opponents. Unfortunately, the focus is not always on policies. Regrettably, too many encourage divisiveness. Too many seek to incite their followers and potential followers to engage in sowing and nurturing discord. In many cases, the comparisons and contrasts are often linked to "non-issues". Political tribalism does not dissipate following the general elections ... even as these same guilty politicians verbalize about the need for national unity. Unfortunately, those who may have been engaged in creating division and championing divisiveness are disqualified from advocating the need for unity and reconciliation. Their followers are unlikely to respond positively and their opponents will understandably not trust the new "all-inclusive" utterances. To them, the spring that provided bitter water cannot now produce sweet water. And so, politicians and their acolytes must commit to avoid speaking with forked tongues. Leaders in business and society must commit to appreciating and encouraging the spirit of diversity. This is critical in avoiding the pitfalls and dangers throughout society when divisiveness is at play. This is as true for those in the developed world as it is for the citizens in emerging economies like ours.

Politicians deepen existing divides when they use inflammatory language, such as hate speech, and this makes their societies more likely to experience political violence and terrorism. The fact that such abusive language was even uttered especially on a public platform is reflective of the shameful levels the opposition is willing to stoop to, under the garb of political criticism. With verbal abuse becoming the new normal in modern Indian politics and ethical standards of political criticism having gone for a toss, it is only a matter of time before respectable political debate is replaced by opportunistic mud-slinging.

More polarised societies are especially susceptible to bouts of political violence and terrorism when politicians use hate speech. Examples include Weimar Germany in the 1920s and 1930s, which featured assassinations of leftist politicians and street brawling by Nazi partisans, Argentina in the 1970s during the so-called "Dirty War" in which government-backed right-wing death squads fought with left-wing political movements who themselves engaged in terrorism and Turkey in the late 1970s early 1980s, when ultranationalist right-wing organisations and leftist opposition movements attacked each other.

When taken to extreme, hateful rhetoric by political leaders can precipitate civil wars and genocides, as was the case in the 1990s in Rwanda, where Hutu extremists used anti-Tutsi radio broadcasts to foment widespread violence. Given the elected nature and political stature of the office, such expletive language tends to incite enmity between people and creates an environment of divisive polarisation that is often characterised by violence, be it physical, verbal or both.

The thoughts shared in the foregoing paragraphs remind us of the dangers that emerge when division is evident among and within groups. Intolerance is often a common trait when differences are highlighted among citizens. That bias, if not managed and curtailed, can be very dangerous and disruptive. History records how well Adolf Hitler (1889-1945), the German politician and leader of the Nazi Party, fuelled division among the German people, highlighting the differences between the "pure Arian race" and those deemed untermenschen (subhuman) or socially unwanted. Jews, blacks, the physically handicapped, and the mentally or emotionally unstable were placed in this category. The division was highlighted and the powder-keg of prejudice ignited. History records that Hitler and his Nazi regime killed 19.3 million civilians and prisoners of war. This example is provided to remind us that fuelling division and prejudice, in whichever forms they are spewed, can be very destructive.

Margaret Cho, an American comedian and songwriter, reminds us to be forever alert to the plight of those who may appear different to ourselves. In her own way, she cautions us about the dangers of the prejudices and divisions that are created when we practice intolerance … and maintain divisions that retard societal inclusiveness. She notes that, "If you are a woman, if you're a person of colour, if you are gay, lesbian, bisexual, transgender, if you are a person of size, if you are a person of intelligence, if you are a person of integrity, then you are considered a minority in this world." Minorities very often discover that they are physically, emotionally, and/or socially maligned and too often unfairly ridiculed. Such behaviours are unacceptable. Such divisions are often unwarranted. While we may not condone some of the behaviours of the individuals Cho refers to in her quotation, we must make sure that we do not infringe on their civil rights or separate/divide them so that they are rejected from mainstream society.

Mohandas 'Mahatma' Gandhi (1869-1948), the Indian lawyer, anti-colonial nationalist and civil rights activist, advocated the need for unity across races, nationalities, and religions. He reminds us that, "Our ability to reach unity in diversity will be the beauty and test of our civilization." This is as true for those who live in developed countries as it is for those of us who reside in developing countries. The test of our civilization will be our ability to reach unity in diversity. It is not beyond us. We have the capacity, the potential, to make this a rea. But each of us must commit (and recommit) to the process. Amidst our differences we have enough in common to appreciate and respect those differences and to work with each other to build and maintain the beautiful and diverse societies of which we are a part. Our fore parents may have resided in the region long before the Europeans "discovered" these territories. Or they may have arrived in our part of the world on slave ships that sailed from the West African coast, or on vessels used to transport indentured servants from India.

Or they may have been among the more recent arrivals to our region having flown in from Syria, Lebanon, North America, or Europe. Regardless of how they came, they had a right to be here. They added to the beautiful societal mosaic of our Caribbean collective tapestry. We are who we are because of who they were and where they came from.

As enlightened citizens, we appreciate the beauty of our diversity. As fair, progressive and open-minded citizens, we will be at the forefront of the opposition to those who may selfishly seek to engender divisiveness and division. Unity, not uniformity, must forever be our focus.

It has become order of day for the politicians to indulge in more divisiveness based on personal ego than the merits and demerits of the issues involved. The ruling party and the opposition parties assume as enemy of each other. In that, the national and peoples' aspirations and interests for their smooth economic development go out of the sight. The persona and not the party becomes more prominent when the party members start worshipping the persona rather than devoting to the party including its ideologies and philosophy promised to and to be fulfilled by them to the people. This results in upmanship of an individual in the party than the party as a collective body. Ego is attached to the person and, if it is pegged up, it encircles the entire party itself leaving no sane and sensible persons in the party to tell the serious implications of such attitude. This is how the present political parties – both the ruling party and the opposition parties – have cultivated a character of hatredness among them that converts into person attachment and ego that aims at creating more and more divisive than unified politics. A situation of this kind among the political parties keep them burning in the heat of arguments against each other and calmness is considered as the weakness. These scenarios one can see today even on a small issue let alone the larger issues.

The democracy demands agree to disagree without being disagreeable which means that the disagreement should not be end rather it should be a beginning to find alternative solution or suggestion to pacify the issues in hand. When one says 'I disagree' means he or she has something in mind as an alternative to the one proposed. It should be the obligation of such person to put forward his or her alternative solution for consideration from the points of view of legislative and legal feasibility. Mere disagreement distances the existing democratic relationship and may turn into interposing as enemies than the learned community sitting in the august Houses of Parliament with competing brilliance among others finding ways and means to address the serious issues the people and the country is facing. This is democratically a positive approach It has become a secondary consideration while disagreement, chaos, criticisms, disorderliness have become the primary considerations in both the Houses. This is democratically a negative approach. The entire purpose of the proceedings in both the Houses is to be constructive unless a constructive proposal, prima-facie, appears covertly as a destructive one, such destructive one needs to be converted into constructive. This should be spirit of the Members of both the Houses. The negative approach that produces vacuum serves no purpose to the people. To serve the people is the crux of both the Houses of Parliament. One needs to find a solution within the differences, the object of the parliamentary proceedings and the duty of both the Houses to serve the people. Weighing of personal attachments or detachments as well as political egoism serves no purpose either of the proceedings or of the people.

Most disturbing factor one witnesses today is the way the Parliament has been working – more noise, less legislative business, increasing expenditure and divisions in the oppositions. Seen from other side, there is growing stubbornness, resistance, noise, lack of respect to listen to the opposition and thumping the debates by the ruling party. Both are at cross roads. There is no mechanism or system for the ruling party and opposition to meet periodically, exchange pleasantries and share as much information as could be within the permissible limits on the developments in the country in the important sectors. Lack of this has widened gap of mutual in understanding each other the broad spectre of priority of the matters to be taken up given the prevailing situation in the country. Absence of basic oral or formal communication among them has been driving towards more confusion, misunderstandings and prejudices. There is, therefore, need for reimagining and refurbishing the working of the parliament with utmost urgency, more so, how to bring the ruling party and opposition as nearer to each other. The citizens are helpless watchers of the ugly political events, the reflections of which are not appreciated by the politicians. It is worthy of the politicians if they could debate and deliberate with mutual understanding rather mutual misunderstanding in the best interests of the people. Some of the suggestions made by the learned former Secretary General {Dr. Kashyap] referred to hereunder are worthy of consideration in the present context.

The politicians have two faces, one of their own and the other that imprints the reflections of the others who may also be politicians or the people in general. The humans have only face. Question, therefore, arises how the politicians could be said to have two faces. They have one original and the other artificial, the difference between them drives towards creating self-conflicts and a sense of hatredness. Truly speaking, hatredness has no place in politics for; if that is to be so, that breeds the same among two divisive communities that support the politicians or the political parties. The hatredness does not stop here; it dives deep into the societies giving birth to the most acrimonious relationships. 'The definition of acrimonious is 'when someone or something is bitter or harsh in manner or speech, or rubs a person the wrong way.'

Lack of reach among the ruling party and the opposition on one hand and among the people and their elected representatives is creating more division even though we as a country are wedded with unity in diversity.

In our country, unfortunately, a dynastic rule for a period of over fifty five years after the country attained independence has led to the creation of dynastic kingdoms in various states of the country. The dynastic rule at the centre was not as a matter choice of the people but those who were in power in dynastic descendant order mesmerized the people that the country is there because of their dynastic presence. They all belonged to an oldest party but made the party as subordinate and subservient to them. The concept of 'High Command' was born in the Indian politics at this juncture of the time. It became a rule of law within that party and no politician belonging to the party had the courage to question it. Any political party is supposed to be governed by its Internal Regulations registered with the Election Commission of India. Sad part was that the ECI did not lay down a standard format of the Internal Regulations for the political parties. The Company Law and the Societies Registration Act, 1860 prescribe the format of the Internal Regulations which are subject to approval after review. Until the regulations are approved and duly stamped under the signature of the authority concerned, they don't come into effect.

Why it was not considered as essential for incorporating under the governing law of the political parties is difficult to understand today but the fact cannot be denied that it was also a political acumanship that would have led to omission of such a provision in the governing law. ECI has power to register the Internal Regulations of the political parties only when the party can be said to have acquired a legal name. This presupposes that the ECI ought to have made a uniform and standardized form of the Internal Regulations for the national and state level recognized parties so that bypassing of the internal regulations by the Office Bearers of the party could be detected. ECI, being the authority for registration of the political parties is deemed to have powers to lay down a standard form of the Internal Regulations for the political parties. Lack of this has given undue and excessive powers to the political parties Office Bearers to regulate the party as they wished. Words such as 'High Command' or Supreme Command' which are not specified in the internal regulations acquired an implicit approval of the party members who faithfully and obediently continued and continue to follow those gracious designations in their way of working subjecting themselves to servitude. This is the state of condition of the dynastic party well rooted into the entire system itself thus becoming a standard practice.

Another unfortunate part of the country was that because of the existence of the dynastic party for more than half century disadvantaged coming up of the two or three major national political parties for sustenance of the democratic system of working rather that led to the evolution of multiparty system which now stand at more than 2500 at the national and state level. Though the constitution of the country is silent on the political parties, it was the constitutional duty of those who were in power for a long period of fifty five years to have encouraged the need for a few political parties according to the size and population of the country as a matter democratic practice prevalent in other democratic countries whose constitutions were taken into consideration while drafting our own constitution. The very fact that the dynastic rule having continued for more than half century, the dynasties believed the people have become used to it rather want that practice to continue like kingdom.

Below are the excerpts from the **'WORKING OF PARLIAMENT AND NEED FOR REFORMS' Ied by the most respected Dr. Subhash C. Kashyap and posted on the Website:** [This is stated to be reproduction from the book Ied by Dr. Kashyap in 2000. The Paper holds its validity even after twenty three years. Other than technological breakthrough, there is no change in the current impression of the parliament in the eyes of the people rather it is more concerning].

"Parliament is the communication link between the people and the government. People talk of happenings in Parliament and of the Members of Parliament as things quite remote and different from themselves. There is little consciousness of Parliament being their own and Members being from among themselves. It is ordinary people who have to be enabled to feel that they are participants in the decision-making and legislative processes and that through Parliament their voice can reach the Government and that it counts. Parliament must have access to public opinion and public must have access to Parliament. If corruption is suspected inside the portals of legislatures, the press and the public must be free to question it and expose it without being threatened under the law of parliamentary privileges. In its own long-term interest, Parliament as an institution cannot afford to place itself beyond all scrutiny by anyone. There is every need for a parliamentary Ombudsman. If stories that are current about payments demanded, offered or paid for favours like gas connections, telephone connections, questions etc. or of subletting of official residences, or of misuse of coupons and passes these need to be thoroughly investigated and, if untrue, publicly contradicted.

A matter often raised is that of the salaries, allowances, amenities, facilities etc. extended to Members. While for some, entering Parliament involves financial sacrifice, for many others it provides much sought for rewards and benefits. There are two extreme views on whether Members are heavily pampered and overpaid or they misunderstood and grossly underpaid. Much can be said on either side. According to one guess, if every member is paid Rs.100,000 to 200,000 per month in cash and all perks and direct and indirect financial benefits from the State are withdrawn, the public exchequer would be a gainer. This would imply that at present, a member on an average gets in cash or in kind not less than Rs. One lakh (One hundred thousand) per month. If the State Legislators are included, the total numbers comes to above 4000. Besides, we have Ministers, Chairmen of Boards, Public Undertakings etc. and politicians occupying innumerable offices with Minister"s status at the State and Union levels, each one costing ten to fifty times the cost of an M.P. All this put together makes the cost of maintaining our huge army of whole-time professional politicians very heavy and hardly commensurate with the returns to society. While stressing the need for cutting down the administrative expenditure under SAP, we have to think of cutting down the staging cost of democracy as well. There is need to drastically slash parliamentary spending under various heads. Even if the resultant economy in the context of the overall national budget may not seem very large, the psychological impact is bound to be massive. Strictest self-control is necessary also because parliamentary budget, by convention, is not questioned or debated.[Author's Note: Figures stated above pertained to 2000 and would have by now multiplied than controlling the expenditure].

Deliberate and concerted efforts are needed also at the professional level to rebuild Parliament's image as the supreme institution of the people. The people should know what their representatives are doing for them. Better press and public relations job and image-building for Parliament are legitimate and necessary and there should be no hesitation to use the latest tools and techniques for the purpose. The mass media - the radio, television, newspapers, films etc. - should all be suitably harnessed to the service of Parliament. These, particularly the print and electronic media can play a vital role in building a healthy image of Parliament……..

Qua of Members is the most important variable in the working of any Parliament inasmuch as a Parliament would be what its Members make of it. It is the primary duty of every Member irrespective of his party affiliations to maintain and project a good image of Parliament by his conduct both inside and outside the Houses of Parliament. Corporate image of Parliament is bound to remain poor unless the qua and conduct of individual Members improve and every Member is imbued with a sense of purpose and responsibility. Also, every backbencher should be enabled to feel relevant and that he matters in what goes on in Parliament. Members of important parliamentary committees need to lay down a strict code of conduct for themselves, never to ask the senior Government officers appearing before the Committee for personal favours, avoid Committee tours unless really necessary and never accept any gifts, dinners, free transport, five star hospital and the like while on tours.

Politics has become a highly professionalised business and should be understood as such. Irrespective of ones talents and professional background, every new member when he first enters a legislature feels completely lost in the dense forest of the mass of conventions, traditions, rules, regulations and formalities of the highly sophisticated parliamentary procedures, processes and practices. Institutionalized arrangements are, therefore necessary to provide the much needed professional training and orientation to every newly elected Member irrespective of his ideological or party affiliations. The curriculum should include, among other things, adequate knowledge of the political system, the Constitution, the Rules of Procedure and Conduct of Business, the practices and precedents, mechanisms and modalities of the working of the Houses and the Parliamentary Committees, the do's and don'ts for Members, the rules of parliamentary etiquette and the like. The emphasis should be on the practical know-how, the technicalities and the operational realities and the concrete situations and not the rule book.

While executive power of the Union is co-extensive with its legislative power, the constituent power under the Constitution belongs exclusively to Parliament. The responsibility of Parliament, therefore, becomes much greater in the case of Constitution (Amendment) Bills. As such, instead of the Constitution Amendments being presented to Parliament like ordinary pieces of legislation in the form of Bills for introduction sometimes at very short notice, it would be desirable if Parliament is associated right from the initial stages of formulation of proposals for constitutional reform, i.e., the actual drafting of a Constitution Amendment Bill may be taken up only after the principles involved have been thrashed out in a parliamentary forum and subjected to appropriate a priori scrutiny by the constituent power. The proposed involvement of Parliament and a priori scrutiny can be achieved through the device of a Constitution Committee of Parliament which may be constituted by resolution or otherwise as a standing joint Committee of the two Houses. The members of the Committee may be elected by the respective Houses. Rather than delay, this might expedite the process of constitutional reforms besides bestowing greater lity, legitimacy and wider acceptability to the reform proposals. As an alternative, after a Constitution Amendment Bill has been formulated but before it has been introduced, it may be subjected to a priori scrutiny of the „Constitution Committee". If this is done, even the Government would be saved many an embarrassment.

"India is the largest populated country and the biggest democratic country in the world. Its democratic pillars are so deep that no one can pull it out. It has been proved so many times and mechanism is set to save democratic values of India. Even though we have the best system to save the democracy, certain gaps created grow unnecessary weed which can bring it to dilapidated state. The political system of India is in such a way that it has expanded its base through its loopholes. Forefathers of Indian constitution have not assessed this much that can curb political defects in India. It is not the mistake of their part but it is the problem which is rising out of situations and loopholes which are not so easily tackled.

Problems in political system of India:

No major party and no perfect choice.	In India, in the beginning there was Congress as major party and had ruled consecutively. The benefit of major and strong political party is that it can do what is good to people and at the same time power can be misused. The strongest party has become degraded due to misuse of power clamping emergency. The misuse of power has shattered the Congress party into pieces. At the same time, negligence towards local feelings gave rise to the regional parties. Regional parties can never think about unity and integrity of nation. They only can think of regional benefit. The negligence of national party at local level has terminated its influence. Now, the Indian political system is run on regional parties and sub-regional parties which are leading to multiple party system at state level.
Coalition governments	The era of coalition governments are running in India. What is the problem with coalition governments? The party should listen to the every party's demands that are walking with it. It cannot breach the line drawn by parties. Decision making will be slow. Few policies may not come into action due to opposition. Every day, the party has to check whether numbers of supporters are good in health. The party which has erred can escape with ease as their support may not be available if government is not helpful to them. The results of coalition governments are delay in decision making and favouritism.
Family politics	Family politics became natural in India. If any person is successful in politics, his total family will be in the political process. It is not bad to an extent but politics is turned to be safe haven for them to be acquitted from any mistake is not appreciable. We can see mother, father, their sons and daughters are in the fray and now in Assemblies and Parliament too. Family politics is dangerous because they can influence more than other can. Their family can be small Assembly and small Parliament. Their opinions can be rubbed on people. It is evident that a single family ruled the most of the time in India till now after independence.
Inheritance in politics is not to be encouraged	Even it is not different from family politics, it differs, as it is given at the time of demise of a leader. Every political party is offering seat to the family members of leader. If this is the situation when we can see normal people rise to power. Youth are completely debarred from politics. The youth in our Parliament are from families which have political backgrounds.
Caste politics is dangerous in political system of India	Caste politics is the worst scenario in India. These are deeply rooted in villages of India. There are villages which support political parties on caste basis. If village has more people belong to one community, the entire community supports the party which belongs to same caste. Through this, other castes of these villages are harassed. They cannot get welfare programmes designed by government. The ineligible persons enjoy

	these programmes. This is the main reason for the high poverty in villages even though poverty eradication specific programmes are launched.
Businessmen in politics and politicians in businesses	This is new trend in Indian political system. Most of our MPs are millionaires. As MLA or MP, they have privileges and with that they are initiating businesses. Most of services were to be in government's hands. But, as there is no proper care, they are left to private sector. As they are left to private sector, our leaders are engaged in businesses. Here, the mistake going on is that they are getting friendly policies related to their businesses using the law. Businessman in politics is not wrong. But, carrying the business attitude is considered to be the fatal blow to democracy. Businessman invests and thinks of profit. If he thinks politics is also like business, then it is problematic. Anyhow, this is the thing which is going on in our present democracy.
Remedies to the problems in political system of India	Our leaders are born with seats beneath them. Few leaders led mostly their lives holding power. Family politics, political inheritance and corruption are situated due to their long term power holding. If they are given few chances to hold power for 2 times in his life time, then it can be suitable. The limit can be increased in Indian context. But, disadvantage is that we lose experienced people in democratic process. Hence, it is good to have reservations which can give chances to the backward communities too. The political empowerment and chances should reach to every person of this country. Few landlords or businessmen should not hold it as their property. India is most democratic country in the world. Every country has its weaknesses and strengths.

Source: India Study Channel Website

[Burning Issue] Intra Party Democracy / Democratization of Political Parties – Political Parties in India: A Backgrounder [Source: https://www.civilsdaily.com/burning-issue-intra-party-democracy-democratization-of-political-parties/ - July 23, 2022]

- A party system is a concept in comparative political science concerning the system of government by political parties in a democratic country.

- In India, there is a multi-party system in place, with the number of parties at the national level fluctuating.

- Furthermore, India has a diverse range of political parties, including left, centrist, and right-wing parties, as well as communal and non-communal parties.

- **Features of Political Parties in India**

    The key features of the Indian Party system are:

    1. Ideology base

    2. Multi-Party System

3. Pre-poll Alliances
4. Coalition System
5. Opposition's Multi-Party Character

Issues with Political Parties in India

- Lack of proper organisation: Another feature of the Indian party system is its lack of structure. Political parties live and die by their organization.

- Groupism inside India's party structure: In India, Groupism is a major problem for every political party. This shatters a party's cohesiveness, causing it to split into several factions. Ex. INC, NCP, TMC.

- Extra-constitutional ways of gaining power: Political parties do not hesitate to utilize uncertain measures to gain political power in addition to legitimate means. Ex. Resort Politics

- Populist tendencies: In India, it is well noticed that political parties turn to populist politics in order to gain power. They take unfair advantage of people's emotions and compulsions, promote populist slogans, and mislead the public. Ex. Temple reconstruction movements

- Lack of discipline among party members: It has been observed that members of various political parties are unconcerned about party discipline, preferring instead to sling dirt at one another. Ex. Undue political statements

- Communal characteristics: The people of India are influenced by caste and religion, and they have a strong sense of allegiance to their caste and religion. Ex. Political party in Hyderabad.

- Criminalization of politics: Leaders are valued for their capacity to attract crowds and raise funds as elections become more and more expensive.

Why are tainted candidates inducted by political parties?

- Innocent until proven guilty maxim: The other reason offered by political parties is summarised by the maxim of Indian law, which is that any accused is innocent until proven guilty.

- Popularity: Such candidates with serious records seem to do well despite their public image, largely due to their ability to finance their own elections and bring substantive resources to their respective parties.

- Prospected victory: The logic of a candidate with criminal charges doing better for the cause of people of is another flawed argument.

- Destabilizing other electors: Others do not seek to punish these candidates in instances where they are in contest with other candidates with similar records.

- Vested interests: Some voters tend to view such candidates through a narrow prism: of being able to represent their interests by hook or by crook.

Why voice for democracy within?

- Dynastic politics: Many political parties in India have charges of dynastic politics irrespective of the political insights of the person who inherits the legacy.

- Opaque appointments: Although election of the party president cannot be the sole criteria for judging intraparty democracy, political parties view the matter only through the procedure of electing the chiefs.

- Dominants: The party head positions are mostly influenced by some external forces which have larger say in finance and caste (or) religion.

- Persona cult: There is a tendency of hero worship in people and many times a leader takes over the party and builds his own coterie, ending all forms of intra-party democracy.

- Centralised power: Most parties are subservient to one supreme leader or a charismatic persona. Such leaders are valued for their capacity to attract crowds and raise funds as elections become more and more expensive.

- Lack of institutionalization: Most of political parties still refuse to lay down settled and predictable procedures for almost everything they do, from the selection of candidates to the framing of a manifesto.

How this impacted election mandates?

- Weaker opposition: In India, strong and well-organized opposition is required for parliamentary democracy to succeed, yet it does not exist.

- Non-coherence: There are several national and regional political parties performing the role of opposition at the moment, both at the national and state levels, but they are not unified on many political topics and do not have a uniform agenda.

- Electoral autocracy: India is often accused to be a flawed democracy on accounts of its alleged far-right-wing political government. There has been increased pressure on human rights groups, intimidation of journalists and activists, and a spate of attacks, especially against Muslims.

- Against public aspirations: People vote for fulfilling their demands and put much effort with aspirations that a stable government would be at their behest to resolve their issues.

- Unstable government: This point needs no explanation. We have largely seen the perils of poor decision-making of politicians due to a lack of consensus among the allies.

Even Monarchies were either elected or limited but never absolute Bhakti or hero-worship sure road to dictatorship, says Dr. Ambedkar

A critical evaluation

- Political parties have become oligarchies: India's success in consolidating a democratic system of government has paradoxically forestalled pressure for party reform. .

- One person diktat rules the parties: Most parties are subservient to one supreme leader who can impose his/her offspring on the party, and even electoral defeat does not loosen their control or hold over the party.

- Election manifesto is nowhere relevant post-election: Political parties with the exception of the Left parties still refuse to lay down settled and predictable procedures for almost everything they do, from the selection of candidates to the framing of a manifesto.

- Party reform is a pressing one in India: While many argue that intraparty democracy is essential to sustain broader political democracy, this is not a panacea for the numerous problems facing parties.

- Vague system is the status-quo: The biggest weakness of parties is that they are leader-centric and most leaders are unwilling to institutionalize the procedures.

- Diktat of the party high-command actually rules a govt.: As a rule, strong leaders rarely support institutionalization because it constrains their discretion and personal power.

- Partisan mobilization of the left-liberals: There is a major challenge facing the party system by party activity driven by partisan mobilisation lies at the root of much of the schism and disruption of Indian politics today. Ex. Leftists frequently meeting the Chinese.

- Sake of electioneering and winning never ends: Another aspect is the reduction of party organisations into election-winning machines. This has become the only role a party envisages for itself.

- Lack of political will persists: If party funds are raised and controlled centrally, this weakens the State units and rank and file vis-à-vis the central leadership on a range of issues including leadership selection and nominations for elections.

Need for imbibing democracy

- Ensuring equal opportunity: The absence of intra-party democracy adversely impacts the constitutional right of all citizens to equal political opportunity to participate in politics and contest elections.

- Less factionalism: A leader with strong grassroot connection would not be side-lined. This will allow less factionalism and division of parties thereby ensuring a stable govt in power.

- Popular representation: A transparent party structure with transparent processes will allow proper ticket distribution and candidate selection. The selection would not be based on the whims of a few powerful leaders in the party but will represent the choice of the larger party.

- Accountability of the legislators: A democratic party will be accountable to its party members, for they will lose elections in the next cycle for their shortcomings.

- Decentralising power: Every political party has State and local body units, an election at each level will allow creation of power centres at different levels. This will allow decentralisation of power and the decision making will take place at the ground level.

- Legal loopholes: Currently, there is no express provision for internal democratic regulation of political parties in India except political defection. The ECI's power to require parties to hold regular internal elections for office bearers, and candidate selection is compromised in the absence of any penal provisions.

How to attain internal democracy within parties?

- Internal elections: It shall be the duty of the political party to take appropriate steps to ensure holding of elections at all levels. The political party shall hold elections in an unpartisan ways by their 'karyakartas'.

- Strengthening Anti-defection Law: The Anti-Defection Act of 1985 requires the party legislators to act according to the party whip which is decided by the diktats of the highest party leadership. One way to democratise political parties is to promote intra-party dissent.

- Limited reservations: Seats can be reserved for women and members of the backward community including minorities.

- Empowering ECI: The ECI shall be competent to inquire into allegations of non-compliance of any of the provisions requiring elections.

- Social audit and penal provisions: ECI should have the penal power to deregister a party until free and fair elections in the party are conducted.

- Encouraging new generation of leaders: For long, there is a widespread impression created that lot of good people shy away from politics. It is therefore necessary that this impression be changed and efficient people brought into political arena.

Way forward

- The 170th report of the Law Commission of India on reform of electoral laws, dedicated an entire chapter on the necessity of providing laws relating to internal democracy within parties.

- It observed that a political party which does not respect democratic principles in its internal working cannot be expected to respect those principles in the governance of the country.

- The National Commission for Review of Working of Constitution states that there should be comprehensive legislation regulating the registration and functioning of political parties or alliances of parties in India.

- The Administrative Reforms Commission II (ARC), 2008 Ethics and Governance Report pointed out that corruption is caused by over-centralization.

Conclusion

- Politics is inseparable from political parties as they are the prime instruments for the execution of democracy in the country.

- We must emphasize our PM's call for a debate on internal democracy in political parties.

- It is imperative that political parties open their eyes to growing calls for electoral political reforms and take steps towards bringing in intra-party democracy.

Above Article speaks the ground realities prevailing right now in the democratic set up of our country. Several committees went into the above aspects but there have been no concrete results pursuant to the recommendations of these committees. That shows what we have been doing in the name of democracy is the showmanship. There is no dearth of intelligentsia and scholars who are the masters in the democratic studies and functioning. Given the position stated in the above Article, do we think we are sincere to our democratic proclamation? Are we not fooling ourselves? The burning issues brought out in the Article have been burning since last fifty years and continue to burn, there being no sense of seriousness on the part of the governance and the concerned authorities. For example, the responsibility to direct the political parties to make up the deficiencies stated before is of the ECI. It obviously shows that the ECI has not been exercising its authority and powers vested in it on the burning issues for; if acted upon in the past fifty years, they would not have continued to show their ugly face today. The ECI occupies the prime place in ensuring sound principles of democracy and is the gateway to maintenance of the democratic system that includes the respect the political parties supposed to accord to their internal regulations.

The Annual Audit Reports of the political parties done by the ECI and posted on the Website cover the accounts part. The role of the ECI goes beyond that boundary, in that, it has to primarily examine and pinpoint the irregularities being done by the political parties with respect to their internal regulations. There is no other authority which is empowered to go into these aspects. Then, which authority is supposed to look into the working manner of the political parties. This is democratically a positive approach parties' vis-à-vis their internal regulations. Lack of this has led to birth of increasing burning issues which have far reaching effects on the democratic spirit enunciated in the constitution.

Though the importance of the ECI includes 'discipline among the political parties with a threat of derecognizing if the parties failed in maintaining inner-party democracy, this needs more effective enforcement considering the way the political parties are working and conducting their activities. This is a critical issue that needs to be accorded utmost importance and priority having regard that in reality, the political parties have been flouting their internal regulations and inner discipline. This is spreading disorderliness in the working of the political parties. Despite ECIs best efforts to curb this tendency, the observance of the internal regulations continues to be the least concern of the political parties. ECI has the authority and powers to act upon the parties defaulting in compliance of the above requirements. Time for ECI to think over on using its powers to derecognize the political party if, on the basis of the findings by an independent agency [like auditors in the case of auditing of the accounts], appointed by the ECI, the degree of irregularities found in the working of the political parties suggests serious deficiencies according to their internal regulations. It is also the time to consider constitutionalisation of the internal regulations of the political parties that would enable ECI to maintain control over the manner in which the regulations are being observed. These are the nerves of the democracy which, unless continued to be strengthened, will start weakening due to unaccountability. Absence of accountability is dominating in our democracy which is spreading different kinds of diseases in political, religious and social fields.

Accountability is how individuals or organizations are evaluated and judged for their performance or behavior related to something for which they are responsible. In democracies, the accountability function is institutionally exercised in the domain of a pluralist democracy, where interest groups can act as accountability holders. Accountability is an essential principle for the construction of publicity for government policies and actions – accountability demanding that democracies' institutional design requires representation and oversight. Interest groups act as intermediaries in the representation process and can influence different policies, and they must also be accountable to their representatives.

.

Unity in diversity is on sound footing in our country but divisions within the diversity based on bias and prejudices in the political, religious and social systems is a continuous cause for concern. There is criticism on every matter without any suggestion. Criticisms cover one or the other of the following:

- Logical criticism assumes that people follow the basic rules of logic and busy with "things just mean what they want them to mean." Logical criticism presumes the people agree about some basic facts and assumptions of the situation and have at least some beliefs in common among themselves. It would not be possible to argue about logical criticism with someone who does not have any common assumptions or who is not willing to even consider the possibiity that given assumption may be correct or incorrect.

- Positive criticism may be overlooked by people who see the only the negative side of something that is why it becomes of paramount importance to highlight the positive side. Positive criticism may also be considered a type of self-defense. Positive criticism is also used as constructive feedback. When an objection what an argument is raised about an idea situation watches something wrong in it with the proof which is relevant to it is called as Factual criticism.

- Factual criticism along with logical criticism is generally considered crucial to ensure consistency predictability and authenticity in the behavior of any manner. To make sense one has to have consistency and predictability of behavior without which there are disorientation and confusion and therefore it cannot guide to making effective choices.

- Constructive criticism aims to show the purpose of something which is but achieved by a different approach. Making criticism is not necessarily incorrect and its reason is also respected but it is claimed that is a similar goal can be achieved by a different method. These criticisms are often considered as tips for improvement that is how things could be better and be done in a more acceptable way.

- Negative criticism may have a bad effect on people who take it seriously. People who insulted react badly to it. Much of it depends on the quantity of negative criticism that is transferred to the other person because some people can handle negative criticism up to a certain extent beyond which it is taken as an insult. The downside of negative criticism is that it shows and tells people what to do, rather than telling them what they should do what they are able to do with sound disabling and not at all encouraging.

- Moral criticism is based on the idea that people should be treated similarly in similar situations and the same norms should be applied to all the people in a similar situation. The exception proves that there exists a certain module which is an exception for some reason and such moral is assumed because human behavior would be unprecedented without it.

- Speculative criticism pleases a crucial role because similar information can be read in a different way by different people. Information when open to interpretation is termed as speculative Criticism since it has different meanings.

The next aspect of diversity and division that has cropped up of late is the Uniform Civil Code [UCC]. The present environment on this subject is very much charged with divergent views propelling the people of different faiths to oppose the subject matter altogether. Let us consider why and how it emerged:

Article 44 of the Constitution reads: Uniform civil code for the citizens - The State shall endeavour to secure for the citizens a uniform civil code throughout the territory of India. This takes back to the making of the constitution by our forefathers. What necessitated for this Article could be more discernable from the Debates of the Constituent Assembly that consisted of the representatives as

Members, highly learned and scholars, of all the Faiths of the country. What went into the Debates on this matter?

In the Draft Constitution adopted by the Constituent Assembly, this Article 44 number was 35. Let us read the CAD [Constituent Assembly Debates] and later developments. It is relevant here to reproduce a paper.

'Debates in the Constituent Assembly and thereafter on Uniform Civil Code Lakshmi Parameswaran published by India Policy Foundation – March, 2020 posted on the Website {Excerpts]:

"The ideas of unity and equa have been at the core of what India represents. Yet the existence of personal laws has been creating divisions in the country from the colonial times. The calls for a Uniform Civil Code (UCC) have always been met with resistance since many are under the wrong notion that is a direct assault on their religion and religious practices. In the haste to ensure that religion remains insulated from the interference of the state, what is often forgotten is that it is the issue of gender justice and national integration that have been pushed to the back burner. It needs to be noted that the early proponents of UCC were women. Among the 15 women, who were part of the Drafting Committee of the Indian Constitution, Hansa Mehta's contribution in trying to make UCC justiciable remains most significant. As a member of Fundamental Rights Subcommittee, she along with Rajkumari Amrit Kaur, Dr B R Ambedkar and M R Masani stressed on the need for establishing a single Indian identity over multiple religious identities and the role that the state has to play in ensuring this. Dakshayani Velayudhan, the first and the only Dalit woman in the cabinet had also made a strong case for UCC. But their motion did not garner any support as the other members of the Drafting Committee felt that by enacting a common code at that point, India may be seen as reneging on its promise given to minorities and this in turn might worsen an already volatile situation. With time, the majority community understood the deeply biased nature of religious laws and subsequently, the government enacted the Hindu Code Bills in 1955-56. Though the original Hindu Code Bill that was wholly supported by Dr Ambedkar could not be passed due to opposition from various quarters, a diluted version which saw the Bill being divided into four parts was passed - : the Hindu Marriage Act, Hindu Succession Act, Hindu Minority and Guardianship Act, and Hindu Adoptions and Maintenance Act.

Welcoming the move, Hansa Mehta said, "This Bill to codify the Hindu Law is a revolutionary Bill and though we are not quite satisfied with it, it will be a great landmark in the social history of the Hindus. But since this Bill was drafted, many things have happened and one of the biggest things that has happened is the achievement of our political freedom. The new State is going to be a democratic State and democracy is based on the equa of individuals. It is from this point of view that we have now to approach the problems of inheritance and marriage etc. that are before us."

Though it was a far cry from the implementation of UCC, it was the first step where one community showed that it was necessary to reform archaic religious practices for ensuring equa and dignity to all. Despite that first step, the many myths surrounding UCC persists even to this day. **A look at the Constituent Assembly debates on the topic further reveals that even though India was celebrated for its syncretic culture, there were clear lines drawn in matters of religion from that time and politics of appeasement practiced in the subsequent years gave immunity to certain communities to continue their religious practices even if they were in clear contravention to human rights. The lack of enthusiasm in even starting a debate on UCC should have ideally raised questions on whether it is the idea of India that is getting eroded in the face of vote bank politics, but those voices never found a platform and the issue was time and again suppressed**.................................[Emphasis added]

"The apprehension felt by the members of the minority community is very real. Secular State does not mean that it is anti-religious State. It means that it is not irreligious but nonreligious and as such there is a world of difference between irreligious and non-religious. I therefore suggest that it would be a good policy for the members of the Drafting Committee to come forward with such safeguards in this proviso as will meet the apprehensions genuinely felt and which people are feeling and I have every hope that the ingenuity of Dr. Ambedkar will be able to find a solution for this," he added.......................

From the Constituent Assembly debates that were against the implementation of UCC, it is clear that the minorities felt that their personal laws cannot be legislated on and the state had no right to interfere in matters of faith. A number of arguments that were raised against UCC were taken up in the counter debate that ensued and many of the fears were dispelled by those who spoke in favour of UCC.

Among the members who felt that UCC was necessary to keep India united, the most vociferous arguments were put forth by K M Munshi. He chose to focus on the two primary arguments that were made against UCC, namely that it infringes on the fundamental rights given in Article 19 and it is tyrannous to the minority. He pointed out that the House has already accepted the principle that "if a religious practice followed so far covers a secular activity or falls within the field of social reform or social welfare, it would be open to Parliament to make laws about it without infringing this Fundamental Right of a minority." This in effect meant that Parliament has the right to enact a uniform code at a time it deems fit.

Regarding the argument that the enactment of a Civil Code would be tyrannical to minorities, he quoted the examples of Turkey and Syria to prove that "nowhere in advanced Muslim countries the personal law of each minority has been recognised as so sacrosanct as to prevent the enactment of a Civil Code."

He stressed that the point of a common code is to ensure that the way of life for the country becomes unified and secular. He questioned how religion can interfere in matters like inheritance and succession which essentially form the tenets of social relations. He said, enactment of a common code affects Hindus equally and the goal of such legislation is to protect the fundamental rights guaranteed by the Constitution like ensuring gender equa. He criticized the isolationist outlook and called for religion to be restricted to spheres that legitimately pertain to it and ensure that the other areas are regulated in the larger interests of national unity.

Munshi also opined that the personal law is part of religion is a mindset that has been perpetuated under the British rule. He gave the example of Allauddin Khilji who made several changes which went against the Shariat when he established the first Muslim Sultanate in India. When the Kazi of Delhi expressed his displeasure in what he saw as blatant violation of the Shariat, Khilji told him that he is ruling in the best interests of the country and for that if he has gone against the Shariat, the Almighty will forgive him…………………..

Dr B R Ambedkar in his response pointed out that there was already a uniform code of laws covering almost all aspects of human relationship which meant that it was possible to have a uniform civil code in the country. Differing on the argument that the Muslim personal law was uniform throughout the country, he reminded the Assembly of the North-West Frontier Province which followed the Hindu Law in the matter of succession and others till, in 1939, the Central Legislature passed a law to apply Shariat to the Muslim dominated area. Even in the United Provinces, the Central Provinces and Bombay, the Muslims to a large extent were governed by the Hindu Law in the matter of succession. He also brought attention to the fact that in North Malabar, the matriarchal form of law, Marumakkathayam Law was applied to both Hindus and Muslims.

Concluding the debate on 2 December 1948 on UCC, Ambedkar said, "All that the State is claiming in this matter is a power to legislate. There is no obligation upon the State to do away with personal laws. Therefore, no one need be apprehensive of the fact that if the State has the power, the State will immediately proceed to execute or enforce that power in a manner that may be found to be objectionable by the Muslims or by the Christians or by any other community in India … Sovereignty is always limited, no matter even if you assert that it is unlimited, because sovereignty in the exercise of that power must reconcile itself to the sentiments of different communities. No Government can exercise its powers in such manner as to provoke the Muslim community to rise in rebellion. I think it would be a mad government if it did so"………….

In the end, it was decided that the amendments proposed to Article 35 do not hold any merit and it was adopted as it is. This article was later moved to the Directive Principles of State Policy as the makers felt that the nation was not yet ready to accept a common civil code. Thus, the goal of a uniform civil code was enshrined in Article 44 of the Indian Constitution and read thus: [Emphasis added]

"The state shall endeavour to secure for the citizens a uniform civil code throughout the territory of India." [Emphasis added]

Debates in the present times:

In September 2019, the Indian Supreme Court lamented that even after 63 years since the codification of the Hindu Law in 1956, the governments in power have failed to take any steps towards implementation of a uniform civil code

The Muslim Women (Protection of Rights on Marriage) Act, 2019 which abolished the practice of Triple Talaq was seen as a progressive step that would realise the goal of UCC. In its judgement4 upholding the constitutiona of banning Triple Talaq, the Court had observed that arbitrary personal laws cannot seek refuge under the rights guaranteed by Freedom of Religion and Equa before Law is supreme. Now the matter is expected to be taken up by the 22nd Law Commission, the formation of which has been officially announced by the government on 25 February, 2020.

Yet the implementation of UCC does not seem to be a goal that can be realized in the near future. Opposition parties like the Congress and CPI (M) have interestingly called the efforts to implement UCC as an offensive attack launched by "communal forces" on the identity of minorities. Though a number of regional parties have come out in support of the statement, it is the stand taken by Congress and CPI (M) that are in direct negation of the values and principles that they have been espousing for so long.

In the case of Congress, it needs to be remembered that Jawaharlal Nehru had clearly stated that UCC will be implemented once the ground is prepared and all parties are taken into confidence. He was of the opinion that changes cannot be imposed from the top and it was the government's duty to educate public opinion and see to it that the changes are imposed only when a community accepts it. He was concerned that many Muslims in the country who decided to stay back at the time of Partition had started believing Jinnah's claims that the Congress rule symbolized "Hindu domination". That is from where the appeasement of minorities first started which continues to leave an indelible mark on Indian po. By not having the courage to implement UCC, Nehru and others lost an opportunity to create an India that could not be destabilized in the name of religion. Instead, they created divisions and created a country where religious sentiments are used to subvert justice.

In addition to Nehru, Dr Ambedkar had also extended his support of UCC during the course of debates in the Constituent Assembly. So now when the Congress says that UCC will divide the country, it needs to be asked if they are disowning their roots and are going against the secular ideals that they have been espousing for so long. Their own leader, Nehru was not against the implementation of UCC in principle and had made it clear that India need to make its environment conducive for such a progressive step to be taken.

The argument put forth by the CPI (M) evokes further curiosity. A party that claims to strongly stand for the ideals of a classless society and which believes that "religion is the opium of the masses" seems to have sudden concerns about each and every religion being able to preserve its own identity. They seem to have forgotten the basic tenets of Marxism that religion is a tool for oppression. Instead of supporting a reform that is in line with their proclaimed principles, the fact that they think, such a reform will be an assault on the country's pluralistic and cultural identity should be seen in the context of them following a partisan agenda.

In the current debates about UCC, there is a wrong notion that is getting perpetuated that it will be a step against Muslims of the country. There cannot be a more flawed argument than this. The implementation of UCC would affect all communities equally and it is not a targeted exercise against any one community. Even though reforms were made in the personal Hindu Laws, it is not without problems. An issue that have been discussed time and again is the registration of Hindu Marriages. Unlike in Islam where marriage is considered a civil contract, Hindu marriages are sacramental even though efforts have been to add the elements of contract into it. This means that the onus is on the persons getting married to prove that they have followed all religious ceremonies and their marriage has religious and legal validity. In a country where customs vary with every region, this particular provision has given rise to a lot of confusion on what are the customs that constitute a legally valid marriage. Also, it needs to be noted that it was not until 2005 that the Hindu Succession Act was amended to give daughters the right to demand partition of parental homes.

When it comes to Christianity, the Indian Christian Marriage Act, 1872 stipulates that a woman has to wait for two years before she can file for divorce. The fact that a Christian marriage is sacramental further adds to the woes of the women. These are clear indications that what a common code does is to address the issues that perpetuate inequalities in society and realise the goal of an egalitarian and just nation.

As Rajkumari Amrit Kaur had pointed out during the deliberation of the 12-member sub-committee constituted to look into the issue of UCC, 'free practice' could legitimise 'anti-social practices' such as Sati, purdah and devdasi customs and nullify laws such as the one favouring widow-remarriage. It is important to deliberate on this topic to understand its implications. A system where multiple people are involved and where they are allowed to come out with their own rules would mean that a platform is being provided to reinforce deep seated biases. In such a scenario, it is often the women who are robbed of their agencies. And what this essentially paves way for is a complete descent into anarchy.

What it also needs to be understood is that UCC is meant to legislate social relations as pointed out by K M Munshi. Matters of marriage, divorce, succession and adoption should ideally have nothing to do with religion as it forms the very foundation of human society. Religion concerns the spiritual space and is something that should remain deeply personal. It is one's relationship with a higher power that cannot be defined and dictated by rules and regulations.

The argument that has often been put forth against the implementation of UCC is that it is a provision under the Directive Principles6 and no law can supersede the fundamental rights guaranteed in the Constitution. The reference here is to Articles 25 to 28 that give everyone the right to practice his/her own religion as propagated by their own religious laws. But the same Constitution has vested Parliament with the right to make laws throughout the territory of India under Article 245. This means political will is the only factor necessary to make UCC a rea.

The question that needs to be asked is which the fundamental rights that require greater protection are Article 14, 15 and 21 ensure equa and dignity for all and protect citizens against all forms of discrimination. Despite constitutional remedies available, a progressive nation like India has been perpetuating gender injustice in the name of religion. Parallel judicial systems have been allowed to continue which goes against the values of democracy and nation-building.

The abolition of triple Talaq was an opportunity for the government and society to initiate the debate on UCC. Yet, a progressive step has over the years been reduced to being hailed as a reform in the personal law. It was also forgotten that to sustain the moment it was necessary to continuously engage with the general public to elicit their opinion as well as to make them understand that UCC will not interfere with religion in any way………………………….

From this it is clear that even Shariat which the Muslims now say cannot be amended is a product of the times it was conceived in. It is imperative for every community to usher in changes according to the way society and the definitions of traditions and culture evolve. Here before voicing opinion against UCC, it may bode well to go back to colonial times to see why despite the Lex Loci Report of 1840 which emphasized the need for uniformity in the codification of Indian law, it was still recommended to keep the Hindu and Muslim personal laws outside of any such codification. This was done with a clear intent of creating a permanent wedge between Indians. As pointed out by Dr Ambedkar, there were several regions in India that were not under any strict personal laws. A Muslim majority region like the North West Frontier Province was following the Hindu Personal laws. Such unity and integration in the long run would have arrested the expansionist ambitions of the British at a very early stage. So today if a particular community believes that UCC is targeted against them, it is important they see it in the right historical context before coming to conclusions of their own.

There have been some powerful voices raised within the Muslim community in support of UCC. Dr. Tahir Mahmood in his book Muslim Personal Laws 1977 had strongly advocated for the framing of a common civil code. He had cited that many Muslim countries have outlawed polygamy – a practice that snatches away the self-respect of women. After the passing of Hindu Code Bills, a noted Islamic scholar Asaf Ashar Ali Fyzee had urged the government to constitute a special committee for examining the personal laws of the Muslim community. More recently, the Governor of Kerala and noted scholar Arif Mohammed Khan had quoted the Pakistani Muslim scholar Syed Abul A'la Maududi to state that the Mohameddan law is very different from the Islamic Shariat and the unjust laws have immensely destroyed the domestic lives of Muslims. The calls for changes are definitely emanating from the community, but they are still too feeble to reach the larger public.

The way forward:

Various courts have been approached regarding UCC. The Delhi High Court has asked the Union government to file its response. The conditions have never been more conducive to initiate a nation-wide debate on UCC. The opportunity has presented itself with enough time for the Centre to start awareness camps on what exactly UCC entails. The root cause for opposing UCC lies in illiteracy that is prevalent. In the case of minorities, this is even more pronounced because if a section of them is educated, their formative years were spent in religious schools and their thoughts have already been moulded in a particular way. It is this vicious chain that the government and civil society need to break in order to usher in reforms that open up minds to new possibilities and help in erasing the artificial barriers.

There are between 200 to 300 personal laws that are operative in India at present. The numbers are staggering and point towards a fragmented society where there is chaos and injustice. In a country where women hailing from a particular religion have no qualms in blocking a major road in the national capital in the name of protecting India's constitutional values, it is rather astounding that none of them ever thought of working towards life and dignity for all. How can women who claim to be so self-aware accept being treated as second class citizens in a society that they hold so dear? Why have voices never been raised against polygamy and the fact that according to Islamic laws, the property is divided in the ratio, 2:1 with two shares to the boy and one to the girl?

The argument that UCC will not work in a country as diverse as India has been flawed from the beginning. One state in India, Goa, has been having a common family law based on the erstwhile Portuguese civil law and even after its annexation in 1961, the state continued to implement the common code. Goa has 65 per cent Hindu population and 25 per cent Christian population, there have been no issues raised till date on its implementation.

India has definitely taken a step in the right direction with the implementation of the Special Marriage Act, 1954 which permits any citizen to have a civil marriage outside the realm of personal laws. It has addressed many of the inherent wrongs of the religious laws. But such a law will be effective only if people voluntarily chose to shun the personal laws in the interests of a just society and consolidated nation.

Amrit Kaur along with M R Masani and Hansa Mehta as members of the Fundamental Rights Sub Committee had in a letter to Sardar Patel said, "One of the factors that have kept India back from advancing to nationhood has been the existence of personal laws based on religion which keep the nation divided into watertight compartments in many aspects of life." They were of the view that UCC should be guaranteed to the Indian people within a period of five or ten years. Yet even after 70 years since the Indian Constitution came into force, UCC remains a distant dream. The time has come for the nation to come together and advocate for a cause that will do away with all barriers and ensure that each and every person gets the dignity and respect that he/she truly deserves."

As noted before, I have reproduced the excerpts from the paper and not its whole text which I considered difficult to accommodate in this book. However, on-going through the full text, I find commona of mind among the Hon'ble Members of Constituent Assembly including the Members belonging to the minority as picked up and reproduced below:

"I submit that the interference with these matters should be gradual and must progress with the advance of time. I have no doubt that a stage would come when the civil law would be uniform. But then that time has not yet come. We believe that the power that has been given to the State to make the Civil Code uniform is in advance of the time......" [Naziruddin Ahmad.]

"Sir, I feel that it is all right and a very desirable thing to have a uniform law, but at a very distant date." [Hussain Imam]

"He expressed the hope that in future, there will be a uniform civil code legislated that will run into every aspect of civil law." [Alladi Krishnaswami Ayyar]

In the end, it was decided that the amendments proposed to Article 35 do not hold any merit and it was adopted as it is. This article was later moved to the Directive Principles of State Policy as the makers felt that the nation was not yet ready to accept a common civil code. Thus, the goal of a uniform civil code was enshrined in Article 44 of the Indian Constitution and read thus:

"The state shall endeavour to secure for the citizens a uniform civil code throughout the territory of India." [Dr. B.R.Ambedkar] [Emphasis added]

"Amrit Kaur along with M R Masani and Hansa Mehta as members of the Fundamental Rights Sub Committee had in a letter to Sardar Patel said, "One of the factors that have kept India back from advancing to nationhood has been the existence of personal laws based on religion which keep the nation divided into watertight compartments in many aspects of life." They were of the view that UCC should be guaranteed to the Indian people within a period of five or ten years." [Emphasis added]

One could infer from the above submissions that the time when it was considered though the need for it was strongly felt, was considered to be not matured and its need was left to the future or at a very distant date.

Question is how to measure the future or a very distant date. Education of the population that existed in 1950 and existing in 2023; if the education has advanced to a respectable level during that period, it has to be presumed that the economic development has also advanced parallel with upward or downward variance. I have given below latest available information on the Website on the religion-wise status of Education and Employment of Muslims in India that contains a comparative analysis with other religions

Following is a comparative the religion-wise status of Education and Employment of Muslims in India and other religions Ied by Mashkoor Ahmad1 and Khalid Khan2 1Assistant Professor, Department of Geography, Aligarh Muslim University, Aligarh 2Assistant Professor, Indian Institute of Dalit Studies, New Delhi published in International Journal of Social Science and Economic Research ISSN: 2455-8834 Volume: 06, Issue: 07 "July 2021"

"Literacy Rate [2011-12]

Religion-wise literacy rate for the population 7 years and above has been demonstrated in Fig. 1.[I's Note: Figure 1 not reproducible]. It is seen that as per the NSS 68th round 2011-12, the average literacy rate (i.e. Was not able to read or write with understanding)in India was 75.0 percent. However, significant inequalities exist in the literacy rates across religious communities in country as the literacy rate varied from the highest of 87.4 percent for Christians to the lowest of 71.6 percent for Muslims. While the literacy rate of Hindus-the majority community was equal to the national average of 75.0 percent. The literacy rate of all the religious minorities except Muslims was above the national average. The low literacy rate among Muslims is a matter of serious concern, it is therefore suggested that efforts should be made to increase the level of literacy among Muslims in particular and among all the population in general so as to improve the literacy rate and minimize the inequalities in the literacy rate among various religious communities in the country.

Levels of Education [2011-12]

The education level of 17.2 percent of the population was below primary level. Primary and middle education level each accounted around 16 percent of the population in the country. Slightly more than one-tenth of the population was having secondary level education. Very sharp disparities have been observed in the education level across the religions in India. The percentage of population with the lowest education level was the highest among Muslims. As high as 21.0 percent of Muslim population was literate below primary level in comparison to 16.8 percent for Hindus, 15.0 percent for other religions, 14.3 percent for Christians. The percentage of population with primary education was found very high among Buddhists (18.9 percent) and Muslims (18.1 percent), Hindus (15.3 percent) and the lowest among other religions (13.3 percent). The secondary and higher secondary education was the lowest among Muslims. Thus, a very high proportion of population of Muslims remained educated below higher secondary. With only 0.6 percent the proportion of diploma holders was also the lowest among Muslims while it was as high as 3.4 percent for Christians and 1.0 percent for Hindus. Again the percentage of education level with graduate and above was the lowest among Muslims (3.2 percent), as compared 7.2 percent for Hindus, 11.1 percent for Christians and 17.9 percent for other religions. Thus, level of education was the worst among Muslim as majority of them having the lowest level of education.

Gross Attendance Ratio in School Education [2011-12]

Though during the last few years many scholarship schemes have been started for the students belonging to religious minorities and other disadvantaged groups in India, yet some of them still are lagging as far as their access to education is concerned. The poor economic background is one reason for this state of affairs. The direct and indirect discrimination of minorities generally their equal access to education which is reflected by inadequate funding, resources, schools etc. in minority dominated areas of the country (UNDP, 2010).

Gross attendance ratio has been measured as percentage of students attending an educational level irrespective of age to corresponding age group population. The value of gross attendance ratio for different education level reveals that huge inequalities exist across religions in India. Among all the religion, Muslims suffer the most as far as their access to education at various levels is concerned. The gross attendance ratio at all level is low for Muslims as compared to all other religious communities. Table 3 reveals that disparities in gross attendance ratio at different levels of education are pervasive across religions. [I's Note: [Table not reproducible]. Up to primary level the gross attendance ratio was the highest among Sikhs (113.1 percent) followed by Hindus (105) while Muslims (98.1 percent) had the lowest attendance ratio at this level. At middle level the gross attendance ratio was the highest among other religions (103.4 percent) followed by Christians (102.7 percent), and Buddhists (101.0 percent) and Sikhs (95.7 percent), while the lowest was found among Muslims (88.3 percent). Huge disparities were found in gross attendance ratio at secondary and higher secondary level. At secondary level the gross attendance ratio was highest among Buddhists (131.5 percent), Sikhs (103.7 percent) while Muslims with only 80.0 percent had the lowest gross attendance ratio among the religious communities. Similarly, at higher secondary level also the lowest gross attendance ratio was recorded among Muslims (51.8 percent) compared to 83.4 percent among Christians, and 73.3 percent among Hindus. Thus, the conditions of Muslims were the most disappointing across the religious communities in the country. Therefore, seeing the present conditions of Muslims in gross attendance ration it is advisable that special effort should be made to have their access to the education at various levels so as to bring them to the main stream population in India.

During the last few years, the scholarship schemes for religious minorities and other disadvantaged groups have enabled many students from these communities to continue their education. However, greater effort is needed to improve enrolment ratios and to reduce dropout rates among minorities (Planning commission of India, 2011) especially among Muslim community which suffers from highest illiteracy in the country.

Gross Attendance Ratio in Higher Education

In the present study the gross attendance ratio has been used to show the participation in higher education and has been calculated as the percentage of students in higher education to the population in the age group of 18-22 years. It is seen that in 2007-08, the gross attendance ratio in higher education was 17.2 percent with significant disparities between urban (30.2 percent) and rural (11.1 percent) areas. Similarly, disparities in gross attendance ratio by religions were also very pronounced and thus are a matter of concern for Muslims who have very low gross attendance ratio in higher education. With only 9.5 percent gross attendance ratio, Muslims were very much below the national average of 17.2 percent while gross attendance ratio of Christians was 29.0 percent followed by others (27.6 percent), Buddhists (20.2 percent), Hindus (18.3 percent) and Sikhs 9.5 percent. Likewise, glaring disparities were found by gender across the religious groups in both the rural and urban areas of the country.

In rural areas the highest gross attendance ratio was found among Christians (20.8 percent) while the lowest among Muslims. In urban areas the highest gross attendance ratio was reported among others religions (52.7 percent) while it was the lowest among Muslims (13.5 percent). In rural areas, gross attendance ratio for females (8.3 percent) was lower compared to males (13.7 percent) on the other hand in urban areas gross attendance ratio for female (30.6 percent) is slightly higher as compared to males (29.8 percent). The high cost associated with higher education was an important deterrent to participation in higher education among Muslims characterised by high incidence of poverty. The low participation of Muslims in higher education may adversely affect their employability in terms of qua of jobs. In fact, high incidence of poverty and low participation in higher education feed on each other (India Human Development Report 2011).

Share of Population in Higher Education

As per the NSS 64th round (2007-08), in India, 4.4 percent of the total population was graduate and above. However, significant disparities were noticed in share of graduate and above by age group and religion. The share of graduate and above population to the total population varied from 10.3 percent for others religion followed by 6.8 percent for Christians, 5.2 percent for Sikhs, 4.7 percent for Hindus and 3.5 percent for Buddhists while for Muslims it was only 2 percent. Thus the share of graduate and above population to total population was the lowest among Muslims and it was less than half of the national average. Similarly, the share of graduate and above was the lowest among the Muslims in all 20 years and above age groups except for 40-49 years of age group in which the share of Buddhists was the lowest. Thus, share of graduate and above population among all the religious communities except Muslims and Buddhists was above the national average. Therefore, emphasis should be given to increase the participation of Muslims and Buddhists in higher education so as to bring them to the mainstream population in the country.

Students in Higher Education by Type of Institutions

It is seen from Table6 [I's Note: Table not reproducible] that around 46 percent of the total students in higher education were enrolled in government institutions. The percentage of students among

Sikhs (56.7 percent), Buddhists (53.7 percent), Muslims (47.6 percent) and Hindus (46.7 percent) was above the national average which indicates that due to lack of money or awareness about qua of education these communities enrol their children in government institutions most of which do not impart good qua education. On the other hand the proportion of students in government institution was below the national average among Christians and other religions. It should be noted here that among Hindus a relatively higher share of students in government institution may be attributed to the higher share of scheduled caste and scheduled tribe students who represent the poorest section of Hindu community. In private added institutions the percentage of Muslim students was the lowest while it was the highest among other religions followed by Buddhists.

Out of School Children

It is very disappointing that in India around 19 percent of the children of age 6-17 years have either never attended school or have attended school in the past but are currently not attending and thus have been identified as out of school (India Human Development Report 2011). Surprisingly, very large variations have been reported in the proportion of out of school children across religions. In this regards Muslim children are the most vulnerable due to higher poverty, low education etc. Among Muslims around 29 percent of the children were out of school. Moreover the proportion of the out of school female children was as high as 31.5 percent. Among Sikhs and Hindus each 17.7 percent of children were found out of school. However, with only 9.7 percent of out of school children the situation was comparatively better among Christians. Among the out of school children, the proportion of female children remained higher compared to male children across all the religious communities in the country.

Major Reasons for Discontinuation/ Drop out

Though, there may be very many reasons for discontinuation or drop out of children from the schools but lack of interest among parents; and children as well as financial problems have emerged as the main reasons in the country. These three reasons accounted around half of the discontinuation or drop out cases in the country. The reasons for discontinuation or drop out varied across religious groups. Among Muslims 18 percent of the discontinuation or drop out was due to lack of interest of parents followed by Hindu (16 percent), Christians (10 percent) and Sikhs (9 percent). Financial constraints accounted highest proportion of discontinuation or drop out of children among all the religious communities especially Muslims (27 percent). Among Sikhs, financial constraints were responsible for 22 percent of the discontinuation or drop out, followed by Christians (20 percent) and Sikhs (20 percent). Lack of interest among the children emerged also one of the main reasons for discontinuation or drop out from the school. This reason accounted 20 percent of the discontinuation or drop out among Sikhs followed by Hindus (14 percent) and Christians (14 percent). Surprisingly, the lack of interest among children accounted for the lowest proportion of discontinuation or drop out among Muslim children (12 percent).

Work Participation Rate

The working population in the labour force has been used to calculate the work participation rate. The NSSO 68th round (2011-12) revealed that in India the work participation rate was 38.4 percent. The rural work participation rate (39.8 percent) was higher as compared to urban work participation rate (35.3 percent). So far as the religion is concerned the highest work participation rate was found among Buddhists (45.0 percent) and the lowest among Muslims community (32.8 percent). A low work participation rate among Muslims community is mainly a result of very low economic participation of Muslim women, especially in urban areas of the country (Papola, 2012; Planning Commission, 2012).However, it is to be seen that contrasting variations were observed in the work participation by gender among different religious communities in the country. With 58.0 percent, the male work participation rate was the highest among other religious communities followed by Sikhs (56.3 percent) while the lowest male work participation rate was found among Muslims (51.1 percent). In case of female, the highest work participation rate was observed among Buddhists (34.2 percent) while the lowest among Muslims (13.4 percent). Thus, in the country the lowest work participation rate for both males and females was found among Muslims. Lower level of work participation rate among Muslims community shows that they have low access to different opportunities including public employment and business, good qua of education etc. compared to all other religious groups in the country (Shariff, 2013).

In rural areas the work participation rate varied from 50.2 percent for Buddhists to 32.8 percent for Muslims. Rural male work participation rate was the highest among other religions (57.9 percent) and the lowest among Muslims (49.8 percent). Similarly, in urban areas too, the male work participation rate was the highest among other religions (58 percent) followed by Hindus (54.9 percent) and Sikhs (54.7 percent). In urban areas, male work participation was 53.1 percent among Muslims while with 50.2 percent Buddhists represented the lowest work participation rate.

Regular Salaried Workers by Type of Enterprise

The distribution of salaried works gives a very contrasting picture by religion and by type of enterprises. It is revealed from Table 9 [I's Note: Table not reproducible] that in India 70 percent of the salaried workers were engaged in private enterprises which are unorganised with limited or no social and economic security to the employees while only 30 percent were engaged in public enterprises which are considered as better paid and gives other social and economic benefits as well as securities to the employees. The data show that among Muslims as low as 17.2 percent salaried workers were engaged in government enterprises compared to 33.9 percent for Christians who enjoy very high literacy rate and higher educational status thereby leading to greater opportunities to enter the government enterprises.

Among Buddhists a higher ratio of salaried workers (33.6) may be attributed to the reservation policies for scheduled castes (Dalits). Hindus were also having comparatively higher ratio of salaried workers in engaged in government enterprises. Muslims are largely engaged in the unorganized sector which shows their precarious situation. The Sachar Committee report (2006) report has revealed, that despite economic boom Muslims have to bear the brunt of the so called competitive forces unleashed by liberalization. Displacement of Muslims from traditional occupations has deprived them of their means of livelihood. Majority of the Muslims, are engaged in the unorganized sector of the economy which hardly enjoys protection of any kind and thus the adverse impact of liberalization has been more acute for them. Moreover many traditional occupations of Muslims in industries like silk and sericulture, hand and power looms, the leather industry, automobile repairing, garment making have been adversely affected during the last three decades."

There is no information available on the Website on the Educational and Employment comparative status of Muslims vis-à-vis other religions that existed on the eve of the India becoming Republic in order to assess the percentage advancement to know the capabilities and competency of the religions as to necessity for need to measure the future or the distant date that could be considered as having arrived for consideration of the introduction of the Uniform Civil Code [UCC} mandated under the Constitution of the country. However, based on the status as given in the Article stated before covering various fields of the status as of recent date among the Muslims and other religions, the status is comparatively appreciable that authenticates upgraded educational and employment status among the religions. In my personal view, it is the time to think about the need for the UCC having travelled a time distance of about seventy three years since the country became Republic. In the absence of any specific time mandate either during the Debates of CA or in the Constitution adopted in 1950 except to the extent of stating at a future or distant date, the future or distant date for the purpose has become indefinable and, therefore, needs to be defined due regard being given to the educational and employment status among the religions as brought out in the various fields in the Article stated before.

The Uniform Civil Code (UCC) is a set of laws that would apply to all citizens irrespective of their religion in matters including marriage, divorce, inheritance, and adoption. The British first mooted the idea of a Uniform Civil Code in the 19th century. However, it was not until the 1950s that the Indian government seriously considered the proposal. In 1954, the Law Commission of India was asked to examine the issue and make recommendations. The Law Commission's report, published in 1955, recommended that a uniform civil code be enacted for all citizens of India. Uniform Civil Code is defined in the Constitution of India under Article 44 of the Directive Principles of the State Policy. According to Article 44 of the Constitution, "the government must make every effort to provide UCCs for its residents across the entire country of India". The UCC aims to protect the vulnerable section of society, including women and religious minorities, while promoting nationalistic fervour through unity. If the code is enacted, it will simplify the laws currently segregated based on religious beliefs. The latest on the UCC is that the Uttarakhand state government has proposed a draft of a Uniform Civil Code. The draft has been met with mixed reactions. Some people have welcomed it, while others have opposed it.

Coming to the law, on June 14, 2023, the Law Commission of India issued a public notice soliciting opinions and comments on the Uniform Civil Code (UCC). This came after a five-year gap since the 21st Law Commission released a consultation paper on the same issue in August 2018. In the Shah Bano case in 1985, regarding the rights of a Muslim woman in divorce, the Hon'ble Supreme Court observed that "Parliament should outline the contours of a common civil code as it is an instrument that facilitates national harmony and equa before law."

The Law Commission of India has received an overwhelming response from citizens across the country to the proposed Uniform Civil Code (UCC) and said it would hold panel discussions and debates amongst all stakeholders. According to sources, over 75 lakh responses have been received by the law panel on UCC. The panel had sought views from various stakeholders, including public and religious organisations, on the contentious issue. If need be, the commission might call upon any individual or organisation for a personal hearing or discussion, the present law panel had said in a June 14 public notice. The consultation paper of the 21st Law Commission headed by Justice B S Chauhan (retd) had said that while the diversity of Indian culture can and should be celebrated, specific groups or weaker sections of the society must not be "dis-privileged" in the process.

The matter is now within the jurisdictional consideration of the Law Commission of India. I have refrained myself to deal with merits and demerits on the issue based on the reactions of the various organizations and religious bodies as appeared in the print and electronic media. What is cogent is whether or not there is need to go into the merits and demerits of the issue at all. The merits and demerits could be on the model code floated by the Law Commission of India but it cannot be on the need or otherwise, the subject matter being mandated under the Constitution which, in turn, is based on the scholarly debates of the Hon'ble Members of the Constituent Assembly that represented the learned Members embracing all the religions of the country, the consent to incorporate the provision on UCC having been based on the consensus of the Assembly. Those who were Members of the Constituent Assembly were our ancestors. Should we disown their consent and, if that be so, do we disown the deeds done and consents given by the ancestors in a family considered from the family obligation and social responsibilities. It is like questioning a grown up tree how it grew up so much large ignoring the fact that its basic formation is its seed. The seeds once merge with the earth take the shape of roots. The leaves of the trees are green. Green colour, according to Online Dictionary, 'This in-depth analysis explains the meaning and symbolism of the color green. Most prominently found in nature, the color green embodies rich foliage, lush greenery, and vast landscapes. This earthy hue is commonly associated with Mother Earth, which is why it's thought to be calming and ubiquitous.'

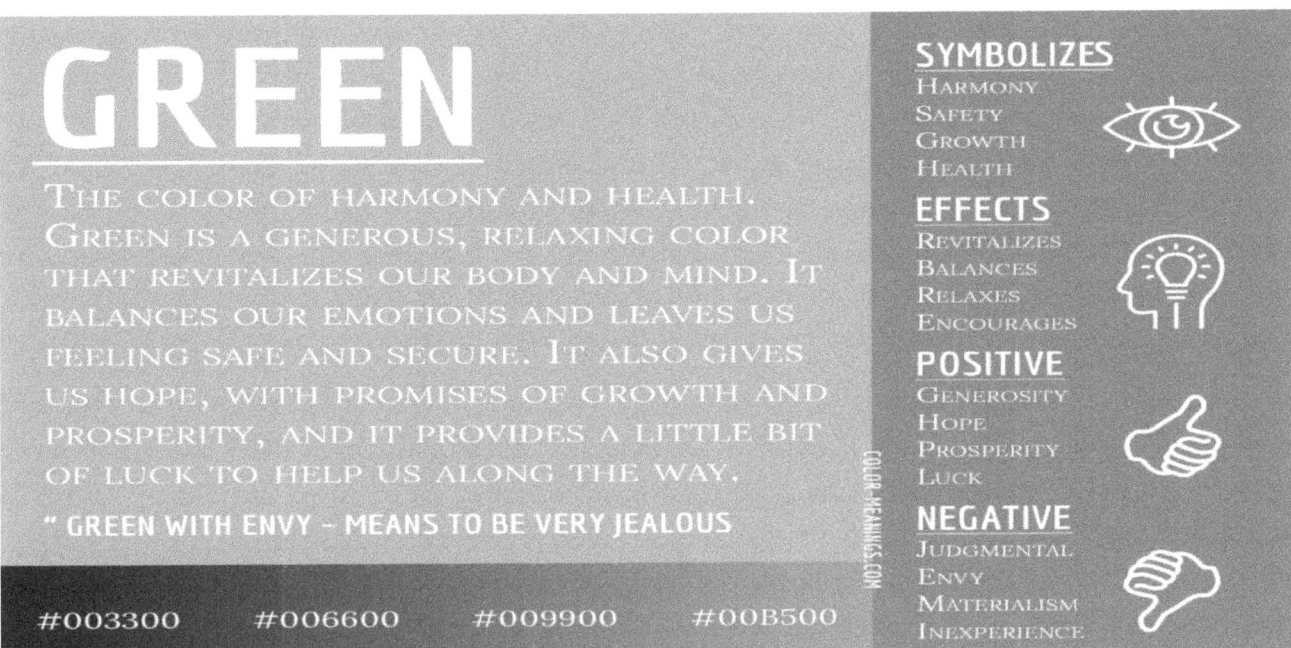

The roots are the strength of the tree which holds on to the natural and the manmade disasters. So also are the scholarly debates of the Hon'ble Members of the Constituent Assembly when they are held together. These debates and consensus incorporated and enshrined in the Constitution of the country are its roots. The Articles in the Constitution represent the characterstics of Green colour stated before, namely, harmony, sanity, growth, health, revitalization, balancing, relaxes, encourages, generosity, hope, prosperity and luck. These are positive aspects of the colour; its negative aspects are judgmental, envy, materialism and inexperience. Let us look at our Constitution in this way. Articles which form its jewels stand at par with the aspects of the Green color. The humans use the trees for various purposes, some for positivity and some others for negativity. So also we consider the Constitution in that fashion. Overall, the benefits the trees bestow upon the humans and other living beings on Mother Earth overweigh the other considerations. If we look at the tree, we exhilarate and exuberate; that should be our chorus when we think through our Constitution like we awoke to a *chorus* of birdsong.

That being so, it is self-questioning if we say what is provided in the Constitution is unconstitutional rather than understanding it as a constitutional mandate on each and every citizen. So, let us confine to model of the Code rather than its moda. It is our duty to honour it as suited best to all the religions together; our earnest efforts should be bring best through our suggestions and negotiations on the model code of the Law Commission of India. Let also stop contesting it from the constitutional point of view which is self-insulting.

Making objections to any matter for the sake of objection is like walking in the air which is not possible in ordinary course but the advancing technology has made it possible. Such technology has not come on earth from elsewhere but is the result of in-depth study, research and experiments. That is the process of technological advancement. But, we don't go through such process while making objections. Any objection without any alternative suggestion is like a balloon bursting in the sky. Objections are the enlightenment not for opposing them but for finding an alternative solution to the problem in hand. Mere objections drive one to avoidable aversions and criticisms which further encourage more acrimony among us. If one has objections, it must be based on sound footing with equally sound solution which is the way for advancement in life of democracy. As noted before, the objections on the UCC could be on the model UCC circulated by the Law Commission which should be accompanied with the rational and reasonable solutions/suggestions.

UCC was never objected during the debates in the Constituent Assembly but differences were with respect to the time, that is, was it feasible to fix a date for its introduction at that time and, if not, it could be left to the future or a distant date. There was unanimity on the merits of the UCC without which there wouldn't have been any provision made in the Constitution. Once it formed integral part of the Constitution, there cannot any debate on its origin and, debate if any, would have to be on the model and the process of implementing it. That is how the UCC has to be looked into and weighed by all the countrymen; there could be no negativity on the origin of source on the need for UCC and the positivity should be the guiding factor on how to evolve the UCC and implement it for the benefit all the religions. That is all what is left for us now. Let us not learn travelling backward in life but let us learn moving forward because the future holds brightness once we believe it would do good for us.

Any division in the diversities is like a tug of war with an understanding that the question of winning or losing it should not be the criteria in democracy though it is the sole criteria in the games. What is needed to be safeguarded in such tug of war on the ground of democracy is that the mid-point of the rope should not break as it would make both participating teams fall flat on the ground causing injuries as well. We need to accord more attention towards the safety of the rope rather than tug of war. So also should be our endeavour on a matter of national interest that should keep accord on upper hand than discord. There have been such divisions in the diversities in the past; some have been solved while some are causing concerns. The concerns root in a negative mind while conquer roots in a positive mind. The negative mind refuses to accept any argument while the positive mind is inclined to accept a reasonable argument and proceed further to the table of negotiations and settlement. The negativity births wilderness and violence in the mind that drives one to the wall rather towards the fresh air. Such infiltration in the mind is dangerous to the individuals, institutions and the nation because its consequences are immeasurable in actions and deeds that start staring at us like a ghost peeping into the home.

There is always a silver lining in every dark cloud which is visible only to those who wish to look at the cloud and not to others who remain looking at the earth.[Website 'Content Iity' defines it as 'This idiom is a metaphorical expression, implying that every single situation has some good or positive aspects. Despite the worst circumstances, there is always some hope or some redeeming qua.] Let us appreciate and admire it for; it gives succour to one and all the moment we are inclined to see the silver lining in our problems, the dark clouds in the democratic system. There is nothing which is insolvable if we think every problem left behind us by the historical events are also intended to be solved through mutua and mutual respect, the only way out God has given to the humans. Arrogance and adamant attitudes create suspicious configurations that when aggravated accelerate the occurrence of negative causes and results in harmfulness in our living together, the breath of our life.

'Will consider proposal for out-of-court settlement' - Hindustan Times (Chandigarh) - 17 Aug 2023 - HT Correspondent

VARANASI: The Anjuman Intezamia Masjid Committee (AIMC), which looks after the Gyanvapi mosque in Varanasi, on Wednesday, said it will hold internal talks on a proposal for a peaceful out-of-court settlement of a legal dispute concerning the religious place.

The AIMC'S remarks came two days after the Vishwa Vedic Sanatan Sangh (VVSS), which represents one of the five Hindu women seeking the right of regular worship at the Gyanvapi complex, wrote an open letter inviting the AIMC to hold discussions for an out-of court settlement. "We have received the letter sent by VVSS chief Jitendra Singh Visen via Whatsapp. We have replied to Visen and (VVSS national president) Santosh Singh. The matter will be placed before the mosque committee for consideration," AIMC joint secretary SM Yasin said.

Visen confirmed getting a response from the Muslim side. "Yes, the (mosque) committee has replied to the letter," he said.

In his letter addressed to the president, manager and joint secretary of AIMC on August 14, Visen said: "It is known to all that the Hindu side and the Muslim side are contesting a legal battle in the court regarding the Gyanvapi campus to prove their respective stand. <u>Some anti-social elements want to take advantage of this legal fight between the both the parties (Hindu side and Muslim side) for their personal gains, which can prove to be harmful for both the country and the society.</u>" [Emphasis added]

He added: "In such a situation, <u>it becomes the duty of all of us to set an example by settling this legal matter peacefully through mutual negotiations, taking care of the safety and security of our country and society. Therefore, I request all of you to accept this invitation with an open and pious mind and come forward for talks to settle the above issue (the Gyanvapi matter). It is possible that a peaceful solution can be found outside the court of the above matter by mutual discussion.</u>" [Emphasis added]

This is known as sighting the 'silver lining in the dark cloud', a reciprocity that is hidden in every national knotty problem or issue but what is needed is looking at it with honest and sincere heart according highest consideration to positivity in the best interests of the people, societies and the country that is what comes out from the letters stated before. The very fact that an inclination is born towards these shows the widening wisdom of the people of the country irrespective of whether or not we would succeed. <u>Failure is the key ingredient for the recipe of success! Embrace your failure, whether it is one failure or many failures, because with the right attitude and a willingness to learn from your mistakes, you are guaranteed a lifetime of success. [Kathryn Sandford].</u> [Emphasis added]

"NEVER LET SUCCESS GET TO YOUR HEAD; NEVER LET FAILURE GET TO YOUR HEART." -ANONYMOUS

Below given is an Image of Silver Lining in Dark Cloud:

[Courtesy: Google]

The divisions within the diversities existed in the past and would continue to be in future. These arose on account of historical, political and religion complexities and, as the time travelled, such divisions received the attention of the kingdoms that ruled our country for about 800 years; some kingdoms made best solutions while some others made worst solutions. History is the witness to such happenings that included, as noted before, political and religious. Those divisions got streamlined as the time passed by and the communities accepted them as a way of life. It is not that such divisions are confronting us today. They were there as stated before. The beauty of the entire process was the positive outlook of the people of the time and the need for adjustment rather than confrontation. The situation under which we stand today is the result of excessiveness in certain cases in the past. Those who were there in the past also faced similar situations as we are facing today. The process of refinement within the religions was born because of the need for the living life on Mother Earth and such refinements were learnt as the process of co-existence, the call of the Almighty in all the religions. Coexist to exist was the voice within everyone. That is there today and would continue to be there in future. Adjustments through mutual respect and sharing sorrows and pleasures among the humans are the tenets of life. These tenets also exist among Other Living Beings on Mother Earth.

"Final Remarks:

27. Discussing secularism in India is usually done by analysing the Constitutional provisions and the acts of judges in their implementation. As the first part of this paper recalls, extended scholarship has underlined the growth and the importance of legal categories such as "secular," "essential practices," "superstition," in shaping Hinduism today. The reformist agenda promoted by some judges in accordance with an interpretation of the Constitution that gives precedence to fundamental rights over the protection of religious freedom has further widened the scope of the law's intervention. However, important changes in religion are also brought forth through action of a less political nature on the part of the courts. Such processes result from systemic properties of Common law and are quite independent from any secularist agenda. One of them, already identified by scholars, is the general effect produced by the fact that the Constitution is centered on individuals on the basis of equa, a legal framework at odds with widely shared Hindu conceptions and practices. The second part of this paper has tried to explore two other characteristics of the legal system that may similarly have a quasi-mechanical impact on religion (not only Hinduism but others as well): the fact that ordinary words are given a legal, technical definition that is sometimes quite different from their usual understanding in the religious realm (for instance "religious service," "religious office," "religious honor"); and the fact that the protection of a civil right such as the "right to worship" imposes on the court the duty to rule on related religious issues, even "essential" ones.

28. As a matter of fact, many of these legal definitions and the whole reasoning behind the discussion on jurisdiction make use of notions that were originally developed for other purposes. A right to an office is taken as an instance of a more general right to property. The right to a religious office does not differ from the right to any other office, which means that it must satisfy the same conditions to be held valid. The right to worship is taken as just one instance of the right to access or use land and water, which is regulated by dispositions of the Criminal Code.

29. This suggests a much deeper-rooted entanglement of law and religion than is usually assumed. At one level it certainly can be approached in terms of heritage, or enforcement of secularism, or religious reform, or a judge's personal agenda. But at a much more fundamental level it also results from the legal system itself which imposes a legal categorization on aspects of religious life: religion has to fall within this legal universe of discourse and of enforceable rules. The kind of religion that is thus eventually shaped is mostly framed by questions and rules that were initially elaborated for other, non-religious litigations. Indeed, nearly all aspects of religious life may thus be re-defined through such legal categories projected and imposed on religious issues, a fact often underestimated in the description of actual attitudes, practices, and institutions in religion." [Source: Excerpts from the Paper "Ruling on Rituals: Courts of Law and Religious Practices in Contemporary Hinduism" - Gilles Tarabout - https://doi.org/10.4000/samaj.4451- posted Open Edition Journals Website]

Despite the Constitution of India declaring India's position as in neutral in respect of all religions, our society has been involved with religion. The growing communal politics is a threat to the growth of real secularism in India. Communalism operates through creating communal disharmony, communal violence, and political violence and also by creating division on the basis of caste, class and/or religion, by spreading myths and stereotypes against minority communities. During the election campaign, the political parties have tended to use different religious communities or group communities and castes for their individual political gains which have greatly diluted the concept of a secular state. Few of the political parties are also identified as parties that are promoting the interests of specific religions or communities. After Independence, political parties in India and politicians started mobilizing voters through elementary identities like religions, communities and castes. These are considered easy ways of strengthening their vote banks. In this way, communalism supported political parties constitute a major threat to the unity of the nation, secularism, and also the concept of democracy.

It is astonishing to note that the "right to form political parties" or any provision regulating the functioning of political parties, do not form part of the Constitution. There is, however, specific provision in the Constitution that Iizes the Parliament to make such laws as necessary in the matter of elections that includes the political parties. It is, thus, imperative to constitutionalise political parties for the effective functioning of democracy in India, if not, make laws in respect thereof under the empowerment provided in the Constitution. This is what is brought out in Part 01 of this book. I have considered them as the constitutional gaps or abeyances while some of them, if not most of them, have the need for constitutionalisation. The wild forest of political anarchy and communalism that have been growing in our country since last fifty years has been due to lack of governing laws in respect thereof. These gaps or abeyances or constitutionalizing matters are invariable and absolute for sustaining and scintillating the democratic way of life. These are interdependent but what is, however, called for is integration and to accord an integral force so that the political parties, the religious bodies, the castes, creeds and classes are made to function within the laid down boundaries. Any trespassing of the boundaries should be dealt in the same manner as the ordinary laws deal with rather trespassing in such cases needs to be more instructive imposing the penal provisions in the form of heavy fines as in the civil law of the land because the criminal law blunts its application in such cases due to the need for the fulfillment of the procedures laid down under the Criminal Procedure Code. That is open to twists and manipulations both by the prosecuting authorities and the offenders that is what we are witnessing in almost criminal cases today.

It is true that the politics and religions have a mixed character. That is also there in individual citizens, bodies and organizations. There are specific laws in place to deal with them that deters them from encroaching upon each other. The political and religious bodies are similarly bodies and organizations to move the democratic functioning. Sadly, the Constitution does not make any specific Article that empowers the government /parliament to prevent excessive mixture of the political and religious bodies, the instances of the nature of which are stated before, in the absence of which, the democracy looks like travelling in a jungle or an event like circus.

Article 327 provides that Parliament may, from time to time, by law, make provisions with respect to all matters relating to, or in connection with, elections to either House of Parliament or the Legislature of a State. The law may include provisions for the preparation of electoral rolls, the delimitation of constituencies and all other matters necessary for securing the due constitution of such House or Houses. The law so made shall be subject to the provisions of the Constitution. Similar power is conferred by Article 328 on the Legislature of a State with respect to the elections to the Houses of the State Legislature. The power of the State Legislature is subjected to the provisions of the Constitution and any law made by Parliament. In my personal view, there being no specific provision with respect to the political parties, the words 'with respect to all matters relating to, or in connection with, elections to either House of Parliament or the Legislature of a State, include the law[s] relating to the political parties because the very next sentence expresses that, 'the law may include provisions for preparation of electoral rolls, delimitation of the constituencies which suggests that the Article 327 is inclusive and exclusive in its spirit and intent. The Representation of the People Acts, 1950 and 1951were enacted under this Article. Without the political parties, the meaning and essence of election is altogether taken away. Election means and includes accordingly 'the political parties' for want of any other specific provision respect thereof and the empowers the Parliament to make laws on political parties. The powers vested in the ECI under the Representation of the Peoples Acts, 1950 and 1951regulate the political parties in so far as the elections are concerned such as registration, model code etc.

I have brought the above provisions before the readers here considering that the divisions among the diversities also attributable in a major way because of increasing mixture of political parties with the religion bodies, castes, creeds and classes which is not intended to be denied but certainly intended to be regulated them as both have by now are showing the signs of uncontrollable horse.

Role of Peace and Value Education for National Integration and Communal Harmony in India by Dr Rachna Pathak, Associate Professor Department of Education, N.A.S. P.G. College, Meerut published in International Journal of Academic Research ISSN: 2348-7666; Vol.4, Issue-1(1), January, 2017 posted on the Website states [Excerpts]:

"…….One of the biggest mobilizing factors is education. Today, the youth is no longer limiting itself to the medical and engineering professions. Now, there is more of an influx into other exciting disciplines like pharmacy, journalism, research, biotechnology, bioinformatics, event management, media, and mass communication etc. This foray into other professions is ensuring an opening up of minds and mentalities like never before. If the youth is empowered with a liberal mindset, it can lead the change which will prod people into overcoming their differences and live as one community, irrespective of caste, creed, religion or ethnicity. Education plays vital role in the man s behaviour. Education gives idea to live and how to communicate each other. It does not change the ideology that could make with once own view point. If education change once ideology then every educated people does not involve in any illegal sources. Today education gives not only language knowledge, but how to live in the society. Education implants values in people s life. People will learn to respect each other and may not hurt the sentiments of others even if don't likes it. It enlightens with the fact that every religion says the GOD is great and none of the belief and its scriptures state to hurt anyone.

Value education is rooted in Indian philosophy and culture and ingrained in every tradition of Indian culture. Educational institutions play a significant role in the promotion of value. The Vedas and Upanishads form the source of inspiration for value education. In the Vedic period, In Ashram education, the Guru insists his sishya to follow certain values throughout his life. Socialist, Secular, Democratic, Justice, Liberty Equa, Fraternity, Dignity of the individuals and integrity of the nation are the ideal conditions in the Constitution. Our values in life must draw their inspiration from these ideals. University education commission 1948- 49 mentioned the various aspects of moral as: loyalty, courage, discipline, self-sacrifice and spiritual. The Secondary Education Commission 1952-53 laid special emphasis on the following values in the formation of character of the students: Efficiency Good Temper Cooperation Integrity Discipline……..

Education highlights the real problem to learners. It gives a clear cut to about what is right and what is wrong. It is believed that teachers are "Visible God" through whom students can understand the rea. Basic learning from an educational institution can be read and write well in once own mother tongue. It makes the people aware about the day to day activity in the society through different sources mainly like News Papers. Education always cultivates good social relationship from the childhood itself. Students belonging to different religion caste and creed study together and a brotherhood love are developed.

The whole enterprise of education is extricably linked with the development of values. Devoid of the potential to nurture values, education losses its heart and soul. No one who attempts to depict the spirit of age in which we live can possibly overlook the importance of education for values. Peace and security are facing new challenges that could have negative implications if we do not address them positively. The malleable years of youth in schools are crucial. Whatever is learnt and imbibed will determine to how students would live out their lives in future. The concern about value degradation is not new to this era. Even before independence such concern were pronounced in policy documents. Policy makers and educators have all along seriously mediated on this concern and have been trying to discern the potential of schooling, pinning their hopes on education to fulfil the aspirations and expectations of the public and the society.

Education has a major role to play in the integration of this country. The way history lessons are presented in the texts and the boring manner they are taught in schools, its become only dates to be remembered. History as a subject lends itself to drama giving emphasis and reasons to events. By dramatizing history lessons learners can realise mistakes of the past and not repeat it but create history by understanding! All of us are taking history only as middle aged people when precious young minds are already corrupted by distorted truths and made distant by disinterested rendering.

Education gives a holistic development to the learners. Education not only restricted in textbook learning but also sports, arts and culture. These aspects help to develop sports man sprit, respect other people s culture etc. Education installs ethical values and makes the learners understand that most aspirations are common in mankind. It installs an awareness and appreciation of not only an individual s cultural heritage but also an awareness and appreciation of the cultural heritage of the others. Education gives the learners knowledge of as individuals and by extension of those around them. Education produces „thinking persons and who can understand their limitations and can learn from those who transcend these limitations. It teaches persons with respect for others. Education produces persons who seek to learn the Wisdom distilled from previous generations and from those of learning and wisdom in their society and the world- at- large. Education understands the distinction between rhetoric and truth/ facts. It helps us to reconcile the dua we see in everything around us and appreciate the whole- the concept of reconciling the opposites. Education is the key in achieving harmony in any society. Education transforms into an "Ethical nation" from one that is built on expediency."

Education of the children of all the religions in our country will be the most helpful, if not sole, consideration for encouraging and ensuring harmony among the diversities with minimal divisions that acts as strength to sustain and maintain harmony among all the diversities and within the, the divisions.

Light up the education in every child to brighten his or her future to learn and earn for self and the family; to enrich the knowledge and to integrate into the national stream. There is no better solution than education for a harmonious life within and among God gifted religions to our country. Be proud and make the country proud.

"Secretary General of the Muslim World League Mohammad bin Abdulkarim al-Issa said India's diversity is a great model for coexistence and praised the Muslim community in the country for their sense of national pride."

Muslim World League secretary general Mohammad bin Abdulkarim Al-Issa on Tuesday praised India's diversity and said "Indian wisdom" contributed a lot to humanity. He also praised the Muslim community in India for their sense of national pride and said, "They are proud that they are Indian nationals and they are proud of their Constitution."

Speaking at an event in Delhi, Al-Issa said, "We have heard a lot about Indian wisdom and we know that Indian wisdom has contributed a lot to humanity...We know that the Indian component with all its diversity is a great model for coexistence not only in mere words but also on the ground and we appreciate all the efforts taken in this regard."

The Muslim World League is an International Islamic NGO that is founded and funded by Saudi Arabia…………..

[Source: India Today News Desk - New Delhi, UPDATED: Jul 11, 2023 17:21 IST]

In September, 2023, the Government of India expressed indicated to change the name 'India' as 'Bharat'. This exploded in verbal, print and electronic media with opposition political parties objecting to any such change. Some of the scholars and historians wrote long articles in the print media and also presented their points of view in the electronic media, for and against the change but most of them were in favour of change of name to Bharat. This is considered as a controversial issue by the opponents and the timing chosen for it. This is the current mood of the country and some took recourse to the debates in the Constituent Assembly on this matter, if any. In nutshell, the debates went as follows:

"In a pivotal moment during the drafting of India's Constitution, the question arose: should the nation be officially named 'Bharat' or 'India'? This debate, which unfolded almost a year after the initial draft, held great significance for the newly formed nation. On September 18, 1949, BR Ambedkar, the chairman of the drafting committee, moved an amendment to draft Article 1, proposing, "India, that is, Bharat shall be a Union of States." However, this proposal sparked a passionate discussion among the Members of the Constituent Assembly.

The Debate: H.V. Kamath, a member of the Assembly, argued that Ambedkar's phrasing was clumsy and suggested two alternatives: "Bharat, or, in the English language, India, shall be a Union of States" or "Hind, or, in the English language, India, shall be a Union of States." He pointed out that in many other countries, India was still known as 'Hindustan,' and its inhabitants were referred to as Hindus, regardless of their religion.

Seth Govind Das, Kamalapathi Tripathi, Kallur Subba Rao, Ram Sahai, and Har Govind Pant joined the debate in favor of 'Bharat.' Das emphasized that 'India' was a relatively recent term introduced after the arrival of the Greeks in the region, while 'Bharat' had deep historical and cultural roots in ancient texts like the Vedas, Upanishads, Brahmanas, Mahabharata, and Puranas. He believed that 'Bharat' better represented the nation's rich history and culture.

Kallur Subba Rao added that 'India' derived from 'Sindhu' or 'Indus,' which was more fitting for Pakistan due to its proximity to the Indus River. He even proposed renaming the Hindi language as 'Bharati' to align it with the spirit of 'Bharat.'

Ram Sahai supported 'Bharat,' citing examples from various Indian regions where it was commonly used, including leaders who referred to the country as 'Bharat' in their speeches. Kamalapati Tripathi passionately argued that 'Bharat that is India' would be more appropriate, resonating with the nation's sentiments and prestige. He asserted that despite centuries of foreign rule, the name 'Bharat' had endured and was deeply rooted in India's culture and history.

Tripathi highlighted the cultural and philosophical richness associated with 'Bharat,' evoking the Rig Veda, Upanishads, teachings of Krishna and Buddha, Shankaracharya, and iconic symbols like Rama's bow and Krishna's wheel. He argued that the name 'Bharat' represented a glorious past that the nation should embrace.

Despite BR Ambedkar's reservations, Assembly president Rajendra Prasad allowed Hargovind Pant to make a case for 'Bharat Varsha,' emphasizing its significance in daily religious practices and its historical usage.

In the end, a show of hands within the Constituent Assembly resulted in 38 in favor of Kamath's proposal and 51 against it. Consequently, the original wording, 'India, that is, Bharat shall be a Union of States,' prevailed." [Source: The Economic Times/News - Bharat vs India also sparked intense debate in 1949: Here is how India got its name in Constitution - ET Online Last Updated: Sep 06, 2023, 09:57 AM IST].

The following information enlightens us on the significance of use of the name 'Bharat' without prejudice to what the Constituent Assembly adopted in the Draft Constitution:

"India is one of those few nations that have two names. How many countries have you heard of that have two names – first that is constitutionally documented, and another name that is perhaps an English translation meant for all those people who cannot pronounce the word? It is often a challenge for people whose first language is English or any other European language to pronounce eastern names. Therefore, in the olden times, it was a norm to change all those names, and people would blindly accept the new names without much resistance.

Take, for example, our country. We go by two names – **Bharat**, the original name and India, the name given by people. People who invaded Bharat arrived at the river Sindhu, and somehow, they changed the name to **Hindu**. Then, the name further changed to Indus. And now, **India** has stuck on as the name of the country for centuries.

In this context, it is essential for historians to come up with a satisfactory explanation that justifies the evolution of the **name "India" and also trace its origin**. It is fascinating to know that the name India does not appear anywhere in the Puranas, Vedas, Itihasa or Amarakosa. Some scriptures of India say "jambu dweepe Bhaarata varshe…." Yet, India was included as the name of our country in our constitution, and everyone was liberally allowed to use this name even after the country attained independence from the British rule.

Whenever we speak in one or more of our regional languages and/or Rashtra Bhasha, the name Bharat or **Bharat Mata** is proudly used. However, when our nation is addressed in English, people often address it as India just like a literal translation for its original name to be understood by the non-Bhartiya people. It is a known fact that Sri Lanka eschewed its name Ceylon a long time ago. Yet, we still cling to the name Ceylon that was given by invaders a long time ago.

The question now is, do we really need to use two names? Is it not possible for us to stick to Bharat and also make others understand why it is crucial for our country to revert to its original name? Talking about our country, it has had multiple names such as **India, Bharat, Hindustan, Hind, Bharatbhumi, and Bharatvarsha**. So, which name should we use? That is a story for another day.

In any case, the word Bharat has a deep-set history behind its name. So, does the other names of our nation. Let's find out the history and etymology behind all these names!

Bharat

The word Bharat comes from the Sanskrit language and is definitely a very ancient name. It has references in the Mahabharata and the Hindu Puranas to "Bharatvarsh." The Puranas describe the word Bharat as a geographical entity that lies between the oceans in the south and the Himalayas in the North. The Puranas also say that Bharat is a politically divided land into several smaller territories.

Yet, it is always referred to together. <u>Therefore, the "Bharatvarsh" stated in the Puranas consisted of the same plura in religion, caste, language, lifestyle, and culture as today's "Bharat." This unity in diversity often makes us think of the most beautiful interpretations of the word Bharat.</u> The word is derived from the dance form Bharatanatyam. "Bha" means expression, "Ra" means melody and "Ta" stands for rhythm. <u>This beautiful interpretation of the word Bharat renders a lovely image of harmonious diversity of our country. It also offers a glimpse and a deep insight into the meaning of "Bharatvarsh" for people in ancient times.</u> [Emphasis added]

The origin of the word Bharat also lies in Sanskrit and Hindu texts, and this gives this word a religious significance for all Hindus too. Bharat can be called a nation where all Hindus feel a deep-seated sense of belonging and identification. This feeling can be rightly inferred from popular slogans such as 'Bharat Mata Ki Jai' that were popular at the time of freedom struggle. Several deliberations took place in the Constituent Assembly at that time regarding whether or not Bharat should precede the name India in the form of "Bharat, or the English language, India…" [I's Note: The debates in the Constituent Assembly on naming of country in the Draft Constitution have been stated before in nutshell]

As is evident in recent years, there have been several Public Interest Litigations that have been filed in the courts of law in favor of the name "Bharat" being adopted in the country as the sole official name of India. The litigations have also favored the idea of India being seen only as a colonial name or hand-me-down. Therefore, today, popular brands such as Patanjali by Baba Ramdev promote themselves as "Made in Bharat" instead of "Made in India." <u>This emphasis on the word Bharat makes it crystal clear that even though the Constitution of India may technically think "Bharat" to the be equivalent of "India" where the meaning of these names is concerned, both the names continue to present different connotations for the majority of the 'Bharatvasis' who might not relate to the name India as much.</u> [Emphasis added]

Hindustan

The Latin name "India" and the Persian name "Hindustan" both come from the ancient Persian term "Hindu." The word Hindu is a Persian word for Sindhu which is the name of Indus River in all the ancient Sanskrit scriptures. Therefore, Hindustan can be called "the land beyond the Indus." The name Hindustan became a very prevalent term in the Mughal Empire before the British rule and primarily comprising of North India. That said, with the passage of time and due to colonization, the term Hindustan expanded in its geographical scope in order to include British-ruled India and all its territories. The old Urdu song 'Tarana-e-Hind' of Iqbal which is popularly known by the name of **'Sare Jahan Se Achcha'** is a well-known and ubiquitous ode to Hindustan, which is the un-partitioned subcontinent of the early 1900s.

If we further delve into the history of Hindustan, several more amusing yet remarkable realizations are revealed. The religious identity of Hindus today has come from the Persians who were perceived by Hindu nationalists as the destroyers of the Hindu culture. After the 19th-century expansion of Hindu nationalism which was led by VD Savarkar, Hindustan was referred to by Sanskrit name "Hindustaan." The Sanskrit name is made up of two words – "Hindu" and "Sthan" for a place. Therefore, the word Hindustaan was born as 'the land of Hindus' rather than giving geographical importance to the name with reference to the Indus River.

Thanks to this name, another slogan appeared that was called **'Hindi, Hindu, Hindustan'** meaning one language, a single religious denomination as well as one territory. This connotation is drastically different from the initial original name of "Bharat" or even "Hindustan."

Talking about the official naming of our country, the Constituent Assembly of India always unwittingly rejected the name "Bharat" throughout their debates. Another reason for the widespread use of "Bharat" by the citizens of India was that people felt that the name "Bharat" sounds significantly more secular than Hindustan. On the flip side, another reason why people often shun the word "Hindustan" is that Pakistan usually calls India "Hindustan." Therefore, people are usually seen avoiding this connotation. Having said that, "Hindustan" is still widely used in various slogans of Subhash Chandra Bose such as "Jai hind or the popular song 'Tarana-e-Hind.'

India

The word "India" shares a lot of its etymology with the name "Hindustan." This is because the Persian "Hind" connects our land from all sides with the Indus River. The name India became popular after the 17th century in English language posts, and ultimately, this word became the popular English reference to our country. Therefore, for everyone who has been brought up in the Western world, our country will probably be known to them as India. This term is also frequently found on television, in conversations, in books or the news. Most people cannot fathom our country being called anything other than India due to its prevalence and popularity.

That said, many people still think that the word "India" is a colonial relic that needs to be discarded immediately, just like Sri Lanka discarded "Ceylon." For other people, India is the equivalent of modern and the most urban regions of India whereas Bharat refers to the "real India." Urbanization and the unequal growth that has been witnessed by our country further exacerbate this massive divide between India and Bharat. However, for many people, especially the youth, India and Bharat and Hindustan are all the same. Bharat and Hindustan are simply inclusive of everything that India stands for!" [Source: Origin of The Word Bharat: Why Did India Come to Be Known as Bharat written by Harinder Singh February 24, 2019 – posted on the Website 'Exploring Bharat'.]

As per the historical points, it may be said that King Bharata was the ancestor of the Pandavas and the Kauravas. It is said that Bharata was a great Emperor who conquered and reigned over the whole Indian sub-continent. The empire of the emperor Bharata was called Bharatvarsha which spread out from the Himalayas to the sea. Regarding Bharatvarsha, one may say that it referred to ancient India. As per records, one may say that there are differing views of various ancient scholars as to how the name Bharatvarsha was derived. However, it can also be said that there used to be a vast spread of Bharatvarsha. Few of the many significant parts of Bharatvarsha included the Himalayas, the Northern plateau, the Ganges region and so much more.

'India, that is Bharat: A short history of the nation's names, from the Rig Veda to the Constitution of India' Written by Adrija Roychowdhury New Delhi | Updated: September 6, 2023 07:28 IST` published in The Indian Express:

"There is speculation of an official change in the name of the country from India to Bharat, even though Article 1 of the Constitution uses the two names interchangeably: "India, that is Bharat, shall be a Union of States."

The roots of "Bharat", "Bharata", or "Bharatvarsha" are traced back to Puranic literature, and to the epic Mahabharata. The Puranas describe Bharata as the land between the "sea in the south and the abode of snow in the north".

In March 2016, the Supreme Court dismissed a PIL (public interest litigation) seeking a name change from 'India' to 'Bharat,' strongly objecting to the petition. A bench, including the then Chief Justice TS Thakur and Justice UU Lalit, told the petitioner that such pleas would not be entertained.

"Bharat or India? You want to call it Bharat, go right ahead. Someone wants to call it India, let them call it India," Justice Thakur had said at the time.

Four years later, in 2020, the Supreme Court once again refused to entertain a similar plea seeking a name change from India to Bharat. The Court, at that time, suggested that the plea could be converted into a representation and forwarded to the Union government for an appropriate decision.

"Bharat and India are both names given in the Constitution. India is already called 'Bharat' in the Constitution," the then Chief Justice of India SA Bobde had stated. [Emphasis added]

So where does the name 'Bharat' come from?

The roots of "Bharat", "Bharata", or "Bharatvarsha" are traced back to Puranic literature, and to the epic Mahabharata. The Puranas describe Bharata as the land between the "sea in the south and the abode of snow in the north".

Social scientist Catherine Clémentin-Ojha explained Bharata in the sense of a religious and socio-cultural entity, rather than a political or geographical one. 'Bharata' refers to the "supraregional and subcontinental territory where the Brahmanical system of society prevails", Clémentin-Ojha wrote in her 2014 article, 'India, that is Bharat...': One Country, Two Names (South Asia Multidisciplinary Academic Journal).

Bharata is also the name of the ancient king of legend who was the ancestor of the Rig Vedic tribe of the Bharatas, and by extension, the progenitor of all peoples of the subcontinent.

Writing in January 1927, Jawaharlal Nehru alluded to the "fundamental unity of India" that has endured from "the remote past": "a unity of a common faith and culture. India was Bharata, the holy land of the Hindus, and it is not without significance that the great places of Hindu pilgrimage are situated in the four corners of India — the extreme South overlooking Ceylon, the extreme West washed by the Arabian Sea, the East facing the Bay of Bengal and the North in the Himalayas." (Selected Works Vol. 2)"

The reasons why it's okay to call India, Bharat - by Dipankar De Sarkar published in Mint Edition 07 Sep, 2023:

What are the ancient references to Bharat?

In Indian cosmology, the earth is flat and circular with a mythical Mount Meru at its centre. It is surrounded by dvipas (islands) separated by oceans. The southernmost is Jambudvipa. In it, to the south of the Himalayas lies Bharatvarsha, named after King Bharata. Jambudvipa is named in Emperor Ashoka's inscriptions (268-231 BCE). An early record comes in inscriptions found in the Hathigumpha caves near Bhubaneswar in Odisha. In giving an account of the reign of King Kharavela of Kalinga (50 BCE), the inscriptions say, "In the 10th year he sent an expedition to conquer Bharatavarsha."

"The fact is that the terms Bharat and India can be used interchangeably, especially in view of the authorized Hindi version of the Indian Constitution, but the government cannot stipulate that everyone use only one name: either is permissible and usable interchangeably," senior Supreme Court advocate and Congress member Abhishek Singhvi told The Hindu.

Mr. Singhvi, who is also a former Chairman of the Parliamentary Standing Committee on Law and Justice, said an amendment would be required only if the government insisted on the use of any one term or wanted to remove a particular term.

Former Additional Solicitor-General and senior Supreme Court advocate Aman Lekhi said it was officially the "Republic of India" and even the G-20 Presidency was known as the "Indian Presidency". He said that any change of name would require a constitutional amendment under Article 368.

"The change is possible but is it necessary? There are certain things that should be free of controversy and the name of the country should highest in that list," Mr. Lekhi said.

"Unless any intention to the contrary is made explicit, the terminology is only a question of semantics. And at this stage, there is no need to read anything sinister," former Law Minister Ashwani Kumar said.

Another top constitutional expert, who did not wish to be named, said there was nothing wrong in sending an invitation as the "President of Bharat". However, it should not be seen as the first step towards doing away with the use of English language……….

The ruling given by the Hon'ble Supreme Court of India supported by the views of the eminent Legal Experts stated before lead to one conclusion that the country should continue to use the names interchangeably in the present circumstances and in the best interests of the country. In no way, the dignity of the country will be diminished by doing so, the same having been in use since seventy three years. It will be sane and sensible to put an end to the present controversy.

PART 03
FUNDAMENTAL DUTIES PARADOX

"....ASK NOT WHAT YOUR COUNTRY CAN DO FOR YOU — ASK WHAT YOU CAN DO FOR YOUR COUNTRY....... - JOHN F. KENNEDY'S INAUGURAL ADDRESS, JANUARY 20, 1961

Every citizen plays a key role in building a New India — a clean, healthy and prosperous nation. Everyone performing their duties, even mechanically, would pave the way for a better neighbourhood, better society, and ultimately, a better country. Let us together build a responsible India. [The Indian Express – November 26, 2019]

"The idea of citizenship has acquired a new meaning, content and purpose in the democratic world. While emphasising on rights, it is very important that one is also sincere about his or her duties towards the society at large and the country, especially its safety and security imperatives.

Universally, great emphasis has been laid on citizens' duties. Article 29(1) of the Universal Declaration of Human Rights states: "Everyone has duties to the community in which alone the free and full development of his persona is possible."

Many nations across the world have transformed into developed economies by embodying the principles of "responsible citizenship" — all the responsibilities and duties that citizens of a nation should exercise and respect. The United States of America is a classic example in this respect. The Citizens' Almanac, issued by the US Citizenship and Immigration Services, details the responsibilities of its citizens — a copy of this document is given to every person on becoming a citizen of the country. Every year, during September 17-23, Americans celebrate the "Constitution Week", using the time to reflect on the rights and responsibilities of citizenship and what it means to be a US citizen." [Source: Written by Ravi Shankar Prasad Updated: November 26, 2019 10:47 IST – Published in The Indian Express].

Fundamental duties are enshrined in Article 51A in the Constitution of India by the 42nd Amendment of 1946. They are listed in Part IV-A of the Indian Constitution and are non-justiciable in nature. The concept of fundamental duties was taken from the USSR (communist countries) as no constitutional concept of it was mentioned in the Constitution of the Western countries. Sardar Swaran Singh Committee made many recommendations but only 10 of them were included in Article 51 A. Later on, by the 86th Amendment of 2002, one more duty was added to the list of duties. Presently, there are 11 duties enumerated in the Constitution.

Historical Context behind the Fundamental Duties:

During the period of internal emergency which was imposed by Prime Minister Indira Gandhi in 1975, people started demanding their fundamental rights as the rights were taken away from the people during emergency time. Indira Gandhi was not in favour of granting fundamental rights to the citizens of India. She decided on a different approach. She asked her Cabinet Minister Swaran Singh to form a committee and make recommendations to the citizens of India which will serve as a reminder to them. By reminder, it was meant that along with the rights there are duties to be obeyed as well. And duties and rights go hand in hand. As a result, Sardar Swaran Singh Committee made recommendations that are now stated in Article 51A of the Indian Constitution.

A Paper posted on the PATHASHALA titled 'ADVANCED CONSTITUTIONAL LAW FUNDAMENTAL DUTIES UNDER INDIAN CONSTITUTION': states [Excerpts]

"**(1) Introduction**

Since time immemorial the emphasis in Indian society in accordance with the dictates of the ancient scriptures has been on the individual's Kartavya, that is, performance of one's duties towards society, the country and especially towards one's parents. The Gita and the Ramayana enjoin people to perform their duties without caring for their rights (or fruits).1 Mahatma Gandhi rightly said that: The true source of right is duty. If we all discharge our duties, rights will not be far to seek. Rights accrue automatically to him who performs his duties. In fact, right to perform one's duties is the only right worth living for and dying for. It covers all legitimate rights.

The law and its prohibitive processes, apprise man of his rights and duties as a unit of the society.3 Right is an interest recognized and protected by a rule or justice4 whereas a duty is an obligatory act.5 Rights and duties are co-relative and therefore no right can exist without a co-relative duty.6 The Constitution of India guarantees Fundamental Rights for the people of India7 under Part III (Article 12 to 35) of the Constitution. The framers followed the American model in adopting and incorporating these fundamental rights in the Constitution. These are certain basic, natural and inalienable rights.8 These have been declared essential rights in order that 'human liberty may be preserved, human persona developed and an effective social and democratic life promoted'.9

Part IV (Article 36 to 51) titled "Directive Principles of State Policy" contains the directives and duties for the State. The inspiration for including in the Constitution such Principles is drawn from the Constitution of Ireland, 1937.10 This part sets forth the ideals and objectives to be achieved by the State for setting up in India a social welfare state as distinguished from a mere police state, which aims at social welfare and the common good and to secure to all its citizens justice- social and economic.11

(3) **Reasons for not Enacting Fundamental Duties in the Constitution**

The framers of the Indian Constitution did not feel the need to enact the fundamental duties in the Constitution as given to us, for the following reasons14:

(3.1) Firstly, the framers of the Indian Constitution were such visionaries as had practiced values in life, discharging their societal and national obligations and had followed noble ideals which had inspired our national struggle for freedom and the need to defend the country, promote harmony, secularism and preserve the rich heritage of the composite Indian culture. To the framers of the Constitution, these were basic and inherent values, which were being practiced by each and every one. These were first nurtured in the home traditionally and were subsequently supplemented by education in schools and colleges. These were integral part of the way of life in India and it was taken for granted that aberrations in the practice of these will not be acceptable to the society. As such no need was felt to incorporate the Fundamental Duties specifically in the Constitution.

(3.2) Secondly, the duties were spelt out by the Preamble to the Constitution, which contains the ideals and aspirations of the people of India and the dedication of Constitution for fulfilling such ideals and aspirations. We have solemnly resolved to secure to all the citizens of India justice, liberty, equa and fraternity. Whatever is needed to achieve these goals is our obvious duty to perform – is a dictate of the Preamble.

(3.3) Thirdly, all the rights enshrined in Part III on Fundamental Rights have inbuilt obligations therein. The need is to read them so as to spell out and understand the duties flowing therefrom.

However, with the lapse of time, degradation of values, particularly values in public life became blatantly evident and the nation felt the need to amend the Constitution and incorporate these values specifically as the Fundamental Duties of every citizens.15

As already stated, those who propagated the inclusion of these duties in the Constitution took a leaf from the Dharamshastras, which stress upon the duties rather than the rights of the people. Geeta aptly declared: "Your duty is your Right". They thought that fundamental duties flow from the fundamental rights and the idea that it was the citizen's duties on which were based fundamental freedoms; and fundamental duties would constitute the corner-stone of the arch of the established socio-political order. They said that the citizens should accept certain responsibilities towards the state, the government, constitutional institutions and fellow citizens.16

(4) Fundamental Duties Part IV-A (Article 51-A) of the Constitution provides the following fundamental duties of every citizen:

a) To abide by the Constitution and respect its ideals and institutions, the National Flag and the National Anthem;

(b) To cherish and follow the noble ideals which inspired our national struggle for freedom;

(c) To uphold and protect the sovereignty, unity and integrity of India;

(d) To defend the country and render national service when called upon to do so;

(e) To promote harmony and the spirit of common brotherhood amongst all the people of India transcending religious, linguistic and regional or sectional diversities; to renounce practices derogatory to the dignity of women;

(f) To value and preserve the rich heritage of our composite culture;

(g) To protect and improve the natural environment including forests, lakes, rivers and wild life, and to have compassion for living creatures;

(h) To develop the scientific temper, humanism and the spirit of inquiry and reform;

(i) To safeguard public property and to abjure violence;

(j) To strive towards excellence in all spheres of individual and collective activity so that the nation constantly rises to higher levels of endeavour and achievement;

(k) Who is a parent or guardian to provide opportunities for education to his child or as the case may be ward between the age of six and fourteen years.17

With the inclusion of these fundamental duties, our Constitution has been brought in line with the Universal Declaration of Human Rights (UDHR, 1948)18 International Covenant on Civil and Political Rights (ICCPR, 1966)19 and also the Constitutions of U.S.S.R20, China21, Sri Lanka22 .

(5) Need and Importance of Fundamental Duties

5.1 Fundamental Duties as enshrined in the Constitution of India have great moral values and may be termed as moral precepts or the expected behavioural patterns of the citizens of India towards the nation. Fundamental Duties of citizens serve a useful purpose. In particular, no democratic policy can ever succeed where the citizens are not willing to be active participants in the process of governance by assuming responsibilities and discharging citizenship duties and coming forward to give their best to the country.

5.2 These duties are intended to create psychological consciousness among the citizens23 and are intended to serve as a constant reminder to every citizen that while the Constitution specifically conferred upon them certain fundamental rights, it also requires citizens to observe certain basic norms of democratic conduct and democratic behaviour.24

5.3 These duties establish and strengthen the democratic balance. These read like a poem, crossing all barriers of politics. They are beacon lights of a citizen, guiding him in his functions.25

5.4 Moreover, the courts can take help of these duties in order to interpret the provisions contained in Part III and IV of the Constitution. The Hon'ble Supreme Court of India has emphasized that Fundamental Rights are not to be read in isolation. They have to be read along with the Chapter IV and IV-A of the Constitution.26

Chapter IV-A becomes an essential feature or basic structure of the Constitution of India and hence Parliament has no power to amend the Constitution with a view to delete it.

(6) Enforceability of Fundamental Duties

It is true that there is no legal sanction provided for violation or non-performance of Fundamental Duties. There is neither specific provision for enforceability nor any specific prohibition. However, Fundamental Duties have an inherent element of compulsion regarding compliance. Out of the ten clauses in article 51A, five are positive duties and the other five are negative duties. Clauses (b), (d), (f), (h) and (j) require the citizens to perform these Fundamental Duties actively.28

As already stated, rights and Duties are co-existent and co-relative. This means right in A implies duty in B. Duty is an inalienable part of right. By the inclusion of a chapter on Fundamental duties, it is the obligation of every citizen to abide by them. Failure on the part of any citizen to perform fundamental duty would imply violation of corresponding right in another person. Therefore, it becomes the duty of the judiciary to enforce those 'implied rights' like other constitutional rights.29

(7) Legal Provisions for the Enforcement of Fundamental Duties

Following are some of the legal provisions already available in regard to enforcement of Fundamental Duties:

7.1 In order to ensure that no disrespect is shown to the National Flag, Constitution of India and the National anthem, the Prevention of Insults to National Honour Act, 1971 was enacted.

7.2 The Emblems and Names (Prevention of Improper Use) Act 1950 was enacted soon after independence, inter alia, to prevent improper use of the National Flag and the National Anthem.

7.3 In order to ensure that the correct usage regarding the display of the National Flag is well understood, the instructions issued from time to time on the subject have been embodied in Flag Code of India, which has been made available to all the State Governments, and Union territory Administration (UTs).

7.4 There are a number of provisions in the existing criminal laws to ensure that the activities which encourage enmity between different groups of people on grounds of religion, race, place of birth, residence, language, etc. are adequately punished. Writings, speeches, gestures, activities, exercise, drills, etc. aimed at creating a feeling of insecurity or ill-will among the members of other communities, etc. have been prohibited under Section 153A of the Indian Penal Code (IPC).

7.5 Imputations and assertions prejudicial to the national integration constitute a punishable offence under Section 153 B of the IPC.

7.6 A Communal organization can be declared unlawful association under the provisions of Unlawful Activities (Prevention) Act 1967).

Offences related to religion are covered in Sections 295-298 of the IPC (Chapter XV).

- Provisions of the Protection of Civil Rights Act, 1955 (earlier the Untouchability (Offences) Act, 1955)

- Sections 123(3) and 123(3A) of the Representation of People Act, 1951 declares that soliciting of vote on the ground of religion and the promotion or attempt to promote feelings of enmity or hatred between different classes of citizens of India on the grounds of religion, race, caste, community or language is a corrupt practice. A person indulging in a corrupt practice can be disqualified for being a Member of Parliament or a State Legislature under Section 8A of the Representation of People Act, 1951.

- Prevention of Cruelty to Animal Act, 1960

- Right of Children to Free and Compulsory Education Act, 2009.

- Water (Prevention and Control of Pollution) Act, 1974, Air (Prevention and Control of Pollution) Act, 1981, the Environment (Protection) Act, 1986. It must be noted that in pursuant to various judgments of the Hon'ble Supreme Court relating to environment issues and having regard to the complex issues of fact of science and technology which arise in environmental litigation and in particular in the elimination of pollution in air and water, in September 2003, the Law Commission of India, in its 186th Report, made a proposal to constitute **"multifaceted" Environmental Court with judicial and technical/scientific inputs.**

(8) Drawbacks in Fundamental Duties

(8.1) The chapter on Fundamental Duties is criticized on the following31 grounds: These duties are non-justiciable like directive principles of state policy. These have been termed or seen merely as moral homilies and platitudes.

(8.2) Certain fundamental duties are so vague in their meaning that they can hardly be perceived by the common people of this country where most of the people are illiterate and poor and quite unaware of their fundamental rights. In other words, these duties are not so worded as to enable a common man to understand the underlying meaning of the words. For instance, different interpretation may be made as to what includes and what does not, in the 'valuation and preservation of rich heritage of our composite culture' or 'spirit of inquiry' or 'striving towards excellence in all spheres of individual and collective life so that the nation constantly rises to higher levels of endeavour and achievement' or 'cherishing and following the noble ideas which inspired our national struggle of freedom'.

(8.3) The chapter on 'fundamental' duties has been inserted after chapter IV that contains directive principles and not after chapter III that contains fundamental rights. Somewhere it gives an impression that, like directive principles, they should also be non-enforceable.

(8.4) Moreover, it is also not clear whether violation of fundamental duties entails any kind of punishment by the Constitution. Chapter IV-A is neither exhaustive nor does it provide the duties in concrete terms. V.D. Mahajan, in his book observed: There is no originalin the idea of fundamental duties of the citizens. They are original in their vagueness. There is nothing fundamental in fundamental duties. They are duties of every individual. These are the qualities, which distinguish human beings from animals. They just lay down what is a normal human behaviour.32

(8.5) Article 51- A has the potential to regenerate and reconstruct the nation. It has been on the statute book for the last 24 years. It commands that "it shall be the duty of every citizen of India", but it is an irony that more than 99 per cent of the citizens of India do not even know about the existence of this article in the Constitution, much less its provisions.33

(9) Role of Judiciary

The apex judiciary in India, in a number of cases, has made harmonious interpretation of part III, part IV and part IV-A of the Constitution, thus signifying the importance of fundamental duties. In Chandra Bhavan Boarding and Lodging v. State of Mysore34, the Supreme Court of India has taken the view that "it is a fallacy to think that under our Constitution, there are only rights and no duties". It has emphasized that Fundamental Rights are not to be read in isolation. They have to be read along with the Chapter IV and IV-A of the Constitution.35

Speaking about the importance of fundamental duties, the Supreme Court in A.I.I.M.S. Student Union v. A.I.I.M.S. 36, held that fundamental duties are not enforceable by a writ of court just as fundamental rights are but it cannot be lost sight of that 'duties' in part IV-A under Article 51-A are prefixed by the same word 'fundamental' which was prefixed by the founding fathers of the Constitutions to 'rights' in part III. Article 51-A does not expressly cast any fundamental duty on the State, the fact remains that the duty of every citizen of India is the collective duty of the State. Fundamental duties though not enforceable by a writ of court, yet provide a valuable guide and aid to interpretation of constitutional and legal issues. Constitutional enactment of fundamental duties, if it has to have any meaning, must be used by courts as a tool to tab, even a taboo, on state action drifting away from constitutional values.

Similarly, in State of Gujarat v.MirzapurMotiKureshiKassabJamat37 the apex court held that directive principles and fundamental duties play a significant role in interpreting the Constitution and determining the constitutional validity of any law or executive action.

In Rural Litigation Entitlement Kendra v. State of U.P. 38, the Supreme Court has issued directions to the State, having regard to Article 51-A (g), the court also reminded that preservation of the environment and keeping of ecological balance unaffected is a task which not only Governments but also every citizen must undertake. It is a social obligation and let us remind every citizen that it is his fundamental duty as enshrined in Article 51-A (g) of the Constitution.

In Shri Sachidananda Pandey v. State of West Bengal39, the court took the view that when the court is called upon to give effect to the directive principles and the fundamental duties, it is not to shrug its shoulder and say that priorities are a matter of policy and so it is a matter for the policy making Authority.

Moreover, in M.C. Mehta v. Union of India 40 the Supreme Court, in order to implement the duty as to improvement of environment, has directed the Central Government: (a) to direct all educational institutions throughout India to give weekly lesson in the first ten classes, relating to the protection and improvement of the natural environment including forests, lakes, rivers and wild-life. (b) To get textbooks written for the said purpose and to distribute them free of cost. (c) To introduce short term courses for training up of teachers who teach this subject. (d) Not only the Central Government but also the State Governments and Local authorities to introduce cleanliness weeks when all citizens, including members of the Executive, Legislature and the Judiciary, should render free personal service to keep their local areas free from pollution of land, water and air. ……..

In Union of India v. Naveen Jindal44, the apex court while declaring that National Flag hoisting by citizens on their premises is fundamental right qua freedom of speech and expression, also took help of the provisions relating to fundamental duties under part IV-A. The court also suggested making an enactment for the matter concerning the National Flag of India.4

State of U.P. v. Yamuna ShankerMisra&Anr.,46 is an interesting case where the object of writing the confidential reports and making entries in the character rolls were read in the light of article 51(j) as giving an opportunity to a public servant to improve excellence. The net of this Fundamental Duty was spread so wide by the court as to spell out the eternal values of honesty, integrity, good conduct and efficiency getting improved in the performance of public duties and standard of excellence in services constantly rising to higher levels so as to be a successful tool to manage the services with officers of integrity, honesty, efficiency and devotion.

Similarly, the Supreme Court in Vishakha and others v. State of Rajasthan47 found it necessary and expedient for employers in work places as well as other responsible persons or institutions to observe certain guidelines to ensure the prevention of sexual harassment of women.

Recently, on 12 April 2012, Hon'ble Supreme Court in Society for Un-Aided Private Schools of Rajasthan vs. U.O.I & Another 48 explained the relationship between Fundamental Right to Life under article 21, Right to Education under Article 21 A, Directive Principles of State Policy under Articles 41, 45 and 46 and Fundamental Duty under Article 51-A (k). The court held that unlike other fundamental rights, the right to education places a burden not only on the State, but also on the parent/guardian of every child [Article 51-A(k)]. The Constitution directs both burdens to achieve one end: the compulsory education of children free from the barriers of cost, parental obstruction or State inaction. Thus, Articles 21A and 51-A (k) balance the relative burdens on the parents and the

State. Thus, the right to education envisages a reciprocal agreement between the State and the parents and it places an affirmative burden on all stakeholders in our civil society.

(10) Recommendations of the National Commission on the Review of the Constitution (NCRC)

The Government of India appointed a committee "to operationalize the suggestions to teach Fundamental Duties to the citizens of India" in the year 1998 under the chairmanship of Justice J.S. Verma. The Committee submitted its report in October 1999. The NCRC examined the report and gave the following recommendations49: For effectuating Fundamental Duties, the following steps should be taken:

(a) The first and foremost step required by the Union and State Governments is to sensitise the people and to create a general awareness of the provisions of fundamental duties amongst the citizens on the lines recommended by the Justice Verma Committee on the subject. Consideration should be given to the ways and means by which Fundamental Duties could be popularized and made effective;

(b) Right to freedom of religion and other freedoms must be jealously guarded and rights of minorities and fellow citizens respected;

(c) Reform of the whole process of education is an immediate but immense need, as is the need to free it from governmental or political control; it is only through education that will power to adhere to our Fundamental Duties as citizens can be inculcated;

(d) Duty to vote at elections, actively participate in the democratic process of governance and to pay taxes should be included in article 51A; and

(e) The other recommendations of the Justice Verma Committee on operationalization of Fundamental Duties of Citizens should be implemented at the earliest.

(f) The following should also be incorporated as fundamental duties in article 51A of the Constitution:

(i) To foster a spirit of family values and responsible parenthood in the matter of education, physical and moral well-being of children.

(ii) Duty of industrial organizations to provide education to children of their employees.

The Supreme Court in Union of India v. R. Padmanabhan50, has directed the Central Government to take appropriate steps for the implementation of the recommendations of the NCRC as expeditiously as possible.51

(11) Suggestions

The recommendations made by Justice Verma Committee on Operationalization of Fundamental Duties of Citizens deserve to be reiterated forcefully. In particular, it is suggested that52:

(11.1) there is imperative need for wider dissemination of information and generating greater awareness in regard to the Fundamental Duties of citizens and obligations of citizenship. This must assume the dimensions of a peaceful, nation-wide, mass-based movement. This can be done through:

(a) organization of advocacy and sensitization programmes,

(b) display of the text of article 51A 'Fundamental Duties' prominently in government publications, diaries calendars, offices and at public places,

(c) radio and video spots highlighting important messages related to Fundamental Duties on AIR, Doordarshan and other channels,

(d) setting up an autonomous body to act like ombudsman on citizenship values and for overseeing operationalization or effectuation of Fundamental Duties,

(e) publication of small booklets on various aspects of Fundamental Duties written in simple language and aimed at different levels of citizens through non-formal education, open schooling, adult education, and universalization of literacy programmes

(f) circumspection by electronic media on programmes, serials, pictures, news and advertisement affecting moral, decency and cultural values and heritage of the country,

(g) activist role by electronic and print media in the matter of Fundamental Duties like protection of the environment,

(h) media avoiding the glorification of acts of violence, armed robberies, and terrorist activities, and

(i) the state machinery ensuring the effectuation of Fundamental Duties, where necessary, by prompt legislation.

(11.2) The benefits from the already existing schemes need to be optimised by monitoring work of NGOs and other institutions operating government-funded schemes focused on aspects of national integration, communal harmony, culture and values, and environment, in tune with the spirit of clauses (e), (f) and (g) of article 51A and making mid-course corrections where necessary.

(11.3) The Directive Principle of State Policy in article 48A, the Fundamental Duty in article 51-A (g) and the existing laws in the area need to be implemented and enforced in the light of the judgments of the Supreme Court.

(11.4) There is need for fundamental transformation in the direction and approach to curricular and co-curricular activities for imparting education in schools and teacher training institutions. This can be done by –

- publishing the content of Fundamental Duties through books published by the NCERT and School Textbook Bureaus,

- presenting each clause of article 51A through anecdotal talks, at morning assemblies at schools,

- organising seminars, debates, competitions on different aspects of Fundamental Duties of citizens, and

- designing an instructional design for education in Fundamental Duties that fits into the present day multi-channel environment where learning accrues from a variety of sources at home, school, community, print and electronic media.

(11.5) In order to ensure dignity of women, gender biases and sex-stereotyping must be eliminated from all textbooks both at state and national levels.

(11.6) Programmes of education for school teachers and higher and professional courses have to be so designed as to enable communication of the content of Fundamental Duties of citizens and the value of abiding by them. What is needed is a vigorous advocacy with state educational agencies, teacher education institutions and university departments for inclusion of Fundamental Duties component in curricula. All courses in Human Rights should also include Fundamental Duties.

(11.7) An independent comprehensive unit encompassing familiarisation with the Constitution of India and Fundamental Duties of citizens there under need to be incorporated in the elementary and secondary teacher education courses.

(11.8) NCC should be made compulsory in all pre-service teacher education institutions. This would promote the values of sovereignty, unity and integrity of the nation.

(11.9) The need to shift emphasis from rights to duties in all walks of life is indeed urgent. Undue emphasis on one's own rights without any awareness of one's duties is not a sign of good citizenship.

(11.10) The Fundamental Duties set out in article 51A were not intended to be legally enforced by one citizen against the other. They are like the Ten Commandments, which every citizen is expected to bear in mind and conduct himself towards the State and society accordingly. Therefore, the endeavour of the State should be not so much to give teeth to the Fundamental Duties but to spread awareness of the duties among the people. It is submitted that in the case of citizens holding public office, each and all Fundamental Duties can be enforced by suitable legislation and departmental rules of conduct. Likewise, sanctions can be provided for professional bodies such as the Bar Council of India, the Medical Council of India, the Institute of Chartered Accountants and the Institute of Engineers, etc.

(11.11) The courts in India have been taking note of the Fundamental Duties in judicial decisions. Being provisions of the Constitution, the courts will have due regard to the Fundamental Duties in interpreting the text of the Constitution. They will also be justified in moulding relief in individual cases having regard to the antecedents of the person seeking relief, particularly judged by the yardstick of Fundamental Duties.

(11.12) Some of the expressions used in the Fundamental Duties may be elaborated or explained to facilitate better understanding and attempts should be made to remove vagueness in them.

(11.13) It is suggested that a few more Fundamental Duties, namely, duty to vote in an election, duty to pay taxes and duty to resist injustice may be added in due course to article 51A in Part IVA of the Constitution.

(12) Conclusion

Emphasizing on the significance of Fundamental Duties, recently, on 23 February 2012, the apex court in the famous case of Re-Ramlila Maidan Incident dated 4/5.06.11 vs. Home Secretary, Union of India and Others53held that a common thread runs through Parts III, IV and IVA of the Constitution of India. While interpreting any of these provisions, it shall always be advisable to examine the scope and impact of such interpretation on all the three constitutional aspects emerging from these parts. It will create an imbalance, if undue or disproportionate emphasis is placed upon the right of a citizen without considering the significance of the duty. The true source of right is duty. When the courts are called upon to examine the reasonableness of a legislative restriction on exercise of a freedom, the fundamental duties enunciated under Article 51A are of relevant consideration. All these duties are not insignificant. They complement the obligations of the State. Thus, all these duties are of constitutional significance.

Thus, fundamental duties are the foundations of human dignity and national character. There is a need to reconcile the claims of the individual citizen and those of the civic society and to orient the individual citizen to be conscious of his social and citizenship responsibilities and so shape the society that we all become solicitous and considerate of the inalienable rights of our fellow citizens. Therefore, awareness of our citizenship duties is as important as awareness of our rights. This should be done by a systematic and intensive education of the people, that is, by publicity or by making it a part of the syllabi and curriculum of education. Homes, Universities, officers and their places of work should be made centres for imparting in the performance of their obligations.55

If every citizen performs his duties irrespective of considerations of caste, creed, colour and language, most of the malaise of the present day could be contained, if not eradicated, and the society as a whole uplifted. Rich or poor, in power or out of power, obedience to citizenship duty, at all costs and risks, is the essence of civilized life.5

It is incorrect to say that Fundamental Duties are not enforceable and are a mere reminder. They have the element of compulsion regarding compliance. So, in order to ensure a faithful and effective implementation of the Fundamental Duties, there is a need to enact suitable legislation wherever necessary to require obedience of the duties by the citizens."

The above Article [Paper] "is pursuant to the study entrusted to PATHASALA by the MHRD, Government of India – [An MHRD Project under its National Mission on Education through ICT [NME-ICT] [Undated] as part of the Courseware.

[Author's Note: Google Search notes 'The National Mission on Education through Information and Communication Technology (NMEICT) is proposed as a Centrally Sponsored Scheme to support the development of ICT in the teaching and learning process for the benefit of all learners in Higher Education Institutions in any time anywhere mode.]

There is no status of Action Taken Report [ATR] on the Paper stated above by the MHRD, Government of India as seen from the Google Website. The effort made in the presenting the Paper is commendable. Though it is stated to be Courseware under the 'Advanced Constitutional Law' - Module: Fundamental Duties under the Indian Constitution, it gets solely attached for advanced education on law and the knowledge built up by the students under that courseware remains with them whereas the subject matter under consideration is such as warranting its spreading out officially throughout the country including its remotest villages. The Fundamental Duties which are more assistive to the Fundamental Rights are like bones in the human body in the sphere of the democratic country. Added to the agony, the Fundamental Rights are justiciable but not the Fundamental Duties though the Hon'ble Supreme Court of India holds them at par with the Fundamental Rights except their enforceability or justiciability. It is also noted by the Hon'ble Supreme Court in some of the famous cases on Fundamental Duties as have been brought out before that if the Fundamental Duties are adhered to by the citizens, there won't be the need for placing greater weight on the Fundamental Rights inasmuch as the Fundamental Rights can be said as non-performance of the Fundamental Duties by the Citizens who are concerned mainly with Fundamental Rights since the time the country became Republic.

The course material combined with the suggestions contained in the Paper under discussion are jewels if not, diamonds. As with any precious metal or stone, rarity is the principal indicator of worth. The more rare the material, the greater is its perceived value, hence the more extortionate the price. Diamonds are more expensive than gold, even though they are far less rare than gold. The attitudinal approach and the suggestions adopted in the Paper are rare to spot in the ordinary course, that is what seems to have been the case in downgrading the Fundamental Duties and upgrading the Fundamental Rights; we having considered rather accorded least consideration to lay increasing emphasis and constitutional Psychological pressures on the Fundamental Duties through various processes as have been mentioned in the Paper especially when those are not justiciable. This is absolutely needed now due to our continuing concern with Fundamental Rights and unconcerned with the Fundamental Duties not appreciating that the second offsets the need for the first.

"To the grumbler all duties are distasteful; nothing will ever satisfy him, and his whole life is doomed to prove a failure. Let us work on, doing as we go whatever happens to be our duty, and being ever ready to put our shoulders to the wheel. Then surely shall we see the light." ~Swami Vivekananda

Besides for the benefit of the Law students, the Courseware could have been, with imperative accent on the Fundamental Duties implemented throughout the country though it is legalistic but the suggestions contained in the Paper are more beneficial to the ordinary citizens who are capable of understanding them provided those are put before them in a proper perspective adopting more generalized usage concept than the legalistic one. The suggestions need to be presented to the citizens in all the officially recognized languages under the Constitution. Appropriate also will be to provide them in bilingual languages. For example, English plus Hindi in the central and northern States, English plus recognized regional languages in the southern states and English plus in the regional languages in the North Eastern States. This is so because the Fundamental Duties which are, otherwise, silently sleeping in the Constitution are to be awakened to every citizen beginning at the villages' level taking through to the small towns, big towns, cities and metros. How this could be done is also suggested in the succeeding paragraphs.

"For breach, statutes in themselves create the remedy. However for constitutional wrong the constitution itself provides the remedy of writ or order. In some matters subsidiary remedy through statute is prescribed. In broader perspective, the wrong may be civil or criminal or taxation etc. as the case may be for which respective regulatory mechanism exists. But a wrong under fundamental duties, if not of gravity lacks statutory remedy for breach. From the study it is gathered that most of the fundamental duties seem to be with no remedy for their breach. Accordingly there is emergent requirement for statutory protection and prevention of breach of fundamental duties as a medicine and not by way of punishment. The remedies suggested being counselling or admonition or obtaining bond and finally if all the measures fail, then fine or imprisonment as a punishment. To be brief, the breach of fundamental duty can be treated as civil misconduct to be met with a statute for honour to duties and preventing the breach. Further, it is also imperative that wherever the intentional breach of duty with gravity is covered by law same to remain undisturbed. But neojurisprudence is imperative to remedy the general breach by providing curative measures at initial stages and obtaining bond for repeated wrong /misconduct. However persistent breach may result in offence after exhausting curative measures followed by obtaining bond for forfeiture if the wrong/misconduct is repeated.

The duties ought to be respected otherwise Law becomes paper tiger when it loses the sanction and enforcement. The short comings of administration of justice are clogged with adjudication and enforcement in the result the sheen of law towards maintenance of social order and national flavor suffers at the altar. As such the fundamental duties to be the form of law ought to have sanction in whatsoever form. To make India great must inculcate obedience to duty. Tree must love the ground on which it stands39 is the thought and ideal of East for adherence to nationalism, social solidarity and mutual co-existence." [Excerpts from the Article 'Jurisprudential Aspects of Fundamental Duties and their Enforceability: A Study Prof. (Dr.) R.L.Koul Amity Law School, NOIDA, AUUP Dr. Meenakshi Koul Assistant Professor, Symbosis Law School, NOIDA].

"In the debate over constitutional rights vs duties, the political thrust on duties is highly problematic in terms of India's deeply intermeshed caste system that implores the individual to perform duties of the caste into which she is born. Besides, caste atrocities are an unfortunate reality even today despite the progress of social mobility made over the decades—enabled by our egalitarian Constitution.

The Constitution of India is a rights-based charter. In simpler terms, it is the founding principle of this republic that citizens are vested with certain inalienable rights that each one can enforce against the State. These are rights of free speech, right to life, right to practise religion, and so on. The Supreme Court has held these rights to be a part of the Constitution's basic structure: not even Parliament in its constituent capacity can abrogate them.

It was alarming, therefore, to hear the Prime Minister observe recently that in 75 years since India's Independence the focus on rights has weakened India and the next 25 years must focus on duties. He made similar suggestions, including on the floor of Parliament, about two years ago, and his Cabinet colleagues have repeated it at various forums over the years. Innocuous as it may sound, what the suggestion effectively does is it turns the Constitution on its head: it seeks to enforce duties that are unenforceable and, under its garb, gives a lowly pass to rights that are strictly enforceable against the state.

FAR-SIGHTED VISION

During the making of the Constitution, our founders were alive to this sociocultural reality. And they had a vision: that from January 26, 1950, all citizens regardless of their caste and socio-political status will be unified by the rights that they have against the state. It was one of the greatest political experiments of the last century, unprecedented both in terms of the population under its sway and the far-sightedness of the vision in a country that was stubbornly conservative at the time. The founders were not naive to think that the dead ink would transform India overnight; indeed the ink was to be enlivened by future generations. Ambedkar expressed the hope that with the enactment of the Constitution, while we were giving ourselves one person one vote, we would not deny the people "one person, one value" for too long.

The judiciary, the bulwark of constitutional morality, has sometimes spoken in the same grammar as the Prime Minister. At an international judicial conference in 2020, the then Chief Justice of India, S.A. Bobde, spoke about the Constitution's Fundamental Duties chapter and quoted Mahatma Gandhi's Hind Swaraj that **"real rights are a result of performance of duty"**. Incidentally, the Prime Minister had quoted those lines just a few weeks before in an interaction with students.

Suggestive, coincidental and innocuous as these statements may sound, when it comes from high offices such as the Prime Minister and the Chief Justice, law-enforcers translate it as a signal from the top that rights are junior to responsibilities. The consequences of it on those who need protection of law are disastrous to say the least. For example, women who seek redress from gender crimes get asked what kind of dress they were wearing to provoke such an attack. [Emphasis added].

Modern democracies are a social contract between adults who elect one of their own to perform certain delegated duties and retain the rights unto themselves. In monarchies, the power and identity are pyramidicaling, insofar as the monarch sits on top axis and the subjects derive their very identity from that axis of power. They ordinarily have no inherent rights and their life and liberty are a largesse or benevolence of the monarch, for which the subject ought to be grateful.

In contrast, in the Indian model, the specific rights of the citizens have been carved out into Chapter IV– Fundamental Rights, in abrogation of which neither the States nor the Union government can make any law. The chapter on rights takes the central place in our constitutional order because, unlike in the U.S., citizens in India have no residuary rights on which the Union cannot legislate. But even in our scheme, the individual owes nothing more to the State than abiding by the laws, paying her taxes, and refraining from committing crimes.

The Prime Minister, before asking citizens to give him more, should look inwards to see how he has discharged his oath to the Constitution from which his office derives its identity. From enabling the greatest economic bust to the meek refusal to confront China within our borders, the list is endless." [Source: Rights & duties Front Line - 25 Feb 2022 - BY KABEER SHRIVASTAVA, AN ADVOCATE]"

It should have first begun with the political parties who capture the peoples' mood and movements and make them to practice what they practice. This is precisely the disconnecting point in adherence to the Fundamental Duties for; the people have become used to political pattern including the language, acts, deeds and behaviour over the years. It has been happening because the political parties that ruled the country and are ruling find no urgency whatsoever to constitutionalize the political parties to bind them to constitutional fundamental duties besides the fundamental rights, the latter is pleaded for every time they want and former has been forgotten. In a democracy, the political parties assume the role of parents to the people of the country similar to the parents to a child. The child follows what is taught by the parents in its teenage; so also, the political parties the guardians of the democracy and of the people must realise the fact that the people walk on their footprints. This is vitiating the social environment that consists of people of all the Faiths in the country and, over a period of time, has formed into a vicious circle that has made everyone to focus on the Fundamental Rights and forget the Fundamental Duties. This is in accord with what the political parties think about and have adopted it in practice. Have we heard any political leader in our country turning the attention of the people on the Fundamental Duties let alone teach them about those duties? I have not come across such talking and teaching on the duties by the political parties to the people so far.

The schools and colleges have also forgotten about the Fundamental Duties. The children are supposed to be inculcated in depth about the Fundamental Duties in the schools and colleges while the people are supposed to be done so by the society. That is not happening because it is neither so in the schools and colleges nor in the society. How Fundamental Duties are a means for achieving responsible Citizenry? It is pertinent to note that, merely because a rule is not backed by sanctions for disobedience, does not mean it has no importance. It is still regarded a rule of law that is expected to be followed.

This proposition was recognised by the Hon'ble Supreme Court in Minerva Mills Ltd. v. Union of India [20] –

"There may be rule which imposes obligation on an individual or authority and yet it may not be enforceable in a court of law and therefore not give rise to a corresponding right in another person. But it would still be a legal rule because it prescribes a norm of conduct to be followed by such individual or authority. The law may provide a mechanism for enforcement of this obligation, but the existence of the obligation does not depend upon the creation of such mechanism. The obligation exists prior to and independent of the mechanism of enforcement. A rule imposing an obligation or duty would not therefore cease to be a rule of law because there is no regular judicial or quasi-judicial machinery to enforce its command. Such a rule would exist despite of any problem relating to its enforcement. Otherwise the conventions of Constitution and even rules of international law would no longer be liable to be regarded as rules of law."

Recently, the **Supreme Court** issued a notice to the Centre and states to respond to a **petition to enforce the <u>Fundamental Duties</u> of citizens**, including patriotism and unity of the nation, **through comprehensive, well-defined laws.**

What is the Significance of Fundamental Duties?

- Rights and duties are correlative.

- The Fundamental Duties are intended to serve as a **constant reminder to every citizen** that while the Constitution specifically conferred on them **certain** fundamental rights**,** it also requires citizens to observe **basic norms of democratic conduct and democratic behaviour.**

- These **serve as a warning to the people against the anti-social activities** that disrespect the nation like burning the flag, destroying the public property or disturbing public peace.

- These **help in the promotion of a sense of discipline and commitment towards the nation.** They help in realising national goals by the active participation of citizens rather than mere spectators.

- It **helps the Court in determining the constitutionality of the law.** For instance, any law passed by the legislatures, when taken to Court for constitutional validity of the law, if it is giving force to any Fundamental Duty, then such law would be taken as reasonable.

What is the Need to Legally Enforce Fundamental Duties?

- Since time immemorial the emphasis in **Indian society in accordance with the dictates of the ancient scriptures** has been on the individual's **'Kartavya".**

- This is the performance of one's duties towards society, the country and especially towards one's parents.

- The **Gita and the Ramayana** enjoin people to perform their duties without caring for their rights.

- In the **erstwhile Soviet Union Constitution,** the rights and duties were placed on the same footing.

- There is a pressing need to **enforce and implement at least some of the fundamental duties.**

- For instance, to uphold and protect sovereignty, unity and integrity of India, to defend the country and render national service when called upon to do so and to disseminate a sense of nationalism and to promote the spirit of patriotism to uphold the unity of India.

- The **Verma Committee on Fundamental Duties of the Citizens (1999) identified the existence of legal provisions** for the implementation of some of the Fundamental Duties. The committee provided with the provisions like:

    - No person can disrespect the **National flag, Constitution of India and the National Anthem under the Prevention of Insults to National Honour Act, 1971.**

    - The **Protection of Civil Rights Act (1955)** provided for punishments in case of any offence related to caste and religion.

It was argued in the petition that the **non-adherence of the Fundamental Duties** has a direct bearing upon the **Fundamental Rights guaranteed under Articles 14 (Equa before Law), 19 (Protection of certain rights regarding freedom of speech) and 21 (Right to Life) of the Constitution of India.**

For example, the need to enforce fundamental duties arises due to the **new illegal trend of protest by protestors** in the garb of freedom of speech and expression.

What is the Supreme Court's Stand on Fundamental Duties?

The Supreme Court's **Ranganath Mishra judgment 2003** held that fundamental duties should not only be enforced by **legal sanctions but also by social sanctions.**

In **AIIMS Students Union v. AIIMS 2001**, it was held by the Supreme Court that **fundamental duties are equally important like fundamental rights.**

Though fundamental duties are not enforceable like fundamental rights they cannot be overlooked as duties in Part IV A.

They are prefixed by the **same word fundamental** which was prefixed by the founding fathers of the Constitution to 'right' in Part III.

Way Forward

There is a need for a uniform policy for the "proper sensitisation, full operationalization and enforceability" of fundamental duties which would "substantially help citizens to be responsible".[Source: Posted on Drishti Website - Enforcing Fundamental Duties - 22 Feb 2022]

The governments should not lose time to implement the above directions/recommendations that would help to clean the political and social environment presently overshadowing the democratic functioning. The state of affair on failure to perform the Fundamental Duties as prevailing today is highly disturbing and yet, the failure of the governments to act upon the directions/recommendations referred to before has been creating continued muck throwing among the politicians, the religious bodies and the citizens in general. Any further delay in acting upon them would cost the country dearly due to widening gap in the political, religious and social environment. Addition to the above directions/recommendations, I wish to humbly submit also the following course of action:

Display the Fundamental Duties in English plus the Regional Language as adopted by the State/UTs on a big size board inscribed in Green or any other colour as considered appropriate and erect and install it throughout the country in the manner stated below:

(a) Outside the Panchayat Office, Schools and Bus Stand/Railway Stations;

(b) In small towns which don't come under the category of Taluka or Block, outside the Administrative Office, the Schools, Bus Stands/Railway Stations in the towns;

(c) In Taluka/Block level towns/semi urban areas, outside the Taluka/Block Office, the Schools, Colleges, if any, Government Hospitals, Bus Stand/Railway Station; Market Places, Cinema Theatres, Courts;

(d) In District level urban areas, outside the District HQrs, its Sub-Offices, Offices, Schools, Universities/Colleges, if any, Courts, Government Hospitals, Bus Stand/Railway Station, Market Places, Cinema Theatres, Airports, Government Libraries, Public Gardens, if any;

(e) In Cities and Metros, outside all the Government Offices, Government Hospitals, Universities/Colleges, Schools, Courts, Bus Stand/Railway Station, Market Places, Cinema Theatres, Public Gardens, Zoos, Residential Welfare Associations [RWAs], Airports,

Government Libraries, the Malls, National Monuments, Memorials, Public Galleries, Inclusion in the National DD Channel in such manner as considered appropriate,

(f) Outside the Exhibitions Grounds

(g) In Metros, outside all the Government Offices/Sub-Offices, Government Hospitals, Universities/Colleges, Schools, Courts, Bus Stand/Railway Stations, Market Places, Cinema Theatres, Residential Welfare Associations [RWAs], Airports, Government Libraries, Public Gardens, Zoos;

(h) Outside the offices of the RBI and its Branches, SBI and its Branches, Nationalized Banks and their Branches, Government owned Insurance Companies, the Public Sector Undertakings and their Branches

(i) At prominent places in the cities and Metros as considered appropriate.

(j) Such other places as may be considered useful.

The steps submitted above would create a compulsive awareness among the citizens by repeated reminding them of their Fundamental Duties. Such constant compelling would, over a period of time, enable the citizens to imbibe their Fundamental Duties and, once it is so realized, it would gradually transform itself into obedience and compliance. Such steps should have been taken from the time the Fundamental Duties were introduced in the Constitution which rather seems to be considered as fulfillment of the duty by the ruling party ignoring on how to educate and activate them among the citizens. The succeeding ruling parties also considered so. This omission on the part of the then ruling party has allowed dusty environment grow than green environment, the fallout of which has reached its extremity and telling its impact on society and citizens. The end result is that it has devastated and demolished the imperativeness of the national spirit on the part of the citizens to abide by the Fundamental Duties. "<u>The Supreme Court has made it absolutely clear in its pronouncements. If not done, then, why the Fundamental Duties in the constitution, laws, rules, regulations to prevent such happenings and who will address this issue?</u>" It seems the political parties, religious and the citizens are allergic to the Fundamental Duties because they believe obedience to the Duties will curtail their freedom of expression they wish to exercise as they like. This is known as walking in the darkness switching off the light. Time we realize this and switch on the light made available for one's own and others responsible and reciprocative growth that would enlighten the democracy and will shine on face of every citizen.

"AVOIDING PROBLEMS YOU NEED TO FACE IS AVOIDING THE LIFE YOU NEED TO LIVE." PAULO COELHO

An essential duty which ought to have been appreciated and by the ECI as a matter of electoral duty which, in my personal view, is equal to fundamental duties has been over looked by the ECI. This is stated below:

Sections 123(3) and 123(3A) of the Representation of People Act, 1951 declares that soliciting of vote on the ground of religion and the promotion or attempt to promote feelings of enmity or hatred between different classes of citizens of India on the grounds of religion, race, caste, community or language is a corrupt practice. A person indulging in a corrupt practice can be disqualified for being a Member of Parliament or a State Legislature under Section 8A of the Representation of People Act, 1951. However, the corrupt practices stated before do not include 'yielding to pressures of the contesting candidates in the elections on accepting bribes or freebies or any other kind of inducement or on castes considerations for voting them though a provision in this regard also needs to be made part of the corrupt practices and included under the above sections. This is particularly so as the said Act places whole burden of compliance on the part of the contesting candidates who, using their money and muscle power have been trying to influence the voters especially those who are under privileged and illiterate but there is no provision in the said Act to educate the voters informing them of the various corrupt practices defined under the said Act so that the citizens stated before are also aware of those provisions are aware in advance or self-informed that creates an obligation on their part to apply their mind before becoming victims to corrupt practices, as also would make them better placed to inform the concerned authorities/observers designated about the contesting candidates inducement trade and tricks so that the authorities or observers get seized of the matter and act upon the candidates timely.

There are a number of documents on the process of election including, in particular, in relation to the candidates but I could not find any such document notified by ECI how the voters should manage the situations where they are subjected to money and muscle power, perhaps that this part concerned the law enforcing machinery. When we talk about 'Free and Fair' election, we need to keep in mind what Sir Winston Churchill said, quoted before "…….It's also essential to this foundation that this man or woman should do this without fear and without any form of intimidation or victimisation, marking his ballot paper in strict secrecy. If that is democracy, I salute it. I espouse it. I would work for it." And so, would I!" Words 'without fear and without any form of intimidation or victimization, marking his ballot paper in strict secrecy…………' are essential to the foundation of democracy, as noted; do not come out in any of the documents of ECI, I tried to find out to the best of my efforts. Above long background given needs to be appreciated in this context.

The Representation of the People Act, 1951 specifies in section 8A Disqualification on ground of corrupt practices. The corrupt practices are defined in section 123 of the Act and include wide range of practices including undue influence. These are for the candidates to abide during the election process, the contravention of which is to be dealt as per the provisions of the Act. This needs to be emphatically brought out to the notice of the voters as well through appropriate method so that the voters understand what a candidate is doing whether is a corrupt practice and, if so, the procedure the voter(s) should follow to instantly report the matter to the designated authority and how the law ensures such voter (s)'s safety in case of the candidate resorting to undue influence defined under the said section against the such voter(s). Such educative information and programs are very important to create awareness among the voters and sensitize them to such situations. As noted, presently, the codes, guidelines, instructions etc. are directed towards the political parties and their candidates. Words "educating the masters" used in the speech of one of the Hon'ble Members in the Constituent Assembly are aimed at educating the voters also on the corrupt practices and the protection available to them from the state to ensure their safety. Only then, the essence of free and fair exercise of the right to vote by the voters could be ensured. In the election process, the candidate is one part and the voter is the other part but so far as the rights and duties are concerned, both stand on equal footing. There exists today an imbalance between the two; in that, the former has received greater attention and the latter received little or no attention from the ECI.

I am of the personal view that ECI also needs to act fast in this regard which also acts as deterrent to the candidate from indulging in corrupt practices. In what manner or method, it could be done has to be considered by the ECI. Most of the voters especially the rural voters and illiterate are hardly capable to understand existence of the mere provisions in the Act on corrupt practices. This would further strengthen and enhance the role of the COMMON PEOPLE and would encourage them to actively participate in the election process. The COMMON PEOPLE would feel proud of having such authority in exercising their voting rights.

This aspect has not received the kind attention of the election authorities since the country became republic and the election process was started. In its absence, the political parties and their candidates had taken for granted, more so, after seventies, to capture the votes by inducement of the voters through corrupt practices including threats. The voter hardly had any knowledge of what are the corrupt practices and how those should be dealt by him if he happened to come under such inducements. The places where the majority of the voters are illiterate and did not have any knowledge about the corrupt practices contained in the Act could have been found most fertile ground for exploitation by candidates through such practices.

Also, due to psychological fear of adverse reaction by the candidate against them including threats as well as in the absence of any protection under the law, they had no option but to accept inducements and vote for the candidate. This could be the main reason why there had been increasing level of corrupt practices. The electronic and print media which are active during elections also brought out such incidences taking place. The political parties and their candidates are wiser to devise various methods to avoid being noticed by the election authorities. Therefore, unless the election authorities educate the masters (voters) such that they are capable of understanding the corrupt practices with backed up assurance by the election authorities of protecting their interests and safety coupled with simple procedure empowering them right to report immediately to the designated Authorities, are made known to the voters educating them on the eve of every election, it is afraid, the election Authorities would not be able to stop the corrupt practices and the candidates so elected would hardly care for decency and decorum expected of them; continue to indulge more and more in corruption during their tenure to make up the money and muscle power they used to get elected. This is critical part of the election process. I believe such serious shortcoming in the election process would receive the kind attention of the election Authorities to ensure free and fair elections. Election Authorities would also come to know through the voters the changing methods of inducements the candidates choose and adopt for corrupt practices.

It is suggested in this regard that the corrupt practices specified in section 123 of the Act may be translated into vernacular languages recognized under the constitution in the form of Booklet and made available to the voters similar to the codes and circulars issued by the ECI on various matters to the candidates/political parties. This would act as a kind of empowerment of the voters which fact would also become known to the contesting candidates/political parties. These copies may be provided in the Panchayat Offices so that the voters could collectively discuss them. This is to be done one time followed by the amendments to the said section as and when made to keep the voters duly updated.

"The Fundamental duties are essentially taken from the Indian tradition, mythology, religions and practices. Essentially these were the duties that are the codification of tasks integral to the Indian way of life. O citizens of the Bharat! As our ancient saints and seers, leaders and preceptors have performed their duties righteously; similarly, you will not falter to execute your duties. (Rig.10.191.2). The reciprocity of right and duties, and the consequent rectification of the wrong done by the non-observance of duty is the edifice on which the functional aspect of our or any legal system rests.

Keeping all this aside, there is a need for adopting curative measures for inculcating duties instead directly adopting coercive measures except in exceptional cases squarely and clearly satisfying the components of offence. All this depends on gravity of breach of duty. Thus, a need arises to make the act as an actionable wrong of a 'civil misconduct' desired to be cured rather punished. Accordingly, innovative solutions may be carved out. Should such course of action is considered as may not be possible, alternative is to give widest publicity to the Fundamental Duties including in the manner submitted before in this Part 03.

Absence of God-fearing culture has become order of the day. This is evident from the types of mishaps and crimes are happening. (God-fearing used to describe religious people who try to obey the rules of their religion and to live in a way that is considered morally right). These are frightening and horrendous. The religious rules and the state laws have little or no concern for those committing such acts. Late APJ Abdul Kalam, former President once said "In India we only read about death, sickness, terrorism, crime. Why are we so NEGATIVE? ...." Negativity has replaced the positivity in our thoughts and deeds.

Growth and security of the nation call for dutifulness and discipline in whatever way of life we are working. This culture was there for twenty five years after independence or becoming democratic; slowly started downgrading when we considered self-interest as greater than the national interest.

This spread in all walks of life, political, religions and society. The constitutional values and principles of governance were side-tracked due to increasing self-greediness, self-adoration, self-worshipping and indifferent attitudes on national issues and security concerns. We need to understand at least at this hour that the politics, religions, castes and creeds must be confined and function within their religious and moral jurisdiction according to the constitution and their own Faiths. Trying to travel beyond undermines the interests of the country. It is like the proverb 'Fence eating the crop' or 'those who break laws they are supposed to uphold.'

"IF YOU WANT TO RAISE A CROP FOR ONE YEAR, PLANT CORN. IF YOU WANT TO RAISE A CROP FOR DECADES, PLANT TREES. IF YOU WANT TO RAISE A CROP FOR CENTURIES, RAISE MEN. IF YOU WANT TO PLANT A CROP FOR ETERNITIES, RAISE DEMOCRACIES." - CARL A SCHENCK

Just while I was completing writing of this book, I came across an Article 'The trolls on social media are Ravanas of present times' by Shashi Shekhar published in Mint dated 22 Oct 2023 {Shashi Shekhar is editor-in-chief, Hindustan. Views are personal.}. I consider it worth reproducing hereunder for the benefit of the readers:

"They have returned like a swarm of locusts. Wars, elections, riots, and natural calamities provide them with the power to expand into hydra-headed monsters. They lurk in the shadows, waiting for such upheavals to emerge. They will not stop until even a tiny spark becomes a major blaze.

I'm referring to trolls, social media's "supari killers" (a slang term for contract killers).

How lethal are they? The following instance gives a picture: A six-year-old Palestinian-American child was found mutilated in Chicago on 14 October. The landlord of the house his family lived in, Joseph Czuba, stabbed the child 26 times and also injured his mother who was trying to save him. According to the mother, Czuba vented communal and racial abuse during the attack. He has been charged with murder, attempt to murder, and hate crime. This murderous act has stunned Americans.

Their fear is justified. The rapid rise in hate crimes has undermined the democratic foundations of this great nation. In 2021 alone, hate crimes have risen by 11.6% in the US. Experts say such crimes could rise in the coming years.

The key reason for this is that some people start portraying incidents such as the killing by Czuba as a threat to a specific community. The worry of majoritarianism spreading has grown as they succeed in spreading confusion with their arguments.

The bloodshed in Gaza is giving them new impetus.

Let me give another example. A Chechen immigrant assassinated a schoolteacher in France last week. Officials believe that the state of affairs in Gaza has played a role in this tragedy. This has given trolls the room to tinker with facts to suit their needs. According to Pew Research, if the present rate of migration from West Asia to Europe continues, it might quadruple France's Muslim population in the next 25-30 years. The hobgoblins of social media are citing the report to claim that refugees were accomplishing what the Arab warriors couldn't in the Middle Ages. The whole of Europe is concerned about such falsification.

This edginess is fuelling neo-Nazism.

The Jews alone had suffered racial hatred under Hitler's time, but now all foreign races and religions are subject to hatred in Europe and the West. Hindu temples in some Western countries, including Canada, have come under attack. Many Sikhs in America have been harmed by rising Islamophobia. People steeped in hatred lack the discernment to distinguish between a Sikh and an Arab.

All this is not to say that such hatred is exclusive to the "liberal" West. Even communist China is under its sway. In Beijing last week, a young man attacked an Israeli diplomat with a knife while shouting religious slogans. The reasons for the attack have not been publicly stated, although most people believe it is related to Israel's conflict with Hamas.

Let us now return to our country.

Because hate crime is not specified in the Indian Panel Code, the National Crime Records Bureau does not collect data on it; nonetheless, this does not mean that hate crimes do not occur in our country. Attacks on alleged cow smugglers, minor occurrences arising from mutual conflicts, the murder of innocent persons in Udaipur or elsewhere, and deadly incidents in Jharkhand in the name of witchcraft are some examples of this. Prime Minister Narendra Modi himself has openly criticized it. Despite this, social media intruders are busy "working" from overseas. The assembly elections in five states, as well as the general elections in a few months, have given them a new opportunity.

The question is, how do you get rid of them?

Elections and conflict have provided them with an opportunity to sharpen their daggers, but our culture has provided us with a boon. Tomorrow is Vijay Dashami, when effigies of Ravana, a symbol of sin, would be burned in a symbolic cleansing. Similarly, we only need to introspect, gather courage and start rebutting social media trolls. It can be our new ritual.

While listening to the family elders and priests speak about Ram Rajya, the question, How was Ram Rajya?, must have crossed your mind several times. In a shloka, Maharishi Valmiki, the sage who composed Ramayana, observed, "Even the words thieves and robbers were not known in Ram Rajya. No one committed evil deeds, nor were elderly men carrying out the last rites of children."

Last rites of children. I hope you got the point."

The foregoing Article is evocative but those to whom this is pointing out need to take note of it and weigh in mind the most damaging and irreparable impressions that leave behind on the youngsters who are just waking up to the learning and living their life. I consider myself not competent to comment upon the Article except admitting what is written therein as the only truth. My understanding so is limited to myself. How those whom it is intended consider it is more important than anything else. It is relevant here to cite the write-up 'Positive and negative impact of electronic media' - By Alan Behrens posted on the Website of the same name:

"Electronic media or for that matter media, in general, continue to play an influential role in our society today-careers are made and destroyed, depending on what gets published in the media. Take Kevin Spacey for example, at one point he was the leading Hollywood icon but when stories of him trying to take advantage of underage actors made the rounds, well, that's the last nail on his career, so as to speak. This only goes on to show you that electronic media can indeed play a pivotal role as it had in the past but it is time that we took a closer look at the same and reviewed the positive and negative impact of electronic media.

The positive impact of electronic media:

Information: Electronic media is one of the effective methods by which you can disseminate information within seconds. So if you wanted certain information including information about an impending tsunami, then electronic media is your best bet to get that information out there, within a short space of time. That's why most politicians utilize all forms of electronic media to publicize themselves and to enable them to reach out to brand new voters.

Educational: Electronic media provides you with a host of information and certain agencies have started using the same to educate their young students. With the help of electronic media young students can learn more about the news, about the process and how reporters often have to report on it while facing a lot of stress and pressure. Some institutions also feature educational modules based on electronic media which can prove to be invaluable for those seeking to establish a career in the same.

Behavioural: various studies have already established that television and other forms of electronic media do continue to influence behavioural patterns in young children. And this can be a positive thing as it helps them to relate to the context and as a result, modify their behavior, As a –parent, you would be required to monitor all their electronic media interaction to ensure that they are not led astray.

The **negative impact of electronic media:**

Psychological: Again various studies have established the fact that the more young children are exposed to scenes of gratuitous violence in television programs, the more likely they are, to act it out. And moreover, television, as well as social media, can have a psychological effect on young viewers and cause them to become more reclusive, and to become addicted to select programs. As a result, this can impact their health in the long run.

Behavioural: Young children often tend to imagine that television programs are for real and naturally when they see explicit scenes and even violent ones, this can have a direct impact on their behavior. This is why it is important for parents to regulate all forms of electronic media; after all, it is for their own benefit. And remember, all it takes is for one show to alter your little one forever.

Health: Being exposed to electronic media 24/7 is not good, not in any sense of the word. For one, binge-watching television programs can impair your vision and even affect your hearing. If that wasn't enough, you would most likely put on more weight as a result of all that inactivity and this can even play a causative role in you developing diabetes.

Social interaction: As a result of being obsessed with electronic media and communication devices, you are more likely to lead a life of a recluse with little or no interaction with others. Soon, you would feel comfortable only when you are sitting in front of your laptop or television which is indicative that you have a major problem.

These are some of the positive and negative impacts of television and other forms of electronic media in our society. This is why we must be on our guard and ensure that our children do not get addicted to the various forms of electronic media from newspapers to androids. You need to carefully monitor your children so that you can be sure that they are watching the right programs, the sort that is educational and nothing gruesome."

I beg to be excused if I submit that the electronic media [also known as e-democracy in a democratic country] seems to be creating an impression of small kingdoms ruled by the capitalists and highly professionalized and advanced journalists. This is so because, as I see it, the electronic media which is supposed to uphold the Fundamental Duties seems to be weakening that constitutional obligation considering greater parts of the presentations made therein are of subsidiary rather than principal characterstics of democratic spirit, in that, the electronic media is getting more indulged in promoting negative formations among the growing children and the social life. It seems to think the sole arbitrator of a matter rather contributing to the arbitration process on public issues. The debates that are organized on the electronic media on certain burning public issues surprises the viewers being so crowded, none is audible of what points of views one is making on a subject matter rather it appears to be a fighting ground and a place for raging against each other. This lacks the maturity of the debates which should be first cool and calm when alone the suggestive ideas for solving or resolving a problem emerge. The debates need to be in a cooling and not heating up temperature.

Another disturbing scenario that has been developing on the electronic media is according increasing attention of the viewers towards the negative events that are multiplying day by day whether in the nature of politics, the social boils and criminal behaviours. I remember to have read in the print media an advisory issued by the Central Government to the electronic media not to give greater coverage and highlight those who have committed or suspected to have committed serious and heinous crimes, religious conflicts including riots. This, I believe, is intended to outsize focussing of the events when the truth gets established only through the judicial process. Such presentations on the electronic media have dangerous tendencies to act upon or counter upon merely from what is shown in the electronic media which is bound to create more social tension. There cannot be any bar in reporting such matters but balance of mind must be the guiding factor. This is where the honesty of the profession of the electronic media journalists stands to the test in the eyes of the viewers and the society in general.

In the judgment declared on 18th January 2021, the Bombay High Court, India has elaborated the position of media trials in India, declaring the judicial point of view. The court viewed the effects and consequences of media trials in the administration of justice, a quintessential factor of modern democracies. The judgment pronounced by Chief Justice Dipankar Datta and Justice G.S. Kulkarni of the Bombay High Court walks on a tight rope navigating the line between the "freedom of the press" guaranteed under Article 19(1)(a) of the Constitution of India and the menace of media trials running contrary to the same Constitution of India. But, in a larger scheme of questions does this case stand as a novelty in the jurisprudence i.e. "Modern Foundation of Media Trials in India" in a world consumed by emerging technologies?

The coverage of the electronic media today has reached the villages where the literacy is yet to grow up matching to the towns and cities. This population becomes victim of reactions to the electronic news items due to lack of knowledgeable information even though their intent may be altogether different. With the digital system spreading fast through the country, the impact of what is seen on the electronic media may sometimes misfire leading to ugly situations and law and order problems. These considerations need to be accorded due place in reporting the news items on the electronic media.

Our country has come out of the clutches of an Empire that controlled us for two hundred years. Time we shed the Empire Jacket in every aspect of our functioning as a democratic country including the Fourth Pillar – the Media - particularly the Electronic Media which has the quickest reach to the people that places on it a higher degree of responsibility and obligation to ensure fairness in all respects of the constitutional spirit including, in particular the obligations prescribed under the FUNDAMENTAL DUTIES IN EQUAL TERMS AS WE MOVE TO CATCH THE FUNDAMENTAL RIGHTS. The democracy rests on this fundamental structure and ensures smoothened passage of life for every citizen.

Electronic Media, in a wider view, includes broadcast by electronic devices, such as social media platforms, the internet, radio, and television. These media types enable the electronic delivery of information and entertainment to a sizable audience. Electronic media can be interactive, like the internet and social media, or broadcast, television and radio.

They are crucial to contemporary communication and are now an integral part of many people's daily lives worldwide. As more and more people now consume media on electronic devices like smartphones, tablets, and computers, electronic media has grown in importance today. It provides an easy and simple approach to accessing a wide range of information and entertainment.

Supreme Court's judgment in the Ranganath Mishra case: The Court observed that fundamental duties should not only be enforced by legal sanctions but also by social sanctions. After all, **rights and duties were co-relative.**

Although it is difficult to foresee exactly how electronic media will change, it will probably greatly impact our lives. Future trends and advancements in electronic media might include the following:

1. Increasing usage of artificial intelligence: Artificial intelligence (AI) will probably be used more and more in electronic media to improve and customise the user experience. A user's interests can be used to promote material, improve search results, and help with chores like translation.

2. Virtual and augmented reality will be more fully incorporated into media: Virtual reality (VR) and augmented reality (AR) technologies are anticipated to increase and be more fully included in electronic media. The uses of VR and AR for gaming, education, and other purposes may fall under this category.

3. Streaming services: will certainly continue to gain popularity and might eventually displace traditional cable or satellite TV subscriptions. Examples of this include Netflix and Hulu.

4. Wider use of 5G technologies: In the upcoming years, 5G technology is anticipated to become more generally accessible, enabling quicker and more dependable internet connections and creating new apps and services.

5. Greater emphasis on cybersecurity: To guard against online dangers and data breaches, there will undoubtedly be increasing emphasis on cybersecurity as electronic media becomes more pervasive and interwoven into our daily lives.

6. Social media platforms will probably keep evolving and might even start integrating more seamlessly with other digital media, such as messaging applications and streaming services.

Time when the Fundamental Duties were incorporated in our Constitution, the Electronic Media in our country was in formative stage. The use and disuse of the emerging information in every walk of life and its impact on the citizens of the country was not then anticipated. This is now outgrowing whereby the central government had to enter this area for regulation. Even there being regulations, the Media Houses are overlooking them in many respects, the examples of which have been submitted before. It will be beneficial to also include pros and cons of the Electronic Media, more particularly, the attitudinal concerns that have direct reflection on the viewers, in the Fundamental Duties and a law need to be made pronouncing the penalties for breach of the Duties. Absence of a law on breach of Fundamental Duties is encouraging the citizens towards more breach than observance of the Duties.

THE ROLE OF LAW IN A STATE OF LAWLESSNESS -) PLEADERS - JUNE 17, 2021 [Excerpts]:

Introduction

"Merriam- Webster defines lawlessness as the state where wrongdoing is widespread and there is disregard for rules and authority. State of lawlessness indicates how the administration of the country has become worse with time. Today, people by grouping together are taking law into their own hands and inventing their own rules and not abiding by the rules of the nation. They are not scared by the law, not even by the Supreme Court. The increase in these situations is making our nation a state of lawlessness.

The norms and the ideas of fairness and decency that were accepted by all the sides in the nation are long lost. It is the same nation that got its freedom way back in 1947 and is still struggling to get justice, not because of outsiders but due to our own people this time. The state of lawlessness is an important issue as it is creating an atmosphere of fear and affecting the faith that the people have in the judicial system of the country…………..

Viewing 21st century India as a state of lawlessness

Threat to constitutional morality:

Several states in India have regulations that prohibit the sale of cows for slaughter. But still, in Uttar Pradesh, the cow vigilante groups are taking the law into their hands and protecting the cows by spreading lawlessness and inflaming communalism within their own community. If the administration of the state does not take action against this then our constitutional morality will suffer.

The major causes responsible for creating a state of lawlessness:

The oppression by the agents of the state and the unwillingness of the political leaders to take action are some of the reasons that are responsible. The practice of taking and giving bribes is not stopping. Even for small needs like water connection, making of birth and death certificate and even to file a police complaint, bribes are taken.

Along with these, the other major causes that are responsible are as follows-

Dying democracy

The methods used by the Britishers at the time when they ruled India, are now being used by the police in our democratic country. If a citizen raises his voice against some wrongdoing or stands in a protest supporting others then they are beaten up by the police mercilessly. This is how our democracy is dying. The day is not far away when we can't even go to these protectors of law to claim our rights.

Paralysed parliament

Parliament being the voice of the citizens has now almost stopped doing that. The political parties have tried to paralyse the parliament; it is being prevented from making the needed laws. There is a large number of absent members in the meeting and day by day, the number of meetings is decreasing.

Time taking delivery of justice

Our judiciary is overburdened with cases. There are over 1.4 judges per 100,000 population in India. For this lawlessness to be abolished, we need speedy delivery of justice so that serious issues that are increasing today in the modern world could be acknowledged and justice to be given.

The possible solution towards curbing lawlessness

We need to take full action to make our constitution work. Firstly, the state must put in the effort to provide speedy delivery of justice. Our judicial system needs a massive investment to face this issue. We need the government to come closer to the needs of the people. The state government must be given an increase in power and resources.

Lastly, those people are needed who do not avoid the call to public service to join the political parties. The recruitment rules of senior bureaucracy must be changed now and deserving people may fill the seats.

There is a chance for communalism to arise by some political design. It is high time for India to have a strong resistance against these communal passions.

Conclusion

The question arises can we stop this injustice and disregard for rules and authority. It is a, yes, we can, we had done it before when the people of the nation stood together against the Britishers and got their freedom. So why not now, when it's our own people of the nation who need to know the power of unity.

With the evolution of society, there is an evolution in the laws. For example, sati pratha and child marriage. With time people realized that these rituals are against the rights of the weaker section and then these practices were abolished. Similarly, in modern times where the crime rate is touching heights, there is desperation to enforce new and strong laws.

The consequences of this lawlessness are more violent and more deaths in the name of fighting evil."

"State machinery has a duty to be committed to the rule of law and demonstrate its ability and willingness to follow the rules it itself makes, for its actions to not transgress into the domain of 'governmental lawlessness- Hon'ble Supreme Court.

These words were recorded by a Supreme Court Bench led by Justice Chandrachud while addressing the appalling working conditions of trial courts in our country. The court was commenting on how the judiciary should be immune from political pressures and considerations.

The court recognised "governmental lawlessness" as one of the threats to keeping the judiciary immune from political pressures. It said that a judiciary that is susceptible to such pressures allows politicians to operate with impunity and incentivizes criminality to flourish in the political apparatus of the state."

What is submitted above is a poisonous mixture of political and police brains. When this happens on any account, one has no option but to say that the rule of law has been brainwashed. Wikipedia states ….' Brainwashing has become a common theme in popular culture, especially in science fiction.[6] In casual speech, "brainwashing" and its verb form, "brainwash", are used figuratively to describe the use of propaganda to persuade or sway public opinion.[7] The brainwashing has now entered into and embraced the investigating agencies and law enforcing authorities. They are guided in their duties more by the state and the politicians than guiding them according to rule of law. [Emphasis added].

Democracy is a mirror where one can clearly see the truth but the mirror also serves as a door to that darkroom just behind it where our chosen representatives are free to take decisions to serve their personal interests to acquire power and property of the people in the name of the people. The representatives are doing so by continuously hammering the minds of its people with their own dreams and desires through promises, planning, theories, concerns, inquiries, and commissions that ultimately take the images on the mirror of democracy as our own, painted by our rulers in the disguise of servants. However, this scenario can be changed if the citizens take effective participation, fulfil obligations, and hold public authorities accountable for their actions. Such behavioural attitudes on the part of the chosen representatives not only their character, also undermines the democratic spirit which is governed by the Rule of Law. First duty to observe the Rule of law is of the legislators, the politicians and the citizens failing that they will be jeopardizing the very democratic functioning.

Rule of law imposes a duty on all citizens in a parliamentary democracy to obey the law and for such obedience the law itself must be just law and not arbitrary or oppressive law. The aim of rule of law like other constitutional principles is the uplifting of freedom and fundamental rights of the people.

The legal system we have and the rule of law are far more responsible for our traditional liberties than any system of one man one vote. Any country or Government which wants to proceed towards tyranny starts to undermine legal rights and undermine the law. Respect for the rule of law is about belief in the capacity of that law to dispense justice, fairness and equa for all. But laws aren't passed by principles - they're passed by governments, and governments can be unjust and unfair. Law is order, and good law is good order. The rule of law doesn't mean the police are in charge, but that we all answer to the same laws. Freedom prospers when religion is vibrant and the rule of law under God is acknowledged.

It is most apathetic that while those who committed minor crimes are caught instantly, tried in a court of law and put behind the bar for months, if not years; those who committed serious crimes enjoying the state and the influential politicians patronage are covered up on one or the other excuse because that suits both most. How can we say we are a largest democratic country when we don't believe that the Rule of Law works like oiling the wheels in democracy? Jungle is the last word one can say when a country works without "RULE OF LAW". Absence of Rule of Law in a country makes its citizens walk just as wild animals walk in wilderness. Let the citizens of the country know that their life itself is in danger when they discard and disrespect the Rule of Law because the Rule of Law is the breathe of the democracy. A practical example of the importance of the rule of law for democracy building is the fact that the rule of law is a fundamental principle embraced in most modern democracies. Constitutions contain the fundamental and, most often, supreme law of the State, and the rule of law dictates the enforcement of those principles above all other laws.

Rule of law and democracy are both desirable attributes of a political system. Scholars writing of democratic transitions from authoritarian rule usually argue that the goal of such a transition is the establishment of democracy with the rule of law, implying that both may be achieved simultaneously. Perhaps that is so.

In reality, what has been happening in our country is the reverse Rule of Law. As noted before, such a situation occurs in a country where the critical organs such as the state, the political parties and the law enforcing authorities establish among themselves an invisible relationship that compromises their fundamental duties under the constitution and the relevant laws and remain outside the purview of the citizens of the country. That is the first reason why the injustice prevails over the justice upon the citizens of the country choking the Rule of Law that has prejudicial effects and unbearable impact on the citizens. The governance, the administrative and enforcing systems once merge within themselves, the citizens are blocked from seeking fair and reasonable response and get tired in trying to pursue it. In certain cases, they become an object of revengeful attitude and action as a matter of vendetta that is inherent in those who control the nerves of democratic working. In such situations, the citizens, although have the machinery and mechanism for redressal and for seeking relief but that lies within the boundary of judicial system which is the one system that gives a ray of hope. The judicial system referred to herein is the higher judicial system for; what I have narrated above about the plight of the people caught in the midstream also happens in the lower judiciary generally leaving a lone choice for the citizens to knock the doors of the higher judiciary which is unaffordable for a common man and is as good as non-existent. The constitution gives guarantees to the citizens for their survival but the survival is interdependent upon the constitutional instruments which is mostly wished for but not able to be sought for.

My foregoing submissions are the result of my inability to resist because the real and reverse rule of law continue to be present in every step of life of an ordinary citizen of the country who hardly understands what the rule of law is about let alone contesting it where it is breached. That capacity is not the one denied by the Creator but denied by the governance for lack of educational ability and economic means to manage self, live with self-respect and self-dignity which is the Chorus of our Constitution that is what the citizens are made to believe but not accessible due to lack of respect for the Rule of Law. So, it remains as a dream and a bubble in the air. Understanding these negative effects upon the citizens by the constitutional authorities is respecting the Rule of Law. That fulfils our duty and obligation towards our Fundamental Duties lest, though they are readable but will remain unread. The Rule of Law has the capacity to make the Fundamental Duties in golden colour with country flying high in every respect. When that transforms in reality, there would be few cries for Fundamental Rights. It is the avoidance of Fundamental Duties that is prompting people to resort to Fundamental Rights.

It is like holding gold in one hand and silver in other hand and advocating that the gold is more valuable than silver forgetting the fact that the gold looks more beautifying when it is mixed with silver and silver looks more beautifying when it is mixed with gold. Gold may be having a higher value than silver but its beautification is much impressive when mixed with silver. That is what the difference between the Fundamental Rights and the Fundamental Duties though the former is enforceable and the latter is not enforceable but that doesn't make difference seen from the intent of their incorporation in the Constitution. Each differs in terms of value but both together make the man and the woman more harmonious.

Online Dictionary states "Yes, silver and gold can complement each other beautifully in various design contexts. The combination of these metallic shades can create an appealing contrast and add visual interest. The key is to balance and harmonize the two colors effectively, considering factors such as the desired aesthetic, overall design theme, and personal preference. When you mix gold and silver together, you get a fascinating color that can range from a greenish yellow to a pale or bright yellow." An Article posted on the Website also states that the resulting color has a beautiful metallic tone that looks elegant and sophisticated. The exact outcome may vary based on how much of each color you use and the lighting conditions.

The Fundamental Rights and the Fundamental Duties are to be considered as having the same character. The Fundamental Rights are incomplete if the same are not complimentary and compatible with Fundamental Duties.

"OUR DUTIES NATURALLY EMERGE FORM SUCH FUNDAMENTAL RELATIONS AS OUR FAMILIES, NEIGHBORHOODS, WORKPLACES, OUR STATE OR NATION. MAKE IT YOUR REGULAR HABIT TO CONSIDER YOUR ROLES-PARENT, CHILD, NEIGHBOR, CITIZEN, LEADER-AND THE NATURAL DUTIES THAT ARISE FROM

THEM. ONCE YOU KNOW WHO YOU ARE AND TO WHOM YOU ARE LINKED, YOU WILL KNOW WHAT TO DO." — EPICTETUS

From the time of the inception of the Constitution and the country becoming Republic, what one could observe is that the governance grossly neglected the due place that was supposed to have been accorded for the Fundamental Duties. With due respects to the Judiciary, it is found that the judiciary also laid more weightage on the Fundamental Rights and later on interpreted that it was due to the non-observance of the Fundamental Duties that has given rise to rush to recourse to the Fundamental Rights by the citizens. We are not immature in understanding in our duties in our daily life towards each other and do observe them but what we do in real in that respect is disrespecting the Fundamental Duties as if these are of a different category and need not be intertwined with Fundamental Rights. That makes us to talk about every now and then about the Fundamental Duties; these are, however, not being enforceable, the aggrieved one feels helpless seeking mercy from the co-citizens and the governing system. Might is the Right that is what we believe most fitting for survival than accepting that the constitutional duties as the Right greater than Might which alone has the capacity to control the Might. Otherwise, the Might will continue to be increasing and the Right will continue to be the victim of the Might.

An individual is the fundamental organ of a State and each organ is required to work unitedly to achieve the means of welfare State. An Individual plays a vital role in a State and its welfare and is entitled to exercise rights. India, the largest democracy in the world, whose Bible is the 'Constitution' enshrines in its Preamble for the "People of India", the principles of Justice, Liberty, Equality and Fraternity[4]. Fundamental rights are guaranteed by the Constitution under Part III and have originated from a collective sourcing of other countries' like USA, Britain, Australia and Canada. Pertinently, it is evident from the Preamble of the Constitution that it primarily focuses on rights in all spheres of life to shelter, protect and secure its citizens. Duties are counterparts of rights. Fundamental duties find their way into the Indian Constitution through the controversial 42nd Amendment....

Duties are an ancient concept encompassed in the eastern jurisprudence as an aspect of human behavior known as "Dharma"[5], staunch admirers, of which were luminaries like Lokmanya Tilak[6] and Mohandas Gandhi. The concept of duties has its origin in the Vedas and they are in the form of religious commands. Epics like Bhagavad Geeta, Ramayana and Mahabharat, also enshrine duty as part of one's Dharma. Thus, the eastern jurisprudence is duty oriented and right is considered as ancillary to duty or consequence of performing duty. It is indisputable, that the framers of the Constitution did not deem it appropriate to incorporate duties in the text of the Constitution, when it was originally promulgated as there would have been several reasons for such omission in light of sufferance....

The Bhagavad-Gita reveals how anyone can perform ordinary duties in the world and yet remain free from the consequences of one's actions. It is not by inaction, not even by doing only the so called good deeds, one attains liberation, but by doing deeds without the sense of doer-ship as a sacrificial offering to God in the true spirit of renunciation and without shunning the responsibility, which comes with birth.

In Islam obedience to the law of the land is a religious duty. The Qur'an commands Muslims to remain faithful to not only Allah and the Prophet Muhammad (sa), but also the authority they live under: O ye who believe! Obey Allah, and obey His Messenger and those who are in authority over you (Ch.4: V.60).

Peter said in the passage just before this one (i. e. verses 11, 12) that the good lives of believers help to win over the unbelieving world. Then he shows us exactly how this works as we do our duty to the civil government. 1 Peter 2:13-14 show what our duty is: Submit yourselves to every ordinance of man for the Lord's sake: whether it be the king, as supreme; or unto governors, as unto them that are sent by him for the punishment of evildoers, and for the praise of them that do well.

The Supreme Court on Monday (February 21)[2022] issued notices to the Centre and states in a writ petition seeking the enforcement of the fundamental duties of citizens as enshrined in the Constitution of India. The petition, filed by advocate Durga Dutt, argues that citizens have a duty to uphold the ideals of the country and to contribute to its growth and betterment, and that not carrying out the fundamental duties of the citizen has a direct bearing on the fundamental rights guaranteed under Articles 14, 19 and 21 of the Constitution.

"The Fundamental Duties are intended to serve as a constant reminder to every citizen that while the Constitution conferred on them certain Fundamental Rights specifically, it also requires citizens to observe certain basic norms of democratic conduct and democratic behaviour because rights and duties are correlative… There have been cases where Fundamental Duties have been brazenly flouted by the people including the officers of the law and which in turn resulted in violation of Fundamental rights of other citizens," the petition argued.

After hearing arguments, the bench also comprising Justice M.M. Sundresh issued notice to Centre and state governments. The plea said: "It is submitted that the fundamental duties are intended to serve as a constant reminder to every citizen that while the Constitution conferred on them certain Fundamental Rights specifically, it also requires citizens to observe certain basic norms of democratic conduct and democratic behaviour because rights and duties are correlative."

The Holy Scriptures of all the Religions command the citizens to be obedient to the Constitutional Duty of the country to which they belong as stated before.

The matter is under Sub Judice in the Hon'ble Supreme Court of India, I refrain myself from making any further comments or pleadings in respect thereof.

However, it may be submitted that the breach of any Official Duty attributable to a citizen under any law is liable for punishment under the applicable law but in the case of breach of Constitutional laid down Fundamental Duties, there is no express law that specifies any punishment in the case breach of Fundamental Duties any punishment, in whatsoever manner. The Freedom of Speech guaranteed to the citizen under the Constitution negates the obligations of citizens imposed under the Fundamental Duties. This is also a paradox much needed to be addressed by the governance but neglected so far. This has encouraged the citizens to speak what they liked against each other individually, in religious and in the political process those otherwise amounts to breach of the Fundamental Duties.

PART 04
GOVERNANCE AND CITIZENS' MORAL VALUES PARADOX

"FUTURE GENERATIONS WILL JUDGE US NOT BY WHAT WE SAY, BUT WHAT WE DO." ELLEN JOHNSON SIRLEAF

Are we abiding the above Quote today? Answer is not assuring rather avoiding looking at the today's political, religious and social environment. The readers are well aware what political, religious and social environment means for; they are going through them grudgingly rather than generously. Anything we do today is not merely for ourselves but for our posterity as well. It thus places a higher level of duty and responsibility upon us that we guard the governance and ourselves as citizens of the country to build robust and sustainable values of life passed on to us by our ancestors and the edicts ingrained in the Holy Scripts of our respective Faiths. I have dealt at length in the succeeding part of this book as to where we stand today in respecting and upholding the values of life both in governance and as citizens. These values are like nectar, that being the reason that our ancestors continued to adopt them as integral to the way of life on Mother Earth. So also is the case with the other living beings on Mother Earth which are also governed by their own way of life laid down by the Nature.

"It is said that "Country is controlled by Laws;

- **Laws are controlled by Politics**
- **Politicians are controlled by Voters**
- **Voters are controlled by Public Opinion**
- **Public Opinion is controlled by the Media and Education**

So, whoever controls Media and Education controls the country. "

William J. Federer [News, Hollywood, Internet]

This Quote aptly applies to the governance and citizens of the country today. Because, what we are doing today is more leaned towards boasting. Online Dictionary defines boasting as – 'To talk or write about oneself or something related to oneself in a proud or self-admiring way.' The ruling political system says what we have done or doing should make every citizen proud of it side-lining the fact that whatever strength the country holds today also holds the past within its fold. That suggests we must give greater respect to the past and make best efforts to safeguard the interests of the generations to come that would acknowledge them with gratefulness. That should be the duty and responsibility of the present generation to ensure what we do today add to the strength of future. The political parties in opposition, on the other hand, never accept whatever is said by the ruling party claiming when they were the ruling party, they had done much more than the present governing system and the present governing system must acknowledge this first before it says what it has done or is doing. A paradoxical situation stands that is affecting affinity of understanding between them. The working of democracy should not be as conferring a right only to criticise but not weigh the criticism in the best interests of the people and country and, if such weighing shows as something not in the interests of the country, the democracy also allows the critics to come forward with alternative suggestions or solutions failing which, one is constrained to think that animosity is more dominating over the search for the alternatives. Such posture either for the party in power or for the opposition continues to inflict increasing width in the parliamentary system of working. This is not being appreciated, as a result of which, the parliament is gradually turning into a ground to play for all kinds of games. It has direct reflection upon the constituents and the younger generation to whom such situations are promoting them to repeat the same outside, highly harmful to the democracy.

The narration in the preceding paragraphs also suggests that neither of the ruling nor opposition parties according at least minimum, if not maximum, attention towards the obligation they hold to do whatever we could that should be in the interests and betterment of future generations that makes them strong enough to face the challenges they confront. The present system should be able to foresee the kinds of challenges to come in future foreseeing the developments on the horizon. This is an essential onus that lies on the present generation that includes sensing of the future based on the extrapolation of the ongoing situations. What lies on horizon for the future generation is unpredictable that does not mean the present dispensation should not have any concern. Our forefathers who drafted the Constitution of the country foresaw the future through their farsightedness which stands as a greatest strength and spirit of the constitution sustaining with such marginal changes as considered necessary in the present circumstances. That is a kind of constitutional strength our forefathers grasped and made over to the coming generation. For that, we remain grateful to them since last seventy three years of the country becoming Republic. There had been and may continue to be there in the future one or other critical time and ups and downs which are possible for the present system to adjust and absorb them within the constitutional framework. That should guide us in building up a solid future.

"I saw behind me those who had gone, and before me, those who are to come. I looked back and saw my father, and his father, and all our fathers, and in front, to see my son, and his son, and the sons upon sons beyond. And their eyes were my eyes.

As I felt, so they had felt, and were to feel, as then, so now, as tomorrow and forever. Then I was not afraid, for I was in a long line that had no beginning, and no end, and the hand of his

father grasped my father's hand, and his hand was in mine, and my unborn son took my right hand, and all, up and down the line stretched from Time That Was, to Time That Is, and is not yet, raised their hands to show the link, and we found that we were one, born of Woman, Son of Man, had in the Image, fashioned in the Womb by the Will of God, the eternal Father.

**I was one of them, they were of me, and in me, and I in all of them."
— Richard Llewellyn, How Green Was My Valley**

The context calls for recalling here UNESCO 'Declaration on the Responsibilities of the Present Generations towards Future Generations which reads as follows [Excerpts]:

"United Nations Educational, Scientific and Cultural Organization. [UNESCO] - Declaration on the Responsibilities of the Present Generations towards Future Generations – Paris, France 12 November, 1997:

The General Conference of the United Nations Educational, Scientific and Cultural Organization, meeting in Paris from 21 October to 12 November 1997 at its 29th session,

Mindful of the will of the peoples, set out solemnly in the Charter of the United Nations, to 'save succeeding generations from the scourge of war' and to safeguard the values and principles enshrined in the Universal Declaration of Human Rights, and all other relevant instruments of international law,

Considering the provisions of the International Covenant on Economic, Social and Cultural Rights and the International Covenant on Civil and Political Rights, both adopted on 16 December 1966, and the Convention on the Rights of the Child, adopted on 20 November 1989,

Concerned by the fate of future generations in the face of the vital challenges of the next millennium,

Conscious that, at this point in history, the very existence of humankind and its environment is threatened,

Stressing that full respect for human rights and ideals of democracy constitute an essential basis for the protection of the needs and interests of future generations,

Asserting the necessity for establishing new, equitable and global links of partnership and intergenerational solidarity, and for promoting inter-generational solidarity for the perpetuation of humankind,

Recalling that the responsibilities of the present generations towards future generations have already been referred to in various instruments such as the Convention for the Protection of the World Cultural and Natural Heritage, adopted by the General Conference of UNESCO on 16 November 1972, the United Nations Framework Convention on Climate Change and the Convention on Biological Diversity, adopted in Rio de Janeiro on 5 June 1992, the Rio Declaration on Environment and Development, adopted by the United Nations Conference on Environment and Development on

14 June 1992, the Vienna Declaration and Programme of Action, adopted by the World Conference on Human Rights on 25 June 1993, and the United Nations General Assembly resolutions relating to the protection of the global climate for present and future generations adopted since 1990,

Determined to contribute towards the solution of current world problems through increased international co-operation, to create such conditions as will ensure that the needs and interests of future generations are not jeopardized by the burden of the past, and to hand on a better world to future generations,

Resolved to strive to ensure that the present generations are fully aware of their responsibilities towards future generations,

Recognizing that the task of protecting the needs and interests of future generations, particularly through education, is fundamental to the ethical mission of UNESCO, whose Constitution enshrines the ideals of 'justice and liberty and peace' founded on 'the intellectual and moral solidarity of mankind',

Bearing in mind that the fate of future generations depends to a great extent on decisions and actions taken today, and that present-day problems, including poverty, technological and material underdevelopment, unemployment, exclusion, discrimination and threats to the environment, must be solved in the interests of both present and future generations,

Convinced that there is a moral obligation to formulate behavioural guidelines for the present generations within a broad, future-oriented perspective,

Solemnly proclaims on this twelfth day of November 1997 this Declaration on the Responsibilities of the Present Generations towards Future Generations ...."

The Quote cited before that those who control the Education and Media control the country seems to have become more attractive and best suited considering the way we are developing the country today. Self-boasting has overtaken the bounden duty of the governance to build the future for the next generation. Media is virtually controlled by the centralized system that consists of the governing system, the opposition system and the tycoons who establish Media Channels. Each is perceptibly supporting the other for self-survival. Media managers are able to read the mood of the public and coin their programmes to show how important is what is shown or what is printed in the newspapers for the public consumption. What we see both in the print and electronic today? We see full page self-made and self-presented advertisement by the state and central governments along with the photos of PM/CM that mesmerises the readers about the developmental programmes and their achievements disregarding the reality that exists on the ground. 'This is known as self-boasting. Boasting is commonly defined as talking in a self-admiring way or glorifying oneself. It is often thought of as excessive pride. We tend to think of people who boast as arrogant, self-preoccupied, or, perhaps, insecure, which may be why they need to boast in the first place.' [Online Dictionary]

Is doing that necessary or use that expenditure for human welfare? Answers to the first part of the question is that it is as good as blinding the eyes of the people for; people are capable to knowing the real development which depends on they experience in their daily life. Why should we show something on paper not verifiable by the people and made believe it to be so? There is no need to talk or show about the economic development in the newspapers and electronic media, except as a quid pro quo deal, because people want daily necessities of life easily accessible and affordable. That is the daily concern of the poor and the poorest people of the country which, if addressed aggressively, no self-demonstration of what I have done need to be made. Let us realize this ethical and moral responsibility on the governing system through ministers, secretaries etc. from the top to bottom level. This should ingrain in every part of the governance and administration of food security and law and order. Don't say we will do, say we have done for the betterment of the people. This has the double power engine capacity that makes the people to accept it as reality than rhetoric. Life cannot survive on rhetoric but on reality. By not realizing this makes reality far from one's reach.

Answer to the second part of the question is that It not only incurs large expenditure from the exchequer or the political parties HQrs but whatever may be the source, the money spent is an expenditure which is otherwise supposed to be earmarked and deployed for the educational and economic development of the country that would ease the yoke of burden on the people reeling under the poverty. The educational and economic development is based on visibility and not invisibility. Truth could be seen only through visibility while the invisibility is one that could hear through ears. Truth lies in eyes and not ears that are what the politicians should learn to understand and practice in a nation's life. What is shown in the print and electronic media about the promises and performance are made to believe for; the need to do that should not have arisen if what is done is visible and truth. It is a kind of political maneuvering that blinds and does not brighten the peoples' eagerness and expectations. Let us save financial resources as much as we can avoiding such moves and apply those resources for real education and economic development that creates indelible truth in the mind of the people and brings them more closure with them who believe in performance in place of promises. This is the sense and essence of the development.

Let me now deal with the electronic media. This is open to one and everyone who wants to build his or her electronic image before the viewers. The channel selects topics and eminent people to speak about a subject matter. The running news items are shown in piecemeal, one neither able to understand the beginning nor the end. Half of the space on the electronic media shown is reserved and used for filmy items and for latest advertisements. There is nothing wrong since electronic media considers it as one way for its own survival. I have seen the companies, an One Man company or private company or public limited company or of group of companies controlled by a holding company, LLP etc. making public their annual financial working and operational results in the media covering both print and electronic. This is so because it is statutorily mandated. There is also a need for adopting such statutory mandate on the media channel owners to publish their annual financial results specially the capital income including the capital contributions, the working and operational results according to the periodicity as may be prescribed by the central government. Time has come to do this now in order to financially regulate the media channels. These channels show the results of others stated before except of their own. I presume the Media Houses are registered and governed under one or the other existing laws. There is need to incorporate in these laws, if not already exist that like others stated before, the Media Houses should also publish their Balance Sheet and P&L Account with all the Disclosures in the Forms laid down under those laws and, if not, a new provision needs to be introduced under the existing laws where under those are registered.

They may be also LLP or companies but whether the financial disclosures are obligatory or not is not known. The Hon'ble Supreme Court of India has been observing on the need for regulating the electronic media especially with respect to the contents of the news items as reported in the newspapers. The central government, as reported in newspapers, issued an advisory to the electronic media channels not to highlight the criminals and anti-social elements. The veracity of the electronic media should be factual without mixing their own presumptions and conclusions. Presenting the facts without any bias and additional comments makes the viewers community free of prejudices; more so, this community has enlarged covering every corner of the country. The biased or prejudicial news items are prone to encourage restlessness in the social environment which also reappears on the electronic media.

Every one of us expects and aspires that our government should be good and effective, we also know that it was for the purpose of securing conditions for safe and happy life that the state came into existence and its continuity is justified in terms of promoting and preserving the qua of life. Kautilya considered it as the bounden duty of the government to act in a manner that realizes the material, mental, moral and cultural wellbeing of the people. It is in this context that the study of good governance has become very important in the study of political science.

Let me narrate here a tiny story titled – 'A BLIND KING NOT BLIND'

'There was a King. He used to walk in the garden of the palace daily morning. One day, he found his younger daughter sitting below a big tree. He walked up to her and asked why she is sitting alone under this tree. 'O' Father King, I sit here to seek solitude. King asked don't you find it within the palace? Your elder sister enjoys within the palace. The daughter replied I cannot find it in the humdrum in the palace.

How do you explain, the King asked? Daughter replied you are King. You need to know which one is Truth, seeing through the eyes or hearing through the ears. King got bit confused. So, he asked her to explain relationship of these characters with the King. She replied, 'O' Father King, you are not King for yourself but for the welfare of your subjects. King asked what is wrong with the welfare of the subjects. She told you spend so many resources for the welfare of your subjects but never have time to test whether that welfare is real or rhetoric. King said that is the function of my Prime Minister and Ministers. She told him that is your assumption but reality stands apart. Because, your subjects are not happy, they being denied the welfare benefits. The subjects say the ministers believe they are also subjects holding different positions and they are also entitle to a share in the welfare benefits that is where lies the gap between what you believe and what your subject say.

She told King 'TRUTH LIES IN YOUR EYES AND NOT EARS'. You are not blind but blind without blindness because you believe what the ears tell and not the eyes see.'

Futuristic financial and economic strength hinges upon to what extent we are honest to the purpose we are pursuing for the sake of the future generations. They also measure up themselves where they stand looking at the past and what past has done for them from where they could proceed to make the nation stronger. What we have done or doing today stands staring at them. It is not known whether and when we would wake up from unconsciousness to understand what real is what honesty is, what integrity is and what commitment and sacrificing mean is, from the point of the future generation. It is so because we have not lived up today to the ethical and moral values our ancestors stood for, our Saints preached for and Mother Earth wished for. Our obsession towards selfishness rather than the service and sacrifice for nation and the people has by now deep rooted. Our first duty now, right now, to uproot it and return to our past noble and valued culture that includes ethical and moral values. Failing to do so now would make us to pass on the same distorted and selfish culture to the future generation.

Above given back up bears the foundation for our capacity to build up resources for the futuristic economic growth and welfare of the people of the country. Though it looks as a different subject from what has been made out above but the nations and people can stand up to the challenges and threats of the times to come only when their body and bones have inherited their our own ethical and moral values that form the ancestors and universal basics. Truthfulness in us cultivates the same truthfulness in others. With this brief background, I now proceed to remind the governments how and from where we could garner wealth and build a reservoir of wealth for the nation.

One, deepening pollution in the political system; second, burning heat in the religious system; third, utter disrespect to the Rule of Law; fourth, political leaders, corporate, those involved in every other activity becoming morally corrupt with no exception of the enforcing authorities; and fifth undermining the education system and loss of moral values among school and college going children have far reaching impact on the overall political, economic and education areas, the spinal cord of the country's and peoples' growth and welfare. Greater than these, every act done to achieve those objects is defended with full force articulating the arguments and trying to provide a sense of superiority as strong enough to sustain their approach and thinking without substance or substantiation. A system grows on validation and substantiation process whether such process is passed on to us by the preceding generation or trying to experiment them in a newer concept by the present generation. This is highly dangerous and self-denigrating. They do not seem to remember the popular Quote "Shameless self-publicity works, of course: living your life as a soap opera." - Chris

Lowe. Let us prevent it as earliest as possible so that it is not passed on to the futuristic democracy and its generation(s).

Existing practice has been made permanent as if the state has no alternative or the state does not want to think about the same at all. As noticeable, the state seems to be more interested in promoting and encouraging the existing system; if that is so; how the society or the people of the country would be able assume elections as fair and transparent elections? Or, does the state want that the present financing system is an accepted practice, fair and transparent, citizens should not question it, the political parties employ it as a right means of financing and the governance would be conducted by the party winning the elections? What a citizen could do under these conditions? At best, go to the highest Court of Law at own cost. Why we are indifferent to ourselves when we know what we are doing about financing election cannot stand to moral and ethical test? Or, should we say moral and ethical tests are nothing to do with election financing? This is an integral part of moral and moral values that, therefore, demand that the extant election financing method must be stopped forthwith and the alternatives should be explored. Otherwise, we will be pouring oil in the fire already lit up not knowing that the fire has the capacity to consume the oil poured until the time there is oil and, when that happens, the fire engulfs the people around. Let us not put this to a testing point and act well in time to prevent such eventuality.

No political party can pretend to have its hands clean, or even cleaner than the other. A handful of individual leaders may be able to claim a kind of personal honesty but none is entitled to a claim of ignorance about his/her party's ability to access dirty money. No political party can claim to be morally superior when it comes to receiving — or extorting —funds from businessmen, big or small.

A country that is assorted, but still it is united, not only joins value to the nation but is also appreciated on international platforms. It sets an example for all nations by highlighting the values and morals of citizens who respect and encourage each other despite their different backgrounds and cultures.

"A machine is a great moral educator. If a horse or a donkey won't go, men lose their tempers and beat it; if a machine won't go, there is no use beating it. You have to think and try till you find what is wrong. That is real education." — Gilbert Murray.

Though the life styles and span coupled with comforts not seen hitherto are advancing along with the advancing technology, research and modernization, it is like a bare body without the spiritual eagerness and desire to acquire it and maintain which makes the body fit to face the oddest times in life, Due to absence of cultivation of the spiritual, all that is acquired in the life sums up to Zero. Moral values form the foundation of humans and whatever kind of superstructure we build must have those as the foundation. The family, social and religious psychological unrest that has been building within us has direct bearing on our way of life. Ancestral moral values handed over to us are the jewels and ought to have been given highest respect and a place of their own by the present generation. Lack of such environment is driving the youngsters who, though educationally highly knowledgeable and well informed, but it is like wearing a new dress concealing the reality of life that needs to be practised as necessarily as food is for the body. There is no objection and any kind of the mistaken notion as to the present way of life but such life if supported by the rich cultural and moral values enhances one's moral strength and the faces will show a shining sign.

ResearchGate posted an Article 'CHILDREN'S MORAL EDUCATION IN THE DIGITAL AGE' – on its Website - December 2022 - Conference: CHILDREN'S MORAL EDUCATION IN DIGITAL AGE - At: UIN KH. ABDURRAHMAN WAHID PEKALONGAN - Authors: Haris Diar Rizki, STAI Brebes, Wahid, author has taken liberty to reproduce below the Article considered beneficial to the readers and in the public interest:

"**A. Introduction**

The sophistication of science and technology at this time has made the world seem to be without borders, various kinds of virtual communication activities to all corners of the world in a short time and the advancement of technology and communication triggered various changes in human life. This is characterized by the increasingly central role of cyber technology in all areas of life.

Digitalization has an impact on all aspects of human life, patterns that are instantaneous, practical and do not pay attention to the process side, and lifestyle changes are inevitable. One of the most worrying problems is the emergence of social media that can damage morals. Children born in this day and age are now directly faced with "two worlds", namely the real world and the virtual world, parents play a very important role in creating environmental conditions so that children are better prepared to face various challenges in the digital era. Therefore, moral education becomes very important, so that the child has sufficient provisions to live the next life.

The key to one's happiness is in one's temperament and character (when one always familiarizes oneself with good character), then this is a sign of one's goodness. On this subject Ibn Qayyim explains that a person's happiness and misery are in his temperament and character, and no one can achieve good in the world and in the hereafter except with good temperament and character (Ibnu Qayyim, 1999, P. 294)

Moral education with the right method is the main key so that children are able to control themselves in using digital media and can take advantage of the sophistication of technology and communication for things that are useful for themselves, but children still avoid the bad influences they cause. So that children can achieve happiness, glory and salvation in the world and the hereafter.

B. Moral Education

In the Big Dictionary Indonesian it is explained that education is the process of changing the attitudes and practices of a person or group of people in an effort to mature people through teaching and training efforts (Departemen pendidikan, 2013, p.236).

In the Islamic context the term education has been known as at-tarbiyah. According to linguistics, tarbiyah comes from three meanings of the word -robbaba-robba-yurobbii which means to fix something and straighten it out. According to Ibn Abdillah Muhammad ibn Ahmad alAnshari al-Qurthubi means that the rabb is the owner, the all-repairing, the all-governing, the all-adding, the all-fulfilling. Meanwhile, according to al-Jauhari, it is feeding, nurturing, (Yatim Abdullah, 2012, p.22). God, because God is educational, nurturing and creator

Tarbiyah according to Ibn Qoyyim al- Jauziyah includes tarbiyah qalb (education of the heart) and tarbiyah of the body at the same time. And he explained the kaifiyah (way) of the heart and the body. He said "Between the heart and the body are equally in need of tarbiyah. Both must be grown and supplemented with nutrition so that they are able to grow perfectly and better than before (Ibnu Qayyim, 1999, p. 46).

From the description of the understanding of education, it can be understood that education is an effort to guide, foster and direct so that children get good. This is very important for parents and educators in the digital era like today so that children are able to utilize technology correctly and avoid damage caused by getting out of control in using information technology.

As for morals according to Hamzah Ya'qub comes from Arabic, plural from the word "khuluqun", meaning action. The word "khuluqun" is commensurate with the word "khalqun", meaning genesis and the word "khaliqun". It means creator and the word "makhluqun", meaning the created one. Thus, the terminological formulation of morals is a close relationship between Khaliq and makhluq and between makhluq and makhluq (Beni Ahmad S, 2010, p. 14).

According to Ibn Maskawaih morals are qualities ingrained in the soul that encourage him to do deeds without requiring thought and consideration (Abu Hasan Al Mawardi, 1985, p.243).

Al-Mawardi revealed: "A person is said to have a noble character if his mind is smooth, has a soft character, his face is cheerful, does not like to rebuke and always speaks a good word (Abu Hasan Al- Mawardi, 1985, p.243).

Shaykh Ibn Sa'di said: "Noble morals are the main and great morals. It is built on patience, gentleness and a tendency to commendable temperament. This moral also gives birth to an attitude of forgiveness, being able to be tolerant of others and happy to share benefits for others.

Commendable morals are also manifested by patience in dealing with the various evils of others, forgiving the mistakes of others and repaying their ugliness with kindness (Abdurrahman As-sa'di, p. 68).

Shaykh Ibn Sa'di said: "Noble morals are the main and great morals. It is built on patience, gentleness and a tendency to commendable temperament. This moral also gives birth to an attitude of forgiveness, being able to be tolerant of others and happy to share benefits for others.

Commendable morals are also manifested by patience in dealing with the various evils of others, forgiving the mistakes of others and repaying their ugliness with kindness.

The human tendency to do good or bad morals, is a form of process, this process is actually very instrumental in shaping the final behavior of human tendencies. This process is then used by educational experts to conceptualize so that human beings can survive in goodness, namely through education. This is where the urgency of moral education, especially children, lies, because to realize a generation of noble character in the digital era like today, the most effective way is to educate children from an early age.

Moral education is one of the educations that must be given to children as early as possible. This is because the child is still holy and clean and has not been contaminated with various bad demons. Therefore, as parents it is necessary to teach and exemplify noble deeds that are in accordance with the teachings of the Quran and the hadith of the prophet Muhammad Shalallahu'alaihiwasalam.

According to Ahmad Amin, there are several things that strengthen moral education and exalt it, namely:

1. Expand the environment of the mind, because a narrow mind is the source of some ugliness and a chaotic intellect cannot produce high morals.

2. Bond with the chosen one, this is because man likes to follow an example.

3. Read and investigate the journeys of heroes and the extraordinary-minded.

4. What is more important to give impetus to akhlah education is that one obliges himself to do good deeds for the public (putting the public interest first).

Trying to do habits with good deeds. The purpose of moral education is given to children in order to cleanse themselves of sinful and evil deeds (Ahmad Amin, 1975, p. 63-66). Because as a human being who has physical and spiritual, the physical is cleansed outwardly through jurisprudence while the spiritual is cleansed spiritually through morals. People who have a clean mind or heart will give birth to praiseworthy deeds so that with praiseworthy deeds it will give birth to a society that respects each other and is happy in the world and the hereafter.

Morals taught to children also aim so that children can know good things and are encouraged to carry them out in daily life and know despicable deeds and dangers so as not to harm the child's life. Thus the child will be able to sort out which things can be done and which man should be abandoned or shunned. Briefly, the purpose of moral education is to educate ethics and the formation of children's souls through lessons, coaching and moral guidance both carried out in schools and in the family environment.

Moral education is the first value education that children get from their families. The results of Rohner's research show that a person's childhood experiences greatly influence the development of his persona. The parenting style of parents, whether accepting or rejecting their children, will affect their emotional, behavioural, socio-cognitive development, and the health of their psychological functions until adulthood.

C. Digital Age

1. Understanding the Digital Era

The digital era is a time when most humans at that time used digital systems in their daily lives. This digital system is more sophisticated than the previous system, namely the analog system. Analog systems produce imitation signals obtained from nature, so there is often signal degradation which results in less clear signals.

Media in the digital era has the characteristic of being able to be manipulated and networked. The media capabilities of this digital era make it easier for people to receive information. The increasingly sophisticated digital technology today makes a big change to the world; the birth of various kinds of digital technologies that are increasingly advanced has emerged a lot.

Various groups have been facilitated in accessing information in many ways, and can enjoy the facilities of digital technology freely and under control. The digital age also makes the realm of people's privacy seem to be lost. Personal data recorded inside the brain of a computer makes internet residents easy to track. The digital age is not a matter of being ready or not and neither is it an option but it is already a consequence. Technology will continue to evolve and move continuously without stopping that runs in the midst of human life. Then there is no other choice but to master and control the technology properly and correctly in order to improve.

2. Positive and Negative Impacts of the Digital Age

In the development of digital technology, there are many impacts felt by humans, both positive and negative impacts. The positive impacts of the digital era include:

a. The information needed can be faster and easier to access.

b. The growth of innovation in various fields oriented towards digital technology that facilitates the process of work.

c. The emergence of digital-based mass media, especially electronic media as a source of public knowledge and information.

d. Improving the qua of human resources through the development and utilization of information and communication technology.

e. The emergence of various learning resources such as online libraries, online learning media, online discussions that can improve the qua of education.

f. The emergence of e-businesses such as online stores that provide a variety of necessities and make it easier to get them.

The negative impacts of the digital era that must be anticipated include:

a. Violation of Intellectual Property Rights (IPR) due to easy data access and causing people to commit fraud.

b. Instant thoughts where such children are trained to think short and lack concentration.

c. Misuse of knowledge to commit acts Criminal is like breaking through the banking system.

d. Decreased moral caused by easy access to and pornography sites.

e. The emergence of anti-social individualist attitudes.

D. Moral Education Methods in the Digital Era

Moral education methods that can be carried out by parents at home and educators in schools include the following:

1. Exemplary Method (Uswatun Hasanah)

Children have enormous imitator tendencies or traits, hence the uswatun hasanah method "a good example of people close to the child.

It's the most appropriate. In this case, the closest person to the child is his parents at home, therefore exemplary examples of his parents have a great influence on the mental and moral formation of children. Exemplary in education is the method that most assures its success in preparing and shaping the child in moral, spiritual and social.

Furthermore, the educator in school is the best example in the child's view that he will imitate in his actions and manners, realized or not, even imprinted in the soul and feelings of an image of the educator, whether in speech or in deeds, whether material or spiritual, known or unknown (Abdulllah Nashih Ulwan, 1981, p. 2).

Without setting a good example, the education of children will not work, and advice will not be imprinted, all forms of speech and actions of parents and educators will be imitated by the child. Gradually a child will know by itself that the actions he does are an obligation that must be carried out not solely because it follows the behavior of parents and educators.

Parents must set an example for children in the use of information technology such as the internet, gadgets, cellphones and others. Tools are used for useful things, always paying attention to the right time and place.

2. Habituation Methods

Since childhood the child must be accustomed to doing good activities, trained to behave well, taught manners and so on. Educating, training, and guiding children slowly are something that must be applied to children so that they can achieve traits and skills well, so that their beliefs and morals are firmly embedded. Morals and principles of belief, including the skills of the limbs, require a gradual process to be achieved and must be carried out habitually or

Repeatedly so that they are achieved and mastered well, and can be carried out easily and lightly, without breaking hard and finding difficulties (Muhammad Husain, 2007, p.11).

7. Method of Advice (Mau'izhah al-Hasanah)

Advice can open children's eyes to the essence of something, push it towards sublime situations, adorn it with noble morals and equip it with Islamic principles. The Qur'an's methods of calling for indictment are manifold. Sincere counsel is imprinted and influential; if it enters a clear soul, an open heart, a wise mind and then the advice will get a response as soon as possible and leave a deep mark (Abdullah Nashih Ulwan, 1981, p.68).

Advice can be in the form of advice or invitations to do or do something good and useful, with the suggestion of instilling discipline, carrying out the obligations of religious orders in children, so that finally carrying out everything with discipline that will later form a noble persona. As in the words of the Prophet that a child when he is 7 years old or perhaps below must be invited to perform the five-time prayer. Children should be invited to do prayers. So that a human being is formed who is in constant contact with his creator. Imam al-Ghazzali explained that a child, who has reached the age of tamyiz, should not be allowed to leave thaharah and prayer. Also began to be ordered to fast a few days in the month of Ramadan (Imam Ghazzali, p.197.)

Advice can also be in the form of prohibitions which is a must not to do acts that could harm yourself or others. This effort is a decisive action to stop deeds that are very clearly wrong. This prohibition is an inappropriate act to do such as stealing, fighting with his friends, and so on. This kind of deed must be so that when he grows up, doing acts that are prohibited by religion is a taboo for him. This strategy aims to form discipline or good behavior for children.

8. Attention Method

The method of education with attention is to devote, pay attention and always follow the development of children in the formation of creeds and morals, spiritual and social preparation in addition to also asking about the situation of physical education and the power of scientific results. This method of attention is the strongest method of education in the formation of a whole man and can encourage him to fulfil his responsibilities and obligations perfectly.

9. Punishment and Reward Methods

This method of punishment is an act given to children who consciously and deliberately make mistakes such as misusing information technology for crimes or obedience to Allah.

Ta'ala, so that with this punishment the child appears a sense of neglect and does not make mistakes a second time. This punishment results in a discipline in the child. . To a higher extent, it is incumbent on children not to do an act prohibited by religion. To do or not to do is not out of fear of punishment, but out of one's own conversion and is obedience to God and always expects His blessing.

Giving gifts to children when doing commendable deeds also needs to be considered, gifts are not always materials or goods, but giving gifts can also be in the form of nods with radiant faces, thumbs up and so on, it all includes gifts that have a very big influence on students. Because, with this gift, it can please children.

10. Surveillance Methods

This method is used to keep unwanted things from happening. Because man is not perfect, so most likely to always make mistakes, these deviations are always present. Therefore, before the mistakes and irregularities are made further, there should always be an effort to hold supervision. Especially nowadays, children are already good at playing gadgets, in this case parents must be able to really supervise, because if they are not supervised later children can open forbidden sites that all damage children's morals and morals.

E. Conclusion

Children's moral education needs special attention for parents. Because of the good and bad behavior of the child, depending on the education given to the child, if the child is educated with good morals, the child must be a good child and vice versa. In today's digital era with all the impacts that occur, the challenges of moral education are more complex. The right method is needed to educate children's morals, so that children in the future become human beings who have noble morals."

Self-beautification is good for person to person but that comes from according higher place over the real life. Beauty that is within is more strong and sustainable. Beauty, if seen in the mirror, hides the real and truth of the person which once disappears when one is off the mirror shows the beauty as originally exists and, at times, one feels self-humiliating when that happens because all the values of life live in the original of the human which erode of their own sooner the person get self-influenced by the external attractions which is good so long as it is within the moral limits. The paradoxes in the human life we are witnessing today are because of self-contradiction. Artificiality exists as long as it is capable of existing and, when that ends, the human comes back to realize the true value of life. There are no values greater than natural values that Mother Earth has blessed upon the humans. Modernity is also born from the original because without it, one wouldn't have understood the comparability between the two values.

Every Form or Object of Manifestation of God embodies something Greatness as made known to us by our ancestors and the Holy Scripts. This, according to me, could be the real purpose of visiting the places of our worship. Second, as earlier noted, is to offer whether by way of prayer or offering, with fullest Belief, Faith and Devotion which are the Real Prayers and Offerings for God which He expects and accepts with greatest pleasure and confers His blessings where one fulfils that oblation. God is not concerned with the size and value of the offer so long as the person offering does not understand the Essence of God manifested in Form or Object on the Earth. That Essence is not to show but share with other humans and other living beings on earth. Because God exists in every human and other living being, what one is doing for them is doing for God. This is the Truth and the only Truth for one who wants to perceive the perceptions of God. This practice in life creates a place of Contentment in oneself which is the Ultimate object of Human Living. Those who practice the Qualities, Justice and Equality in their life are able to cut the negativity at the root.

GOD IS THE LIGHT SHINING IN THE MIDST OF DARKNESS, NOT TO DENY THAT THERE IS DARKNESS IN THE WORLD BUT TO REASSURE US THAT WE DO NOT HAVE TO BE AFRAID OF THE DARKNESS BECAUSE DARKNESS WILL ALWAYS YIELD TO LIGHT." –HAROLD S. KUSHNER

This portion is not dealing with ritually written historical background of corruption, black money and fake currency nor their changing causes and channels nor it is measuring the their length and width in terms of statistical presentation which are available already in various reports, books, lectures, seminars etc.. This portion makes an earnest effort to touch the core curiosity of the people being attracted towards corruption, black money and fake currency undertaking innovative avenues that offer scope for trials and errors and, once through, expand their operative motives and methods by blinding the checks and balances in the laws and systems to enrich themselves, pass a part thereof to the people including the enforcing agencies as a cost free cake to cushion in case of need, after doing due diligence of the response that would be of such people. It is human instinct to be attracted by wealth when offered where such instinct is bereft of honesty and integrity, otherwise known as soft targets for complicity.

The causes which breed the corruption are the conversion of the loopholes in the laws, rules, regulations, procedures, systems, guidelines etc. to suit one's own occasion, situation and circumstance for financial gain individually or collectively exploiting hapless citizens as well as political platforms and conduits specially designed to surreptitiously amass as much wealth as the circumstances permit for doing one or other favor. Have laws made and numerous measures taken by the governments helped curtailment, if not, elimination of corruption from the national map? As reports pour in day in and day out, they have neither helped curtailment nor elimination of corruption in the country, rather newer and newer corruption scandals have been surfacing. When laws, procedures, audits, checks, supervision, controls etc. said to have been in place cannot deter the corruption, to whom else the worst affected ordinary citizens of the country should look for extricating from corruption ruthlessly reining in every functional and administrative mechanism?

This question raises a further question as to what the institutions and utilities entrusted with full responsibility and functional powers at the national and state level as well as in every department of the government, central and state undertakings, organizations, government autonomous bodies, banks controlled by the governments had done or have been doing in diagnosing the processes and procedures functioning and operating and plugging the loopholes in the entire gamut of governmental systems to precisely detect the causes of the disease called corruption rather than waiting for the post-mortem report of the corrupt officials as and when caught and then repeating and reiterating the same rules, guidelines etc. and submission of their annual reports to the appropriate authority? This is what seems to have been the progress we have made for containing the corruption. National and state level organizations have mammoth organizational structure equipped with adequate powers with latest available diagnostic and detection techniques. Don't they owe an explanation to the nation?

During the past three decades or so, the corruption has been growing in a monstrous shape entrenching every organ of the governance, the public and private utilities and companies and even among the organizations and institutions operating for so called social orderliness. This speaks the truth that we have reached a state of abysmal depth of dishonesty where even a ray of sunlight pierced through a hole beseeches one to correct oneself does not seem to have any effect on the persons addicted to corruption. This also speaks the enormity of the problem.

The game rule of corruption is that it starts from the top pilfering down to the bottom. Upper echelons set the corruption into motion preaching to the downward hierarchy and in parliamentary and public speeches as a precept that the corruption is a necessary evil and must be rooted out for the welfare of the people and the country. It is a simple principle of life that a child understands by example and not by precept. It is also true that child observes its parents' doings at home. Precept for the child becomes a bubble to burst when the child observes the parents doing something other than what they are preaching.

Likewise, in a functional hierarchical set up, one cannot blame persons in lower hierarchy if they follow the same practice as the persons in upper hierarchy do, both being well aware that such practice is unwholesome, against public interest and forbidden by laws. Thus the corruption outgrows the width and breadth of public interest and laws so much so that it becomes unreachable to the enforcement authorities. An outcry of the corruption compels the higher level persons to start pestering the enforcing authorities to, somehow or the other, act to cool down the outcry. The lower level persons in hierarchy become easy prey to the enforcement authorities net them drumming high sound publicity against them as if they have been found guilty for punishment. This is also known as scapegoating the innocent persons by building against them superficial criminal cases ruining their official and social life forever. By the time their case comes up for final orders in a court of law, either they would have dead or would have become super senior citizens to undergo punishment having no means to challenge in higher courts but to silently get used to swallow pains of the prison. The law becomes blind when it imposes punishment on an innocent person.

There have been umpteen outcries against public leaders and the bureaucrats mindlessly indulging in corrupt practices for self-gain or for the gain of some unknown and unidentifiable persons in the system. Thus, there is ample evidence to show that the birth of corruption takes place at the higher level and becomes a core curiosity for amassing unearned wealth which leads to further down corrupt practices. Such amassing of wealth starts wielding arrogant power and harassment of persons connected one way or the other in the outcry. Those who actually amassed or amassing the wealth have the benefit of influencing the process of justice or engaging legal luminaries to defend them. This is the order of day.

Enforcement authorities have two modes to deal with corruption cases, one is to inflict upon an innocent person the injury of corruption wantonly under the political and bureaucratic irresistible influence of the higher level commands who is made to languish either in jail or on bail for indefinable because of investigating agency's dilly-dalling process and judicial prolonging process, in both the cases, the person is made to mentally disturbed with no window to see the light outside. Because, if he or she were to be honest to the core through out the sevices, there was no recovery whatsoever during the raids and there was no financial loss caused to the serving Organization.

This state of condition of the person does not appeal to anyone, neither to the enforcing agency nor to the trial court of law. Criminal law in our country is bereft of humanitarian essentialities for; the investigating agency thinks its job is completed once the charge sheet is filed while the judicial process has no humanitarian compulision to weigh the weight of excessive inhumanity being imposed for fulfilling the procedural compliances, considered more pressing than testing on the face of the charge sheet whether or not there is any case that should be made for proceeding with the trial.

The charge sheet is taken cognizance once it is filed without any arguments on both the sides, whether it is factual or facial, before taking cognizance. This is one of the causes for heaping up of the pendency of the criminal cases. The Hon'ble trial court does not subject the charge sheet to at least preliminary arguments/submissions by the accused person with seriousness whether or not the charge sheet should be admitted. This opportunity to the accused peson does not exist once the Hon'ble Trial Court takes cognizance and issues summons. This has become as a matter of practice. The next stage at which the accused is given opportunity to argue upon is when the court takes up arguments on charge. In a case, to my knowledge, the charge sheet was filed in 1994, the Approver's Statement was filed in 1996 and the arguments on charge commenced in 1996 and continued till 2016. It is humby submitted that there is also need to give an opportunity to the accused person and the prosecution soon the charge sheet is filed to contest/defend the charge sheet and, after hearing the arguments of both the parties,orders need to be passed whether or not the chargesheet should be taken cognizance of and summans should be issued. It is critical moment for the accused because it is possible that the accused would be in a position to place his or her submissions before the Hon'ble Trial Court, based on the documdents of the prosecution that the charge sheet does not make out any charge against him or her.

The Hon'ble Supreme Court of India held that "All told, we thus see that the **Apex Court has sought to make it pretty clear that unexplained inordinate delay can be a very crucial factor in quashing a criminal complaint.** What the Apex Court has held in this leading case must definitely be adhered to without fail by all the Courts in quashing a criminal complaint in any given case. No denying it!" [Citation: Hasmukhlal D Vora & Anr vs The State of Tamil Nadu in Criminal Appeal No. 2310 of 2022 and cited in 2022 LiveLaw (SC) 1033 that was pronounced as recently as on December 16, 2022 in the exercise of its criminal appellate jurisdiction has laid down unequivocally that unexplained inordinate delay can be considered as a '**very crucial factor**' for quashing a criminal complaint.] It is not kown whether the ruling of the Hon'ble Supreme Court cited above has been or is being followed at the lower courts, presumably,

it is not being followed as found from the news items in print and electronic media that the charge sheet once filed is taken cognizance of by the Hon'ble Trial Court and summons are issued to the accused person[s]. There is need to give a reasonable opportunity at this stage for the accused person[s] to present his or her positition vis-à-vis the allegations made in the charge sheet more so, the charge sheet cannot sustain if there were to be no recovery from the accused person or loss to the serving Organization under the the Prevention of Corruption Act, 1988. To this end the central government has already issued instructions that sanction for prosecution should not be accorded by the competent authority in the Organization where there was no recovery from the accused. Similar should be the case where there is neither recovery nor financial loss to the Organization. The associated provisions of the sections such IPC linked to the case under PCA 1988 cannot have substance and veracity in the absence of the recovery and/or financial loss to the Organization. The allegations of the prosecution bcome fictitious which aspect is not being considered by the Hon'ble Trial Court at the time of taking cognizance of the charge sheet which is possible if due opportunity is given to the accused to bring out that the charge sheet does not make any allegation about the recovery or loss. Despite that, the Hon'ble Trial Court takes cognizance of the charge sheet and issues summons to the accused person[s], that amounts to travesty of truth and justice which are the fundamental core for proceeding in the criminal case under PCA 1988..

"The Court before taking cognizance needs to be satisfied about existence of prima facie case on basis of material collected after conclusion of investigation. The magistrate has to apply his mind to the facts stated in the police report or complaint before taking cognizance for coming to the conclusion that there is sufficient material to proceed with the case. Taking of cognizance is a judicial function and judicial orders cannot be passed in a mechanical or cryptic manner." [Citation: Sanjit Bakshi v. State of NCT of Delhi & Anr. in CRL.M.C. 4177/2019 & CRL M.A.34231/2019 and cited in 2022 LiveLaw (Del) 533]

The other mode is not to file the charge sheet or seek for closure of the case under the shadow of the most powerful persons.

Justice is the ethical, philosophical idea that people are to be treated impartially, fairly, properly, and reasonably by the law and by arbiters of the law, that laws are to ensure that no harm befalls another, and that, where harm is alleged, a remedial action is taken - both the accuser and the accused receive a morally right consequence merited by their actions (see: due process). [Source: Legal Information Institute – LII Website] Who should ensure this, the Hon'ble Trial Court, High Court or the Supreme Court? This gives no option to the accusd person but to silently undergo the process until it is completed, continuing delay being of no significance in law or until death of the accused person especially when he or she is in advanced age of his or life, whichevrer is earlier.

Gap between enormous investments by the governments for economic development and welfare aimed at accelerating the measures for alleviation of poverty under various nomenclatures is widening year after year as the ground realities of the intended beneficiaries bemoan. This is stated to be mainly due to disregard to defined procedures or a twist to them in a way that opens up scope for corrupt practices presenting overtly as if there is nothing wanting in the implementation. Social and statutory audits have been highlighting discreet presence of such practices in their reports but their findings and recommendations are by and large overshadowed by most influential people in power and overlooked. The constitutional bodies and enforcement Authorities entrusted with the responsibility of overseeing the expenditure from the exchequer are overawed by overtures and invisible threats.

Every year 'Vigilance Awareness Week" is observed in all the governmental systems with great fanfare and the following rituals are repeated:

(a) To display banners, posters etc. at prime locations in the office;

(b) To organize seminars/workshops inviting prominent faculty;

(c) To organize competitive debates/lecture/essays on anti-corruption topics amongst the employees and the students in the colleges/schools and to distribute prizes;

(d) To bring out special issue of journals during the period; and

(e) To request the non-government organizations, institutions and service associations in the local area to participate in the Vigilance Awareness campaign.

(f) A Pledge is read by the Head of the Organization/Department and repeated by the employees present on the occasion. Text of Pledge reads as:

"We, the Public Servants of India, do hereby solemnly pledge that we shall continuously strive to bring about integrity and transparency in all spheres of our activities. We also pledge that we shall work unstintingly for eradication of corruption in all spheres of life. We shall remain vigilant and work towards the growth and reputation of our organization through our collective efforts. We shall bring pride to our organizations and provide value based service to our countrymen. We shall do our duty conscientiously and act without fear or favor."

Logically such pledge ought to be made obligatory at the time of one's entry into service rather than repeating it every year which does not appeal because pledge is supposed to be taken once; otherwise it becomes a ritual losing its essence.

A big question? This raises one's eyebrows with awesomeness. Why then all this ritual exercise?

In one's home, office, pubic services, places of worship and what not, one is told to be conscious of the acts one does and be guided by one's own Conscience which is the human virtue handed down to us by our great saints of yesteryears. Whether or not to follow them is for each person to think himself or herself.

Asking for a favor while discharging one's duty as a human over and above what one rightfully earns is no less than stealing. The difference between a corrupt person and a thief is the former does it as if it is honorable knowingly it be dishonourable while the latter does it as a profession for survival willing to undergo the punishment. A beggar begs because he has nothing and no person who has something will ever go for begging. Those have wealth in hand to live with dignity of life yet, are consciously are corrupt are worse than a beggar.

Moral values and ethics when ignored by human, such human becomes inhuman and the corruption is the process of dehumanizing oneself. Once one is dehumanized, the consciousness and Conscience remain in a state of dreadful darkness and such person becomes more hardening towards humans compulsively creating a situation which compels the other human to oblige bribing through bargaining, if there is scope, to get one's work done, otherwise supposed to have been done as part of one's duty.

There is other face of corrupt tendencies - interpretation of applicable laws and rules and inbuilt insurability and assurance from mechanisms of justice with integrity and honesty to protect the innocent and punish the guilty and administration of the regulatory system established in various sectors. These institutions are supposed or presumed to be self-insulated from corruptive practices in every inch of their functioning and discharge of duties, being the foundation of faith for an indicted person. This is an objective outlook but the subjective outlook of what is actually happening on the ground in these institutions is best left to the institutions to make their own moral assessment and satisfaction.

Then, why, knowingly well what is moral, what is amoral and what is ethical and what is unethical, we get detached with the positives of those values and embrace their negativities that is the first sign of birth of selfishness within us that is capable of rejecting any kind of talk on any kind of values inviting dejection in life. This is where we erred and continue to err thinking that human can earn, besides legally, also illegally under the overbearing shadow of the selfishness. The corrupt practices are the products of rejection of life values and, when that happens, the human becomes blind to the values and those having sight think using the magnifying glass to search for the ways and means for corruptive practices.

When this spreads through the societies, the beauty of whiteness in the societies becomes blackish detaching the humans in all and every respect with the values that makes the humans to indulge freely into the corrupt practices. Are we not dishonouring what we learnt about those values in our schools and colleges or religious practices? Answer is 'who cares for honour today' when dishonour empowers more enrichment of illegally earned wealth in all the societies and the governing systems including the enforcement Authorities with or without the patronage of political figures? The Organs of the Constitution are thus infested with chronic influences which support the present scenario of committing more illegal than legal or treating illegal is as good as equal to legal. Why it has become so? I have answered this question before but wish to add that purity grows in oneself only through self-realization of what is good and what is bad for oneself, for the society and the country. Until we consciously think over this right up to touching our Conscience which resides adjacent to Soul in human body, we cannot conceive of purity, leave alone understanding and practicing it in one's own and everyone's life, the foundational base for the wellbeing of one and all.

In the present political, religious and social spheres, we believe preaching on the life values is more impressive to the audience than teaching about practising them in life for; both the preacher and the audience are in agreement in one sense that it is difficult to practice in life and the preaching is the only best way. Read the following Quote and learn what to say in our public talks and speeches:

"AN OUNCE OF PRACTICE IS WORTH MORE THAN TONS OF PREACHING." - MAHATMA GANDHI.

"The Greatest Crimes Are To Associate Another With God, To Vex Your Father And Mother, To Murder Your Own Species, To Commit Suicide, And To Swear To Lie" - Muhammad

The Quotes are valid eternally

By now, I believe, we are able to grasp the essence of the moral values in the individual's, societal and national life. These values work like construction of a beautiful structure or building. This is so because if everyone who works in such an effort would have to have imbibed the moral values that breathe honesty in every step of the construction of the structure or building. So, such values have to be inculcated in the individual, society and nation if we want that the structure of democracy is free from dirtiness that represents the dishonesty and criminalized mind. It is easier said our country is a great democracy but the meaning of great is limited to the size and population of the country but not the qualitative considerations of its people.

To put a stop to the caste system, **untouchability, prejudice, and other forms of oppression** that have existed in our culture for generations, Article 17 was included in the Indian Constitution. It provides security not only against the government but also against private individuals.

The state has a legal obligation to take the appropriate efforts to ensure that it is not violated. (People's Union for Democratic Rights v Union of India Case)

- Of all the rights articles established in the Constitution, Article 17 is the only one that is absolute. That is, practicing untouchability in any form is prohibited and there are 'no ifs, no buts,' only punishments if you practice untouchability.

- The inclusion of this article in the Constitution demonstrates the priority placed by the Constituent Assembly on the abolition of this heinous practice.

- **Article 17** is also a key clause in terms of equa before the law (Article 14). It ensures social justice and human dignity, two rights that have been denied to a large segment of Indian society for millennia.

- **Article 17** is absolute in nature, which means it cannot be violated under any circumstances.

Indian culture is more than five thousand years old and is one of the few ancient cultures that still survive today. Language, arts, spiritual, music, dance, literature all form a part of this culture. Indian culture has responded differently to influences of different cultures, especially those of invaders and it has preserved, absorbed and assimilated the different elements and this is the secret of the success of Indian culture and civilization. Inspite of its diversity, there is a 'fundamental unity' which makes it unique. Indian culture has many different parts and each is closely related with the other and has intricately woven values. Families are essential in preserving and transmitting culture. It is in the family that the child first experiences and absorbs the values of sharing, caring, unselfishness, tolerance. Unity, loyalty, integrity are key features of an Indian family with emphasis on interdependence and concern for others. In India, food is valued not only because it is nutritious but also for it is a gift from God. Clothes are associated with tradition, diversity of culture. The national symbols in India symbolize unity, truth and patriotism. National symbols are distinctive to the country. Teachers are to be aware of integrating values into the curriculum in all subjects. Often we carry within us many prejudices or wrong beliefs and do not think whether these are right or wrong.

With due respects to the Hon'ble Supreme Court of India and to the Hon'ble High Courts, in my personal view, the Untouchability Practices should also include naming of caste of a person in the print, electronic media and by the political parties, the governing system except for educational and economic considerations. These together have been provoking, if not promoting, the persistence of the caste system in the country thereby rendering the constitutional provisions ineffectual. It is high time for the Government of India and Hon'ble Courts of Justice to bar the above system prevalent in the social environment of the country. Naming of a person by caste is not an educational degree or title but forced upon us by the traditions. If we look back to our traditions prevailed centuries ago and modern traditions, numerous changes had taken place in way of our living. I believe, this would go a long way in restoring the dignity and respect to the persons coming under the caste system. If not, we should admit that we are consciously encouraging the use of the caste system defeating the very object and purpose of Article 17. Inclusion of such practice among the practices mentioned in the said Article would, over a period of time, consign the naming of the caste to oblivion.

Whatever the information we are able to collect through Population Census or Economic Surveys periodically is aimed at finding the status and economic standing of the population necessary in the education, planning of the economic development and for evolving appropriate policies and programmes to upgrade the education and economic development wherever we find it is warranted. This is the sole purpose of the census and surveys and not to pinpoint the castes and make it habitual to name the persons by castes. We have no right to name the person by caste pursuant to Article 17 of the Constitution of our country. Every educated person would have read the Constitution but the constitution is not merely for reading; it is to imbibe the human values enshrined therein. This we don't want that leads to discriminations within ourselves. The discriminations are our own products preserved and sold according to the needs of the times. This needs to be rooted out and to be replaced by enlightened outlook.

Also, what we find from the recent developments that the states and the politicians are interpreting the population census and surveys are most suited for self-presentation of the reports and by relying upon that for pleading for increase in the reservation of quotas intended initially for ten years but with self-interest dominating their desires, the quota practice has been opted for its continuance even up to the seventy third years our country becoming Republic. What does it suggest? Our utter failure to sincerely and honestly to implement the education and economic development policies and programmes including diversion and self-consumption of the funds earmarked for both during the above years.

There shouldn't have been any need for continuing quota regime had we uplifted the poverty level people to a dignifying status of educated, self-earning and living with self-respect which we could have done when we claim we are an advance country with latest technologies in every field but we didn't want.

That we didn't do believing that quota regime is the best game the politicians can play whenever and wherever they so desire on two considerations; one is to keep the names of castes alive to reap rich dividend for their political consolidations and second, for using them as the best tossing coin during the elections. Our elections today are completely adulterated with castes, black money and freebies. The citizens of the country challenged this practice through petitions in the Courts of Law who considered the petitions and directed the ECI to take note of them and regulate the system. ECI, despite best efforts, found it beyond its control, the reason being that the ruling party was itself a part of the process along with other political parties. ECI is not free to breathe natural air, the air system being controlled by the ruling party. Since the time we became Republic, the ECI's independent status is regulated by the ruling party whereby it works like a smoke screen overshadowing the ECI.

The purity of the election system is the strongest breathing strength of the democratic country. It is not so in our country since the dawn of democracy. Like weather is poisoned due to the extreme pollution, so also, the independency of the ECI is polluted because of political extreme bad weather that entered every part of its lung system. Then, how can we expect ECI to control the black money and caste considerations during the elections. We have become indifferent to our own systems and enforcement of laws and rules in most of the matters including the election process. Then, whose job it is to do this job. Every part of the administrative and enforcement system is rusted and is resting.

Thus, we cannot blame anybody for the widening gap in promises and performance and, when that happens, finding a medial mode seeking for increasing the Quotas and allocation of additional public funds based on the census and surveys as sacrosanct documents whereas the population census is envisaged for every ten years by the Centre and not by the States which have learnt the art of crossing limits of the constitution on one pretext or the other. This needs to be stopped forthwith, the intentions being biased and prejudicial to the democratic process contemplated in the constitution and highly harmful in upbringing the poorest of the poor to the ground level. I also beg to be excused if I submit that the constituents of our Constitution have developed hesitating attitude to call a spade a spade without beating about the bush.

Time we wake up to the call of the day and fight to the finish the wrongs that are dominating our democratic functioning. **What do we owe to future generations? And what can we do today to make their world a better place?** These Questions should be our main concern today.

"THE CASTE SYSTEM HAS DIVIDED PEOPLE AND DILUTED THEIR COLLECTIVE STRENGTH." – BABA AMTE

OPINION: All caste-based reservations should be abolished - Reservations serving the policy of divide and rule, says Justice Katju - By Markandey Katju Updated: November 01, 2022 14:02 IST

Representational Image | PTI

"I am against any caste-based reservations for admissions in educational institutions or jobs. Instead, special facilities and help should be given to poor children of all castes (even upper castes) or religions, to ensure them a level playing field.

For instance, a child of poor parents may not have the money to buy school textbooks. He should, therefore, be provided the text books free of charge by the state. This, however, is different from providing reservations on caste basis, which I strongly oppose, for the following reasons:

1. Reservations can only benefit less than 1 per cent SCs or OBCs, while creating an illusion that all are benefited. SCs in India are about 25 crores, but reserved jobs for them would be only a few lakhs. So very few will get the benefit of reservations, and even these will be mostly from the 'creamy layer'.

2. Reservations are doing great harm to the SCs/OBCs for two reasons:

    (a) They act as psychological crutches to them, thus, weakening them. In other words, an impression is created among SC/OBC youth that they need not study and work hard because even without doing so they will get admission or a job. SCs and OBCs must throw aside the crutches of reservation and say that they will work hard and show by competing with upper castes on merits that they are not intellectually inferior to upper castes.

    (b) Reservations are serving the policy of divide and rule of the political rulers, as they create animosity between SCs/OBCs and upper castes. An upper caste youth who got 90 per cent in his exams may be denied admission/job, while an SC/OBC who got 40 per cent may get it, by virtue of reservation. This naturally causes anguish in the former. India's massive problems can only be overcome by a mighty united people's struggle which will totally transform the country and bring it into the ranks of the developed countries, but for that unity among the people is absolutely necessary, but reservations divide us.

    SCs must realise that they cannot succeed in their struggle for social amelioration if they are isolated. They must join hands with the enlightened section of the upper castes, and fight along with them. But this will be difficult as long as reservations continue.

3. Our politicians use reservations for their vote bank politics. So the real purpose of reservations is not to benefit the SCs/OBCs but to benefit the politicians.

4. Caste reservations have further perpetuated the caste system, instead of helping in destroying it. Caste is a feudal institution, which has to be destroyed if India is to progress, but reservations further entrench it.

The time has now come when all Indians, including SCs/OBC, see through this political fraud and charade, and demand the end of all caste-based reservations. [Justice Markandey Katju retired from the Supreme Court in 2011. The opinions expressed in this article are those of the author's and do not purport to reflect the opinions or views of THE WEEK.]

Let the castes and creeds remain in their respective homes, in their respective worshipping places and in their respective understanding so as to keep their fundamental values alive but let us not drive them to street corners where people of different castes gather and gossip that makes mockery of the citizens, the humans. The humans are to be seen through the human heart that is what God has gifted to humans.

The castes census, according to my thinking, should be to identify the deprived and suppressed citizens by the age old social practices, to establish criteria to measure their level of education and economic life considering the average living standard of the citizens **[Golden Line]** and that should be the benchmark for extending all kinds of support by the central and state governments as a national necessity and priority until the time there is tangible evidence that such class of citizens are making up their lives upward which should continue until they reach the national average standard of living. Turning this into political opportunity would inject more negativity in the living conditions of such citizens and, there would never be a day when we can say there is no need for caste based reservations. Let the approach submitted above be the golden line for educational and economic improvement and upbringing of such citizens. The present political tones and tunings for the caste based census need to be taken out from the shadow of politics so that the class of the citizens who are standing below the national average standard of living, regardless of the castes they belong, are fully covered, protected and made to move towards progressing and prosperity. To make this actionable, the constitution, if necessary may be amended so that there would be a clear Vision for the future irrespective of the political party in power.

What is needed is to establish the principles of democracy and governance first in one-self, then in the social life, then among the political arena and then in political administration and justice. This is not happening rather disorderliness is growing. The huge gaps that are continuing to exist in our democratic framework have also been pinpointed in this book.

Evidence of a Democratic system of government in India is originally found in the Vedas. There is distinctive evidence from Rig Veda, which mentions a thriving republican form of Government in India. We may quote a few beautiful slokas from Rig Veda which were to be sung in unison at the beginning of the republican assembly –

"We pray for a spirit of unity; may we discuss and resolve all issues amicably, may we reflect on all matters (of state) without rancor,
may we distribute all resources (of the state) to all stakeholders equitably,
may we accept our share with humility" – Rig Veda – 10/191/2

PART 05
HUMAN DEVELOPMENT PARADOX

"ALL THAT IS VALUABLE IN HUMAN SOCIETY DEPENDS UPON THE OPPORTUNITY FOR DEVELOPMENT ACCORDED TO THE INDIVIDUAL."

- ALBERT EINSTEIN

'What is Human Development'?

"**UNDP Report** states Human development grew out of global discussions on the links between economic growth and development during the second half of the 20th Century. By the early 1960s there were increasingly loud calls to "dethrone" GDP: economic growth had emerged as both a leading objective, and indicator, of national progress in many countries even though GDP was never intended to be used as a measure of wellbeing. In the 1970s and 80s development debate considered using alternative focuses to go beyond GDP, including putting greater emphasis on employment, followed by redistribution with growth, and then whether people had their basic needs met."

These ideas helped pave the way for the human development approach, which is about expanding the richness of human life, rather than simply the richness of the economy in which human beings live. It is an approach that is focused on creating fair opportunities and choices for all people. So how do these ideas come together in the human development approach?

- **People:** the human development approach focuses on improving the lives of people lead rather than assuming that economic growth will lead, automatically, to greater opportunities for all. Income growth is an important means to development, rather than an end in itself.

- **Opportunities:** human development is about giving people more freedom and opportunities to live lives they value. In effect this means developing people's abilities and giving them a chance to use them. For example, educating a girl would build her skills, but it is of little use if she is denied access to jobs, or does not have the skills for the local labour market. The aspects of human development are foundational (that is they are a fundamental part of human development); and aspects that are more contextual (that is they help to create the conditions that allow people to flourish). Three foundations for human development are to live a healthy and creative life, to be knowledgeable, and to have access to resources needed for a decent standard of living. Many other aspects are important too, especially in helping to create the right conditions for human development, such as environmental sustainabi or equa between men and women.

- **Choices**: human development is, fundamentally, about more choice. It is about providing people with opportunities, not insisting that they make use of them. No one can guarantee human happiness, and the choices people make are their own concern. The process of development – human development - should at least create an environment for people, individually and collectively, to develop to their full potential and to have a reasonable chance of leading productive and creative lives that they value.

The human development approach, developed by the economist Mahbub Ul Haq, is anchored in Amartya Sen's work on human capabilities, often framed in terms of whether people are able to "be" and "do" desirable things in life. Examples include

- Beings: well fed, sheltered, healthy

- Doings: work, education, voting, participating in community life.

- Freedom of choice is central: someone choosing to be hungry (during a religious fast say) is quite different to someone who is hungry because they cannot afford to buy food.

- As the international community seeks to define a new development agenda post-2015, the human development approach remains useful to articulating the objectives of development and improving people's well-being by ensuring an equitable, sustainable and stable planet. [Source: UNDP Reports Website]

According to the ancient concept, the goal of democracy is to uplift mankind. But according to the latest thinking, this concept has got more expansion. In today's context, the real goal of democracy is to conduct governance with equal participation of the entire public, in which the real interests of the people are protected and all round development. To put it simply, human development with full of co-ordinance is an important goal of democracy.

The constitution of India, the laws and rules incorporate essential ingredients bestowed by the Nature on the humans how to deal the welfare of the state and its people. Ancient rulers and judicial pronouncements laid down certain doctrines to deal with various situations, all for betterment and not for bitterness. The doctrines evolved over centuries remain valid for ever for, they imbibe values gifted by Nature and the Nature expects the humans to uphold them as long as the humans are integral part of the Mother Earth. Great legal luminaries since centuries were couched with these doctrines; they believed legalistic interpretation solely based on statutes blinds one to the natural justice that flows from nature and ingrained within the statutes. Their sagaciousness rested upon searching for truth within the statutes understandable by a common man and impressionable upon presiding judge. Laws are made for architecting citizens to respect rule of law. Lest laws become mockery and the race for disrespecting the rule of law tends to rise.

How the journey had been through the period of seventy years as an independent and republican country? Answer to this can be found in books written by great historians and experts – both ways –

in favor or disfavour of the governments in power at the relevant times. The common man is one among the very ordinary people (VOP); has little or no say in the matter of government or governance rather there is no mechanism by which he could say and, if there is one, that is through his elected representative whom he voted rightly or wrongly being illiterate, in majority of the cases. Already he is so much burdened either because of his very survival for lack of economic security or always busy for earning something for a day's survival. Elections bring him a kind of festive season where the parties and their contesting candidates offer attractive and varieties of gifts including monetary benefits making him or her mentally surrender to vote for candidate. This has been the trend of our democracy everyone embraces but never battles. Time does not predict what would happen and lets the humans know when it would happen without differentiating whether one is rich, middle class or the poorer class or a leader.

Every child born is an asset for its parents, the society and the country if the newly born child is well nursed to mould it for the welfare of the parents, society and the state. This is the Truth that every child holds in its eyes soon it is born. Denial of this places responsibility squarely on the governance and on us. This entails individually, socially and nationally the consequences. Lack of understanding this is driving growing children towards committing crimes and unhealthy social activities resulting into a liability to parents, society and the nation. Let us remember if every human is able to live with self-dignity, he or she hardly cares for crimes and anti-social or anti-national activities.

Nature has bestowed our country with vast Natural Resources and Manpower. Their exploitation is the essence of National and Self-Growth. If not, manpower would manifest into liability to the state that may grow beyond one's control inflicting more damage than happiness to the society and the nation. This is not realized by the political parties and the governments in power. They grant approvals for increasing the force to control the crimes; it is recurring expenditure but will not be able to see the end of the problem. Because, it is human instinct to react to injury that creates multiplying injuries. The governing system has been merely an onlooker displaying differences between the local government and central controlled government. These differences are good to satisfy each other's ego and political blames which has become so common that we hardly care for our constitutional obligations and rule of law.

"A POLITICAL PARTY IS A GROUP OF HUMAN BEINGS, WHICH IS STABLY ORGANIZED" - EDMUND BURKE.

Once harnessing of Resources and Human Development available starts, welfare of the society accompanies by itself. What we have been doing for decades or so moving towards Reverse Social Welfare – Spending Spree of available financial resources without application to material and human development. In this process, the financial burden is put back again on the people and society. End result of performance of all the sectors is the outcome of Economic Development of Nation which, in turn, transforms living standard of its citizens - it may be growing prosperity or increasing miseries depending entirely upon national character imbibed in every individual, business, national commitment, governance, self-respect; mutuality of national religions, castes and creeds; and each other's faith. Is it happening in India? Let this be first assessed before comparison of our own image with those of others.

The initial reservations were only for SC and ST [Article 15 (4) and Article 16 (4)]. OBCs were included in the ambit of reservation in 1991 [Article 15 (5)]. The percentage continued to be extended from time to time. Promises are pouring of late for reclassification of the castes and for increasing the existing percentage of reservation. The governments have undertaken various social and welfare scheme for upliftment of the weaker sections of the society with main impetus on increasing the income capacity. UNDP in its reports states "Income is a means – an important one, but not the only one – to human development. Income is not the sum total of human lives. Through various measures, the benefits of income need to be translated into enhancing different aspects of human well-being. Thus economic growth is a necessary, but not a sufficient, condition for human development. It is the qua of growth, not its quantity alone, which is crucial for human well-being. As the 1996 Human Development Report put it, growth can be jobless, rather than job creating; ruthless, rather than poverty-reducing; voiceless, rather than participatory; rootless, rather than culturally enshrined; and futureless, rather than environment-friendly. Economic growth which is jobless, ruthless, voiceless, rootless and futureless is not conducive to human development. If income is not the sum total of human lives, the lack of it cannot also be the sum total of human deprivation either. Thus impoverishment, from a human development perspective, is also multidimensional. The lack of income or income poverty is only one aspect of human impoverishment; deprivation can also occur in other areas– having a short and unhealthy life, being illiterate or not allowed to participate, feeling personal insecurity, etc. Human poverty is thus larger than income poverty.

According to the hazards of caste-based reservation quotas, shedding light on the challenges faced by India's education system and government job sector.

Hindrance to Meritocracy:

One of the fundamental issues arising from caste-based reservation quotas is the erosion of meritocracy. By reserving a specific percentage of seats or positions based on caste, the system inadvertently places more emphasis on social identity rather than individual merit and qualifications. This approach undermines the principle of rewarding excellence and hinders the growth of a competitive environment, which is essential for the overall development of a nation.

Educational Challenges:

Caste-based reservation quotas impact the education system in various ways. Firstly, the quotas may discourage students from general categories, who are often more financially and socially disadvantaged, leading to a sense of injustice and decreased motivation to strive for academic success. Secondly, the system creates an atmosphere of divided classrooms, where students may feel stigmatized or labelled solely based on their caste. This can hinder social cohesion and limit the potential for intellectual growth and exchange of ideas among students.

Inefficiency in Resource Allocation:

The implementation of reservation quotas has often resulted in a misallocation of resources. The limited availability of seats for students belonging to general categories, despite their academic competence, has led to a situation where deserving candidates are denied opportunities while seats remain vacant due to a lack of qualified applicants from reserved categories. This imbalance not only undermines efficiency but also perpetuates the cycle of inequality and hampers the overall progress of the nation.

Disincentive for Skill Development:

The reservation system can inadvertently discourage individuals from marginalized communities from pursuing skill development and higher education. With assured reservations in government jobs, some individuals may feel less compelled to acquire new skills or explore other employment avenues outside the protected domain. This can have long-term implications on the nation's workforce, hindering the development of a diverse and skilled workforce capable of driving economic growth.

Deepening Social Divisions:

While the intention of reservation quotas was to bridge the gap between different castes and promote social equa, it can also inadvertently contribute to the perpetuation of caste-based divisions. The emphasis on caste identity and the categorization of individuals into different groups can reinforce societal divisions and hinder the progress towards a truly egalitarian society. This can impede the collective efforts required to transcend caste barriers and foster a sense of unity and nation-building.

Conclusion:

While the caste-based reservation quota system in India was introduced with the noble objective of rectifying historical injustices and promoting social equa, it is crucial to recognize the potential dangers it poses to the education system and government jobs. The erosion of meritocracy, educational challenges, inefficient resource allocation, disincentives for skill development, and the deepening of social divisions are significant concerns that need to be addressed. As the nation moves forward, it is imperative to find a balance that ensures equal opportunities for all while promoting a merit-based system that rewards talent, hard work, and dedication, irrespective of social backgrounds. Only through such balanced reforms can India strive towards a more inclusive and prosperous future for all its citizens

Time immemorial it is known that India is predominantly an agricultural based country and its population in rural areas represents much larger than that in urban areas. On becoming republic, we seem to have believed the growth originating from the industrialization compared to agricultural and agro-industries. The first industrial policy of the government dominated this understanding and continued for many years to come and then new industrial policy was introduced. There was no such scientifically developed agriculture and agri-products development policy around the same time other than the green revolution introduced in early sixties. Industrialization was necessary especially steel, fertilizer, electricity etc. to significantly supplement the agriculture and agro-industries development. What we forgot in the entire process was the need for equal, if not more, investment in rural areas, more importantly, education and health sectors. Semi-urban and urban areas saw multitudinal growth of schools, colleges and universities; the rural areas were denied the same. The heart of India lives in rural areas and the other parts of the body lives in urban areas. This difference was not appreciated at the relevant time. Those living in rural areas constituted human capital much larger than in urban areas, have all the similarities as of those living in urban areas other than education, health, life style and living standard. The reverse education and economic growth represented the difference between the two. The governments of the time did not realize that education was more needed in rural areas to conjugate with the development of urban areas.

Cardinals of socio-economic growth, as one can understand from the definition of "social welfare" defined by the United Nations 1967 are: "Social welfare as an organized function is regarded as a body of activities designed to enable individuals, families, groups and communities to cope with the social problems of changing conditions. But in addition to and extending beyond the range of its responsibilities for specific services, social welfare has a further function within the broad area of a country's social development. In this larger sense, social welfare should play a major role in contributing to the effective mobilization and deployment of human and material resources of the country to deal successfully with the social requirements of change, thereby participating in nation-building."

Underlying essence of socio-economic development, as the writer understands, is money spent whether it is public or private should produce a compensatory product or service, except limited subsidization based on merits, that enables one to build up with ability to self-earn to live with dignity of life; the government to earn estimated revenue against the expenditure and the corporate to earn profit and sustain with well-built up reserves for the future growth.

"I will give you a talisman. Whenever you are in doubt, or when the self becomes too much with you, apply the following test. Recall the face of the poorest and the weakest man [woman] whom you may have seen, and ask yourself, if the step you contemplate is going to be of any use to him [her]. Will he [she] gain anything by it? Will it restore him [her] to a control over his [her] own life and destiny? In other words, will it lead to Swaraj [freedom] for the hungry and spiritually starving millions? Then you will find your doubts and yourself melt away." - Mahatma Gandhi.

The debates and discussions on the subject matter confined to exchange of political language vocabulary among the political parties, media debates, scholars writings in the print media. What, however, one could find was there was no reference to or reflections of the Constitution on the point of discussions and debates. 'Beneficiary' cannot be substituted for the 'Creativity' for; the creativity is inborn in every human to understand and act upon economic opportunities created by the governance under the Directive Principles as also confer right to citizens under the Fundamental Rights that convey the realistic meaning of what welfare and equa fundamentals are enshrined therein. That is beneficial to any one; more so, to the poor which confers as a birth right to learn, earn and live with self-dignity. Such welfare measures envisaged under the Constitution of the country do not empower the ruling political party converting them into welfare schemes as self-defined by them. Doing so, amounts to overriding the obligations of fulfilling aspirations of the citizens for their self-sustenance, also as application of the public funds on selective basis and purposes that cut the umbilical cord of equa guaranteed under the Fundamental Rights. The silence of the provisions of the Directive Principles of State Policy to spell out in broad terms what welfare policies and programs mean on the lines as well stated therein is free legal aid, emboldened the governing system to draw their own definitions or conclusions about those two critical words, the umbrella of the weaker sections of society and further different political parties understood them in their own way but not in the same way as contemplated under the Principles.

What the politicians of the day thought and found more convenient to bestow physical benefits including in cash and those who received them were designated as 'Beneficiaries'. Investopedia defines Beneficiaries as:

- A beneficiary is an individual who receives a benefit which is often a monetary distribution.

- Distributions can have tax consequences.

- Beneficiaries who inherit a retirement account may have various options for the distribution of its funds.

- Options for distributions from Inherited IRAs [Individual Retirement Accounts] depend on whether the beneficiary is an eligible designated beneficiary or a designated beneficiary.

- You can change the beneficiaries on financial accounts at any time, though doing so requires completing and returning the relevant paperwork.

Let us compare it with the definition of 'Creativity'.

"By formally announcing 2021 as the **'International Year of Creative Economy for Sustainable Development',** the United Nations has acknowledged the creative economy's status as a driving force in building a future that respects the environment, workers and the basic principles of democracy....."

The politicians considered the word 'beneficiary' is more suited to economic development than 'creativity' such as, in particular, 'Universal Basic Income [UBI]' introduced in some of the advanced countries but found it more economically burning and abandoned it. In our country also, there was a strong attempt to provide cash under Universal Basic Income (UBI) scheme by introducing which many of the countries have burnt their fingers. This was not pursued further, a sensible step. The primary function of the economic development is to bring about a sustainable economic development which alone has the answer for removal of poverty. The cash-based economic development opens up more leakages and eats away the treasury leaving the targeted communities to continue to wait for their welfare and betterment of life.

Schemes should be such that open up newer opportunities continually to the people in the fields of education, skill development, health and sanitation, infrastructure development that has great potential to absorb the human capital and also open up industries, services and commerce in order that the obligation of creativeness if generated among the people, their living aspiration, that help them to learn and earn themselves contributing to the wealth of the nation as well as to make themselves self-sustaining. This is the sense and essence of welfare schemes and not free distribution of cash that attracts and addicts them towards beggary snatching away their life spirit, inspiration and aspirations for their self-growth, the Mother Earth offers through Nature she has created for the benefit of every Living Being including the humans. That is what the God's desire to be fulfilled by the rulers of the countries.

It is extremely sad to note that the infrastructure development in the various sectors which alone has the enormous capacity to create wealth for the people and the country that includes welfare but breaking the same infrastructure earmarked resources into various parts highlighting them having inbuilt strength to augur welfare to the people is a misplaced economic development concept. The world moves through newer and newer creations and subjecting such creations to human exertions which has the urge and capacity of one having self-earned for self-survival with self-dignity, a perennial contentment and satisfaction. If this substantive and self-assured confidence and enthusiasm does not exist in every human effort, it is as good as a void effort. Humans live in this world that included our country and they know that without making their muscles moving and straining to the last breathe of the body, the body would not have resources and means to sustain itself.

Another standard statement one gets from the planners and politicians, also now the media - what all is happening is due to increasing population. Contrarily, family planning is given a higher priority than provision for food, vegetables and fruits to the people. Simple arithmetic of planning and policy making is that every plan that is developed takes into accounts the latest available population census figures to measure the population growth for prioritization, planning and fund allocation for development envisaged during plan period. This makes to call population growth a misnomer especially when effective family planning program is well in place for past several years. What is tried to hide is the implementation process of planned program..

At what point of time of the development process, one could say balancing has been achieved between the population growth and the economic development process? Assuming there could be a point of time one could say so, should family planning continue to be given same rigor in its implementation, more so, when the people have understood its need and urgency for their own self-development? Why then blame games on planned development and population growth. It seems to have been made a hysteria ever chasing the people in the country. Let us also look at the countries which practiced family planning since long and found themselves in a state of shock when they saw turning their country into becoming an aging nation with no bloom of youths and, then, started adopting the children of other countries. They attained fastest economic development and comfort of living, yet found themselves in state of discomfort and unhappiness. Nature knows balancing the population – births and deaths and it never intends to make births alone as the increasing burden on Mother Earth. Inventions and technological advancement have their own limitations and stretching them beyond their limitations invites a state of imbalance in the Nature.

Instead of reducing fertility or promoting contraception, programs must be built around the goal of empowering individuals and families to make informed and responsible choices for themselves and their families. This freedom has intrinsic value for all human beings. Treat the human as an asset as we consider non-human assets of utmost importance for economic development. We forget that any asset other than human being cannot function independently and its dependency on the human beings is the natural necessity. Unless human hands are made to touch other kinds of assets, such assets don't work of their own. That is why the entire world accords highest importance and urgency for the human development. The human development has a wide connotation. As we keep searching for its invisible benefits to the self, society and the nation, we are walking in darkness. The only way put aside the darkness that confronts humans is to understand the need for the continued search for the light in human life. Darkness is death in the sense it makes everything standstill and creates increasing economic burden upon the humans, the society and the nation. Light is hope and darkness is despair.

BJ [Business Journal] published an Article 'Mass ageing poses a challenge we've never faced before' in its Website that enlightens human ageing:

"The world is ageing quickly. In 2022, there have been practically 800 million individuals aged 65+ years, globally, representing 10% of the world's inhabitants. This is more likely to improve by 5-6% each 30 years to succeed in 16% by 2050 and practically 1 in 4 individuals by the tip of the century. The wider implications of ageing societies will more and more occupy our mind-space within the many years to come back.

What's quick changing into a actual is that ageing is the dominant international demographic development. Rapid and accelerating ageing is going down on account of declining fertility, rising longevity and the motion of enormous cohorts into the ranks of the aged. The inhabitants construction has modified considerably through the years. Global life expectancy has greater than doubled during the last century and is anticipated to proceed climbing alongside that path. At the identical time, fertility has dropped in each nation worldwide. In many developed nations, fertility charges, recorded as variety of births per girl, have dropped to just about 1.3 or decrease. South Korea lately reported a fertility charge of 0.9. India's fertility charge has greater than halved to 2.0 in simply 4 many years.

The energy of this mega-trend is so nice that even an international occasion just like the covid pandemic has solely barely affected inhabitants measurement and development, regardless of an estimated 15 million direct and oblique covid-related deaths and a two-year decline in life expectancy in the course of the pandemic. Any long-run impression on fertility from the outbreak of Sars-CoV-2 continues to be unsure.

All nations face main challenges to make sure that their social and wellbeing techniques are ready for this variation. The shift in age distributions started in high-income nations like Japan and Germany; however it's now low and middle-income nations which are experiencing the largest adjustments. By the center of this century, two-thirds of the aged will stay in low and middle-income nations. **Since that is taking place over the identical time span as local weather change, it's going to add to the monetary burden of every nation at a time when their assets are already stretched.** [Emphasis added].

There are alternatives and challenges that come up from this dramatic shift. As societies age, it provides a chance to faucet the expertise of aged people who possess a wide selection of useful capabilities. If carried out systematically and creatively, what would possibly in any other case be perceived as a legal responsibility will be transformed into an asset? The largest challenges, after all, are associated to revenue safety, healthcare (and associated prices) and, no much less importantly, guaranteeing lives of dignity for the aged.

Many in India in all probability take into account this difficulty as one for the longer term. Au contraire, India already has the second largest inhabitants of aged people at practically 100 million. By the tip of this century, that quantity will rise to 330 million individuals, practically the identical because the inhabitants of the whole US at the moment. With that measurement, problems with elder care, wellbeing techniques and revenue and pension safety are already upon us.

The 'wicked' drawback for India is that even because the nation works on the vital difficulty of offering employment to younger individuals, it might want to take into account extending the retirement age, rising what employers put in for pensions, and offering incentives for family financial savings and elder care.

The difficulty is additional sophisticated by the truth that there's a stark distinction between states in demographic construction. Many of the states with greater GSDP per capita, like Maharashtra, Tamil Nadu, Gujarat, Karnataka and Kerala, have fertility charges properly beneath 2.0, whereas Uttar Pradesh (UP) has a fertility charge of two.4 and Bihar (highest of all states) of three. While the median age of India will rise from the mid-twenties to the mid-thirties over the following decade, Tamil Nadu and Maharashtra might be nearer to 40 and Bihar and UP nearer to 30.

Additionally, ladies outlive males by about 3-4 years on common, which compounds the revenue safety drawback.

Like many different creating nations, India is underprepared for this advanced demographic evolution. Defined profit pensions (DB, the place advantages of revenue and healthcare are assured) have given method to Defined Contribution plans (DC, the place tax-advantaged contributions are made). DB plans are unaffordable to employers and DC plans are usually inadequate to cowl the price of will increase in lifespan. **The internet result's a family deficit for elder care. As absolutely the variety of school-going kids reduces in some states, faculties must be closed and hospitals opened as a substitute**. [Emphasis added].

A complete vary of options will must be tried. The first is to extend the productive lifespan of individuals by steadily elevating the retirement age, in order that in each full-time and freelance capability, the aged can contribute and in flip obtain some revenue safety. Healthcare and wellness must be strengthened from start to outdated age together with early-motherhood prevention and mitigation of way of life illnesses like diabetes and hypertension. A 'calorie' mindset ought to give method to a 'balanced nutrition' mindset; all this to extend 'health spans' and reduce the monetary burden on households and society at massive. An improvement in permissible contributions to DC plans might be required, in order that the magnitude of financial savings work for longer lifespans.

As it occurs, humankind has never faced this drawback earlier than.

P.S: "In the tip, it's not the years in your life that depend. It's the life in your years," said Abraham Lincoln."

This Article is somewhat frightening for India unless the central and state governments seriously rethink on this subject matter and encourage growth of new human asset rather than emphasizing for its discouragement. Both the governments should open their eyes to the ensuing glaring at our population control system. Let us not be proverbial attributing 'population growth' as the main cause for slowing down our economic development whereas the cause has been due to the continued failure of the governments to draw up realistic plans and programs and ensure their implementation to 80-90 percent if not one hundred percent. For every kind of economic development failure, we find it more convenient to blame the population to gain immediate political mileage whereas the planning and programming done is based on the latest available Census and not on artificial assumptions. That being so, it categorically contradicts the statements being made by the economists in the government and the politicians, even though not acknowledged and admitted, the very failure in maintaining a systematic balancing of the targets and achievements amounts to self-admission of the economic development failure.

The World Bank in an Article 'Invest in People to Improve India's Human Capital' dated 17 November, 2021 on its Website states "vesting in human capital - people's health, skills, knowledge, and potential - is the most important long-term investment any country can make for future prosperity and well-being. In India today by the time children grow up and start working, they are likely to be just half as productive as they could have been with full education and good health. A strong focus on human capital development can help India achieve higher economic growth, more and better jobs, and improve the qua of life of its population. The COVID-19 pandemic risks wiping out some major human capital gains that India has made over the years, while slowing progress in other areas. This film highlights the importance of human capital for India. It narrates the story of a young girl and a boy and their growth towards becoming a productive member of society.

In not so understanding indicates the human development failure on the part of the governance. Once born on Mother Earth, no one has right to make human die. The birth of suicides is the cause of the governing system negligence though, in political language, it can be attributed to many causes other than the negligence. All kinds of suicides have direct bearing on the utter negligence towards needs that have their own various characters and compulsions. Tracing such characters and compulsions on a continual basis is the fundamental function of the educational and economic development which cannot be detached from the humans and attached to inexcusable excuses. The real education and economic development alone have the strength and capacity to prevent the tragic suicides. Why a man or a woman is forced to resort to this last call of life? Denial of opportunities for self-growth and absolute carelessness to take such person in the arm of the governing system, the society and the individual citizens and comfort him or her with creative life that alone has the sense of life.

The spate of suicides, of late, occurring in the country for one other reasons of which, the crucial reasons being the increasing signs of depression trends among the students aiming at higher studies, among the married couples for reasons of self-assumed negativity in mind or pressure of In-laws either on account of dowry or the desire to hold control over the newly married girl directly or through her husband. This is the second largest category that comes within the meaning of suicides. Third and last category is the aged parents or elders left uncared by the family thereby creating a hell in their livelihood and bid Question Mark, how to live in future which, if does not offer any seeable solution, their last resort is also the suicide. Our education and social systems must accord highest importance and urgency right from the school level emphatically making the children and youngsters the dangers of isolating their grandparents at the critical moment of the lives. A psychological awareness must dawn in the minds of the children which is achievable only through moral and ethical based education system. Today's parents would be tomorrow's grandparents and as noted in one of the Articles given above, there is also need for the governing system to enlarge their participation in the nation building that would assure them a second line of protection for their livelihood.

I have suggested below the need for an independent body to realistically address this growing tendency on the part of the youngsters, the old aged and among the married couples. There is something wrong somewhere that is needed to be investigated with human and not mechanical mind. If we save one human today from suicides, we are going to create millions of humans for the future generation. Life is not the birth right of only those who have learnt to live happily with possessions acquired illegally which is worse than suicide because it amounts to snatching away from others something available. The first degree of obligation and responsibility for the suicides rests upon the governing system, its policies and programmes, all of which are launched and implemented for human welfare, lack of which is human suicide.

SUICIDE ISN'T COWARDLY. I'LL TELL YOU WHAT'S COWARDLY; TREATING PEOPLE SO BADLY THAT THEY WANT TO END THEIR LIVES." - ASHLEY PURDY

Let the nature and the population grow. Let us be honest to ourselves how best we can serve both. Young generation is conscious and aware of how to plan their life and future whether in metros, urban or rural by now and leave the choice to them about the population growth. Let us not invite a time when we would be needed to go to populated countries for adoption of the children. This is also one of the causes for forced family planning programs, the anti-thesis of creativity for economic development and self-development. It is the governing system invention to blame the population growth rather than blaming itself for its utter failure to meet the human growth challenge through sensible education and economic development.

It is rightly said — if you educate a man, you educate an individual. But if you educate a woman, you educate whole family and nation. Education is an integral part of every individual's life but when girls are educated, countries become stronger and prosperous. It is time the chorus for family planning is shifted to 'educate woman, she will educate the family and nation'. There is still a significant 'gender-bias' in offering the opportunities of education to male and female children. Men have more access to education. Education helps women attain economic independence and social status. It enhances their earning capacity as well. Education for women makes a favourable impact on the fertility rate and health care of women and children. It tends to bring down the birth rates that help in reducing the population growth rate. This suggests also the need for shifting at least fifty percent of the funds allocated for family planning for education of women that helps develop cognition of family planning among the women of its own. A recent news item notes that the Indian youths are aging. A balanced growth will by itself address the aging problem – births and rebirths are continual and not constrictive. That is how Mother Earth provides the guiding light. The nation should not lose its human assets other than natural deaths which is inevitable.

Hindustan Times in an Article 'Govt issues draft norms to prevent student suicides' By Fareeha Iftikhar posted in Edition dated October 4, 2023 states:

"The guidelines have been drafted at a time when a spate of suicides has been reported among school students preparing for competitive exams in Rajasthan's Kota, India's test prep hub.

To prevent suicides among school students, Authorities must be able to identify early warning signs of self-harm by forming wellness teams, fostering a supportive environment and integrating mental well-being in everyday functioning, draft guidelines released by the education ministry said on Tuesday.

There is a need to promote mental health and well-being among students, said the draft document titled UMMEED (understand, motivate, manage, empathize, empower, develop) by the ministry's department of school education and literacy, in line with the National Education Policy 2020. The draft document was released for public consultation.

Noting that the reasons for suicide are complex and differ from individual to individual, the draft said it was important to be aware that at times, suicide can be an impulsive act that can take place due to immediate events causing extreme stress.

"Students go through many transitions during their school life which can cause extreme stress, for example, transition from home to school, from one school to another, school to college, losing a parent, sibling, friend, near and dear one, etc.," the guidelines said. "Along with this, children also experience changes as they progress through the developmental stages, leading to concerns such as those related to physical changes and appearance, peer pressure, career decisions, academic pressure, and many more."

"It is important to discard damaging notions, including comparisons with peers, the perception of failure as permanent, and the sole measurement of success based on academic performance," they suggested.

The guidelines have been drafted at a time when spates of suicides have been reported among school students preparing for competitive exams in Rajasthan's Kota, India's test prep hub. There have been 25 cases of death by suicide among students in Kota so far in 2023.

The guidelines emphasize the formation of school wellness teams led by the principal, and having school counsellors, students, teachers, a representative of the school management committee, and a school supporting staff as members. The team will play an important role in implementation of school activities directed towards creating awareness about mental well-being that lead towards suicide prevention.

"When a student displaying warning signs has been identified by any stakeholder, they need to be reported to the SWT, which takes immediate action," the guidelines stated.

They divided warning signs into three categories– feelings, behaviour and actions. Students who exhibit feelings of hopelessness, helplessness, worthlessness, guilt and shame, or having lack of concentration, withdrawal from social interactions and sudden mood swings are at risk. They also place students with reckless behaviour, talking about self-harm or ending life and becoming detached, among others, as those displaying warning signs.

"The warning signs are indicators that a student is at risk of suicide. Identifying the warning signs is important to provide timely support to students, as it is these signs which would lead to identifying those at risk of harming themselves," the guidelines stated.

The wellness teams would listen to the identified students and encourage them to talk to counsellors. The counsellors would interact with the students through counselling sessions. The team will maintain records of such students and will keep following up with them, the guidelines recommended.

Emphasising the importance of building capacity of stakeholders, which includes teachers and school staff, students, families of students and other stakeholders, the guidelines stated, "An important step in this direction is to enhance their knowledge and skills in recognising warning signs, providing support, and responding promptly to students at risk."

They also suggested to de-stigmatising mental health concerns such as anxiety, depression, suicide, substance abuse through storytelling, rallies, posters, exhibitions and other activities.

The wellness teams should be reconstituted regularly to provide all stakeholders an opportunity to build awareness, the guidelines said, suggesting periodic review of their functioning.

"These guidelines align perfectly with the NEP's vision of holistic education. They emphasize not only academic excellence, but also the emotional well-being of our students," said Jyoti Arora, principal of Mount Abu Public School in New Delhi. "By nurturing partnerships between schools, parents and the community, we can collectively work towards preventing suicide and reducing the stigma surrounding mental health issues."

'**YOUTH KI AWAZ [YKA]** has posted an Article '**The Silence Epidemic: A Closer Look at Student Suicides -** by Kunaljha94 dated 15 March, 2023 on its Website which is reproduced hereunder:

"TW: SUICIDE AND DEATH

Losing a student to suicide is a devastating experience that can leave friends and family feeling helpless and hopeless. However, in times of darkness, it is essential to hold onto hope and remember that there are reasons to keep fighting. As I *Jamie Tworkowski* once wrote, *"Don't give up on your story. Don't give up on the people you love. Hope is real. Love is real. It's all worth fighting for."* These inspiring words remind us that, despite the difficulties we may face, there is always a reason to persevere. This article will delve into the complex issue of student suicide and explore ways we can come together to prevent it.

Introduction

While farmer suicides in India are generally known as a crisis, student suicides are becoming more and more covert. In fact, more students died by suicide than farmers. In two separate occurrences, three students who were studying for admission exams in Kota, Rajasthan, allegedly committed suicide.

India has a lot of untapped potential, which is revealing itself in the youth and students who are replacing even grownups in the workplace and advancing themselves in every way. This youth is made up of many students from different parts of the nation who are pushing themselves beyond what is reasonable for teenagers or college students to accomplish. However, among this large group of students, many are struggling with trauma, depression, and anxiety due to various career-related issues.

The third most common cause of mortal amongst young adults worldwide is suicide. Preventative measures need to be conducted with cultural sensitivity and customized to the region-specific characteristics of a country; it is becoming increasingly clear. Youth are now the group most at risk in one-third of both developed and developing nations due to the sharp rise in suicide rates within this age group. Because the employment of new suicide methods is linked to pandemic rises in overall suicide rates, the problem of "Cyber-suicide" that is rising in the internet era is also cause for concern.

Why Suicide?

Only Indian households and educational establishments can provide the solution to this problem. Children in India are forced to study hard for a secure future while also being strongly influenced by the multifaceted socio-economic, cultural, and psychological atmosphere and milieu present in higher education institutions, which stimulates drastic measures such as suicide. When a person is at their lowest point, it may appear like their only alternative is to die since they are unable to understand their own feelings and thoughts.

Causes of Student Suicides in India

Many theories and explanations have been offered for suicide. Emile Durkheim offered a solid foundation for a sociological approach on teenage suicide, arguing that suicide has a societal component. He said that communities with the correct balance amid individual initiative and community cohesion also have the lowest suicide rates. Suicide is more complex than being only a manifestation of mental disease.

Integration and regulation are two important aspects, in Durkheim's view, that have an impact on suicide rates. According to Durkheim, regulation refers to the presence and significance of norms, regulations, and laws, both informal and official, while integration refers to a person's interactions with others and their role in their communities. Both of these things must be in balance. Suicide may happen from having too much or not enough of either.

With over 1 billion people, India is the second-most populated country in the world. It additionally has one of the biggest rates of suicide among people between the ages of 15 and 29 and third-most female suicides worldwide each year. Academic stress is the most well-known cause for both male and female students' suicide in India, and it is a common cause. One recent instance of this is the 10th-grade girl student who died by suicide on March 3 in the Dausa district of Rajasthan. In her suicide note, the student stated that she was stressed out about her upcoming board examination and that she had no way to cope with the pressure of getting more than a 95% on her exams.

The stress extends much beyond high school and college. The stories of successful students receiving top grades and top job offers that make headlines significantly contribute to parents asking their kids to follow in such footsteps.

Reasons

Academic Pressure

Academic strain is a key cause of student suicides in India. Throughout a student's academic career, there is frequent pressure to perform well in the classroom. Parents and society have lofty aspirations for students' academic performance, frequently equating it with future employment opportunities and social standing.

The competitive pressure in India's educational system puts greater strain on students. Students must indulge in fierce competition to gain admission to the top colleges and universities because there are only a limited number of seats available. This competitiveness fosters a climate of extreme pressure and stress that could be harmful to a student's mental health.

Moreover, India's educational system frequently emphasises memorization and rote learning while putting less of an emphasis on critical thinking and innovation. This strategy can be particularly difficult for students who, despite their best efforts, may find it difficult to achieve academic success. The strain is too much to bear because each person is born with unique talents, aptitudes, and abilities. Academic pressure can increase if a student feels inadequate, ashamed, or unsuccessful as a result of not meeting expectations in the classroom.

The nature of university environment, particularly one that places a focus on examinations, the stress of studying, and competence are critical attributes in student suicides. Parents have a vital role in unsettling the children. Yet, parents place responsibilities on their children who have been victimized by the exam-centric system in order to fulfil their own aspirations and to perform well on the exam.

Former University does not grant Commission head Professor Armaity Desai is adamant that state-level nor are federal governments doing enough to prevent student suicides. The superior education being provided in educational institutions is severely harmed, and our educational system forces pupils to learn things they may never use in the real world. This increases the pressure to perform, particularly during exams. Suicidal thoughts could result from the worry.

Competitive Environment

For students, the competitiveness in India's educational system is a very stressful and difficult component. There is fierce rivalry for the few available places in top colleges and institutions, with a huge number of applicants. Students may experience significant levels of stress, anxiety, and depression as a result of this very competitive environment.

Early in a student's academic career, competition and academic achievement are prioritised, and students frequently attend private tutoring alongside their usual classes. The overwhelming pressure to achieve well in school can cause people to prioritise grades above a comprehensive approach to learning. In order to strengthen their college applications, students can feel pressured to join in extracurricular activities, which increase their workload as well as stress levels.

Ragging and Bullying In Educational Institutions

In India, ragging refers to the negative interactions between juniors, freshmen, or first-year students and the seniors in an institution or school. It frequently entails insults, doing errands for seniors, and numerous other intricate tasks. Many serious injury claims against the victims have resulted from it. In India, ragging is subject to strict legal restrictions.

Today's ragging has made a comeback under the cover of cyberbullying. Children have been ridiculed and made a spectacle of through cyber bullying. This causes low self-esteem, which eventually causes various other issues to arise, including depression as well as other psychological disorders. This could ultimately result in their killing themselves.

Breaking the Silence: The Impact of Social Stigma on Accepting Sexual Orientation

One's sexual orientation becomes clearer mostly while they are young. If they come to terms with their sexual—gay, lesbian, bisexual, or any other—it presents its own set of challenges. Because to the stigma attached to it, it is very tough to accept and to communicate with family, friends, and classmates.

The young person is under tremendous strain because most parents and family members do not understand their sexual orientation.

In addition to the high prevalence of bullying and jeering directed at LGBTQ children by classmates in schools and universities, the following factors have been linked to high suicide rates among this group of young people.

– Lack of emotional support when relationships fail;

– The belief that a relationship cannot progress to its logical conclusion;

– Concern that a partner will submit to family pressure and get married;

– Concern that one will never find love again given the low number of LGBT people in society;

– The pressure to keep the relationship a secret at all times.

Dr. Shreyas Magia, a psychiatrist, argues that because their relationship was viewed as "abnormal" by society as a whole, a Gay person was unable to communicate the specifics with their family or friends, which intensified their distress and made them emotionally more frail and susceptible. The fact that the relation can rarely progress to a point of resolution worries these kids a lot. This adds to the chaos and lowers the person's self-esteem.

Financial Pressure and Emotional Neglect

Students may experience emotional neglect, identity issues, social isolation, and financial strain to maintain their studies.

Due to their busy schedules, parents frequently disregard the warning indications of suicide. The emotional pressure is increased by the teen's sense of emotional deprivation and neglect, combined with his or her sense of being abandoned and forgotten. They feel as though their absence won't even be noticed if they disappear because of this emotional neglect.

Lack of Adequate Support

When it comes to their children's educational choices, parents in Indian families frequently have significant influence and may even put pressure on them to choose certain subjects or professions that they perceive to be more prestigious or socially acceptable.

In Indian society, there is often a pervasive **"Log Kya Kahenge"** mentality that can affect school and university going students as well as aspirants preparing for competitive exams. This mindset is the result of a ubiquitous stimulus for behaviour and decision-making in people: fear of social rejection or judgement.

Instead of letting their children pursue their interests and passions, parents often push them to pursue jobs in engineering, law, or medicine, for instance. Given that their families may have higher hopes for their academic success and in their careers.

Parents may object when their children indicate interest in choosing a different course of study or career because they are concerned about what other people may think or say. For students, this pressure can be detrimental because it can result in a loss of autonomy as well as more stress and worry.

It is critical to foster an atmosphere where students may follow their hobbies and interests without worrying about being judged or criticised by their family or society. This can improve students' general wellbeing by lowering anxiety and psychological stress among them.

Forced Career Choices and Not Speaking Up

In general, a lot of children in our nation give in to intense pressure, particularly from their household and professors, regarding their academic pursuits and job choices. In India, it has long been a problem that young people are frequently pushed in a particular direction by family and societal pressures irrespective of their own inclinations or abilities. This might cause kids who are required to do well academically and find well-paying careers to feel forlorn and dejected, in particular.

Many incidences of student suicide in recent years have been related to the anxiety and stress of being compelled to make a professional decision. Students who don't live up to their families' or society's expectations may feel like failures, which can lead to melancholy and feelings of futi. These emotions may be made worse by the fierce battle for employment in some industries, which may prompt some students to act in an extreme manner.

This issue is exacerbated by a number of variables, such as a lack of vocational counselling and assistance, limited or no access to educational and employment possibilities, and cultural mind-sets that place a high value on academic and financial achievement. High tuition costs and outstanding student loans are two additional financial struggles that many Indian students experience, which can increase the pressure to perform.

Socio-Economic Factors

Socioeconomic issues, like poverty, inequality, and social standing, can have a significant impact on a student's educational prospects and performance in India. It can be extremely difficult for students from low-income families to get the education and resources they need to excel academically.

A student's academic success and mental health may suffer as a result of poverty restricting access to needs like food, shelter, and healthcare. Another important socioeconomic aspect influencing pupils in India is educational inequality. Students from underrepresented groups may experience bias and discrimination, which will restrict their access to resources and high-qua education. Additionally, a student's social standing can affect their educational chances and achievements, with a higher social standing granting them access to more opportunities and resources.

Impact of Student Suicides on Society

A. Impact on Families

The death of a child to suicide is a painful experience that can cause the members of the family left behind to feel overwhelming grief, guilt, and anger. Relatives of children who have committed suicide could feel a variety of things, such as shock, bewilderment, and extreme sadness. They could feel bad for missing the red flags or not supporting their child enough. They might also experience blame and stigma from society, which would make their suffering and loneliness worse.

Families who lose a child to suicide may suffer long-term effects on their psychological health and general wellbeing. Post-traumatic stress disorder, anxiety, and depression are all possible among parents and siblings (PTSD). They might also experience monetary and interpersonal difficulties.

B. Impact on Educational Institutions

When a student takes their own life, it can affect the institution's academic performance as well as cause trauma and mourning among the students, professors, and staff. Lower attendance rates, less involvement in leisure activities, and a lack of a desire to study can all be caused by a drop in student morale.

Following a student suicide, institutions may also be subject to legal and financial repercussions. If they don't give the kid enough help or resources, they can be held accountable, which could result in legal action and financial losses.

Measures To Prevent Student Suicides in India

Government Initiatives

The National Mental Health Program (NMHP)

In order to address the issue of mental health and prevent suicides, the Government of India introduced the National Mental Health Policy in 2014. The goal of the policy is to raise awareness of mental health issues and improve mental health services.

The National Suicide Prevention Strategy

The National Suicide Prevention Hotline was established by the Indian government in 2018 to offer those who are having suicide thoughts round-the-clock emotional support. The phone number to call is 080-46110007.

The Mental Healthcare Act

It was approved in 2017 to establish a legislative structure for the nation's promotion and defence of mental health. The act has provisions relating to the advancement of mental health services and the prevention of suicide.

Youth Red Cross

It is a non-profit group that collaborates with the government to stop teen suicides. The group supports those who are dealing with mental health problems and raises awareness about preventing suicide.

Data on Student Suicides:

According to *NCRB Statistics*, 12,526 students committed suicide in 2020, and 13,089 did so in 2021. The report omits mentioning the precise causes. Nonetheless, it claims that 864 out of 10,732 children under the age of 18 committed suicide as a result of "failure in exams". "Family issues" was the leading factor in suicide among individuals under the age of 18.

According to the most recent report for 2021, suicide cases also rose. 13,089 pupils, 56.51 percent of whom were men and 43.49 percent of whom were women, committed themselves.

- People under the age of 25 make up 53.7% of India's population, which includes adolescents and young adults. However, because they lack the necessary skills, the majority of these youths are not employable.

- In 2020, a student committed suicide every 42 minutes, or more than 34 students committed suicide each day, according to the *National Crime Record Bureau (NCRB)*. 13,089 student suicides, or 8.4% of all deaths, reached a record high in 2022.

Conclusion

In India, student suicides in higher education institutions have become a significant social issue. The causes of student suicides are a complex web of problems and influences. What drives someone to make such a drastic choice as ending their life? What is it about this age, which is viewed as the most exciting and hopeful time of life, that makes life not worth living? Are the youth's tolerance waning or are mistakes not being accepted with grace? Such inquiries on student suicide are numerous. Suicides are caused by many socioeconomic, psychological, and cultural factors.

To reduce the danger in India's higher education institutions, several actions have been started. Nonetheless, the aforementioned debate amply illustrates the fact that risk factors for student suicide are not limited to academic institutions. There are a number of other factors that are outside of educational institutions' purview. Hence, macro and micro level interventions are required for suicide prevention programmes. Also, it is necessary to conduct detailed study on the efficacy of various therapies. This will make it easier to strengthen the interventions that work.

It is crucial to realise that suicide is not a reasonable solution. It destroys many other lives in addition to their own. There is assistance out there. There are those who are more than willing to support them in coping with it, including counsellors, psychologists, and even close friends."

[This post has been self-published. Youth Ki Awaaz neither endorses, nor is responsible for the views expressed by the author.]

The Draft Norms issued by the Central Government on prevention of suicides among the students at the places of educational institutions and coaching hubs need to take into consideration the Articles on the subject matter stated before. The articles throw wider aspects of the reasons for the suicide which have to be addressed truly and honestly by the central and state governments as integral part of the human development. Failing that, we should know, the death of youngsters does not bring back life. This group of the generation resorting to such extremity to end life has to be considered as loss of golden ornaments in hand for the sake of human growth and development of future generations. Giving the picture what has been brought out in the Articles given before to the present generation for reading and understanding would precariously haunt them psychologically for their self-growth, the basic asset for the self, family and national development. The draft norms look like sermons without any pointed action oriented measures which have the capacity to console and comfort the youth community, especially, the ones who are on the brink of their life as well as compel the educational institutions and coaching hubs to comply with. There has to be a national body or commission to keep constant watch over such happenings at the national level and to take rigorous measures against defaulting institutions in order to sensitizing such institutions and their obligations towards the safety of the students under their control.

A body or commission to be known as "National Commission for Prevention of Student and Other Suicides [NCPSOS] has to be conferred adequate powers to deal with the student and other suicides. Committees for such purpose exist in some of the countries including China [Hong Kong]. This is suggested keeping in view the fact that the central and state political leaders first want to save their skin blaming each other ignoring the impact of the tragic incidents which could be controlled and solved only through affection and redressal methods of the students prone to suicides. This task if left at the mercy of the institutions and the coaching hubs, they become more pressurized within themselves to safeguard their interests and standing reputation whereby the seriousness of the preventive and investigative measures miss in their initiatives that could at best be a routine exercise for them. The central and state governments though react to such tragic events including the setting up of committees, ministers and political leaders visiting the institutions and the coaching hubs, such exercise is to silence the public outcry as far as possible thinking human memory is short.

An Article posted on the WIRE Website written by Sepoy Sarveswar and Johns Thomas dated 02/Jun/2022 , "More students died by suicide than farmers in 2020, yet, while farmers' suicides are widely recognised as a crisis in India, students' suicides are increasingly swept under the rug.' notes, among others, scholars have long linked farmers' suicides to India's agrarian crisis; it is time that civil society starts looking at students' suicides as an indicator of a grave crisis of the country's educational structure – including the institutional structure, curriculum, and the like. The few publicly-funded educational institutions in the country, such as Indian Institutes of Technology (IITs) and medical colleges, see huge numbers of applications as students compete for a limited number of seats; those who can afford it either go to foreign countries to study or join private universities in India. The failure of the Union government to improve the country's educational infrastructure means that exam-oriented coaching had become the norm. Cashing in on the 'hope for a better future,' coaching centres emerged as one of the predominant industries in the education sector. However, these centres are now being seen as prisons for the many youngsters who join them; where *their bodies, souls and dreams are tamed.* What's more, students from marginalised sections are pushed further to the margins through a number of factors, such as the lack of English-medium education; private institutions charging high fees; poor qua education in government-run schools and institutes; ever-growing economic inequality; graduates not having the adequate skills to secure jobs; and caste discrimination. The rise of neoliberalism as an economic and social ideology has pushed the youth to blame themselves for their failure to secure their 'dream job' while the government continues to shirk its basic responsibility. The neo-liberal agenda keeps propagating the belief that it is not that hard to find success if one works hard enough, normalising the notion that the youth should blame themselves for their 'failures". [Emphasis added]

What is one good thing, however, to be noted is that the need for addressing the student suicides has at last dawned in the mind of the central government. The state governments are still in the state of slumber, hardly have any time to think such serious incidents happening under their nose because they try to be busy to find out political blames against each other rather than collectively finding solution to the problem. Appointment of committees and the routine police investigations are the anti-thesis of the solution. This is known as constitutional indifference to the treatment of humans, their own citizens. The norms, circulars and dry speeches get swept away in the sorrowful wind the country is facing right now. Think about that and act on that to provide timely and realistic breathing to the affected student community. The norms and circulars are bare bodies without intent or any commitment. The affected students are someone's son and daughter who they consider as the blossoming flowers and shelter for their future. One suicide may multiply the suicides within the family and society for want of assured protection of life growth to younger generation and a secured protection to the family.

The central and state government also need to consider providing financial aid to the poor students for pursuing higher education including for undergoing coaching at the privately established recognized coaching centres in form of aid though higher educational loans are available to them from the State owned Banks. This is normally availed by the students going abroad for higher studies. The suggested aid is intended for the students who are identified as prone to extremities due to financial pressure and inability of the family to meet the ends for higher education within the country but have an intent aspiring for higher education. If this is addressed to the satisfaction of the youth community, there won't be need for being guided by the Caste System presently occupying upper most mind of the political community. Their purpose is to divide and rule for their own self-benefit of gaining the political power. If we go back on historical background on the caste based reservation, this was intended for a limited time from the date of coming into force of the constitution. This went on extending ten yearly basis every time. Now, the politicians want this to be placed on permanent basis. This is not for welfare of the castes but for their own self-interest since, they believe, it works like magic wand during elections.

The question we must, therefore, ask ourselves is who amongst us needs rights the most? Certainly not those who sit on the top of the caste and gender hierarchy. As Justice D.Y. Chandrachud pointed out at the B.R. Ambedkar Memorial Lecture in January, most upper castes have already converted their historical privileges into contemporary socio-political capital. But it is the poorest, the underprivileged among us to whom the Constitution gives the equa that the society denies them in everyday life. [Emphasis added]

Hindustan Times, New Delhi Edition published an Article 'can't target coaching centres for suicides, parents to blame: Supreme Court' By Abraham Thomas - Nov 21, 2023:

"The Supreme Court on Monday said that blaming the mushrooming of coaching institutes for the rising suicides among students, primarily in Kota, was not correct because it is the high expectations put by parents in a competitive environment that is driving children to end their lives.

Refusing to entertain a petition that sought regulation of private coaching institutes and a law to prescribe their minimum standards, a bench headed by justice Sanjiv Khanna said, "The problem is of parents and not of coaching institutes."

Conscious of the fact that nearly 24 suicides have been reported this year in Kota district in Rajasthan, where such institutes offering engineering and medical coaching for school going children have grown, the bench, also comprising justice SVN Bhatti, said, "Suicides are not happening because of the coaching institutes. They happen because the children cannot meet the expectations of their parents. The number of deaths could be much higher."

The court was hearing a public interest litigation (PIL) filed by a Mumbai-based doctor Aniruddha Narayan Malpani who blamed coaching institutes for driving students to the point of death by using children as "commodity" for selfish gains.

The petition argued by advocate Mohini Priya said that while suicides in Kota have grabbed headlines, the phenomenon is common to several private coaching institutions, and there is no law or regulation that holds them accountable.

"Most of us would like not to have coaching institutes," the bench said. "But nowadays, the examinations have become so competitive and there is a lot of expectation from parents. Students lose out by half a mark or one mark in competitive exams."

Court suggested the petitioner to either approach the Rajasthan high court as suicide incidents cited in the petition largely pertained to Kota, or move a representation to the Union government. "How can we direct a legislation on this issue?" it asked.

At this point, advocate Mohini Priya sought permission to withdraw the petition, indicating that the petitioner would prefer moving a representation, which the court permitted.

The petition argued that student suicides is a grave human rights concern and the "lackadaisical attitude of the Centre in enacting a law despite the rising number of suicides clearly reflects upon state's apathy towards protecting young minds who are the future of our country". It said that it was their constitutional right to live with dignity guaranteed under Article 21 (protection of life and liberty).

The Rajasthan government recently introduced the Rajasthan Coaching Institutes (Control and Regulation) Bill, 2023, and Rajasthan Private Educational Institutions Regulatory Authority Bill, 2023, as steps to control and regulate the functioning of private coaching institutes. The two bills are yet to become a law."

India Today's Article 'The Kota student suicides and why we need to stop normalising academic pressure' - On World Suicide Prevention Day, here's a deeper look at the staggering rise of student suicides in the pressure-filled competitive exam coaching centres of Kota written by Roshni Chakrabarty - New Delhi, UPDATED: Sep 10, 2023 23:05 IST.

This Article is an enlightening presentation on the students' suicides and endeavours to address every aspect of the subject matter. It reads as follows:

"It is no secret that a vast majority of Indian parents want to see their children succeed as doctors and engineers. Around 93% of students were aware of just seven career options as per a 2019 study. While the awareness among students may have increased in the digital surge during the pandemic years, the numbers may not have changed much for parents.

But this unawareness of the large number of booming career options and a pressure to perform academically, fuelled by relentless pressure exerted by families and institutions to excel, shrinking employment opportunities, and a toxic competitive culture in coaching institutes, is costing India dearly – it's pricier than the whooping Rs 12,000 crore coaching industry of Kota.

On World Suicide Prevention Day, we need to note that among the estimated 7 lakh suicides occurring worldwide each year, quite a significant number comprises India's youngsters -- suicide is the leading cause of death among those aged 15 to 30 here.

The National Crime Records Bureau reported that a student took their own life every 42 minutes in 2020, totalling 34 student suicides per day. In the same year, 11,396 children below 18 years old ended their lives.

The warning signs date back to 2015 when a National Crime Records Bureau report showed a 61.3% increase in student suicides at coaching centers. A recent survey indicates that four out of ten students in Kota grapple with mental health issues such as depression.

Around two lakh students flock to Kota annually, hoping to prepare for competitive exams like the Joint Entrance Exam (JEE) and the National Eligibility-cum-Entrance Test (NEET). In 2023, authorities reported 24 student suicides related to the pressure of competitive exams in the district in 2023, the highest number in any year.

According to Rajasthan police data, the figure was 15 in 2022, 18 in 2019, 20 in 2018, seven in 2017, 17 in 2016, and 18 in 2015. No student suicide was reported in Kota in 2020 and 2021 for the coaching institutes were shut due to the Covid-19 pandemic.

Currently, around 1.77 lakh students from across India are enrolled in nine major institutes, including Allen Career Institute, Motion Education, Resonance, Bansal, Aakash, Career Point, Physics Wallah, and Unacademy.

The coaching institutes are the lifeblood of the city, with over 4,000 students' hostels and 40,000 paying guest facilities.

It is true that many of the 2 lakh-odd students going to Kota every year end up succeeding. But not every student can handle the pressure that on psychological terms is quite abnormal.

The relentless competition among aspirants is fuelled by weekly tests, publicised results, and a fast-paced curriculum. Students find themselves trapped in gruelling 12-hour work schedules, seven days a week, far from their families and friends.

There's a lack of support for those who struggle, and the pressure to succeed is immense.

Nitin Vijay, the CEO of Kota's Motion Education institute, says that student suicides are a national issue spurred by parental pressure and over-expectations and that coaching centres shouldn't be blamed for the same.

"Before sending children to prepare for medical and engineering exams, parents need to see if their child is interested in pursuing the course. At the same time, they should focus on preparing the child to take the pressure that is required to crack competitive exams," he says.

He vouches for building self-esteem in students so they can handle the pressure of preparing for national-level competitive exams better.

Last year as well, experts suggested grooming students before sending them to Kota.

"We need to make them understand that facing failure in the process is a part of the journey, and they should not be disheartened by it," Vijay says.

"In fact, over the years, there has been a lot of enhancement in the education system, where technology is easing the learning process for students and allowing for personalised education to give a complete support system to aspirants," he says.

He feels that encouraging students to view lower grades as opportunities for improvement can not only assist them in managing exam-related stress but also equip them with valuable problem-solving skills.

While the Kota coaching industry appears more interested in financial gain than student welfare, Nitin Vijay rejects it, saying that fees are standardised across the board, including government institutions.

After Maharashtra's Avishkar Sambhaji Kasle and Bihar's Adarsh Raj couldn't withstand the intense grind of coaching institutions and ended their lives on August 27, a meeting was held the very next day in Rajasthan to address the problem.

The administration had issued directives last year, including providing weekly off days for students and conducting psychological evaluations for both students and teachers. Regrettably, these directives have yet to be fully implemented.

Now, the government aims to ensure compliance with guidelines and round-the-clock support for students' well-being. A committee led by Bhawani Singh Detha has been formed to propose preventive measures.

Recent preventative measures include a police helpline for distressed students, directives to coaching institutes to stop tests for the next two months, suggestions to organise fun activities, offering motivational content online, reducing the syllabus, and providing counselling for poorly performing or absent students.

Additionally, coaching institutes will implement a "half-day study, half-day fun" approach on Wednesdays and will not conduct routine tests for two days. A daily mental status assessment form will also be introduced.

However, these solutions do not completely address the core underlying issues.

A survey by MindPeers revealed that a staggering 75% of individuals in need of regular professional mental health care in India receive no support. This treatment gap exacerbates the mental health crisis among young people, pushing them toward despair.

The lacklustre attitude towards the seriousness of mental health issues in the country forms the foundation of this problem.

While celebrity suicides and other social issues grab headlines, the alarming rate of student and youth suicides often goes unnoticed. Society needs to recognise the complex factors leading to suicide, including parental expectations, the unforgiving education system, and societal pressures.

Administrative responses, like ordering the installation of springs and sensors on ceiling fans, only place blame on students and increase surveillance, boosting anxiety.

<u>Long-term solutions require a collaborative effort from parents, educators, institutions, policymakers, mental health professionals, and young people who have experienced the impact first-hand.</u>
[Emphasis added]

THE UNDERLYING ISSUES

Going beyond the statistics, it's crucial to delve into the underlying issues that drive students to take such drastic measures. The pressure-cooker environment in Kota's coaching centres is a glaring problem.

Students are compelled to study for about 16-18 hours a day in cramped classrooms, leaving them with little or no time for recreation or relaxation. Exams are even scheduled on weekends, adding to their stress.

As told by an ex-student from Kota's rigorous system, exams are taken every two-three weeks to assess the preparation levels. The deal breaker is the public display of the marks scored. There are separate lists for the top 10, the top 100, and those who didn't clear the test.

Moreover, the coaching centres cover the syllabus at a rapid pace. And if one cannot keep up, they will fall behind and face a syllabus that just keeps piling up. It is almost impossible to catch up.

The financial pressure from middle-class parents is also immense as these students constantly face the imminent responsibility of paying of lakhs of money – but only after they get a decent job which again, they can get only if they crack the exam they are studying for and secure a seat in a desired institute.

Many of the students who died by suicide in Kota came from small towns and middle-class or lower middle-class families. These students were likely the top of their class in their hometowns and full of hope of a successful future wherein they emancipate their parents from their restricted settings and opportunities.

It's a starry-eyed dream that they climb towards. And if one rung of the ladder breaks, or they lose their footing, they come crashing down, dreams and all.

WHY DO SUICIDAL THOUGHTS ARISE?

Suicide or suicidal behaviour results from a complex interplay of biological, socioemotional, cultural, political, and social justice factors.

In the case of young people, these influences manifest as developmental differences, parental expectations, the rigorous education system, and the marginalization faced due to factors like race, religion, or socio-economic background.

Over time, these pressures accumulate, leading to feelings of hopelessness and despair. It's important to note that the development of a mental health disorder may occur along this path, but it is not a necessary precursor to suicidal behaviour.

While short-term goals include ensuring students' mental well-being through counselling and awareness programmes, we must also question society's tendency to demand unrelenting excellence from young minds.

<u>The primary cause behind the rise of student suicides in Kota seems to be the high-pressure environment with little to no relief for students. The human psyche is simply not built to work optimally in such a setup for an extended period.</u> [Emphasis added]

<u>Over time, this intense competitiveness, lack of friendship and support among peers, the physical absence of parents, and unhealthy eating and sleeping patterns, coupled with financial pressure and lack of motivation towards the chosen career path breaks down the mental stability of the teens.</u> [Emphasis added]

Moreover, the media coverage of suicides also impacts the family and peers of the victims due to the sheer emotional upheaval that is caused by such an event that they are not taught how to deal with.

THE NEED FOR A DEEPER UNDERSTANDING

The Rajasthan government appears to have taken a proactive stance on the crisis in Kota and promises to investigate and find solutions.

While these may be welcome changes in the right direction, knee-jerk reactions and band-aid solutions like fans with springs, CCTVs, and punitive actions against scapegoats will not bring lasting change.

What is required is a much deeper and continuing engagement with all stakeholders, including parents, educators, pivotal institutions, policymakers, professionals, people with lived experiences, and young people who have faced the brunt of these tumultuous times and survived.

A deeper understanding of child psychology, including what is considered a healthy lifestyle for effective functional of developing minds is urgently needed among coaching centre officials, teachers, parents and the students themselves.

"Education and awareness campaigns are instrumental in destigmatising mental health issues and normalising conversations around them. When we encourage open, non-judgmental communication, we create a vital lifeline for those who may be struggling silently," says Dr Krishna Veer Singh, Co-Founder and CEO of Lissun.

"Recognising the warning signs of distress, such as extreme mood swings, social withdrawal, or expressions of suicidal thoughts, is equally vital. These signs should never be dismissed, and intervention should be immediate," he says.

"Seeking professional help is paramount, and individuals in distress should be empowered to reach out to mental health professionals or helplines without hesitation. Timely intervention can quite literally save lives," he adds."

I have submitted before a detailed account on the need for prevention of the suicides including, in particular, the suicides by the youngsters especially the students. I have also submitted before the valuable views of the learned writers gathered from the Google Website on the same subject matter. With due respects to the Hon'ble Supreme Court, my submissions on the Observations made by the Hon'ble Supreme Court on the subject matter in hand are given below for active and positive consideration by all those concerned with the matter:

The subject matter relates to human lives that begs for highly sympathetic and compassionate approach which is well reflected in the Articles and my own submissions made before. It is submitted that the observations made by the Hon'ble Supreme Court that the parents are to blame for suicides does not seem to be the sole cause. The causes for the suicides of the order presently taking place among the students community are hidden somewhere else but brushed aside in the storm of suicides attributing them to the parents, the students and the coaching centres. We have not travelled beyond this boundary so far to ascertain what other causes could be that are hidden and continue to be ignored at various levels. It is to be appreciated that the aspirations of the students are unstoppable which is but natural considering the present employment market conditions. Their struggle begins from the stage of nursery admission, primary, secondary, senior secondary school, then colleges and thereafter the coaching centres. Coaching centres became immensely popular throughout the country ghost town to a thriving coaching hub. Ever 1991 coaching centres attracted students like bees to honey. Singh (2018) asserts nearly two lac children study in Kota in the city's top 12 coaching institutes. These students migrate to Kota every year to receive the best. The causes for the mushrooming coaching centres are, in my personal view, are:

a. The syllabus set out by agencies concerned for the competitive examinations are of much higher level than the level of education at which the students undergo in the senior secondary schools according to the syllabus set out for such schools. The syllabus in the latter case nowhere near comparison from the competitiveness compared to the syllabus prescribed for the competitive examinations. This creates a wide vacuum between the two.

b. It could be said in percentage terms that the widening gap noted before may be 40 percent as between the syllabus for senior secondary schools and the syllabus for the competitive examinations. In other words, the standard of syllabus for the senior secondary schools is lower by 40 percent compared to the syllabus for the competitive examination. That put the students in a state of fixation that compels them to run to the coaching centres to make up the gap of 40 percent in order to gain competitiveness for appearing for the competitive examination.

c. This loophole in the senior secondary schools syllabus was found to be a golden opportunity for those whose brain started exploiting the students aspiring for competitive examinations and they converted that loophole into coaching centre system. It is like someone who is taking food at home is given 40 percent of his appetitive capacity daily, that someone would have to search for food outside the home to make up the food deficit of 60 percent.

d. This is not to suggest that there is no need for the coaching centres. Our education system right from the nursery to the senior secondary is not measurable with the standard of syllabus the competitive examinations demand for. The basic cause for the students getting depressed to compete in the competitive examinations based on the syllabus they studied in the schools is accordingly attributable to under preparation of the students capacity at the school level, particularly, in the senior secondary school.

e. But students know they can't get good employment opportunities in the fields they aspire for considering the further learning and earning capacity they hope for.

f. Those are bygone days when the parents used to put heavy pressure on their children to studying hard to be able to secure a decent job which was too much to bear in the competitive environment as then existed.

g. Education has no meaning unless it keeps updating itself with changing scientific, technological, administrative and societal environment. That is the process for updating and upbringing of the knowledge of the students in the schools. The Online coaching facilities coupled with digital system available now offers alternative scope for self-enhancement of the knowledge and competency to face the competitive examinations.

h. Every child born is an asset for its parents, the society and the country if the newly born child is well nursed to mould it for the welfare of the parents, society and the state. This is the Truth that every child holds in its eyes soon it is born. As it grows, it yearns to learn to make its own life worthy of living and respectful. All this depends upon the educational and employment environment prevailing at a given time.

i. Today's children are different compared to what they were fifty years back. They are of demanding nature and hungry for knowledge and adequacy of edging approach. This should be fundamental understanding of the developing of education system of the country. If the education system is made a barren land, the students would have to remain searching for water and shadow to sustain in such land.

j. What I am endeavouring to bring home to the educational authorities, the schools and colleges as well as those agencies who are assigned with the job for setting up syllabus for competitive examination that either the syllabus at the senior secondary schools must be upgraded comparatively nearer to the syllabus for the competitive examinations or syllabus for the competitive examinations has to be made slightly lower comparable with the syllabus for the senior secondary schools bridging up the existing gap. If the ratio between the two today is 80:110 [i.e. 80 percent at the senior secondary schools and 110 percent at the competitive examinations level, the ideal ratio will have to be 95:110 or 85:100 respectively..

k. It also needs be appreciated that there were no coaching centres in the nineteen fifties or sixties or seventies barring few for IAS examination [such as Rau's Study Circle] but the standard of syllabus at the edge of the school education was much higher that enabled the students to either to make self-studies using the past patterns or to join the available coaching centre for a short period. The coaching centre appeared on the horizon sometime in 1990s onwards. That suggests downward trending of the curriculum at the senior secondary schools.

l. To do what is submitted at [k], it is absolutely essential that the standard of syllabus at the senior secondary school level should be enhanced so that those students who are able to secure high percentage in the school level examination can make up the gap through self-study or take the help of individual coachers or institutions for a short while mainly to catch up with the trends of the competitive examinations.

m. Today we have been downgrading the standard of syllabus of the senior secondary schools and encouraging the coming up of new coaching centres.

n. It is not correct to blame the parents singularly. The parents once agree to their son's or daughter's desire to join the coaching centre to make up the gap for the competitive examinations, the parents readily agree and provide the financial assistance and what all else is needed even if they have to borrow or beg.

o. Once the son or daughter joins the coaching centre situated at different places than their residential place, the parents are entrusting them to the complete care of the coaching centres having paid the requisite fees and charges. The onus of protecting the interests of the son or daughter in such cases primarily rests with the coaching centres which they are neglecting to the extent of the scope available to them to do so in the absence of the state regulations on the setting up and working of the coaching centres.

p. If what is submitted at [o] is altogether absent, the coaching centres will have absolute freedom and free will to deal the students without anybody's control that creates psychological and physical pressures on the students driving them towards suicides, the extremity of life.

q. What impact such eventuality would bring upon the parents could be understood only by such persons who have the human heart. They also would have lost their lives not literally but physically and psychologically.

r. The coaching centres always maintain a nexus with the politicians and the police for seeking their help when the coaching centre is in deep water – looks for political and police blessings.

s. "Beyond the Classroom: Exploring the relevance of Coaching in Class 11th and 12th – Article posted on the Website of LORDS International School reads as under:

As students enter the crucial years of classes 11th and 12th, the question of whether coaching is necessary often arises. While some argue that coaching provides valuable guidance and support, others believe it may be beneficial for students to have some time off from their regular academic routines. Coaching in classes 11th and 12th can be seen as an opportunity for teenagers to have an enjoyable time without strict discipline. However, it is important to note that attending coaching classes is not always necessary if the teachers in school are providing effective instruction. Here are some key considerations to help parents and students make informed decisions about their educational journey: [Emphasis added]

When evaluating the need for coaching, consider the following:

Quality of School Teaching: Assess the quality of teaching in your school. If the teachers are experienced, knowledgeable, and provide comprehensive instruction, attending coaching classes may not be essential.

Personal Learning Style: Consider your personal learning style and preferences. Some students may thrive in a classroom environment, while others may prefer self-study. Understanding your learning needs can help you make an informed decision.

Individual Academic Goals: Reflect on your academic goals and aspirations. If you have specific targets, such as excelling in competitive exams, coaching classes may offer specialized guidance and support.

Availability of Resources: Evaluate the availability of resources and study materials in your school. If your school provides access to comprehensive materials and additional support, you may not require coaching classes.

Time Management and Balance: Consider your ability to manage your time effectively and balance academic commitments with other activities. Coaching classes can provide structure, but it is important to maintain a healthy work-life balance.

Financial Considerations: Coaching classes can be an additional financial burden on families. While some students may benefit from coaching, it may not be financially feasible for everyone. It is important for parents to assess their financial situation and prioritize their child's academic needs accordingly.

Ultimately the decision to enrol in coaching classes for classes 11th and 12th depends on the individual student's needs, aspirations, and circumstances. Striking a balance between coaching classes and personal time for self-study and relaxation is key. The goal should be to empower students to become independent learners, critical thinkers, and well-rounded individuals who are *prepared to face academic challenges and excel in their chosen paths. Whether you choose coaching classes or rely on school teaching, discipline, and dedication are key to achieving academic success."* [Emphasis added].

The Online coaching facilities coupled with digital system available now offers alternative scope for self-enhancement of the knowledge and competency to face the competitive examinations.

The Article reproduced above supplements, if not, supports the personal views submitted by me at [a] to [r] above.

My above submissions are intended to entreat the authorities concerned and judicial system to appreciate the saddest happening in reality and be kind enough to give effective directions through the regulations to make the coaching centres to whom the parents have entrusted their son or daughter to accord highest degree of humanistic considerations and financial concessions to make them achieve their life goal safely and securely so that their inbuilt tensions and anxieties are minimized to the maximum extent who would remember the coaching centre for ever during their life time. This should be sense and essence of coaching centres lest, the coaching centre would become walking in the wilderness.

In electoral democracies, that pyramid is inverted. There are no subjects but citizens. Elected representatives derive their power and identity from citizens and not the other way around. Her rights are not subject to anyone's benevolence but are inherent in her birth as a citizen and nothing can abrogate those inalienable rights from her. In the United States, for example, citizens retain unto themselves the right to do everything except those baskets which they delegate to their respective State governments (like law and order), and the States in turn delegate certain baskets (like foreign relations) to the federal government. By the virtue of the 10th Amendment, the residuary basket of rights is reserved unto the citizens themselves.

"A mother is she who can take the place of all others but whose place no one else can take." Gaspard Mermillod.

Such role and duty should not be converted into and assumed as of a 'step mother'. This understanding is posing presently most dangerous attitude towards the downtrodden communities in the country. Assurances are many but the actions are not even one third of the assurances. The gap has been widening and continues to widen for lack of oneness and belongingness among the upper castes and the lower castes that is what could be said 'divisions within ourselves' which is harmful for a country which is based on 'Unity in Diversity', when one acts contrary to the other. This is the cause which is not curing the differential caste system prevailing in the country with the patronization by the politicians. One hand, they are supposed to work together for its upliftment and, on the other hand, one could see its more mesmerisation than materialization. We will keep on talking about the castes but those will remain where they were due to lack of strict and merciless enforcement of the provisions of the Constitution and the laws made thereunder. This is bounden duty of the governance system that failed to root out the problem during the last seventy three years. To act on the problem, the governing system should have approached it from three angles. First, passive patch up, second, strict enforcement of law and the third, most important of all, the lower castes citizens should have been strongly supported to educate them from the down below with integrated system of education-cum-skill development and its continued upgradation. The ruling parties that ruled the country till the of Eleventh Five Year Plan [2012] made provisions in the plans but their implementation was uncared for and the third, added to both, the provisions of election law which should have found some way out to ban the political parties running for votes putting the castes in the front. This has reached a stage of incurability.

LET US TALK LESS ABOUT THE CASTES AND MORE ABOUT THEIR UPLIFTMENT THROUGH OPENING UP MORE AND MORE EDUCATION AND EMPLOYMENT OPPORTUNITIES, OTHERWISE WE WOULD CONTINUE TO TALK MORE WHICH IS LIKE OUR SITTING IN A BOAT THINKING THE BOAT IS FLOATING WHEREAS WE WOULD FIND LATER THAT THE BOAT IS SECURELY TIED TO THE PILLAR AT THE BANK OF THE RIVER. THIS IS KNOWN AS DAY DREAMING AND SELF-FOOLING.

Human Development

We have considered so far in terms of the Articles and the Draft Norms of the central government which talk so much about so many things about the student suicides but forget to remember that the human is made up of spiritual essence to sustain oneself. This aspect is missing in our efforts and official language of norms and circulars both of which are dispirited and, therefore, fail to sensitize the spiritualisation gifted by God to humans. It is like searching for sweet fruits in a wild forest which is the dense of the wild animals whose food is flesh and bones that makes them wilder in their attitudes.

HOPE THAT IS LIFE. THIS SHOULD BE THE BEGINNING OF THE FIRST LESSON IN THE EDUCATIONAL INSTITUTIONS AND COACHING HUBS THAT FILLS THE STUDENTS AND CHARGE THEM WITH HOPE.

"This crippling of individuals I consider the worst evil of capitalism. Our whole educational system suffers from this evil. An exaggerated competitive attitude is inculcated into the student, who is trained to worship acquisitive success as a preparation for his future career." - — Albert Einstein,

It is my sincere appeal to those thus affected is not to give any focus to the object encountered in life and never allow that object to stick in the mind by itself as an object. This does not call for great efforts. It is simpler. So many things happen in life, hang and pass away of their own. Never try to stop them. Try to face them as they come and think giving self-confidence, reasoning and control more dominance to overcome when something starts troubling. Get out of that dangerous trap surfacing around and stand firmly on the ground; it is bound to go of its own when it is not focussed and get exhausted of its own. Whatever could be the oncoming cause, build up strong confidence within with determination to overlook it, howsoever serious it may be and wait for the good things to emerge to make life worth living. It is the natural process in any one's life to come across quarrels, provocations, threatening, browbeating, mistreating, betrayal of trust and challenges and so on, face them with full self-confidence and positivity which prevents formation of any negativity. Some source living on the earth comes to help if one's intent is to avoid negativity honestly and with all the self-belief. One is not alone on earth. There is Living God in everyone, that is the bestowment of Atman (Soul) and one of everyone would be there to help representing the Spirit of the Soul. Absolute Belief that one would cross over the hurdle is the essence and existence of life. That is the greatest strength and that one should realize. Focus only on Self (Soul) within with all humbleness and gratitude. Self-prevention is better than searching for cure from somewhere that costs unsure of relief. Never lose confidence which acts as a strongest stone to stand and those who try to hit it hurts one who hits. That should be the spirit of life.

The negativity injures human in deep because, as we stand today, majority of our parents, brothers and sisters not only experiencing this factor with unbearable mental and physical pains, also coiled in them like a lady coiled the loose thread around her finger or a long scarf around her neck as if the factor is permanently planted in them not knowing that if the negativity becomes so dominant, the presence and essence of positivity disappears from life which is also there enjoyed by millions in their life.

Make the spiritual Sayings of Great Saint as part of the curriculum in the educational institutions and the coaching hubs and reserve minimum fifteen minutes to recite them and practice them by the students in every class every day after the Prayers in the schools and in the class rooms in the colleges, institutions and coaching hubs before start of the class so that they touch the Conscience of the students which has the awakening power being adjacent to the SOUL IN THE BODY. These are available in the regional languages as well, as I believe. This is one way to throw out the negativity and invite the positivity like holding a perfumed flower in hand. This is the secular way of doing that does not injure the sentiments of any religion.

Speeches by 'saints' in schools on the third Saturday of each month have been made a mandatory part of extracurricular activities by the Rajasthan Education Department.

Though there are existing many laws and Acts for the protection of Women and Children but these are not be able to protect women and Child's rights and their fundamental freedom because of the mind set of our society. We have seen that the women and children are being exploited from the ancient time and at present 21st century. We have seen in our day today life women are rape, murder, sexual harassment in their works place, public place etc. Likewise children also exploited due to their vulnerary nature. Thus, it is indicated that women and child are exploited in various aspects like economic, social etc. So, it is time to change our mind set view on women and child in our society and we should take care of them.

Paper – World Economic Forum [WEF] -Here's what young Indians really want from life – Oct 5, 2018

"India's young population is its most valuable asset and most pressing challenge."

"As the fastest growing economy today, India is home to a fifth of the world's youth. Half of its population of 1.3 billion is below the age of 25, and a quarter is below the age of 14. India's young population is its most valuable asset and most pressing challenge. It provides India with a unique demographic advantage. But this opportunity will be lost without proportionate investment in human capital development. At the same time, the world today is more dynamic and uncertain than ever before. As India undergoes rapid and concurrent economic, demographic, social and technological shifts, it must ensure that its growth is inclusive and is shared by all sections of the society. India will not be able to realize its true growth potential its youth is not able to participate adequately and productively in its economy.

In order to understand which skills and jobs India's young people want, and assess whether the current education system meets these aspirations, the World Economic Forum and the Observer Research Foundation collaboratively conducted a survey of more than 5,000 youth in India.

The results indicate that young Indians are ambitious and show greater autonomy in their career decisions. They acknowledge changing skill requirements and are eager to pursue higher education, undergo additional training and enrol in skill development programmes. At the same time, various factors are blocking their ambitions and preventing them from adapting effectively to the changing nature of work. The survey's insights can inform policies and strategic action to ensure that India's young people transition smoothly from from education to economic activity. Here are some key findings:

1. Indian youth are independent, optimistic and open to a changing labour market

The influence of family and peers on the career and educational choices of India's youth is in decline. Young people are increasingly seeking productive employment opportunities and career paths that reflect their individual aspirations. Around half of the respondents cite interest in their field of study as the primary reason for their choice, while 19% report being influenced by their families. Moreover, a third of the respondents report being interested in entrepreneurship, and 63% report being highly or moderately interested in supplementing their income with gig work. This shows a degree of openness towards alternative forms of employment.

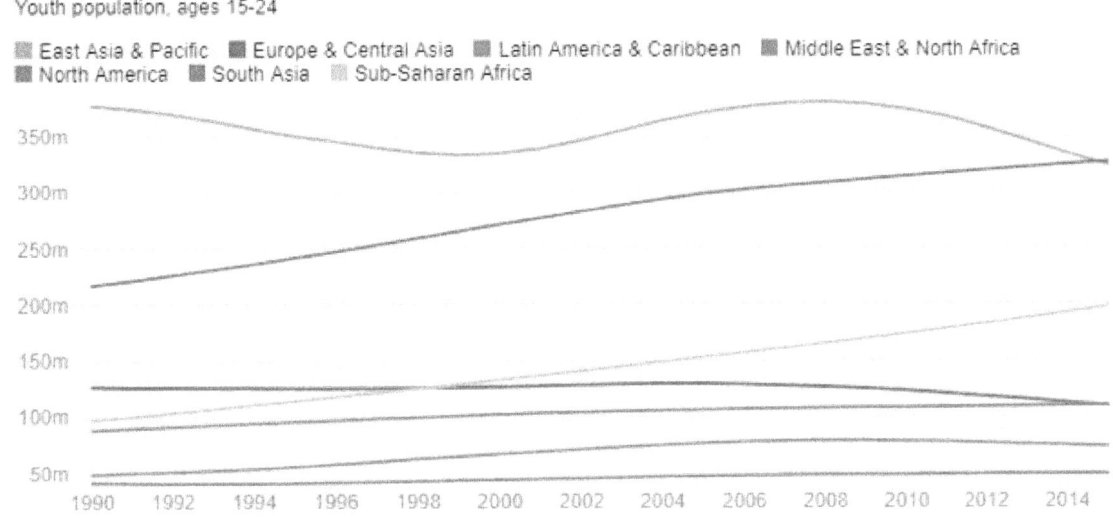

Image: World Bank Atlas of Sustainable Development Goals 2017

2. Indian youth need more guidance and career counselling

Many youth report to facing multiple barriers to finding desirable and suitable job opportunities. Factors like information asymmetries on jobs and skills, and lack of guidance for setting realistic career goals and making professional choices, are holding back young Indians. 51% of respondents report that a lack of information about available job opportunities that match their skill sets is a significant barrier. Around 30% report a lack of access to any kind of counselling or mentoring opportunities. 44% of respondents view this as the most important factor in the demand-supply mismatch.

Greater access to career counselling and mentoring services can help to address these misalignments between skills and aspirations, and improve young Indians' career choices.

3. Young Indians are interested in pursuing higher education and skills development

84% of respondents consider a post-graduate degree as a requirement for their ideal job, while 97% aspire to a degree in higher education. They are also keen on other forms of ongoing education, with 76% of youth reporting that they are very interested in participating in a skills development programme. Increased employment opportunities and higher wages are the main motivators for this goal.

This contrasts with the fact that less than 3% of the country's total working population is vocationally or professionally trained, compared to between 60-70% among developed countries.

India must leverage the optimism of its youth and support the proliferation of high-qua education and training opportunities. At present, there is an acute lack of awareness of available government-run skill development programmes. There is also significant scepticism about their qua and relevance. In order to enhance the uptake of existing programmes, it is critical to make them relevant, affordable and accessible.

4. The private sector must do more to bridge the skills gap

The private sector needs to play a more active role in enhancing the capabilities and skills of India's youth. India is faced with a paradox: there is significant youth unemployment, and yet the private sector bemoans a lack of adequately skilled and market-ready workers. Notwithstanding the government's role in providing basic education and training, there is a significant need for greater private sector involvement. This will ensure that training initiatives are demand-driven and impart skills that match industry requirements.

These programmes can be supplemented with career guidance activities with industry professionals, such as talks, seminars and workplace visits.

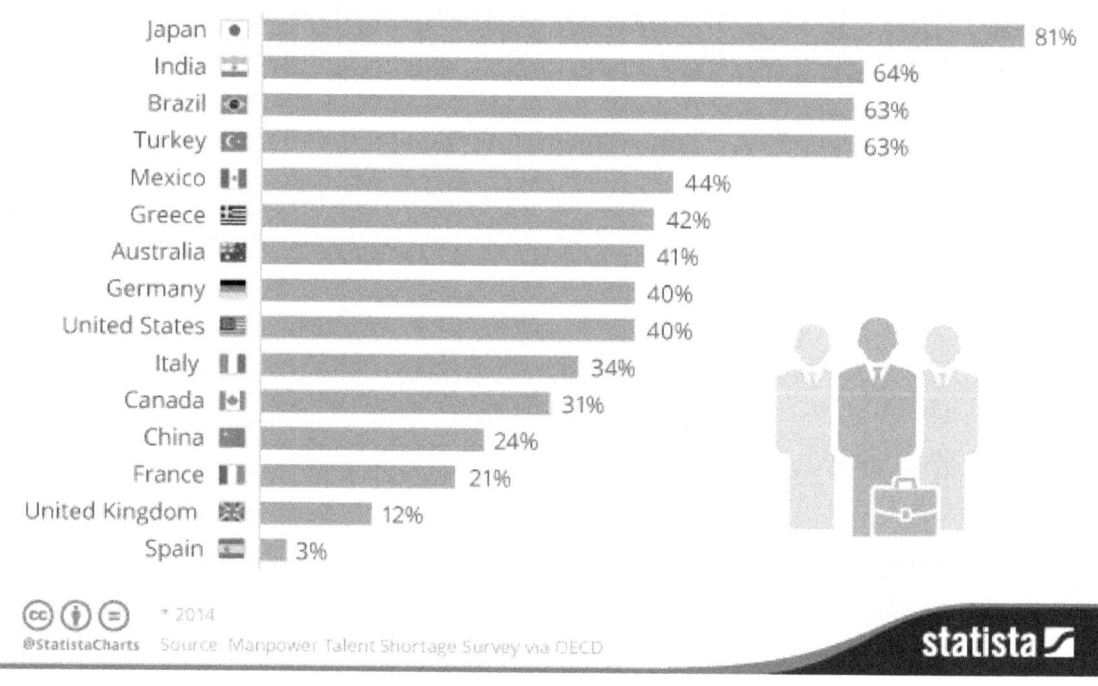

Image: Statista

5. India's socio-cultural norms add further complexity

34% of the surveyed youth report that discriminatory and personal biases related to their marital status, gender, age or family background are a major barrier when looking for a job. 82% of female respondents said their ideal employment would be full-time, disproving the stereotype that women prefer part-time jobs. Similarly, despite the persistent view that household work and unpaid work are suitable and desirable for women, only 1% of surveyed female youth report this as being a desirable option for them.

As the nature of work changes with the Fourth Industrial Revolution, existing gender-based biases are likely to widen if dedicated policies and initiatives are not implemented to address them. Efforts are needed to reduce rather than replicate the biases of today in the future workspace.

6. Social Media and the internet can play a bigger role in effective job-hunting

81% of survey respondents rely on media and internet sources for obtaining information about employment opportunities. This is particularly insightful in light of the finding from the Future of Work, Education and Skills Survey which reveals that just 14%t of surveyed firms reported using online recruitment channels.

The prevalence of social media and internet use among India's youth presents an opportunity to expand their awareness about education pathways, employment opportunities, skill needs, and available skill development programmes.

For 63% of the respondents, a good salary is the most important criteria for choosing a job. The perception of higher pay and job security is consequential in a majority of Indian youth preferring to work in the public sector and exhibiting scepticism for unconventional employment options like gig work and self-employment. More information on the changing labour market and emerging job roles through internet can help break these stereotypes and boost Indians' appetite for diverse professional and educational pursuits.

There are steps in the right direction, such as the Indian government's Start Up India initiative to boost entrepreneurship; the launch of the Skill India mission; the establishment of a dedicated Ministry of Skill Development and Entrepreneurship; the establishment of industry-led sector skills councils, and the overhaul of the Industrial Training Institutes.

While these initiatives indicate the Indian government's commitment to skilling initiatives, it is imperative to devise specific strategies that address the schism between youth employment preferences and labour market realities. As the nature of jobs and work changes with the Fourth Industrial Revolution, this gap is likely to widen. Moving forward, collaborations between various government agencies and ministries, the private sector, academic experts, training organizations, civil society and youth themselves will be critical for enhancing young India's potential. Our abi to meet the next generation's aspirations is crucial in boosting labour productivity and driving inclusive growth."

Howsoever the world makes advancement in technology, as its stands today and as may be continued to be developed, such technology has not come to Earth from blue sky but created by the humans for the convenience of and for comfort of the humans which suggests no technology could evolve of its own without the magic touch of the humans in different fields of expertize and for different purposes of the humans. The technology advancement for war games is known as negative technology inasmuch as it has to be used for killing of the humans in the name of terrorism or war games. How these games give birth also has the human touch when human is in egoistic state of mind and resorts to destructive acts. One may ask, how then would we be able to defend ourselves, our societies and our nation?

Experts are debating on this topic for years. Also, the technology covered a long way to make human life easier but the negative aspect of it can't be ignored. Over the years technological advancement has caused a severe rise in pollution. Also, pollution has become a major cause of many health issues. Besides, it has cut off people from society rather than connecting them. Above all, it has taken away many jobs from the workers class. Although technology is a good thing, everything has two sides. Technology also has two sides one is good and the other is bad. [Toppr Website]. Technology is essentially for beneficial purposes of human which if viewed with negativity becomes hurtful to the humans. Understanding this lies within the human Conscience and not in the technology.

Here lies the answer. The technology for good purposes enhances the life of humans while the technology for bad purposes, annihilates the humans. Wars are not born today. These were there since the time the human civilization dawned on Mother Earth. Two does not make one because it is sum of two ones, understanding of which provides harmony and happiness to humans while contesting that Two represents 1+1 gives birth to division of mind that infests a sense of ego and both Two and 1+1 stand opposite to each other to fight each other until each has lost the physical and spiritual strength within and fall flat on the ground. That is the end of the argument of Two and 1+1.

"Just to add, I don't agree that the formal proof is a good reason to say it's not obviously true. The logical system there gains some credibility because it proves that 1 + 1 = 2, not "1+1= 2" has credibility because the logical system proved it. If the logical system had instead come out with "1+1 does not equal 2" then we would most likely reject the logical system because it doesn't agree with our rules for addition. I would very much say that 1+1 = 2 is true by definition, it's a bit like the statement "the standard metre is one metre long" before the redefinition in terms of light speed" – Franz - May 27, 2017.

Social Isolation and Loneliness

WHO in an Article posted on its Website notes: "High-qua social connections are essential to our mental and physical health and our well-being. Social isolation and loneliness are important, yet neglected, social determinants of the health of older people.

Social isolation and loneliness are widespread, with some countries reporting that up to one in three older people feel lonely. A large body of research shows that social isolation and loneliness have a serious impact on older people's physical and mental health, qua of life, and their longevity. The effect of social isolation and loneliness on morta is comparable to that of other well-established risk factors such as smoking, obesity, and physical inactivity.

A wide variety of face-to-face or digital interventions have been developed to reduce social isolation and loneliness among older people. These include social skills training, community and support groups, befriending, and cognitive behavioural therapy. Creating more age-friendly communities, by improving access to transportation, information and communication technologies and the built environment can also help reduce social isolation and loneliness. Laws and policies that address marginalisation and discrimination can also foster greater social connection.

Social isolation and loneliness are increasingly being recognised as a priority public health problem and policy issue for older people. During the course of the UN Decade of Healthy Ageing (2021-2030), the Demographic Change and Healthy Ageing Unit will be addressing social isolation and loneliness as one of the themes that cuts across the four main action areas of the Decade."

'Public Health Concern': WHO Looking for Experts to Treat Loneliness Epidemic - Story by Times Now Digital • 3h, also notes:

"To address unanswered questions on rising loneliness among people, silently taking the form of an epidemic, the World Health Organisation (WHO) is looking for experts to join its recently announced technical advisory group on the issue.

Notably, many countries, including the United States, have already declared loneliness and self-isolation epidemics in their respective nations. US Surgeon General Dr Vivek Murthy went on to describe it as bad as smoking dozens of cigarettes.

According to the United Nations nodal agency on public health, the experts will assist in identifying strategies that might be applied to reframe the issue as an actual worldwide public health concern. Earlier, the WHO formed a panel to find ways to address social isolation and loneliness affecting people of all ages.

Globally, loneliness and social isolation are thought to be linked to a 25–33 per cent higher risk of death.

The WHO states that social isolation and loneliness, which are symptoms of a lack of social connections, impact individuals of all ages and have a major negative impact on well-being and physical and mental health, including the risk of suicide and death.

In comparison with problems like obesity, lack of exercise, and smoking, loneliness also has many health risks attached to it. For instance, social isolation and loneliness are associated with 25 to 33 per cent increased risk of morta, especially among senior citizens.

"A very miniscule percentage of old people are digitally literate today and remain self-conscious about it. This is widening the gap between generations and leading to an uncomfortable undercurrent within the four walls of almost every family across the country," TOI quoted Agewell Foundation founder Himanshu Rath as saying.

A recent survey by Agewell in 2021 among 10,000 senior citizens revealed a significant increase in a sense of loneliness or isolation among the respondents. Surveys and publications have confirmed the significance of bridging the digital divide and generation gap. In order to achieve digital equa for individuals of all ages, United Nations Secretary-General Antonio Guterres recently called for more inclusive policies, strategies, and activities."

Humans have both intrinsic and extrinsic values, of which, which is good is up to the choice of the humans. What are the human intrinsic values are given below based on the Article posted on the Website "Clearer Thinking" - Clearer Thinking Team - Sep 28 - Your intrinsic values: why they matter and how to find them - Updated: Oct 6: [Excerpts]:

"Your *intrinsic values* are the things you value for their own sake, regardless of whether they bring you anything else. This means they are the things you value most fundamentally.

Potential intrinsic value	% of respondents reporting this is an intrinsic value for them that is...		
	important (or higher)	very important (or higher)	incredibly important
That I have agency and can make choices for myself	82%	64%	37%
That I continually learn new things	78%	60%	35%
That I avoid taking actions that significantly harm others	74%	54%	28%
That the basic rights of all people are protected	73%	55%	34%
That I believe true rather than false things	72%	52%	27%
That we protect from harm those who can't easily protect themselves	72%	52%	30%
That I feel happy	69%	45%	23%
That I protect my friends and family	68%	49%	27%
That my family members have happy and successful lives	67%	47%	25%
That I am always fair in my dealings with other people	67%	41%	17%
That I show courage in the face of difficult challenges	64%	42%	20%
That I get to experience a wide variety of different things during my life	64%	42%	21%
That beautiful things come into existence (e.g., art or music)	64%	43%	24%
That I feel connected to other people	63%	42%	20%
That we do not destroy the natural environment	63%	44%	24%
That the people I know personally feel happy	60%	35%	16%
That people all around the world do not suffer much during their lives	60%	37%	19%
That I maintain my humility and don't become too prideful or boastful	59%	39%	19%
That I am able to express myself creatively	59%	38%	19%
That I am honest and don't lie	58%	38%	15%

We also ran a study to investigate whether particular intrinsic values are more associated with particular demographics. To be clear, we weren't looking to see which intrinsic values were *most common* in those groups; the most common intrinsic values (e.g., "That I feel happy") were very common across all demographics, which is not very interesting. Instead, we were looking to see which intrinsic values were *most predictive* of being a member of particular groups. We found the following:

Intrinsic values most associated with being right wing / conservative in the U.S:

1. That god is pleased with me

2. That humanity worships god

3. That those who do bad things are punished

4. That people are religious

5. That humanity is not replaced by another, more intelligent life form

6. That my values do not change to something different than they are right now

7. That I have children

Intrinsic values most associated with being left wing / progressive / liberal in the U.S.:

1. That animals (non-humans) feel happy

2. That animals (non-humans) suffer less than they do normally

3. That nature is protected from damage by humans

4. That people I don't know feel happy

5. That the world is a fair place

6. That there are lots of different kinds of humans

7. That animals (non-humans) experience more pleasure than they do normally

Intrinsic values most associated with being female:

1. That humans are kind to each other

2. That there are lots of different kinds of humans

3. That humans have the freedom to pursue what they choose to pursue

4. That I get to experience a wide variety of different things during my life

5. That I continue to care about other people

6. That I love other people

7. That not all humans have the same experiences as each other

Intrinsic values most associated with being <u>male</u>:

1. That I myself experience more pleasure than I do normally

2. That I myself am able to get the things that I want

3. That the people I know personally are able to get the things that they want

4. That the people I know personally experience more pleasure than they do normally

5. That people I don't know experience more pleasure than they do normally

6. That animals (non-humans) feel happy

7. That those who do bad things are punished

Intrinsic values most associated with being <u>older</u>:

1. That other people continue to care about me

2. That humanity becomes more moral than it is right now

3. That people trust me

4. That I avoid saying things that are false

5. That the world is a fair place

6. That I believe true things rather than false things

7. That the nature of what humans are is not one day radically altered by advanced technology

Intrinsic values most associated with being <u>younger</u>:

1. That the animals that are currently alive live longer than they normally would

2. That I am admired by other people

3. That the people I know personally experience more pleasure than they do normally

4. That people I don't know are able to get the things that they want

5. That I myself am able to get the things that I want

6. That I myself suffer less than I do normally

7. That I myself experience more pleasure than I do normally

We've developed the following categorization of intrinsic values, based on our findings across our research on the topic:

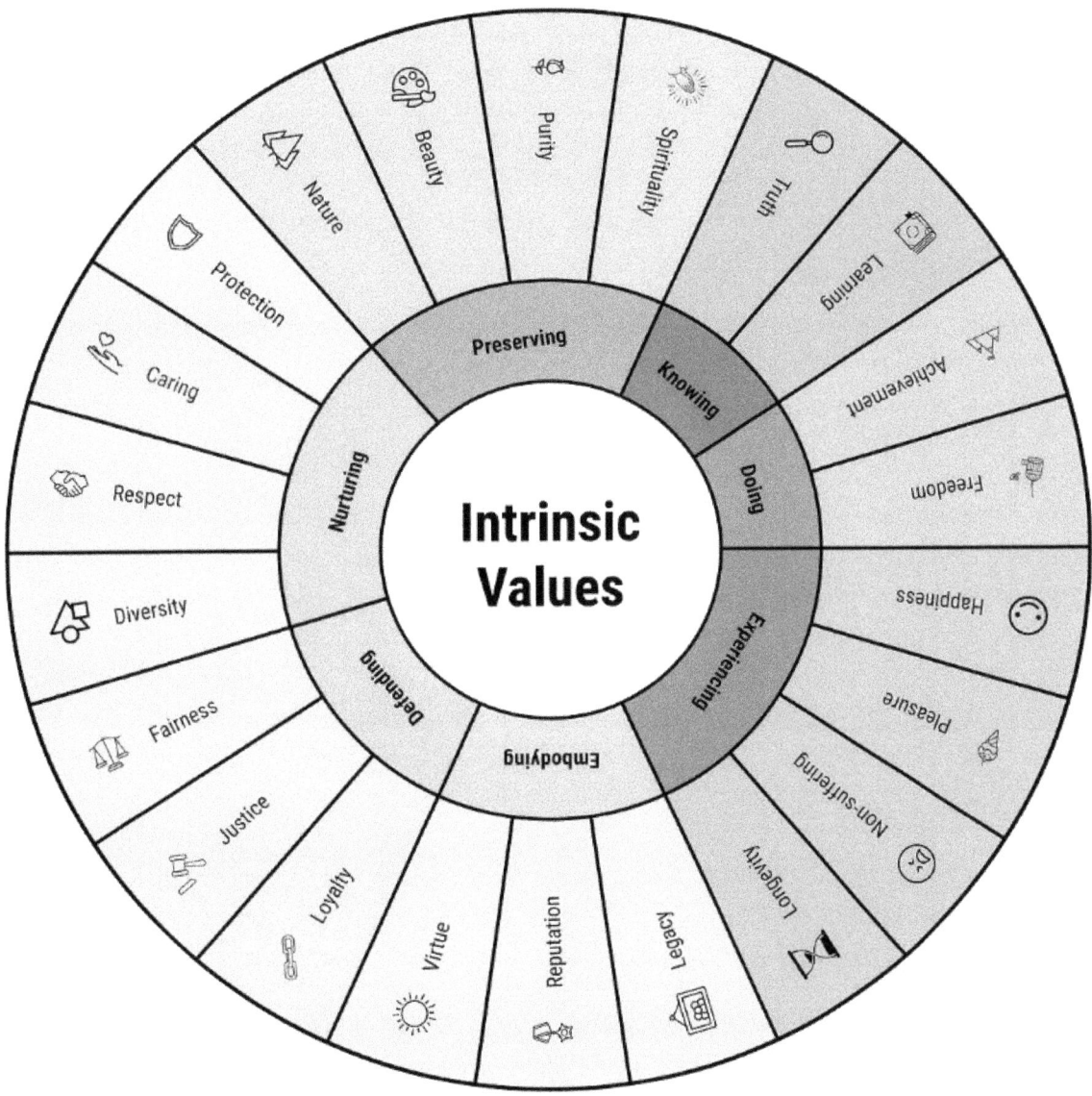

Ok, but why should you identify your intrinsic values?

Why should you care about these values? Well, there is evidence that they affect you in all sorts of ways! We've listed just a few, below.

Note: Psychological research on values often does not differentiate between intrinsic and non-intrinsic/instrumental values (this distinction is much more popular in philosophy, and we think it's an important one!); instead, it tends to focus on broad values that our studies have found it is very common for people to count among their intrinsic values (e.g., justice or happiness), just as we have in our wheel above! For this reason, although some of the research discussed below doesn't explicitly use the phrase 'intrinsic values', we think that it's reasonably accurate to characterize it in those terms.

1. **Romantic Relationships:** Research indicates that romantic partners often harbor similar intrinsic values. There is some evidence that the alignment of these values contributes to interpersonal attraction and might also play a role in overall relationship satisfaction.

2. **Boosting Feelings of Acceptance and Closeness:** There is some evidence that, for individuals grappling with lower self-esteem, reflecting upon shared values with a partner can foster a heightened sense of acceptance and emotional intimacy.

3. **Motivation:** Theories in psychology and philosophy both independently argue that intrinsic values are a key source of motivation and reasons for action. Knowing what yours are could help you make decisions and help you better understand your relationship with motivation.

4. **Grit:** The points about motivation are taken even further by work on 'grit'. Grit is a trait that combines *perseverance* and *passion* for long-term goals. It's the ability to persistently pursue challenging objectives over extended periods, even in the face of adversity, setbacks, or failures. Work on this trait emphasizes that it is easier to achieve when your long-term goals are deeply connected with your deepest values.

5. **Advocacy:** Historically, environmental conservationists have relied on the significance of intrinsic values in their advocacy. They have argued that natural environments should be preserved for their own sake, rather than because they serve some other (usually human) purpose. In doing so, those conservationists encourage you to include natural environments among the things you value intrinsically. This is a strategy that can be applied to anything that you value intrinsically and want to advocate for! Though keep in mind it's very unlikely you'll change people's intrinsic values, but you can tap into latent values they already have."

The human values that contradict the intrinsic values of the human are the extrinsic values of humans. The genesis of loneliness lies not in the humans who have state of mind of loneliness but in the state of mind of the humans who are habituated contradicting the intrinsic values of humans. That suggests what is needed is to aggressively address the humans considering the extrinsic values as of more importance in their life, the basic cause of birth of loneliness among the young and older generations. Humanistic attachment and its demonstration among the humans have the capacity to keep the loneliness at bay. Let us also read the following.

Let us now talk about two godly qualities – compassion and forgiveness – their impact on co-humans and other living beings.

Compassion is the ability to feel for someone or to have the same feeling as that of someone else. ... In kindness, a person may feel sorry for some person but will not reflect the suffering person's feelings. But with compassion, a person may have the same feelings as that of the suffering person.

Compassion is stronger than kindness. Compassion is a concept that is deeply embedded in our human consciousness. It may also prove to be crucial to our well-being in a world. Indeed, the capacity for compassion in the human mind and heart, recently a topic of study in the neurosciences and the subject of ongoing discussions in psychology, ethics, literature, and theology, may be key to the very survival of humankind as well as the environment we share with other creatures. According to Wikipedia – "Compassion motivates people to go out of their way to help the physical, mental, or emotional pains of another and themselves. Compassion is often regarded as having sensitivity, an emotional aspect to suffering, though when based on cerebral notions such as fairness, justice, and interdependence, it may be considered rational in nature and its application understood as an activity also based on sound judgment. ………." I understand that love and kindness are subjective and individualistic considerations, the compassion is to feel for someone or to have the same feelings as that someone.

Fredrick Boehner describes what it means to have compassion in this way: "Compassion is sometimes the fatal capacity for feeling what it is like to live inside somebody else's skin. It is the knowledge that there can never really be any peace and joy for me until there is peace and joy finally for you too." Compassion always stands for positivity. It is an instant instinct in human, also other living beings trying to reach out to one who is suffering in whatever nature assuming the same suffering as if of one's own. It is not concerned with goodness or badness or harmfulness in human or other living beings and feels compassion as one for all of them. The compassion thus wants to give to the suffering person more than love and kindness, natural emergence from the consciousness and heart. One who thinks and acts so assumes godly qua and runs to soothe one who is suffering. Compassion thus is an integral part of the divinity.

Greater Good Magazine – Science-Based Insights for a Meaningful Life of the Greater Good Science Center at the University of California, Berkeley answers 'What is Forgiveness?' thus:

"Psychologists generally define forgiveness as a conscious, deliberate decision to release feelings of resentment or vengeance toward a person or group who has harmed you, regardless of whether they actually deserve your forgiveness.

Just as important as defining what forgiveness is, though, understands what forgiveness is not? Experts who study or teach forgiveness make clear that when you forgive; you do not gloss over or deny the seriousness of an offense against you. Forgiveness does not mean forgetting, nor does it mean condoning or excusing offenses. Though forgiveness can help repair a damaged relationship, it doesn't obligate you to reconcile with the person who harmed you, or release them from legal accountability.

Instead, forgiveness brings the forgiver peace of mind and frees him or her from corrosive anger. While there is some debate over whether true forgiveness requires positive feelings toward the offender, experts agree that it at least involves letting go of deeply held negative feelings. In that way, it empowers you to recognize the pain you suffered without letting that pain define you, enabling you to heal and move on with your life.

While early research focused on forgiveness of others by individuals, new areas of research are starting to examine the benefits of group forgiveness and self-forgiveness."

Same Magazine further asks "Why Practice It? Thus answers:

- Forgiveness makes us happier: Research suggests not only that happy people are more likely to forgive but that forgiving others can make people feel happy, especially when they forgive someone to whom they feel close.

- Forgiveness protects our mental health: People who receive therapy designed to foster forgiveness experience greater improvements in depression, anxiety, and hope than those who don't. Forgiveness may also play a role in preventing suicide.

- Forgiveness improves our health: When we dwell on grudges, our blood pressure and heart rate spike—signs of stress which damage the body; when we forgive, our stress levels drop, and people who are more forgiving are protected from the negative health effects of stress. Studies also suggest that holding grudges might compromise our immune system, making us less resistant to illness.

- Forgiveness sustains relationships: When our friends inevitably hurt or disappoint us, holding a grudge makes us less likely to sacrifice or cooperate with them, which undermines feelings of trust and commitment, driving us further apart. Studies suggest that forgiveness can stop this downward spiral and repair our relationship before it dissolves.

- Forgiveness is good for marriages (most of the time): Spouses who are more forgiving and less vindictive are better at resolving conflicts effectively in their marriage. A long-term study of newlyweds found that more forgiving spouses had stronger, more satisfying relationships. However, when more forgiving spouses were frequently mistreated by their husband or wife, they became less satisfied with their marriage.

- Forgiveness boosts kindness and connectedness: People who feel forgiving don't only feel more positive toward someone who hurt them. They are also more likely to want to volunteer and donate money to charity, and they feel more connected to other people in general.

- Forgiveness is good for kids and teens: Kids who are more forgiving toward their friends have higher well-being. Forgiveness training can help adolescent girls who are bullies and bullied decrease their anger, aggression, and delinquency, while increasing their empathy and improving their grades.

- Forgiveness is good for workplaces: Employees who are more forgiving are also more productive and take fewer days off, partly thanks to reduced stress around their relationships.

- People who practice self-forgiveness tend to have better physical and mental health. Forgiving ourselves may also improve our relationships.

Love, Kindness, Compassion and Forgiveness are the most powerful weapons in the Universe. I also add Trust – the bridge between God and humans and hence within the humans. I have made my best efforts to highlight the sanctified significance of the godly qualities, practising of which in one's daily life would systemize and purify the body expanding the human capacity to create a treasure of positivity in mind and overcome negativity altogether. These godly qualities, individually and collectively act as 'The Living God on Earth" in human relationship and in relationship with other living beings on earth.

Trust is important because it is the basis around which all human relationships revolve. Without trust there can be no relationship. A good husband and wife are trustworthy if they express it in words and actions. The basic needs are for human values. These values are rooted or based in trust affection. Trust, in the dictionary, is defined as being confident, believing, or relying on someone or something to do what is expected. Imagine what a world would be like without trust. Why Is Trust important in the Workplace? If a workplace is able to foster a strong sense of trust within their organisation they can see a number of benefits including: increased productivity amongst staff, improved morale amongst employees and staff. In family, people are able to trust and rely on each other for support, love, affection and warmth. Why Trust is Important for business. Trust is the most important business and brand asset to manage, especially in relationships with customers, clients, employees, and stakeholders. A person hurting the Spirit and Soul is bound to fall in his own pit. First trust in oneself and then, one will be able to trust others. Trust is the moral obligation in humans and other species. Trust and that trust turns into trustworthiness.

Mistrust or breach of trust is cheating creating chaotic psychological and physiological effects. Mistrust is individualized while breach of trust is protected in law. Law compensates the one affected due to breach of trust. Mistrust is a valid response to feeling betrayed or abandoned. But pervasive feelings of mistrust can negatively impact a person's life. This can result in anxiety, anger, or self-doubt. It is said that suspicion creates mistrust. The root of suspicion is lack of knowledge; as such, the remedy to suspicion was to learn more about the issue that is troubling one. It is also said that suspicion also leads to self-liquidation. Suspicion is a floating thought and, if it is to be trusted as true, it should be made true through verifiable facts. Or self-assessed satisfaction that convincingly concludes the suspicion or otherwise. Believe in trust unless and until the symptoms of mistrust become perceptible. The person who is entertaining mistrust in mind suffers most than the person who is causing mistrust. Mistrust and, as part of it, the suspicion is also responsible for the birth of negativity which is more painful, the reason being the mistrust and suspicion hold strongly and todisplace them takes a longer time. Sometimes it leads to permanent loss of trust. One, therefore, needs to be careful in forming a mistrust or suspicion. Better to avoid them. Mistrust and suspicion act like devils. A devil is the personification of evil as it is conceived in many and various cultures and religious traditions. It is seen as the objectification of a hostile and destructive force.

"Until a century or so ago, almost no one lived alone; now many endure shutdowns and lockdowns on their own. How did modern life get so lonely?" - By Jill Lepore.

Let us read the following Article that answers what Jill Lepore wrote:

<u>A history of loneliness - Published: March 19, 2018 10.36am GMT posted on 'THE CONVERSATION' Website</u> :

"Is loneliness our modern malaise?

Former U.S. Surgeon General Vivek Murthy says the most common pathology he saw during his years of service "was not heart disease or diabetes; it was loneliness."

Chronic loneliness, some say, is like "smoking 15 cigarettes a day." It "kills more people than obesity."

Because loneliness is now considered a public health issue – and even an epidemic – people are exploring its causes and trying to find solutions.

While writing a book on the history of how poets wrote about loneliness in the Romantic Period, I discovered that loneliness is a relatively new concept and once had an easy cure. However, as the concept's meaning has transformed, finding solutions has become harder.

Returning to the origins of the word – and understanding how its meaning has changed through time – gives us a new way to think about modern loneliness, and the ways in which we might address it.

The dangers of venturing into 'lonelinesses'

Although loneliness may seem like a timeless, universal experience, it seems to have originated in the late 16th century, when it signalled the danger created by being too far from other people.

In early modern Britain, to stray too far from society was to surrender the protections it provided. Distant forests and mountains inspired fear, and a lonely space was a place in which you might meet someone who could do you harm, with no one else around to help.

In order to frighten their congregations out of sin, sermon writers asked people to imagine themselves in "lonelinesses" – places like hell, the grave or the desert.

Yet well into the 17th century, the words "loneliness" and "lonely" rarely appeared in writing. In 1674, the naturalist John Ray compiled a glossary of infrequently used words. He included "loneliness" in his list, defining it as a term used to describe places and people "far from neighbours."

John Milton's 1667 epic poem "Paradise Lost" features one of the first lonely characters in all of British literature: Satan. On his journey to the Garden of Eden to tempt Eve, Satan treads "lonely steps" out of hell. But Milton isn't writing about Satan's feelings; instead, he's emphasizing that he's crossing into the ultimate wilderness, a space between hell and Eden where no angel has previously ventured.

Satan describes his loneliness in terms of vulnerability: "From them I go / this uncouth errand sole, and one for all / myself expose, with lonely steps to tread / The unfounded deep."

The dilemma of modern loneliness

Even if we now enjoy the wilderness as a place of adventure and pleasure, the fear of loneliness persists. The problem has simply moved into our cities.

Many are trying to solve it by bringing people physically closer to their neighbours. Studies point to a spike in the number of people who live alone and the breakdown of family and community structures.

British Prime Minister Theresa May has set her sights on "combating" loneliness and appointed a minister of loneliness to do just that in January. There is even a philanthropy called the "Campaign to End Loneliness."

But the drive to cure loneliness oversimplifies its modern meaning.

In the 17th century, when loneliness was usually relegated to the space outside the city, solving it was easy. It merely required a return to society.

However, loneliness has since moved inward – and has become much harder to cure. Because it's taken up residence inside minds, even the minds of people living in bustling cities, it can't always be solved by company.

Modern loneliness isn't just about being physically removed from other people. Instead, it's an emotional state of feeling apart from others – without necessarily being so.

Someone surrounded by people, or even accompanied by friends or a lover, can complain of feelings of loneliness. The wilderness is now inside of us.

Populating the wilderness of the mind

The lack of an obvious cure to loneliness is part of the reason why it is considered to be so dangerous today: The abstraction is frightening.

Counterintuitively, however, the secret to dealing with modern loneliness might lie not in trying to make it disappear but in finding ways to dwell within its abstractions, talk through its contradictions and seek out others who feel the same way.

While it's certainly important to pay attention to the structures that have led people (especially elderly, disabled and other vulnerable people) to be physically isolated and therefore unwell, finding ways to destigmatising loneliness is also crucial.

Acknowledging that loneliness is a profoundly human and sometimes incurable experience rather than a mere pathology might allow people – especially lonely people – to find commona.

In order to look at the "epidemic of loneliness" as more than just an "epidemic of isolation," it's important to consider why the spaces of different people's minds might feel like wildernesses in the first place.

Question is whether Soul protects the human or human should make efforts to sustain Soul? Soul is not responsible for what human does and the human has to bear the consequences of what he or she does or has done in the present or past life. It is the duty of the human to obey the Law of the Nature and adopting that as part and parcel of life. Where human departs from that duty, the Soul is hurt. That means, Soul protects the human when the human is in right path, the path whether right or wrong being ascertainable from one's Conscience adjacent to the Spirit linking the Soul. Doing injurious acts to co-humans triggers self-fearsomeness. Humans are born on Mother Earth to complete the obligated duties during life time. One should never think as alone living on Mother Earth who has blessed the Nature for the sole benefit of the humans and the other living beings. If this is understood, loneliness leaves the body behind opening up the blind eyes towards what exists – humans and other living beings all around to associate and enjoy with them, a sense of zeal to live. This is the God given path for human development in whatever conditions or circumstances the human is placed – HOPE IS LIFE. Object should be to contribute for the wellbeing of oneself, of the society and of the country, the ultimate object and purpose of the humans born on Mother Earth. Fulfil it as a Command from God.

About the 'Loneliness' along with the enlightened write-ups [Articles] and Quotes stated before, I believe, would inculcate a fresh air of perfumes to those affected by 'loneliness' that will enthuse them to merge with the reality of life rather than remaining in a hypothetical life. Let us not wish or seek for something which is beyond our reach. If a kite is flying in the sky, we should not jump to catch it which injures to the body. To get the kite in hand, use its controlling method, that is, thread in one's hand that helps to bring it in one's hand. So is the life. Be content with what God has given. Greatness of life lies in approaching for something or the other through the positive process. Be satisfied with that which is the sense and essence of life. There is nothing more or less beyond this.

"THE PURPOSE OF LIFE IS TO CONTRIBUTE IN SOME WAY TO MAKING THINGS BETTER." — ROBERT F. KENNEDY

There should not be any hesitation to say that the suicide has also become a kind of virus. The debates going on in the electronic media and print media in India, presumably also in other countries right now, relate to curing the mental stress and disorders that have developed and developing in the people who survived the suicide virus. The situation seems to be such that mothers died leaving the newly born or growing children, fathers left leaving the dependents in increasing anxiety about the future survival economically, brothers and sisters left leaving the dependents in the same conditions and many of the children became orphaned with Children Care Centres. These developments did not differentiate the social classes – rich or the poor, making, however, the poor more particularly to live in a miserable state of condition. This continues to happen and the doctors and psychologists have been comforting this class of people on the electronic and print media. That is comfort but not a cure that happens depending wholly on the self-correction of the mental status using the clues given by the doctors and psychologists combined with Nature's Spiritual cure.

There is no such medicine or vaccination that can claim to provide permanent cure for such class of people; it could only soften the shocks to some extent for those using the medicines regularly. Author believes that those who are employed whether in government, semi-government service, autonomous bodies or private sector services, deserve to be given highest consideration by the employers extending highest level of love, affection, assistance, comfort and diversions that would gradually bring down the impact to a state of normalcy. Once this happens, they will be able to see a new ray of light and hope to live as they lived and continue their life in a normal way. Over and above this, they need to do themselves nature and spiritual cure practices regularly.

Making mockery in such cases is a severest sin. Save the life should be the sole purpose of everyone. The saver and the saved will experience the greatest.

Solace. Knowledge is Supreme. Use it for good only. Read the following Quotes about the LIFE to regenerate your Spirit within yourself:

A DAY WITHOUT LAUGHTER IS A DAY WASTED - CHARLIE CHAPLIN

"LIFE ISN'T ABOUT FINDING YOURSELF. LIFE IS ABOUT CREATING YOURSELF." - — **GEORGE BERNARD SHAW**

It is humans who undergo trying times in life which should be taken as strength to sustain and move forward and not to succumb. There is nothing that cannot be overcome but what is needed to overturn the bad times in life and snatch the opportunities hidden therein.

Uttarkashi tunnel rescue timeline: How team effort saved lives of 41 trapped workers in 17 days - Here is a timeline of how the rescue efforts unfolded over the past two weeks - Web Desk Updated: November 29, 2023 08:19 I

November 12: A landslide strikes the Brahmkhal-Yamunotri highway on the day of Diwali, resulting in the partial collapse of the Silkyara-Dandalgaon under-construction tunnel around 5.30am and 41 workers at the site get trapped.

A multi-agency rescue operation begins with teams comprised of personnel from NDRF, SDRF, BRO, ITBP and NHIDCL, which was executing the project. Authorities ensure supply of oxygen, food and electricity to the trapped workers

November 13: Recue team manages to contact trapped workers through a pipe used to supply oxygen. More rubble keeps falling with the debris accumulation spreading from 30 metres to 60 metres.

November 14: Preparations begin to insert 800mm diameter steel pipes through the rubble using an auger machine via horizontal digging. More rubble falls and two workers suffer minor injuries.

November 15: NHIDCL asks for a state-of-the-art auger machine, which is airlifted from Delhi to speed up the operation after the earlier machine is unable to perform the required task.

November 16: New diesel-driven 1,750-horse power American auger machine starts drilling through rubble after midnight.

November 17: Around afternoon, drilling team clears 24 metres of rubble out of the total 57-metre rubble stretch by the afternoon and inserts four steel pipes. Fifth pipe hits an obstacle.

Another state-of-the-art auger machine brought to speed up the rescue operations. However, operation gets suspended after a cracking sound is heard in the tunnel, sparking worries about further collapse of rubble.**November 18:** Experts warn of further collapse of debris due to vibrations created by the auger machine that could risk the lives of the rescue personnel. Drilling remains halted and PMO officials mull alternative options. They along with experts chalk out five evacuation plans that could be implemented simultaneously. One of the plans was to drill vertically through the top of the tunnel.

November 19: Union minister Nitin Gadkari reviews the rescue operation and says horizontal drilling appeared to be the best bet. Drilling remains suspended.

November 20: PM Narendra Modi dials CM Pushkar Dhami to take stock of the operations. A boulder blocking the progress of the auger machine keeps the drilling suspended.

November 21: The first video of the trapped workers released. It showed the workers, donning yellow and white helmets, talking to each other. Rescue team simultaneously begins drilling at the other end of the tunnel in Balkot though experts said it could take up to 40 days to reach the workers. Horizontal drilling from the Silkyara end using auger machine begins.

November 22: Horizontal drilling reaches about 45 metres with only 12 more metres remaining. Ambulances, doctors and hospital beds on standby. Auger machine hits some iron rods overnight.

November 23: The iron rods blocking the way removed after six hours and the drilling reaches 48 metres. Drilling halted again after cracks appeared in the platform where the drilling machine rests.

November 24: Drilling which resumes after the auger machine is restarted gets suspended again after the machine hits a metal girder.

November 25: The auger machine blades are stuck in the debris, with the rescue team being forced to go for alternate options that could take several days. Officials decide to manually bore through the remaining rubble and simultaneously drill vertically 86 metres from above.

November 26: Vertical drilling completes 19.2 metres of 83 metres and 700mm pipes are being inserted.

November 27: Rat-hole miners join the rescuers to dig through around 10 metres of horizontal rubble. Vertical drilling from above reached a depth of 36 metres.

November 28: Rat-hole mining experts break through the last stretch of the rubble at about 7 pm. Trapped workers are brought out on wheeled-stretchers one by one with all 41 men being evacuated safely. "

On reading the above Article, it could be said that **"HUMANS ARE MIGHTIER THAN THE MACHINES, MORE SO, WHEN IT WAS ACCOMPLISHED THROGH THE HUMAN UNITY IN DIVERSITY THAT IS THE ULTIMATE OF HUMAN EFFORT AND JOY"**

Tzu Chi Med J. 2020 Oct-Dec; 32(4): 339–343. - Published online 2020 Aug 14. doi: 10.4103/tcmj.tcmj_71_20 - PMCID: PMC7605294 - PMID: 33163378 - The impact of artificial intelligence on human society and bioethics - Michael Cheng-Tek Tai* - Author information Article notes Copyright and License information PMC Disclaimer

What is artificial intelligence?

Artificial intelligence (AI) has many different definitions; some see it as the created technology that allows computers and machines to function intelligently. Some see it as the machine that replaces human labor to work for men a more effective and speedier result. Others see it as "a system" with the ability to correctly interpret external data, to learn from such data, and to use those learnings to achieve specific goals and tasks through flexible adaptation [1].

Despite the different definitions, the common understanding of AI is that it is associated with machines and computers to help humankind solve problems and facilitate working processes. In short, it is an intelligence designed by humans and demonstrated by machines. The term AI is used to describe these functions of human-made tool that emulates the "cognitive" abilities of the natural intelligence of human minds [2].

Along with the rapid development of cybernetic technology in recent years, AI has been seen almost in all our life circles, and some of that may no longer be regarded as AI because it is so common in daily life that we are much used to it such as optical character recognition or the Siri (speech interpretation and recognition interface) of information searching equipment on computer [3].

Different types of artificial intelligence

From the functions and abilities provided by AI, we can distinguish two different types. The first is weak AI, also known as narrow AI that is designed to perform a narrow task, such as facial recognition or Internet Siri search or self-driving car. Many currently existing systems that claim to use "AI" are likely operating as a weak AI focusing on a narrowly defined specific function. Although this weak AI seems to be helpful to human living, there are still some think weak AI could be dangerous because weak AI could cause disruptions in the electric grid or may damage nuclear power plants when malfunctioned.

The new development of the long-term goal of many researchers is to create strong AI or artificial general intelligence (AGI) which is the speculative intelligence of a machine that has the capacity to understand or learn any intelligent task human being can, thus assisting human to unravel the confronted problem. While narrow AI may outperform humans such as playing chess or solving equations, but its effect is still weak. AGI, however, could outperform humans at nearly every cognitive task.

Strong AI is a different perception of AI that it can be programmed to actually be a human mind, to be intelligent in whatever it is commanded to attempt, even to have perception, beliefs and other cognitive capacities that are normally only ascribed to humans [4].

In summary, we can see these different functions of AI [5,6]:

1. Automation: What makes a system or process to function automatically

2. Machine learning and vision: The science of getting a computer to act through deep learning to predict and analyse, and to see through a camera, analog-to-digital conversion and digital signal processing

3. Natural language processing: The processing of human language by a computer program, such as spam detection and converting instantly a language to another to help humans communicate

4. Robotics: A field of engineering focusing on the design and manufacturing of cyborgs, the so-called machine man. They are used to perform tasks for human's convenience or something too difficult or dangerous for human to perform and can operate without stopping such as in assembly lines

5. Self-driving car: Use a combination of computer vision, image recognition amid deep learning to build automated control in a vehicle.

Do human-beings really need artificial intelligence?

Is AI really needed in human society? It depends. If human opts for a faster and effective way to complete their work and to work constantly without taking a break, yes, it is. However if humankind is satisfied with a natural way of living without excessive desires to conquer the order of nature, it is not. History tells us that human is always looking for something faster, easier, more effective, and convenient to finish the task they work on; therefore, the pressure for further development motivates humankind to look for a new and better way of doing things. Humankind as the homo-sapiens discovered that tools could facilitate many hardships for daily livings and through tools they invented, human could complete the work better, faster, smarter and more effectively. The invention to create new things becomes the incentive of human progress. We enjoy a much easier and more leisurely life today all because of the contribution of technology. The human society has been using the tools since the beginning of civilization, and human progress depends on it. The human kind living in the 21st century did not have to work as hard as their forefathers in previous times because they have new machines to work for them. It is all good and should be all right for these AI but a warning came in early 20th century as the human-technology kept developing that Aldous Huxley warned in his book *Brave New World* that human might step into a world in which we are creating a monster or a super human with the development of genetic technology.

Besides, up-to-dated AI is breaking into healthcare industry too by assisting doctors to diagnose, finding the sources of diseases, suggesting various ways of treatment performing surgery and also predicting if the illness is life-threatening [7]. A recent study by surgeons at the Children's National Medical Center in Washington successfully demonstrated surgery with an autonomous robot. The team supervised the robot to perform soft-tissue surgery, stitch together a pig's bowel, and the robot finished the job better than a human surgeon, the team claimed [8,9]. It demonstrates robotically-assisted surgery can overcome the limitations of pre-existing minimally-invasive surgical procedures and to enhance the capacities of surgeons performing open surgery.........

The impact of artificial intelligence on human society

Negative impact

Questions have been asked: With the progressive development of AI, human labor will no longer be needed as everything can be done mechanically. Will humans become lazier and eventually degrade to the stage that we return to our primitive form of being? The process of evolution takes eons to develop, so we will not notice the backsliding of humankind. However how about if the AI becomes so powerful that it can program itself to be in charge and disobey the order given by its master, the humankind?

Let us see the negative impact the AI will have on human society [10,11]:

1. A huge social change that disrupts the way we live in the human community will occur. Humankind has to be industrious to make their living, but with the service of AI, we can just program the machine to do a thing for us without even lifting a tool. Human closeness will be gradually diminishing as AI will replace the need for people to meet face to face for idea

exchange. AI will stand in between people as the personal gathering will no longer be needed for communication

2. Unemployment is the next because many works will be replaced by machinery. Today, many automobile assembly lines have been filled with machineries and robots, forcing traditional workers to lose their jobs. Even in supermarket, the store clerks will not be needed anymore as the digital device can take over human labor

3. Wealth inequality will be created as the investors of AI will take up the major share of the earnings. The gap between the rich and the poor will be widened. The so-called "M" shape wealth distribution will be more obvious [**M-Form Society** is a term that describes the demographic distribution of wealth in a society in which the statistical curve appears roughly in the form the letter "M". The term was first used in the writings of William Ouchi - *"The M-Form Society: How American Teamwork Can Recapture the Competitive Edge."*[11] Subsequently in 2006, it was used again by the Japanese economist and corporate strategist Kenichi Ohmae (大前研一) in his work. According to his observation, Ohmae argued that the structure of Japanese society has emerged into a 'M-shape' distribution. It refers to a polarized society with the extreme rich and the extreme poor.]

4. New issues surface not only in a social sense but also in AI itself as the AI being trained and learned how to operate the given task can eventually take off to the stage that human has no control, thus creating un-anticipated problems and consequences. It refers to AI's capacity after being loaded with all needed algorithm may automatically function on its own course ignoring the command given by the human controller

5. The human masters who create AI may invent something that is racial bias or egocentrically oriented to harm certain people or things. For instance, the United Nations has voted to limit the spread of nucleus power in fear of its indiscriminative use to destroying humankind or targeting on certain races or region to achieve the goal of domination. AI is possible to target certain race or some programmed objects to accomplish the command of destruction by the programmers, thus creating world disaster.

POSITIVE IMPACT

There are, however, many positive impacts on humans as well, especially in the field of healthcare. AI gives computers the capacity to learn, reason, and apply logic. Scientists, medical researchers, clinicians, mathematicians, and engineers, when working together, can design an AI that is aimed at medical diagnosis and treatments, thus offering reliable and safe systems of health-care delivery. As health professors and medical researchers endeavour to find new and efficient ways of treating diseases, not only the digital computer can assist in analysing, robotic systems can also be created to do some delicate medical procedures with precision. Here, we see the contribution of AI to health care [7,11]:

Fast and accurate diagnostics

IBM's Watson computer has been used to diagnose with the fascinating result. Loading the data to the computer will instantly get AI's diagnosis. AI can also provide various ways of treatment for physicians to consider. The procedure is something like this: To load the digital results of physical examination to the computer that will consider all possibilities and automatically diagnose whether or not the patient suffers from some deficiencies and illness and even suggest various kinds of available treatment.

Socially therapeutic robots

Pets are recommended to senior citizens to ease their tension and reduce blood pressure, anxiety, loneliness, and increase social interaction. Now cyborgs have been suggested to accompany those lonely old folks, even to help do some house chores. Therapeutic robots and the socially assistive robot technology help improve the quality of life for seniors and physically challenged [12].

Reduce errors related to human fatigue

Human error at workforce is inevitable and often costly, the greater the level of fatigue, the higher the risk of errors occurring. AI technology, however, does not suffer from fatigue or emotional distraction. It saves errors and can accomplish the duty faster and more accurately.

Artificial intelligence-based surgical contribution

AI-based surgical procedures have been available for people to choose. Although this AI still needs to be operated by the health professionals, it can complete the work with less damage to the body. The da Vinci surgical system, a robotic technology allowing surgeons to perform minimally invasive procedures, is available in most of the hospitals now. These systems enable a degree of precision and accuracy far greater than the procedures done manually. The less invasive the surgery, the less trauma it will occur and less blood loss, less anxiety of the patients.

Improved radiology

The first computed tomography scanners were introduced in 1971. The first magnetic resonance imaging (MRI) scan of the human body took place in 1977. By the early 2000s, cardiac MRI, body MRI, and fetal imaging, became routine. The search continues for new algorithms to detect specific diseases as well as to analyse the results of scans [9]. All those are the contribution of the technology of AI.

Virtual presence

The virtual presence technology can enable a distant diagnosis of the diseases. The patient does not have to leave his/her bed but using a remote presence robot, doctors can check the patients without actually being there. Health professionals can move around and interact almost as effectively as if they were present. This allows specialists to assist patients who are unable to travel.

SOME CAUTIONS TO BE REMINDED

Despite all the positive promises that AI provides, human experts, however, are still essential and necessary to design, program, and operate the AI from any unpredictable error from occurring. Beth Kindig, a San Francisco-based technology analyst with more than a decade of experience in analysing private and public technology companies, published a free newsletter indicating that although AI has a potential promise for better medical diagnosis, human experts are still needed to avoid the misclassification of unknown diseases because AI is not omnipotent to solve all problems for human kinds. There are times when AI meets an impasse, and to carry on its mission, it may just proceed indiscriminately, ending in creating more problems. Thus vigilant watch of AI's function cannot be neglected. This reminder is known as physician-in-the-loop [13].

The question of an ethical AI consequently was brought up by Elizabeth Gibney in her article published in Nature to caution any bias and possible societal harm [14]. The Neural Information processing Systems (NeurIPS) conference in Vancouver Canada in 2020 brought up the ethical controversies of the application of AI technology, such as in predictive policing or facial recognition, that due to bias algorithms can result in hurting the vulnerable population [14]. For instance, the NeurIPS can be programmed to target certain race or decree as the probable suspect of crime or trouble makers.

THE CHALLENGE OF ARTIFICIAL INTELLIGENCE TO BIOETHICS

Artificial intelligence ethics must be developed

Bioethics is a discipline that focuses on the relationship among living beings. Bioethics accentuates the good and the right in biospheres and can be categorized into at least three areas, the bioethics in health settings that is the relationship between physicians and patients, the bioethics in social settings that is the relationship among humankind and the bioethics in environmental settings that is the relationship between man and nature including animal ethics, land ethics, ecological ethics…etc. All these are concerned about relationships within and among natural existences.

As AI arises, human has a new challenge in terms of establishing a relationship toward something that is not natural in its own right. Bioethics normally discusses the relationship within natural existences, either humankind or his environment, that are parts of natural phenomena. But now men have to deal with something that is human-made, artificial and unnatural, namely AI. Human has created many things yet never has human had to think of how to ethically relate to his own creation. AI by itself is without feeling or personality. AI engineers have realized the importance of giving the AI ability to discern so that it will avoid any deviated activities causing unintended harm. From this perspective, we understand that AI can have a negative impact on humans and society; thus, a bioethics of AI becomes important to make sure that AI will not take off on its own by deviating from its originally designated purpose.

Stephen Hawking warned early in 2014 that the development of full AI could spell the end of the human race. He said that once humans develop AI, it may take off on its own and redesign itself at an ever-increasing rate [15]. Humans, who are limited by slow biological evolution, could not compete and would be superseded. In his book Super intelligence, Nick Bostrom gives an argument that AI will pose a threat to humankind. He argues that sufficiently intelligent AI can exhibit convergent behavior such as acquiring resources or protecting itself from being shut down, and it might harm humanity [16].

The question is–do we have to think of bioethics for the human's own created product that bears no bio-vitality? Can a machine have a mind, consciousness, and mental state in exactly the same sense that human beings do? Can a machine be sentient and thus deserve certain rights? Can a machine intentionally cause harm? Regulations must be contemplated as a bioethical mandate for AI production.

Studies have shown that AI can reflect the very prejudices humans have tried to overcome. As AI becomes "truly ubiquitous," it has a tremendous potential to positively impact all manner of life, from industry to employment to health care and even security. Addressing the risks associated with the technology, Janosch Delcker, Politico Europe's AI correspondent, said: "I don't think AI will ever be free of bias, at least not as long as we stick to machine learning as we know it today,".… "What's crucially important, I believe, is to recognize that those biases exist and that policymakers try to mitigate them" [17]. The High-Level Expert Group on AI of the European Union presented Ethics Guidelines for Trustworthy AI in 2019 that suggested AI systems must be accountable, explainable, and unbiased. Three emphases are given:

1. Lawful-respecting all applicable laws and regulations
2. Ethical-respecting ethical principles and values
3. Robust-being adaptive, reliable, fair, and trustworthy from a technical perspective while taking into account its social environment [18].

Seven requirements are recommended [18]:

- AI should not trample on human autonomy. People should not be manipulated or coerced by AI systems, and humans should be able to intervene or oversee every decision that the software makes
- AI should be secure and accurate. It should not be easily compromised by external attacks, and it should be reasonably reliable

- Personal data collected by AI systems should be secure and private. It should not be accessible to just anyone, and it should not be easily stolen

- Data and algorithms used to create an AI system should be accessible, and the decisions made by the software should be "understood and traced by human beings." In other words, operators should be able to explain the decisions their AI systems make

- Services provided by AI should be available to all, regardless of age, gender, race, or other characteristics. Similarly, systems should not be biased along these lines

- AI systems should be sustainable (i.e., they should be ecologically responsible) and "enhance positive social change"

- AI systems should be auditable and covered by existing protections for corporate whistle-blowers. The negative impacts of systems should be acknowledged and reported in advance.

From these guidelines, we can suggest that future AI must be equipped with human sensibility or "AI humanities." To accomplish this, AI researchers, manufacturers, and all industries must bear in mind that technology is to serve not to manipulate humans and his society. Bostrom and Judkowsky listed responsibility, transparency, auditability, incorruptibility, and predictability [19] as criteria for the computerized society to think about.

SUGGESTED PRINCIPLES FOR ARTIFICIAL INTELLIGENCE BIOETHICS

Nathan Strout, a reporter at Space and Intelligence System at Easter University, USA, reported just recently that the intelligence community is developing its own AI ethics. The Pentagon made announced in February 2020 that it is in the process of adopting principles for using AI as the guidelines for the department to follow while developing new AI tools and AI-enabled technologies. Ben Huebner, chief of the Office of Director of National Intelligence's Civil Liberties, Privacy, and Transparency Office, said that "We're going to need to ensure that we have transparency and accountability in these structures as we use them. They have to be secure and resilient" [20]. Two themes have been suggested for the AI community to think more about: Explain ability and interpretability. Explainability is the concept of understanding how the analytic works, while interpretability is being able to understand a particular result produced by an analytic [20].

All the principles suggested by scholars for AI bioethics are well-brought-up. I gather from different bioethical principles in all the related fields of bioethics to suggest four principles here for consideration to guide the future development of the AI technology. We however must bear in mind that the main attention should still be placed on human because AI after all has been designed and manufactured by human. AI proceeds to its work according to its algorithm. AI itself cannot empathize nor have the ability to discern good from evil and may commit mistakes in processes. All the ethical quality of AI depends on the human designers; therefore, it is an AI bioethics and at the same time, a trans-bioethics that abridge human and material worlds. Here are the principles:

1. Beneficence: Beneficence means doing good, and here it refers to the purpose and functions of AI should benefit the whole human life, society and universe. Any AI that will perform any destructive work on bio-universe, including all life forms, must be avoided and forbidden. The AI scientists must understand that reason of developing this technology has no other purpose but to benefit human society as a whole not for any individual personal gain. It should be altruistic, not egocentric in nature

2. Value-upholding: This refers to AI's congruence to social values, in other words, universal values that govern the order of the natural world must be observed. AI cannot elevate to the height above social and moral norms and must be bias-free. The scientific and technological developments must be for the enhancement of human well-being that is the chief value AI must hold dearly as it progresses further

3. Lucidity: AI must be transparent without hiding any secret agenda. It has to be easily comprehensible, detectable, incorruptible, and perceivable. AI technology should be made available for public auditing, testing and review, and subject to accountability standards ... In high-stakes settings like diagnosing cancer from radiologic images, an algorithm that can't "explain its work" may pose an unacceptable risk. Thus, Explainability and Interpretability are absolutely required

4. Accountability: AI designers and developers must bear in mind they carry a heavy responsibility on their shoulders of the outcome and impact of AI on whole human society and the universe. They must be accountable for whatever they manufacture and create.

CONCLUSION

AI is here to stay in our world and we must try to enforce the AI bioethics of beneficence, value upholding, lucidity and accountability. Since AI is without a soul as it is, its bioethics must be transcendental to bridge the shortcoming of AI's inability to empathize. AI is a reality of the world. We must take note of what Joseph Weizenbaum, a pioneer of AI, said that we must not let computers make important decisions for us because AI as a machine will never possess human qualities such as compassion and wisdom to morally discern and judge [10]. Bioethics is not a matter of calculation but a process of conscientization. Although AI designers can up-load all information, data, and programmed to AI to function as a human being, it is still a machine and a tool. AI will always remain as AI without having authentic human feelings and the capacity to commiserate. Therefore, AI technology must be progressed with extreme caution. As Von der Leyen said in *White Paper on AI – A European approach to excellence and trust*: "AI must serve people, and therefore, AI must always comply with people's rights…. High-risk AI. That potentially interferes with people's rights has to be tested and certified before it reaches our single market" [21].

The biggest threat waiting on the shore is the extent of impact the ongoing technological breakthroughs including AI would have upon the human development, more so, human skills, employment opportunities and productivity levels. The extant education system in our country is far behind the technological breakthroughs taking place in the world. One hand, we say underutilization of our human capacity and, on the other hand, we are fast thinking about the technological inventions and innovations. We want to embrace every technological breakthrough not giving any thought whether such breakthrough would be useful for ever ignoring weighing them in terms of positivity and negativity on the human life. We made a breakthrough in AI, rejoiced but now regretting for the fear on how to distinguish between the real and the duplicate and even found necessary to test whether what is seeable is real or AI. In this, the missing point is that how we would be able to skill developed humans placements vis-à-vis technological breakthroughs including Artificial Intelligence [AI] that is presently confronting the whole world. How we are going to balance the both in every field of industrial, information technology, agriculture, research and economic development. It is easier to uphold the technological breakthroughs but more worrisome how to match the developing technology with the human employment/deployment? True that productivity is much higher through the application of technology than the human efforts. Nevertheless, the technology by itself cannot function in aloof with humans, the human touch being God gifted capability more so; the technology development is also integral part of that human touch.

Looking solely at the higher productivity through technological applications is like closing one eye to see the world. In other words, the human aspirations to undergo best education, especially the youngster, incurring huge expenditure in the upgradation of the learning process hoping to get good employment opportunities for self-sustenance get darker once the technology overtakes the human ambitions and efforts. These are contrasting; yet, what is sought for is the need for policy regulations to regulate optimum use of available human reservoir using the technology as a supporting strength but if it is reversed, the worst victims will be the humans. This is a very touchy and tactical issue that calls for an in-depth study and research work both theoretical and empherical at all levels of human activities so as to first safeguard the interests of humans born on Mother Earth than technology which is not born on Mother Earth but developed by the humans to supplement their efforts and not to substitute them in one and every sphere of human life.

As Stephen Hawking once said, "The development of full artificial intelligence could spell the end of the human race", this is still circling as a current issue in everyone's conversation. As we know, AI is the future, and especially in this digital age, its multitasking ability makes it a boon. It reduces the time for data-heavy tasks, and consistent results all make it one of the best inventions of the 21st century. At the same time, the reason that AI can give better results in less time than humans makes it a bane to the entire human society. As it completely replaces human beings and can interrupt human presence in every field.

The term "artificial intelligence," or AI, has become a buzzword in recent years. Optimists see AI as the panacea to society's most fundamental problems, from crime to corruption to inequality, while pessimists fear that AI will overtake human intelligence and crown itself king of the world.

Underlying these two seemingly antithetical views is the assumption that AI is better and smarter than humanity and will ultimately replace humanity in making decisions.

It is easy to buy into the hype of omnipotent artificial intelligence these days, as venture capitalists dump billions of dollars into tech start-ups and government technocrats boast of how AI helps them streamline municipal governance. But the hype is just hype: AI is simply not as smart as we think. The true threat of AI to humanity lies not in the power of AI itself but in the ways people are already beginning to use it to chip away at our humanity..........[Source: Artificial Intelligence and the Loss of Humanity – Berkeley Political Review Website - By Xiantao Wang on November 15, 2020]

The foregoing observations are eyes opener for the humans and the humanity with the extent of catastrophic effects the humans are going to face in future are unknown today unless AI itself tells the humans who is going to control whom – whether human is capable to control AI or AI is capable to control humans. This question though by itself seems to one as artificial today but from what is being foretold by the experts concerned such as those noted before; there is every possibility of dangers of AI out throwing human life than the human life to AI.

In Hinduism, Bhasmasura (Sanskrit: भस्मासुर, Bhasmasura) is an asura or demon, who was granted the power to burn up and immediately turn into ashes (bhasma) anyone whose head he touched with his hand. The asura was tricked by the Vishnu's only female avatar, the enchantress Mohini, to turn himself into ashes.[Wikipedia]. So could be the boon of AI to humans.

"THE CREATION OF A JUST SOCIETY WAS NOT SIMPLY UNDERSTOOD AS A PRACTICAL MEANS OF SURVIVAL BUT AS THE NOBLEST EXPRESSION OF HUMAN TALENT AND INGENUITY." - BY INGRID ROSSELLINI

Let us thus understand the above Quote as Gift for the Human Development.

REFERENCES

1. India that is Bharat: A short history of the nation's names, from the Rig Veda to the Constitution of India – The Indian **Express** dated Written by Adrija Roychowdhury - New Delhi | Updated: September 9, 2023.

2. When and how Bharat did become India? – The Times of India - Rajni Pandey / TOI Education / Sep 5, 2023.

3. Who coined the term 'Jambudvipa' and 'Bharat' for India as a country? – Hinduism Stack Exchange. Com - Translation is a bit lengthy, a reference of which could be read here: proframanathan.blogspot.com/2014/05/- Vikrant -May 31, 2018.

4. 'India' or 'Bharat'? What does the Constitution say? – India Today - Nalini Sharma - New Delhi, UPDATED: Sep 5, 2023.

5. India' and 'Bharat' interchangeable, can be used in official invitation, say legal experts - September 05, 2023 10:54 pm | Updated September 06, 2023 06:59 am IST - New Delhi - SANDEEP PHUKAN – **TH.**

6. How did India get her Name Bharat?- Unacademy.

7. Bharat vs India also sparked intense debate in 1949: Here is how India got its name in Constitution SECTIONS – ET Online Last Updated: Sep 06, 2023.

8. Why arithmetic isn't enough for opposition unity – The Indian Express – written by Written by Rupak Kumar **-up**dated: September 7, 2021.

9. Quote Interpretation No. 2 written by Plutarch: 'To find fault is easy; to do better may be difficult.' - https://www.socratic-method.com/quote-meanings/plutarch-to-find-fault-is-easy-to-do-better-may-be-difficul

10. [2014] 3 S.C.R. 1 2 COMMERCIAL TAX OFFICER, RAJASTHAN v. M/S BINANI CEMENT LTD. & ANR. (Civil Appeal No. 336 of 2003) FEBRUARY 19, 2014 [H.L. DATTU AND S.A. BOBDE, JJ.]

11. Law Sikho - 3 Day Boot camp On Corporate Litigation And Arbitration- 5th to 7th January, 2024, 7-10 pm (IST) - Abhyudaya Agarwal COO & CO-Founder, LawSikho, Harsh Jain CO-Founder, LawSikho.

12. "Is It Necessary?": PM Requests Couples To Not Hold Weddings Abroad – NDTV - News Press Updated: November 26, 2023.

13. https://byjus.com/free-ias-prep/oath-and-resignations-for-upsc-exam/
14. Equal Pay For Equal Work: Concept and Case Laws By Sanam Bhatia Published on 21 Oct 2020. – Legal Bites – Law and Beyond.
15. INDIA TODAY - Ahead of 2024, how Opposition unity is a jigsaw puzzle that just won't fit – written by Shikha Mukerjee - UPDATED: Mar 15, 2023.
16. **Political participation and representation of Women in India -** https://www.civilsdaily.com/news/political-representation-of-women-in-india/
17. Indian Party System: Patterns, Trends, and Reforms - July 2020 - DOI:10.13140/RG.2.2.34407.68004 – Authors - Mahendra Prasad Singh - University of Delhi – ResearchGate.
18. Equal pay for equal work - Wikipedia
19. Can i offer worship/prayers in Shiva or Shakti temples after having meat and without bathing? - Ask Question - Asked 7 years, 3 months ago - Modified 7 years, 3 months ago – Hinduism - Stack Exchange
20. Who will deliver us from the poison of Communalism – March-April, 2009 – All World Gayatri Parivar?
21. Reason and science in Islam – Faith in Allah - https://www.abuaminaelias.com/reason-science-islam/#:~:text=Reason%20%28al-%E2%80%98aql%29%2C%20the%20God-given%20ability%20to%20acquire%20knowledge,revelation%20and%20its%20relationship%20to%20the%20natural%20world.
22. THIRD SCHEDULE [Articles 75(4), 99, 124(6), 148(2), 164(3), 188 and 219]* Forms of Oaths or Affirmations - https://www.mea.gov.in/Images/pdf1/S3.pdf
23. How 'WE, THE PEOPLE OF INDIA' Have Performed As A Republic? – Outlook - Abhik Bhattacharya - UPDATED: 25 JAN 2023.
24. Diet in Hinduism – Wikipedia
25. ROLE OF WOMEN IN STRENGTHENING DEMOCRACY - by Dr. Ranjana Kumari January 27, 2020 –GenderMatters.in
26. Burning issue] Opposition in India: Role, Challenges and Way forward - [Burning issue] Opposition in India: Role, Challenges and Way forward - Civilsdaily
27. Roles and Importance of Political Party in Democracy - https://bscholarly.com/roles-and-importance-of-political-parties-in-democracy/
28. The Epistemic Consequences of Paradox

29. Published online by Cambridge University Press: 30 June 2022 - Bryan Frances – Cambridge University Press.

30. Reality checks for the Opposition's unity project

    Since 2014, the Opposition parties have been divided and ineffectual; merely beating the drum of oneness is not enough - December 20, 2021 - <u>M.K. NARAYANAN- https://www.thehindu.com/opinion/lead/reality-checks-for-the-oppositions-unity-project/article37992567.ece</u>

31. Eight-in-ten Indians limit meat in their diets, and four-in-ten consider themselves vegetarian - BY MANOLO CORICHI – July 8, 2021 – Pew Research.

32. What is Constitutionalisation? - Martin Loughlin - https://doi.org/10.1093/acprof:oso/9780199585007.003.0003

33. List of Political Parties in India – Wikipedia.

34. MARRIAGE IN THE MODERN INDIAN SOCIETY: AN OVERVIEW Dr. Navneet Saini - IJCRT2202118.pdf

35. **Democratising Political Parties -** https://www.drishtiias.com/daily-updates/daily-news-editorials/democratising-political-parties - 25 Oct 2021

36. **Freedom of Marriage World Map -** https://marriage.hiddush.org/table

37. <u>Freedom of Conscience and its contours – A look into the legality of it</u>

38. <u>In Focus - Updated Nov 20, 2018 | 16:53 IST | Udit Chauhan – MirrorNow News. Com</u>

39. The Principle of No Work No Pay – INBA VIEWPOINT – August 2, 2019 written by Surya Pratap Singh Naruka.

40. Vantage | Why foreign weddings are not good news for India-Firstpost - The Vantage Take November 28, 2023.

41. 6 Indian Temples Where They Serve Non-Veg Prasad – By Yash Lakhan

    Updated: Nov 29, 2022 - https://www.slurrp.com/article/6-indian-temples-where-they-serve-non-veg-prasad-1657996595637

42. The real reason behind a political party's decline - January 31, 2023 RUCHI GUPTA

43. Reflections on Culture - Insights of Swami Chinmayananda - - Arundhati Sundar – 23rd October, 2017 - - Preksa – A Journal of Culture and Philosophy.

44. The fallacy of 'Opposition unity' – written by Praveen Chakravarty Last Updated 19 February 202 – Deccan Herald.com

45. INDIA TODAY - No work, no pay debate: Privileges your MPs already have - Shreya Biswas - New Delhi, UPDATED: Aug 13, 2015.

46. India Forum - Indian Democracy's Paradoxical Moment - RAHUL VERMA, ARMAAN MATHUR - NOVEMBER 15, 2022.

47. Understanding Roles & Responsibilities Of Member Of Parliament - By B.PAC|December 15th, 2021|Categories: B.ENGAGED|

48. Temple 'purified' with Gangajal after Muslim MLA's visit in UP – By HT Correspondent – November 28, 2023.

49. Blessed Is He — Whose Own Faults Keep Him From Seeing The Faults Of - Others: S.a.n.a.h - Follow - Published in

50. Dissecting the Evasiveness of Inner Party Democracy - Vivek Mishra, Ambar Ghosh.

51. International marriages - International marriages - Federal Foreign Office (auswaertiges-amt.de).

52. 18 Different Types of Criticism - February 17, 2019 | By Hitesh Bhasin |

53. Accountability in Democracies - Fernando Filgueiras - Living reference work entry - First Online: 02 December 2020

54. INDIA TODAY - How much of Indian land is occupied by China? As Centre, Congress trade barbs, truth lies in Parliament records - Rahul Shrivastava

    New Delhi, UPDATED: Jun 23, 2020

55. What is UCC? – written by Gurpreet Kaur Dutta – FINOLOGY BLOG

56. A Background Paper* on WORKING OF PARLIAMENT AND NEED FOR REFORMS - This Paper is reproduced from Dr. Subhash C. Kashyap's book "Reviewing the Constitution?" (New Delhi, 2000 Edition) and also based on his History of the Parliament in India, Vol.6, New Delhi, 2000, pp. 541-559. The views expressed are personal to the author.

57. THE Indian Parliament - LARRDIS (L.C.)/2012 © 2012 Lok Sabha Secretariat, New Delhi - Published under Rule 382 of the Rules of Procedure and Conduct of Business in Lok Sabha (Fourteenth Edition).

58. Understanding Secularism In Indian Democracy: Concept, Crisis And Fate - Subhasri Chatterjee 30 October 2020 – LAWYERSCLUBINDIA.

59. Ruling on Rituals: Courts of Law and Religious Practices in Contemporary Hinduism - **Gilles** Tarabout - Introduction. Through the Lens of the Law: Court Cases and Social Issues in India [Full text] - Published in *South Asia Multidisciplinary Academic Journal*, 17 | 2018.

60. Right to religion does not include right to convert: MHA to SC – THE HINDU BUREAU – NEW DELHI

61. The Diversity, Divisiveness and Division – VINCENTIAN – February 27, 2020. Democracy of India: Ruling Party Vs Opposition Party – by Dr. Neelam Seam.

62. Two Fighting Cats and Monkey Bread Dividing - https://www.fablesbook.com/two-fighting-cats-and-monkey-bread-dividing/

63. Muslim conquests in the Indian subcontinent – Wikipedia.

64. Why India Must Crack Down on Abusive Language Against Constitutional Functionaries - Curated By: V Vijaya Sai Reddy - Last Updated: OCTOBER 26, 2021.

65. Green Color Meaning: The Color Green Symbolizes Harmony and Health -

    Green Color Meaning: The Color Green Symbolizes Harmony and Health - Color Meanings (color-meanings.com)

66. INDIA TODAY - Uniform Civil Code: Tough challenges and raging debates over the years - Aneesha Mathur - New Delhi, UPDATED: Jun 28, 2023.

67. Will Consider Proposal for out-of Court Settlement – 17 Aug, 2023 - https://www.pressreader.com/india/hindustan-times-chandigarh/20230817/281956022322914

68. Disagreement Doesn't Have to Be Divisive by Francesca Gino - November 16, 2020

69. Times of India - Islam preaches co-existence, says Muslim World League chief Al-Issa - Ambika Pandit / TNN / Updated: Jul 12, 2023.

70. Why words matter: Political violence increases when politicians use inflammatory language - Research shows that hate speech is not just political theatre. - Why words matter: Political violence increases when politicians use inflammatory language (scroll.in)

71. STATUS OF EDUCATION AND EMPLOYMENT OF MUSLIMS IN INDIA Mashkoor Ahmad and Khalid Khan - International Journal of Social Science and Economic Research ISSN: 2455-8834 Volume:06, Issue:07 "July 2021"

72. Role of Peace and Value Education for National Integration and Communal Harmony in India - Dr Rachna Pathak - International Journal of Academic Research ISSN: 2348-7666; Vol.4, Issue-1(1), January, 2017.

73. Debates in the Constituent Assembly and thereafter on Uniform Civil Code – Lakshmiparameswan – India Policy Foundation.

74. Fundamental Duties as a mean to achieve responsible Citizenry by Amogh Dabholkar* & Vaishnavi Kamble) Published on July 1, 2020 By Bhumika Indulia- SCC [ONLINE] BLOG.

75. Significance of Fundamental Duties - Indian Polity Notes - Patil Amruta - Mar 30, 2023 – prepp.

76. Jurisprudential Aspects of Fundamental Duties and their Enforceability: A Study Prof. (Dr.) R.L.Koul Amity Law School, NOIDA, AUUP Dr. Meenakshi Koul Assistant Professor, Symbosis Law School, NOIDA.

77. Enforcing Fundamental Duties - https://www.drishtiias.com/daily-updates/daily-news-analysis/enforcing-fundamental-duties

78. Need to remember our fundamental duties as we remember our fundamental rights - Written by Ravi Shankar Prasad -
Updated: November 26, 2019 – The Indian **Express**

79. Rights and Duties – by Kabeer Shrivasta – 25 February, 2022 - Frontline

80. Religion in India –Tolerance and Segregation – 4.- Attitudes about castes - BY NEHA SAHGAL, JONATHAN EVANS, ARIANA MONIQUE SALAZAR, KELSEY JO STARR AND MANOLO CORICHI – PEW RESEARCH CENTERJUNE 29, 2021.

81. Caste and Politics: An inseparable concoction - Simran Dey @Digital Well Being in the times of Rising Screen Time JUN 19, 2021.

82. Significance of Fundamental Duties - Indian Polity Notes - Patil Amruta - Mar 30, 2023- prepp.

83. Shortcomings of Indian democracy - June 17, 2021 -)*Pleaders.*

84. Fundamental Duties: Concept, Importance and Relation By Sheen Kaul Published on 9 July 2020 - https://www.legalbites.in/fundamental-duties.

85. Fundamental duties must be enforced, says plea in Supreme Court: February 24, 2022February 24, 2022 by Insights Editor – INSIGHTSIAS.

86. The role of law in a state of lawlessness - June 17, 2021-)*Pleaders.*

87. FUNDAMENTAL DUTIES: THE FORGOTTEN PART OF THE INDIAN CONSTITUTION – Developed by NIMACTIVE @2023 Jus Corpus Law Journal

88. US History.Org: "Ask Not What Your Country Can Do For You" - John F. Kennedy's Inaugural Address, January 20, 1961.

89. Search only for what is the meaning of 'duty' according to Bhagwad Gita - Yahoo India Web Search

90. Making Sense of the House: Explaining the Decline of the Indian Parliament amidst Democratization - December 2013 - Studies in Indian Politics 1(2):153-177

91. DOI:10.1177/2321023013502907 – Authors: Rahul Verma - University of California, Berkeley, Vikas Tripathi, Gauhati University – ResearchGate.

92. What do we owe future generations? And what can we do to make their world a better place? - Published: September 18, 2022 9.15pm BST – The Conversation.

93. Is 1+1=2 true by definition? –

https://philosophy.stackexchange.com/questions/8738/is-11-2-true-by-definition

94. Merely naming caste not an offence- under SC/ST Act: Karnataka high court –Vasantha Kumar / TNN / Updated: Jan 29, 2023.

95. HINDUISM - WHAT ABOUT CASTE AND UNTOUCHABILITY? - MAY 21, 2011 PROUDHINDU.

96. Role of Ethics in Media and Technology -)Pleaders - July 1, 2020.

97. Topic: - Meaning, Nature and Functions of Law Topic: - Meaning, Nature and Functions of Law - https://law.uok.edu.in/Files/5ce6c765-c013-446c-b6ac-b9de496f8751/Custom/jurisprudence-Unit-I.pdf

98. Information provided about Jodo): (Jodo) meaning in English - Translation (hinkhoj.com)

99. Rational Choice Theory Of Criminology – By Ayesh Perera - Updated on April 20, 2023 - Reviewed by Saul Mcleod, PhD – Simply Sociology Website.

100. Politicization of Bureaucracy- Insights IAS.

101. The Link between Crime and Morality Published by Admin on April 11, 2023.

102. Supreme Court frowns on mentioning caste in cause titles: What courts have earlier said on this - Written by Khadija Khan -
New Delhi I Updated: March 20, 2023 – The Indian **Express.**

103. Census 2021Will Not Include Caste-Wise Data Despite Demands From

    Activists, Politicians [The Union government on Tuesday noted that the upcoming 2021 census will enumerate only Scheduled Castes (SC) and Scheduled Tribes (ST) to chart India's caste-wise population. The data will not include Other Backward Castes (OBCs)].

104. 10 Difference Between Animals and Humans (With Table) – Animal Differences.

105. Democracy in Ancient India- ANUARY 3, 2017 I BY: RAKESH GOYAL – PRAGYATA.

106. Do Animals Have Feelings? Examining Empathy In Animals - Posted April 3, 2019 by UWA I Psychology and Counselling News.

107. Indian black money – Wikipedia.

108. Vol. 2 | Issue 1 | August, 2020 The Concept and Significance of Political Justice under the Constitution of India Prof. (Dr.) P. Ishwara Bhat* - https://www.cmr.edu.in/school-of-legal-studies/journal/wp-content/uploads/2021/03/Article-3-2.pdf

109. Call a spade a spade - Wikipedia

110. Caste census: Constitution and power of states to hold such enumeration of population – The New Indian Express - Published: 07th July 2022 03:02 AM | Last Updated: 07th July 2022 08:41 AM – by Preetha Nair.

111. INDIA TODAY - Who created the caste system in India and how it changed over time? - India Today Web Desk

112. New Delhi, UPDATED: Feb 6, 2023.

113. Everything You Need to Know About Pus – Healthline.

114. OPINION: All caste-based reservations should be abolished - By Markandey Katju Updated: November 01, 2022 –[Reservations serving the policy of divide and rule, says Justice Katju].

115. CHILDREN'S MORAL EDUCATION IN THE DIGITAL AGE - December 2022 - Conference: CHILDREN'S MORAL EDUCATION IN DIGITAL AGE-At: UIN KH. ABDURRAHMAN WAHID PEKALONGAN - Authors: Haris Diar Rizki, AI Brebes Wahid – ResearchGate.

116. Declaration on the Responsibilities of the Present Generations Towards Future Generations – unesco - Paris, France - 12 November 1997 - Theme: Social & Human Sciences - Authoritative texts: Arabic, Chinese, English,French,Russian,Spanish

117. Chapter 14 - Democracy as a Moral Challenge from Part III - For the People Published online by Cambridge University Press: 24 February 2022 – By Gian Vittorio Caprara Edited by Ashley Weinberg

118. Public/Civil service values and Ethics in Public administration: Status and problems - https://www.civilserviceindia.com/subject/General-Studies/notes/public-civil-service-values-and-ethics-in-public-administration.html

119. UNIT 1 INDIAN CULTURE AND HUMAN VALUES - https://egyankosh.ac.in/bitstream/123456789/8857/1/Unit-1.pdf

120. The Unsettling Consequences of Justice Delay in India: A Grave Situation with Alarming Data - gaurav pandey @The Legal Perspective

121. Issues with the Indian judicial system - July 5, 2016)Pleaders.

122. INDIA TODAY - Indians' funds in Swiss banks climb to Rs 20,700 crore, highest in 13 years - Press Trust of India - New Delhi, Zurich, UPDATED: Jun 17, 2021.

123. THE TELEGRAPH ONLINE - What ails the Indian Administrative Service - https://www.telegraphindia.com/opinion/what-ails-the-indian-administrative-service/cid/1705431

124. Crime and Politics in India - April 2020 - Publisher: Blue Diamond Publishing - ISBN: 978-93-86518-67-5 - Authors: V.V.L.N. Sastry.

125. List of Indian states and union territories by Human Development Index

126. World Economic Forum: How to build a better India by 2030 - Jan 17, 2020.

127. Mass ageing poses a challenge we've never faced before-Business Journal – BJ.

128. UNDP: India ranks 132 on the Human Development Index as global development stalls - SEPTEMBER 8, 2022

129. List of countries by Human Development Index – Wikipedia.

130. The World Bank - Invest in People to Improve India's Human Capital.

131. Where the two paths meet: Krishna's message in the Bhagavad Gita

132. The Bhagavad Gita presents a balanced philosophy of life

    August 30, 2018 03:30 pm | Updated 05:31 pm IST - SWAMI YADAVENDRANANDA - Krishna's message for an overall human development - The Hindu

133. Human Development Index (HDI) by Country 2024 - Human Development Index (HDI) by Country 2024 (worldpopulationreview.com)

134. The Future of Reservations in India-By Akhilesh Pillalamarri – THE DIPLOMAT November 20, 2022.

135. How to stop violence against women in India — it starts with training police officers - Published: January 23, 2018 – THE CONVERSATION.

136. Unyielding Human Spirit: The Successful 17-day Rescue Operation in Uttarakhand, India - By: Dil Bar Irshad Published: November 28, 2023 – bnn.

137. India has strength; it's one of most important countries in world: Harvard Prof - 30 Aug 2022 – [Professor Michael E Porter] – LIVE MINT.

138. Are freebies affecting the economic growth of India? - **April 29, 2022 12:15 am | Updated 06:03 pm IST -** PRASHANTH PERUMAL J. – THE HINDU.COM

139. How The Constitution Helps To Maintain The Integrity And Unity Of The Nation V.Sudhish Pai 30 Nov 2020 – LIVELAW.

140. Reservation in India – Explained in Layman's Terms - LAST UPDATED ON SEPTEMBER 30, 2023 BY ALEX ANDREWS GEORGE – ClearIAS.

141. INDIA TODAY - The Kota student suicides and why we need to stop normalising academic pressure - Roshni Chakrabarty - New Delhi, UPDATED: Sep 10, 2023.

142. THE IMPACT OF CORRUPTION ON GROWTH AND INEQUALITY - Transparency International.

143. Your intrinsic values: why they matter and how to find them - Updated: Oct 6, 2023 – Clear Thinking.

144. The Times of India - WHO looks for treatment for epidemic of loneliness - Durgesh Nandan Jha / TNN / Updated: Oct 25, 2023,

145. Artificial Intelligence and the Loss of Humanity - BY XIANTAO WANG ON NOVEMBER 15, 202

146. The Indian **Express** -Rajasthan: Listening to speeches by 'saints' must for students - Written by Deep Mukherjee – Jaipur | Updated: June 13, 2018.

147. Human development: definition, concept and larger context –

148. https://www.undp.org/sites/g/files/zskgke326/files/migration/arabstates/ch1-e2002.pd

149. Religion and Economic Development - The advantage of moderation - March 28, 2008 - by: Rachel M. McCleary – Hoover Institute.

150. World Economic Forum – India: Here's what young Indians really want from life - Oct 5, 2018.

151. Is Artificial Intelligence A Boon Or Bane? - Technology / By Praveena V -

    Fegno Technologies.

152. Academic Distress' and Student Suicides in India: A Crisis That Needs to be Acknowledged - 02/JUN/2022 – The WIRE.

153. Rise in student suicides a wake-up call for coaching centres - ABHISHEK SAHU - MAY 09, 2023 – Money control.

154. Human Values - Definition of values – INSIGHTIAS.

155. Govt issues draft norms to prevent student suicides – By Fareeha Iftikhar, New Delhi

156. Bhasmasura – Article – Wikipedia.

157. The impact of artificial intelligence on human society and bioethics – Michael Cheng-Tek Tai - National Library of Medicines.

158. TRUIMPHIAS - GROWTH OF WELFARE: BAN ON CORRUPTION & LEAKAGES – 16 March, 2021.

159. The Perils of Caste-Based Reservation Quotas: Unveiling the Challenges in India's Education System and Government Jobs – I Rajwani – Published July 13, 2023. – LinkedIn.

160. World Health Organization – Social Isolation and Loneliness.

161. THE ECONOMIC TIMES Technology to bring down corruption and leakages in public distribution system and other schemes – By Jayadevan PK , ET Bureau Last - Updated: Aug 11, 2011.

162. SELF STUDY HISTORY - MORAL ATTITUDES – Posted on March 23, 2015.

163. Can't target coaching centres for suicides, parents to blame: Supreme Court - By Abraham Thomas - Nov 21, 2023.

ABOUT THE AUTHOR

Graduate in Commerce 1961. Completed short term Vigilance Course organized by the Institute of Secretariat Training & Management and in Parliamentary Procedures and Practices organized by the Bureau of Parliamentary Studies & Training, Ten days on job training in World Bank (1990), Washington. I was a Team Member of the World Bank and ADB Teams for Project Appraisal and Special Studies. A Member of the Loan Negotiation Team of the Government of India for ADB Loan for financing power projects in the country.

I served Rural Electrification Corporation Limited {REC} for 18 years and Power Finance Corporation Limited {PFC} for 12 years, overall 30 years.

While I was working in Rural Electrification Corporation Limited (REC) as Deputy Secretary, my services were sought by the erstwhile Ministry of Energy [now Ministry of Power] for drafting of Memorandum of Association [MOA] and Articles of Association [AOA'], other related documents and for registration/incorporation of PFC. PFC was incorporated on 16 July, 1986 under the Companies Act, 1956 after due approvals and as per the procedure prescribed under Company Law. My services were again sought by the same Ministry on immediate basis in the first week of September, 1987 for raising Rs. 100 Cr. from the financial market [Public Issue] including its utilization for critical power projects selected by the Planning Commission by end of March, 1988 as per the mandate stated to have been given to the Ministry by the MOF/PMO. I joined PFC on 17th September, 1987 on deputation as Senior Manager [Bonds] for a period of one year. Besides registration,

CMD was yet to be appointed. I was reporting to Joint Secretary (F) in the Ministry. CMD assumed office on 14th January, 1988

The printed Bonds stated before along with Interest Warrants [Transferable by Endorsement and Delivery] were issued to the Public through Offer for Sale [OFS] and were listed on the BSE and DSE as per the Guidelines issued by the erstwhile Controller of Capital Issues [CCI] in 1986. The approvals exempting the Bonds from Stamp Duty and Income Tax were printed overleaf of the Bond for the convenience of the Bond Holders, for the first time in the history of Capital Market in the country in March, 1988 which were fully subscribed.

I functionalized and operationalized the PFC.

The entire amount was mobilized and utilized for the projects as mandated by the end of March, 1988 after due approvals and loan documentation by the Board of Directors [BOD] of PFC. PFC awarded to me honorarium and commendation letter. As per the desire of CMD, I absorbed in the services of PFC after one year in the same post as Employee Number One (001) of PFC. I was promoted from that post to the post of Deputy General Manager [Finance & Financial Operations] in 1989 in PFC..

As my moral duty, I wish to state that at the fag end of my services in PFC, I was implicated in a politically motivated criminal case when the security scam broke out in 1992, in connection with investment transactions of around Rs. 419 Cr. made with a UCO Bank, Hamam Street Branch, Mumbai, even though the fact being that the investment transactions related to 1988-90 and had no relationship with security scam for which the government established a Special Court under the Special Court [Trial of Offences Relating to Transactions in Securities] Act, 1992 in Mumbai.

The entire invested amount alongwith the interest due and payable thereon was received back by PFC on due dates. The need for investment with the above Bank arose as the New Delhi Local Branch of the said Bank to whom PFC approached for empanelment of its name for absorption of short term surplus funds for investment in Government Securities/Public Sector Bonds. Such letters were addressed by the then CMD to the Chief Executives of the SBI, its subsidiaries and Nationalized Banks in April, every year. The said Branch advised PFC that the investments in securities are dealt by its Branch at the Hamam Street Branch, Mumbai, which was said to be solely dealing in securities transactions through its Official Brokers under the instructions of its Head Office.

PFC did not file any complaint against me with the CBI. CBI registered the case suomoto.

The then CMD appeared before the Joint Parliamentary Committee (JPC) in connection with investment of Rs. 300 Cr in March, 1992 made by him, the period covered under Securities Scam by obtaining offer directly from Harshad Mehta's firm which was the officially appointed broker firm of the UCO Bank, Hamam Street Branch, Mumbai. The amount was invested by him in equal amount with UCO Bank, Hamam Street Branch through the said Broker's firm and the Citi Bank, New Delhi. Ex-post facto approval of the BOD of PFC stated to had been obtained after the issue of Bonds. It is also understood that the then Director [Finance] recorded his dissenting note on the issue of the Bonds by CMD. The then CMD admitted before JPC having invested the above amount and through said banks and broker.

Due to tremendous political pressure brought upon due to JPC findings, soon thereafter, I was placed under suspension in November 1992. On appeal in the Hon'ble High Court of Delhi and the Orders passed by the Hon'ble High Court, the suspension order was revoked in May; 1996. I remained under suspension for four and a half years.

The then CMD who was examined by JPC in connection with the investment of Rs. 300 Cr. stated before, accorded sanction for prosecution against me. The Charge Sheet was filed in 1994 and the Approver's Statement was filed in 1996.The charge sheet and Approver's Statement do not mention a word about any allegation against me of corruption or recovery from me or any of my relatives or of any financial loss to PFC. The Search Report given to me by the CBI was submitted to the said CMD the same day for his kind information.

The Statutory Auditor's Report incorporated in the Annual Report of PFC for 1992-93 {P 39, Para 1. Page 40 Para 11.6 and Page 41 Para 4, 5, 9 Point 26.1} regarding investment of Rs. 300 Cr. stated before supports the mala-fide intention of the then CMD in sanction of prosecution against me. PFC suffered financial loss of Rs.15 Cr under the above investment. The amount is stated to have been written off in the books of accounts. There was no criminal or departmental action against those who caused financial loss of Rs. 15 cr. the said CMD. This was a blatant discrimination on the part of CBI to have charge sheeted me despite no financial loss having been caused by me to PFC. Those who caused financial loss of Rs. 15 Cr were not considered for any action by the investigating agency [CBI]. The sanction for prosecution accorded by the then CMD was malicious. PFC thus made me a Scapegoat under the political pressure and public cry.

So long as I was entrusted investment department, PFC did all its investment of short term surplus funds through the SBI and its subsidiaries, Nationalized Commercial Banks and their subsidiaries. PFC did not deal investment transactions with any Broker's firm as a matter of policy although its Articles permitted dealing with brokers.

On the written mandate of the Nationalized Bank at Mumbai with whom the investment transactions were done, PFC obtained quotes from the Representative of their Official Broker's firm in New Delhi and all the investments, were based on merits of rate and absorbing capacity, duly approved by the then CMD were made in the name of UCO Bank, Hamam Street, Mumbai. The short term funds available for short term investment on day to day basis were spread out among four to five Banks based on the highest rate offered and the capacity to the absorb the funds. In no case, the funds were invested with a single Bank except once with said UCO Bank as other Banks indicated their inability to absorb the same.

All the investment transactions with the aforesaid Bank were made by RBI Cheques (Banker's Cheques) crossed A/c Payee initially through the New Delhi Main Branch and later, as mandated by the UCO Bank Branch at Hamam Street, Mumbai, the investments were routed through a designated foreign Bank (ANZ Grindlays Bank, Parliament Street, New Delhi) which had said to have the online money transfer through SWIFT transfer facility [Society for Worldwide Interbank Financial Telecommunication] since investment amount was to be transferred on the same day as the interest thereon was to start from the date of the cheque.

PFC had given specific written mandate in the form of letters along with the Banker's Cheque crossed A/c Payee to the said foreign Bank with copy to the Hamam Street Brach of UCO Bank at Mumbai for transfer of money to the invested Bank at Mumbai. The designated foreign bank for transfer, as per the Charge Sheet, credited the proceeds of the banker's cheque to the account of the

Broker's firm. It is also stated in the Charge Sheet that the forwarding letters and the banker's cheques were handed over by the concerned Officers in PFC to the local representative of the Harshad Mehta's firm, the Official Broker of UCO Bank, Hamam Street, Mumbai. This was being done by the PFC officials as per the mandate and authorization given in writing by the UCO Bank, Hamam Street at Mumbai to PFC. PFC had also received such mandates from five to six other banks and Crossed RBI Cheques handed over to their Agents under the letter of authorization. The investments made with these banks were properly invested and invested amounts along interest payable were received back by PFC on due dates from all of them. There was no default whatsoever as far as done by the investment department under me.

I was not aware of crediting the banker's cheque proceeds to the account of said Broker's firm by the said foreign bank since all the monies invested together with interest due and payable were received back by PFC on due dates with no loss of funds, thus leaving no scope for suspicion on misuse inasmuch as also, the RBI Crossed cheques were to be deposited in the A/c of PFC maintained with RBI. The Charge Sheet states the Approver had replaced the letter given by PFC enclosing the cheques by the letter of Harshad Mehta firm as per the instructions of Harshad Mehta, the fact of which was not known to PFC which presumed the proceedings of cheques were transferred to UCO Bank, Hamam Street Branch through its designated ANZ Grindlays Bank, New Delhi since Bank Receipts [BR] for the invested funds duly signed by the authorized signatories of the said Bank were furnished to PFC with particulars of securities in which funds were invested and the invested funds along with interest payable thereon were received back by PFC on the due dates and the BR was duly discharged by PFC officials and returned to the said Bank. All these documents form part of the Documents attached by the CBI to the Charge Sheet. The BRs were signed by the authorized signatories of UCO Bank under the Power of Attorney [POA}.

The said CMD ordered special audit of the investment transactions of the value stated before. The special audit report contains the complete procedure followed by the investment department with no adverse comments or qualifications, thus authenticated the investment procedure followed with the approval of the then CMD. The special audit report also specifically confirmed in Part III to the specific queries of CMD to the effect there were no deviations in the investment procedure followed with the said UCO Bank, Hamam Street Branch and the transactions had the approval of the competent authority i.e. the then CMD.

This report was considered by the Central Vigilance Commission (CVC) which requested the Ministry of Energy to forward it to the Director of CBI for taking into consideration while investigating the case. This was accordingly done by the Ministry of Energy (now Power). CBI, except attaching a copy of the same with Charge Sheet as part of the documents (D23), did not mention a single word about the same in the Charge Sheet, thus had not taken the report into consideration during the investigation. The report would have bared the allegations made in the

Charge Sheet had CBI taken same into consideration during investigation and had dealt it also in the Charge Sheet. This was biased and prejudicial on the part of the CBI.

I was under depression for about six months after the suspension. I made written submissions to the CMD, PFC, then Secretary in the Ministry and the Hon'ble Minister of Energy but there was no response from any one. My wife developed hypertension in 1993 which could not be controlled despite best medical treatment. She suffered brain stroke 12th May, 2005 midnight, admitted to the hospital, remained in coma for 28 days. On regaining on the 29th day, the Doctors found her having completely paralyzed right side and loss of speech. She remained bed ridden for eight years and passed away on 7th Dec 2013.

The case though registered under the PCA associated with the provisions of IPC was transferred to THE SPECIAL COURT AT BOMBAY Constituted under the Special Court [Trial of Offences Relating to Transactions in Securities] Act, 1992 in Mumbai on the petitions filed by some of the accused persons residing in Mumbai sometime in 2017. On appeal by CBI in Hon'ble Court of Delhi, in 2017, the transfer of case was stayed. Final Order is still awaited. The regular trial is yet to begin. The case has thus been pending for the last more than 30 years.

I was due for retirement on 31st December, 1996; my service was extended up to 31st July, 1997, the date on which I retired from the services of PFC. There being no Pension Scheme in PFC at that time, I served as Consultant in Multinational Consultancy Organizations for 18 years post retirement to financially support myself and my family. PFC engaged me as consultant in May, 2006 for assisting PFC on policy, procedural and compliance matters of SPVs set up by PFC [PFC was the Nodal Agency] under Ultra Mega Power Projects, an Initiative launched by the GOI/MOP in 2005-06, served PFC in that position for two years on contract basis. In June, 2008 joined another multinational subsidiary company (a Subsidiary of German based Parent Company) as Senior Advisor [Finance, Commercial and Regulatory Affairs], Best Professional Employee and Special Contribution Awards were given to me while working in this company.

I am now aged 87 years and, on that ground and there being no allegation of any recovery nor any financial loss to PFC, filed petition for discharge in the Hon'ble High Court of Delhi which, though appreciated the facts, dismissed the petition as not a fit case on the ground that other accused persons had not filed any such petition. Among the accused persons in the case, I was the only person oldest of all others.

Though I have been Employee No. 001 of PFC, I retired in the same post I was holding on the date of my suspension [DGM-Fin] [November, 1992] while my most of the juniors retired as Director and CMD. I thus lost my entire professional future career and the consequent financial benefits.

My Advocate whom I engaged for filing the Petition in the Hon'ble High Court of Delhi and his Associate Advocate filed SLP in the Hon'ble Supreme Court against the Order of Hon'ble High Court of Delhi. On the date of hearing, the Associate Advocate who was Advocate on Record [AOR] withdrew the SLP of his own. AOR did not inform me about the withdrawal of SLP. I came to know about the same after about two months when I contacted his junior Advocate. This also entailed additional expenditure on my part which was met by my elder son who was working in a foreign country.

On completion of the contract in 2018 with multinational Consultancy Company, I took up writing of books. The List of Books published by me numbering 16 is appended. Another book [Project 17] is under publication.

More than thirty years are over; the trial is yet to begin. The mental and physical pain is curable by the Doctors but there is no Law under which an accused person can approach for relief for the inordinate and continuing delay in a case in which there was no recovery at all, is, according to me, also a kind of cruelty.

I had submitted several emails to CVC, CBI and PFC for expediting the case but no response. This is the case of victimization of an honest semi-government officer under the criminal system.

It may look to the readers that I have written about the thirty years old pending criminal case against me to gain sympathy of the readers which is not so because according to Maya Angelou " "You alone are enough. You have nothing to prove to anyone."

LIST OF BOOKS PUBLISHED BY PRAHALAD RAO

01. A WAKE UP CALL FOR EVERY INDIAN {2019}
02. JAMMU & KASHMIR – THE TRUTH OF THE MATTER – 2019
03. THE LIVING GOD ON EARTH - 2019
04. PRITHVI PER JEEVIT ISHWAR {2020} { THIS BOOK WAS TRANSLATED IN HINDI LANGUAGE ON DEMAND}
05. SOUNDS OF SILENCES IN INDIA'S CONSTITUTION-DANGERS AHEAD – 2020-
06. COVID-19 – NOT A NATURAL CALAMITY – AN ANALYSIS OF ITS ORIGIN AND THE FALLOUT {2021}
07. INDIA'S POLILTICAL BLUNDERS BLEEDING ITS BOUNDARIES 2021.
08. SOCIALIST, SECULAR & RELIGION IN INDIA – THE MISCONCEPTIONS 2021
09. INDIA'S STRESSED ASSETS CONUNDRUM- SUGGESTED WAYOUT – 2021
10. ANYONE WHO CAN TELL WHERE DID COVID-19 COME FROM THAT KILLED MILLIONS HUMANS IN THE WORLD – IS SILENCE AN ANSWER? {2021}.
11. ABOUT CERTAIN DECISIONS ON TARIFF UNDER ELECTRICITY ACT, 2003 – IN RETROSPECT {2021}
12. INDIAN PARLIAMENT MONSOON SESSION {2021} RUCKUS – TIME TO THINK ABOUT COURSE OF ACTION.
13. INDIA'S FUTURISTIC DEMOCRACY – THREATS OF CONSTITUTIONAL GAPS AND DIGITAL ERA – DECEMBER, 2022.
14. INDIA'S ELECTIOIN FINANCING, FREEBIES AND WELFARE – A FISCAL DISASTEER [2023].
15. WE ARE ONE INDIA ONE PEOPLE – 2023
16. TRUTH ABOUT THE SECURITIES SCAM 1992 [2023]
17. INDIAN DEMOCRACY'S PARADOXES [2024] [THIS BOOK]
    [PUBLISHERS: M/S BLUEROSE PRIVATE COMPANY LIMITED]
    [The books hereinabove mentioned are registered under The Copy Rights Act, 1957 and ISBNs are incorporated therein]